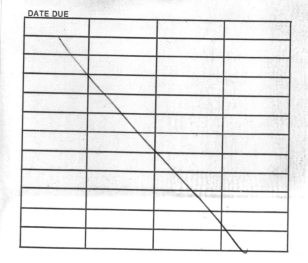

THE JAPANESE MIND:
ESSENTIALS OF JAPANESE PHILOSOPHY AND CULTURE

the Japanese Mind

Essentials of Japanese Philosophy and Culture

Charles A. Moore, editor
With the assistance of Aldyth V. Morris

HONOLULU

East-West Center Press

University of Hawaii Press

CHARLES A. MOORE, for many years senior professor of philosophy at the University of Hawaii, died in April, 1967, before his work on this volume had been completed. Long an advocate of the promotion of greater understanding between people of the East and West, Professor Moore was known internationally as the innovator and driving force behind the East-West Philosophers' Conferences (held in Honolulu in 1939, 1949, 1959, and 1964) which brought together leading philosophers of the Orient and the Occident to exchange ideas and to enhance their understanding of other traditions. His career as teacher, conference director, editor, and author was distinguished in its breadth and effectiveness in achieving East-West rapport.

Every effort has been made by those involved in finishing this book to maintain the high standards set by Professor Moore. A special recognition is owing to Professors Minoru Shinoda, Yoshifumi Ueda, Yukuo Uyehara, Kenneth K. Inada, Beatrice Yamasaki, Mr. Masato Matsui, and Mrs. Wake Fujioka.

WINFIELD E. NAGLEY
University of Hawaii
Department of Philosophy
Chairman

Preface

THE PUBLICATION OF THIS VOLUME completes a three-volume undertaking to make available to non-Oriental peoples the fundamental principles of the philosophies of cultures of China, India, and Japan. This is the third volume in the series in order of publication.

Like the others, this volume consists exclusively of papers—in whole or in part—taken from the books resulting from the four East-West Philosophers' Conferences held at the University of Hawaii in 1939, 1949, 1959, and 1964. There are no papers in any of these volumes written by people who did not participate in the conferences themselves—one or more of them.

A selection had to be made for practical reasons, and so not all of the papers presented on Japan at the four conferences are included here. The chapters in this volume are all written by Japanese scholars of top rank who bring to their work—as do the authors in the other two volumes—not only the highest possible competence in intellectual understanding of Japanese philosophy but who also live that philosophy in their culture. (Some scholars object to this exclusive dependence upon the Oriental himself to interpret his own culture, thinking that the outsider might be more objective and less idealistic in interpretation, but, for good or for bad, the policy of the conferences has been that we must understand other people as they understand themselves, and the chapters in these volumes represent that philosophy.

It would be best, of course, for the scholar at least, if the Japanese characters were included with the romanized Japanese in the text—the romanized Japanese is given along with the English in cases where there might be any possibility of misinterpretation. However, it has been decided that a more practical alternative for a book of this sort, which is meant, in general, not for the academic scholar alone, who is naturally well acquainted with most of the material involved, but for the general educated reader, to include an appendix which will list on one side the romanization in the text and on the other the Japanese characters that correspond to that romanization. This is such a complicated situation that some discrepancies between the romanization in the text and the romanization in the appendix are inevitable. It is the opinion of the editor that these are very few in number and are practically unavoidable in view of the great complexity of the situation and a great number of the items involved. Extreme appreciation is hereby expressed to Professor Yoshifumi Ueda, who went through the entire list of cards on which the romanization and the characters for the appendix were given in preparation for the Appendix and eliminated as many errors as possible. However, even for such a scholar as he is, there were still difficulties, and all that we can do—in the editor's name and in that of Professor Ueda—is to apologize for any discrepancies that might persist. Of course, anyone knowledgeable about Japanese in the scholarly world will know from the characters what the romanization should be—although this is not always the case, because, although this is less true than in the case of Chinese, there are differences of opinion concerning romanization. The matter of romanizing Chinese and Japanese is always a complicated problem and this volume is no exception.

There are some—but very few—cases of catering to the reader by employing forms of common usage. If this is objectionable, the editor apologizes, but he does not feel it is objectionable occasionally; and if it helps the reader—who is expected to be a Westerner—understand the material involved, the technical inaccuracy is of little real importance. Clarity and ease of reading, as well as technical accuracy, are the ideal sought. There is, however, no catering to the reader in such cases as the indicating of plurals and the matter of using the technically correct Japanese name-order, in which the family name precedes the personal name. In a few instances, however, the Western form is indicated in the cases in which books have been published under the author's Westernized name—as, for example, D. T. Suzuki.

In the first paragraph of this Preface it was said that not all the papers presented on Japan are in this volume. However, practically all of them are here in whole or in part. There are some cases where excerpts from particular papers are included, although the papers themselves as a whole are not. There is such an excerpt from Dr. Suzuki, one from Dr. Junjirō Takakusu, and a long comment from Dr. Shōson Miyamoto in relation to the paper by Professor Yukawa. (In the case of Dr. Takakusu, his excerpt is merely the very last part of his extremely complicated and technical article and refers exclusively to methods of contemplation. This is included after one of the chapters by Dr. Suzuki in order to supplement Dr. Suzuki's presentation and to give details of the methods of contemplation which Dr. Suzuki does not present. The main part of Dr. Takakusu's paper—peculiarly, if you will—is in the volume *The Indian Mind,* because his paper is not really on Japanese Buddhism but on basic Buddhism, technical Buddhism, Buddhism as contrasted with and in relation to Hinduism. Since the writers of *The Indian Mind,* give less attention to Buddhism and to its fundamental seriousness and depth than it deserves, since Buddhism is a tremendous contribution of India to the entire continent of Asia and to the philosophical world, it was felt quite appropriate— though Dr. Takakusu is Japanese—to include at least the main part of his paper in the Indian volume.)

One will notice that there is no general introduction to this volume, although there are full-length introductions to both of the other volumes in this three-volume series, that is, *The Chinese Mind* and *The Indian Mind.* There is a one-paragraph Introduction which brings to the attention of the reader the extreme value of the study of Japanese philosophy and culture—as well as its possible contributions to the philosophical mind of the world because of its many unique and novel points of view.

This paragraph was originally the first paragraph of an Introduction by the editor. However, speaking frankly, the Introduction got somewhat out of hand, because the editor felt that certain matters deserved mention which were more controversial than anything mentioned in the other Introductions. Consequently, the first paragraph was excerpted from that Introduction and is here on a separate page opening the volume. The rest of that "Introduction" is an article called the Editor's Supplement. It is presented at the end of the volume, not because it is not significant—the editor hopes it is—but because the editor does express there some controversial interpretations, many less idealistic interpretations, and many more or less unmentioned ideas as compared with the content of the volume itself. It is meant for controversy. It is meant to be provocative. It is meant to encourage thinking about instead of merely understanding or knowing about facts of Japanese philosophy and culture. If it is objectionable to certain Japanese, all that we can do is to apologize—again—but also to avow complete sincerity, both personally and in the name of philosophy and understanding.

Special attention probably should be called to one discrepancy that is actually a mistake—in the text—which Dr. Ueda called to the attention of the editor and about which he felt very strongly. Almost throughout the volume the word "sect" was substituted for the Japanese word "*shū*,"—an example of catering to the reader—such that, for example, "Jodo Shinshū" became "Jodo Shin sect." This is utterly inaccurate to a Japanese and is taken care of in the Appendix. Apologies again.

The editor found the papers in this volume among the most exciting he has ever read and the ideas most provocative. It is hoped that the general reader will have a similar reaction.

As is usually the case, many colleagues, friends, and scholars elsewhere who are knowledgeable about Japan helped and offered suggestions in connection with the formation and contents of the book and with the Supplement. Special appreciation must go to Dr. Kenneth K. Inada, Mr. Masato Matsui, Mrs. Floris Sakamoto, Dr. Minoru Shinoda, Professor Yukuo Uyehara, and Professor Beatrice Yamasaki.

Charles A. Moore

Honolulu
January 23, 1967

Contents

Contents (*continued*)

THE JAPANESE MIND:
ESSENTIALS OF JAPANESE PHILOSOPHY AND CULTURE

CHARLES A. MOORE   *Introduction*

THE JAPANESE thought-and-culture tradition is probably the most enigmatic* and paradoxical of all major traditions, but—partly for that very reason—it presents more intellectual and cultural challenges, more unique and interesting suggestions, and more provocative reactions than any of the other great traditions of Asia. The paradoxical character of the Japanese mind has been inevitable and unavoidable for the Japanese—in adopting, adapting, and attempting to harmonize such differing and conflicting philosophies and religions as Confucianism, Taoism, Buddhism, German idealism, and indigenous Shintō. And it is also inescapable and beyond clear-cut comprehension for all but the Japanese, especially the West. It makes an exciting study but a demanding one. It can also be a rewarding experience, and one of serious practical significance on the contemporary world-scene, especially if, and to the extent that, traditional values and attitudes continue to—or again—prevail, as some with a sense for history predict, and if the enigma continues.

The basic and very technical chapter on Buddhism by Dr. Takakusu Junjirō is not included in this volume—except a very small excerpt to supplement Suzuki's treatment of methodology. Takakusu's chapter is in the Indian volume rather than here, even though he is a Japanese, because the papers by the Indians do not treat Buddhism sufficiently fully, whereas Takakusu's chapter deals with the fundamental and technical aspects of Buddhist philosophy and specifically in contrast to Hinduism this is a loss to this volume

* See footnote 1 to the Supplement, pp. 306–307.

but, as a matter of fact, he says very little about Japanese Buddhism except what is in this volume.

Besides the technical papers presented at the Conference meetings, there were Public Lectures at some of the Conferences. Some of these are included in these volumes. In this volume the Lecture by Suzuki entitled "The Individual Person in Zen" is included. An apology is due to the late Dr. Suzuki because the Public Lectures were being televised and therefore were limited to one-hour in duration.

Suzuki's lecture was not timed in this way, and consequently he did not actually finish all he had to say on the subject. What was omitted from the Public Lecture as printed here, however, was very technical—though extremely important. It was presented voluntarily in a second lecture—a lecture given exclusively to the members of the Conference—the following day, in a gesture of generosity typical of the great man Suzuki.

In detailed style, the traditional Japanese or Far Eastern pattern is followed. This may cause some Westerners difficulties until they get used to it. At first, the editor decided to make concessions to Western readers and add the "s" for plurals and to use the Western style of names—at least for contemporary names as is the style now—in which the personal name comes before the family name. It was decided, however, that this concession to Western convenience was unjustified in a scholarly volume. Consequently, there is no use of the "s" for the plural—there are no such usages in Japanese. Also the family name always appears first here, even in the modern or contemporary names which are now tending to follow the Western style. This may eventually develop more fully, but it is not actually correct according to Japanese tradition, and so it is not used here.

The non-use of hyphens in this volume on Japan may confuse those who have read the other two volumes—on India and China—because hyphens are used somewhat profusely in those volumes. The reason for this difference is that hyphens are almost always incorrect in Japanese, and therefore they are not used.

Nor is capitalization used except where it must be in cases of proper names. One might expect every word in the title of a book to be capitalized as in the West, but this is not the Japanese style.

One of the main features of this volume and of the Conferences is that not all of the representatives writing here are technically trained philosophers. These have been philosophers' conferences, to be sure. The books resulting from them are intended to present the basic philosophies of the country in question. However, each book is also presented—as a philosophical explanation of the basic principles underlying the culture of the country, so that we are trying to explain here both the philosophy and the culture, in their relationships. This qualification—of non-philosophers—applies very seldom, however. It is used when the field covered by the chapter is so particularly applicable to one aspect of the culture that an expert in that field—religion, social customs and practices, and law, as examples, must be presented by experts in those particular areas.

Usually, the style used in the Conference books has been to use small superior letters at every Japanese word or name in the text followed by a list of those letters and their corresponding Oriental characters at the end of the chapter. This system has not been used in these volumes. Instead, in an Appendix, there is a composite list of Japanese characters in their romanized form, along with the corresponding Japanese characters. The romanized form is in the text itself along with its English equivalent, and the reader who happens to be interested and qualified in the Japanese language can easily find it in a composite list at the end of the volume. It may as well be admitted that the compilation of this list has been very difficult. If mistakes appear, all the editor can do is offer his apologies. Every effort has been made to provide accuracy and consistency—and, in the text itself, clarity.

It might be admitted, too, that clarity has *sometimes* been given priority over technical usage. Occasionally, common usage has been applied, even though it might not be accurate from the scholar's technical point of view. After all, this book is not exclusively for the scholar; it is primarily for the general educated reader.

This book is not intended as a textbook. However, it is extremely suitable for this purpose, providing the instructor has comprehensive and basic background material upon which to base discussion.

One of the fine things about this volume is that every chapter (with one exception) is written by a Japanese who is not only academically and intellectually fully acquainted with the substance of Japanese philosophy and culture but who is a living representative of that philosophy and culture. The theory underlying this is that we must understand other people as they understand themselves.

MIYAMOTO SHŌSON   *The Relation of*

Philosophical Theory

to Practical Affairs in Japan

I. Prince Shōtoku's Ideal of a National State [1]

Prior to the introduction of Buddhism into Japan in the sixth century, there was no philosophical activity in the country. The people of the time were nurtured in the traditional Shintō awe for Nature and its simplicity. That tradition still remains as an "exact reproduction of the ancient creed, just as the wooden temples of Ise, which are rebuilt every twenty years, preserve the architecture of almost prehistoric times." The beauty of its simplicity in the form of straight lines is viewed in the quietness of the precincts. The aged trees and serene streams represent the beauty of the primitive life. Early Japan had a quite natural life. This way of life was decidedly practical, although not so conducive to conceptual reasoning. Influence from China by way of Korea changed this simplicity.

The contact with the Asian mainland was to effect a tremendous change and complex development in Japanese thought and culture. An ancient record states:

In 538 [the *Nihongi* says 552], the King of Paekche (Kudara), Syŏng-Myŏng, sent a mission to Kimmei, the Emperor of Japan, with presents consisting of an image of Shaka Butsu (Śākyamuni Buddha) in gold and copper, several flags and umbrellas, and a number of Sūtras, saying: "This is the most excellent among all doctrines, but it is hard to explain and hard to understand. Even the Duke of Chou and Confucius did not attain a knowledge of it. It can give merit and reward without measure and without bounds and thus leads to a grasp of highest wisdom. Imagine a man possessing treasures to his heart's content and able to satisfy all his wishes. So it is with this wonderful doctrine. Every prayer is fulfilled and naught is wanting. Moreover, it has spread from distant India to the Three Han (Korea), where all receive it with reverence. Your servant therefore has humbly dispatched his retainer to transmit it to the Imperial Court and to spread it throughout the home provinces, in order to fulfill the words of Buddha: "My *Dharma* shall spread to the East." [2]

The Emperor admired profoundly the beauty of the Buddha statue. This is a very important event for understanding the reason for the swift spread of Buddhism among the Japanese and for its impact on the practical affairs of their life. Ancient Shintō art and ceremonial worship had no images, while Buddhism inspired sculpture and painting of the image of the Buddha in India, Central Asia, China, and Korea. The great Kamakura Buddhist art had for several hundred years, up to the year 538 during the reign of Emperor Kimmei, already cultivated deep spiritual realization in the countries of its influence.

By the end of the sixth century, a great crisis developed in Japan as the result of losing the ancient Japanese domains on the Korean Peninsula and also the defeat of her ally, the Kingdom of Paekche. But Japan was favored with a large number of Korean refugees, including many Buddhist artists and artisans, just as at the time of the crisis caused by the Mongol invasions many Zen masters fled to Japan during the Kamakura period (1192–1331) from the China of the Southern Sung Dynasty (1127–1279). The revolution wrought by Buddhism was moral as well as literary and artistic. It was the wish of Shōtoku Taishi (574–622), who may be regarded as the real founder of Japanese Buddhism, to give his people a better moral code. He was the type of genius and philosopher-statesman needed to mold the form and feature of the Japanese national state in the most critical period of her debut into the civilized nations of the world.

Prince Shōtoku [3] ("*shōtoku*" literally means "sovereign moral power"), a contemporary of Augustine of Canterbury and Muhammad of Arabia, was a prince regent of Empress Suiko. He took office in 593, which is approximately half a century following the official introduction of Buddhism into Japan. Buddhism was at this time mainly a religion of immigrants, refugees, diplomats, those involved in commercial trade, and the royal family, who sought to utilize foreign economic, political, religious, and cultural means to gain distinction over powerful clans and feudal lords. The common people remained ignorant of Buddhism. The Japanese royal family in those days had yet to achieve its hegemony, and the clans and feudal lords were almost equal in distinction with the royal family.

The Buddhist idea of Mahāyāna (Great Vehicle) and Ekayāna (One Vehicle) of truth, and of the enlightened spirit of humanity, was conducive to the consolidation of the royal family as the sovereign power. This is the first attempt to apply philosophic thought to practical affairs.

From the earliest times it has been characteristic of Japanese Buddhism to worship the Buddha, rather than the *Dharma* (Law) or the *Saṅgha* (Assembly), of the Three Treasures. With the exception of the Zen (Ch'an) sects, which worship Śākyamuni Buddha, the principal object of worship (*honzon*) has been the cosmic or eternal Buddha. And this was always connected intimately with emperor-worship and ancestor-worship. This is the reason Buddhism became so much more pietistic and nationalistic in character than in either China or India, which emphasized the *Dharma* as philosophical thought and the *Saṅgha* in monastic life. Later, the unbroken imperial lineage influenced the Shin sect to adopt blood-succession, rather than *dharma*-succession, as was traditional in Buddhism, and so the eldest in the succession of the lineage of Shinran becomes the head, the pope, of the Shin sect. We may find a clue to this unusual system when we consider the reason for Shinran's paying special homage to Prince Shōtoku, dedicating many songs of praise (*wasan*) to him, saying: "*Wakoku no kyōshu Shōtoku wō*" (Shōtoku is really the king of Japan). Prince Shōtoku "found in Buddhism a universal basis for the relationship of the ruler and the ruled. His inspiration helped in achieving national unity and in subduing the clannish spirit under it." [4]

Prince Shōtoku also utilized the Confucian idea of Heaven, Earth, and man to establish the central authority of the court. It is reflected in the famous third Article of his *Seventeen-Article Constitution* (*Jūshichijō kempo*): [5]

III. When you receive the imperial commands, fail not scrupulously to obey them. The lord is Heaven, the vassal is Earth. Heaven overspreads, and Earth upbears. When this is so, the four seasons follow their due course, and the powers of Nature obtain their efficacy. If the Earth attempted to overspread, Heaven would simply fall in ruin. Therefore it is that, when lord speaks, the vassal listens; when the superior acts, the inferior yields compliance. Consequently, when you receive the imperial commands, fail not to carry them out scrupulously. Let there be want of care in this matter, and ruin is the natural consequence.

He neglected, however, the idea that Heaven's will and movements may remove the Imperial Sovereignty if it becomes unsuitable. The emphasis on the need of public discussions and the people's co-operation is due to the influences of the Taoist *yin-yang* reciprocal-circulation principle, the Confucian principle of the Mean, and the Buddhist democratic equality; for example, as:

X. Let us cease from wrath, and refrain from angry looks. Nor let us be resentful when others differ with us, for all men have hearts, and each heart has its own leanings. Their right is our wrong, and our right is their wrong. We are not unquestionably sages, nor are they unquestionably fools. Both of us are simply ordinary men. How can anyone lay down a rule by which to distinguish right from wrong? For we are all, one with another, wise and foolish, like a ring which has no end. Therefore, although others give way to anger, let us on the contrary dread our own faults, and, though we alone may be in the right, let us follow the multitude and act like them.

XV. To turn away from that which is private, and to set our faces toward that which is public—this is the path of a minister. Now, if a man is influenced by private motives, he will assuredly feel resentment, and, if he is influenced by resentful feelings, he will assuredly fail to act harmoniously with others. If he fails to act harmoniously with others, he will assuredly sacrifice the public interest to his private feelings. When resentment arises, it interferes with order and is subversive of law. Therefore, in the first clause it was said that superiors and inferiors should agree. The purport is the same as this.

Shōtoku sought to maintain harmony under the imperial throne, as seen in the First Article:

I. Harmony is to be valued, and an avoidance of wanton opposition is to be honored. All men are influenced by partisanship, and there are few who are intelligent. Hence, there are some who disobey their lords and fathers, or who maintain feuds with the neighboring villages. But, when those above are harmonious and those below are friendly, and there is concord in the discussion of business, right views of things spontaneously gain acceptance. Then, what is there which cannot be accomplished?

Prince Shōtoku contributed much to enrich the nation's life. The arts and sciences known on the continent were introduced and adapted, and it is interesting but not unnatural "that in the later ages, architects, and carpenters, sculptors and painters, artists of flower arrangements, masters of archery, adored the Prince as their patron saint, by organizing Taishi-kō, i.e., Shōtoku Taishi Union, each according to the groups and localities, and by celebrating their Taishi festivals." [6]

Prince Shōtoku died in the year 622 at the age of 49. His wife died a year later. His eldest son, Yamashiro, was popular as the heir apparent, but he and his wife committed tragic suicides when attacked by the arrogant Soga clan, who were merciless to exclude any power which would prove an obstacle to their clannish ambition. It is to be noted that the Shōtoku family was of the closest kinship relation with the Soga family. "He died like a martyr, amid celestial portents, as we are told, and worthy of his father. 'If,' he said, 'I had raised an army and attacked Soga, I should certainly have conquered. But for the sake of one person, I was unwilling to destroy the people'!" Thus he and his family took their lives before the statue of the Buddha. The whole family of Shōtoku had kept the motto: "Everything is evanescent, and the only truth is the Buddha's teaching." This motto can be seen embroidered in the *tenju koku maṇḍara* [7] (*maṇḍara* depicting the land of Heavenly Life) tapestry, which was made in his memory by Lady Tachibana-no-Ōiratsume. In this early period of the introduction of Buddhism, the life and the way of conduct of the Shōtoku family were extraordinary examples in which we can see how Buddhist teachings guided practical affairs.

Many historians and scholars of the present think that Prince Shōtoku is the founder of Japanese civilization, for to him is ascribed the Seventeen-Article Constitution, the commentaries on the *Saddharma-puṇḍarīka*, the *Śrīmālā*, and the *Vimalakīrti Sūtra(s)*, and so on. The reason for ascribing these achievements to Prince Shōtoku, though they might be of later composition, is that his personality, his tragedy, and his sacrifice of his whole family led the people to worship him. Japan as a nation was not unified before this time, for she lacked an ideal personality for the unification of the country. Since that time Prince Shōtoku has been the idol of Japan, from whom everything ideal and cultural is believed to have originated. Seven great temples are also ascribed to him, namely, Hōryūji, Shitennōji, Chūgūji, Hachiokadera (Kōryūji), Ikejiridera (Hōkiji), Tachibanadera, and Katsuragidera.

Shitennōji was a Buddhist sanctuary, a place of worship, which remains even today the central temple of Osaka. Originally, it included four institutions: (1) Kyodenin (literally, temple of reverence-field) . . . for discipline and learning; (2) Seyakuin (temple of the dispensary); (3) Hidenin (temple of compassion-field), and asylum for the helpless; (4) Ryōbyōin (temple of the hospital or sanatorium). It was erected on a hillside on the eastern end of the Inland Sea. The Inland Sea was and is the maritime highway connecting central Japan with the western provinces and with Korea and China. Thus, the temple was erected at the post where the immigrants, artisans, missionaries, and envoys coming from the Continent finished their sea routes and landed in central Japan. . . . We can imagine how those newcomers from the Continent on landing at this port were impressed by the all-embracing spirit of the Buddha embodied in this sanctuary established by the ruler of the land. . . . Shitennōji was partly intended for the reception of the foreigners.[8]

II. Buddhism as a Guardian Religion of Japan— and the Persecution of Its Critics

In describing Japanese Buddhism, the expression "state religion" and "guardian religion" are often used, but it is important to know that, when a nation is still in its formative stages, the meanings of these terms are quite different from what we might understand them to be. The first form of Japanese Buddhism was a complex of faiths held by immigrants, a religion imported from abroad, a source of material and worldly blessings, etc. The emphasis was on the worldly gains and benefits to be derived from praising the Buddha's virtues, and there was an almost total lack of real faith in or understanding of the teachings. A popular idea was that by worshipping the Buddha "calamities will be avoided and happiness will be brought about." This basic attitude continued even after Buddhism gained popular approval by the imperial courts and eventually came to have a determining influence upon the ceremonies of the state. Even today, the new post-war religions which promise the healing of sickness and the abolition of poverty in return for oblation reveal the basic attitude which made the Japanese worship the Buddha for the sake of worldly blessings. This is not a trait of the primitive religious consciousness of the Japanese alone, for throughout the world, even in this modern scientific age, faith has a worldly and material attraction for the masses of the people. It is human nature to want a long life, a life free of sickness and disease, days filled with happiness, etc. The important thing is whether this basic desire of man is developed to include blessings for all of humanity. In Japanese Buddhism, prayer and worship are generally directed to the Buddha, not only for the sake of self, but for the sake of all people, for the country as a whole, and for society. In the early stages of the introduction of Buddhism into Japan there was no imperial or national state. With the introduction of Chinese culture, the people attempted to establish a society based upon the T'ang (618–907) court, and, though they attempted to utilize the ideals of Buddhist philosophy to establish a peaceful society, using such statements as "protecting and strengthening the country by the true *dharma*" (*shōbō gokoku*), what actually happened was that prayers in ceremonies and rituals were offered for the prosperity and weal of society and the elimination of calamities and sickness.

Those who engaged in such pursuits consisted mainly of the upper classes connected with the imperial court, and thus it can be said that Japan was formed by the activities of the aristocracy, rather than by the lower stratum of society. This is evident in the famous statement: "*Kyūchū Shingon Kuge Tendai*," that is, "Esoteric Shingon for the imperial court ritualism, and Esoteric Tendai for aristocratic ritualism."

Gradually, the structure of society changed as the imperial state was solidified, and in the Kamakura period the lower stratum of society became dominant and in control of the reins of government. In the beginning of the modern period, at the time of the Meiji Restoration (1868), the powers of government were returned to the imperial household.

In the Kamakura period, radical changes in Japanese society occurred. Kamakura is the new capital of the militarist Shōgunate. The military are quite close to the farming class, who constitute 70 to 80 per cent of the Japanese population. This marks the new era—the era of the masses—warriors, peasants, and merchants, all of whom are non-aristocratic. This is especially true of the areas in the eastern part of Japan. This was the expansion of Japanese colonization; and Kamakura Buddhism was the frontier culture. The royal family and aristocracy in Kyoto became weakened. It is also interesting that such leaders of new religions as Hōnen (1133–1212), Shinran (1173–1262), and Nichiren (1222–1282) (except Dōgen, 1200–1253, who went to China for Buddhist studies) were all persecuted and exiled by the pressure of the old established churches in Kyoto and Nara, giving them the opportunity to make contact with the common people. Although Hōnen, Shinran, Dōgen, and Nichiren achieved their religious reform in different ways, there was one way in which they were united: in the common cause of reformation and in the spirit which demands a religion of simplicity, practicality, absolute faith, individual spiritual awakening, and a new and vital aspiration.

It is interesting to note the reason for the persecution of the reformers, Hōnen and Shinran, by the traditional sects of the ancient city of Nara to the south and the monastery of Hiei to the north. They claimed [9] that Hōnen and Shinran disgraced the various deities and *buddhas;* that they were anti-socials who acknowledged the evil acts of men; and that they were anti-nationalistic. The traditional priests criticized Hōnen and Shinran as responsible for the weakening and disintegration of the imperial state, and advocated their banishment to distant and remote places and the promotion of the "various sects which would guard and strengthen the nation." They looked upon the reformers as mere agitators and not as men who attempted to develop new spiritual insights. A famous statement of Shinran reads: "Even the good man is saved; how much more so the evil man." The "evil man" (*akunin*) was a deep spiritual realization of Shinran, but critics saw this as mere acknowledgement of the evil tendencies of men. Scholars say that this concept of "evil man" refers to the warrior class, the *bushi,* or *samurai,*[10] and others hold that it refers to the merchants [11] and workers of the day; but what is clear is that it does not refer to the aristocrats of olden days, who were upholders of the "guardian religion."

Shinran's name is not included in the traditional histories of Japan, though historically it can be shown that he was banished to Echigo, spent a number of years in this remote northern province, then went to eastern Japan, and later returned to Kyoto, where he spent the remainder of his 20-odd years. Today, however, Shin, or Jōdo shin, the sect founded by Shinran, who mingled only with the masses, is the most aristocratic of the Buddhist sects. The aristocratic coloring of this sect began with Rennyo (1415–1499) and was developed along this line in the Tokugawa period (1571–1867).

Dōgen, who also propagated a new type of Buddhism, avoided contacts with the imperial court, although he was of aristocratic birth. He practiced meditation and the disciplines of Buddhism away from the cultural center of Japan, deep in the remote hills of Eihei. Both Eisai and Dōgen studied in China and, respecting the tradition of Buddhism, transmitted the Rinzai and Sōtō sects of Zen Buddhism. Shinran and Nichiren never went abroad, and they can be considered purely Japanese in the development of their thought.

Shinran, however, selected as the transmitter of his Buddhism two thinkers from India, Nāgārjuna and Vasubandhu; three from China, T'an-lüan, Tao-ch'o, and Shan-tao, and two from Japan, Genshin and Hōnen. He selected Prince Shōtoku and called him the "King of Japan." He thus maintained a balanced view of Japanese culture. His consideration of the Original Vow of Amida as "non-dual" is in accord with Dōgen's non-duality of practice and *satori*, original Buddhism's Middle Way, and Mahāyāna Buddhism's ideal of non-duality.

As opposed to this, Nichiren had as the principle object of worship the phrase, *"Namumyō Hōrengekyō"* (*Saddharma-puṇḍarīka-sūtra*), and the four guardians of the nation in the four quarters, and placed alongside it Tendai Daishi and Dengyō Daishi, and also Hachiman Daibosatsu and Amaterasu Ōmikami. This is significantly different from Shinran, who revered Prince Shōtoku as the founder of Japanese Buddhism, for Nichiren worshipped the national god, or *kami*, Amaterasu Ōmikani. This is the reason that Nichiren is closely connected with modern Japanese nationalism and Shintōism. In modern Japan there have been many military men, scholars, and politicians who have followed the faith of Nichiren. It is an interesting sidelight that the great majority of the "new religions" in Japan have their origin in Nichiren's Buddhism.

III.   Shinran's Naturalness (Jinen Hōni)

The most outstanding figure among the leaders of new religions in the Kamakura period was Hōnen. He was "the real founder of Japanese Amidism. It is true that his followers were not officially recognized as a sect until the time of Tokugawa Ieyasu (1542–1616), though in practice they formed a religious body from Hōnen's lifetime onward which Shinran developed with great precision." [12]

His name originated in the saying *"Hōnen dōri no hijiri,"* [13] that is, the saint of *dharmatā-yukti* (the saint as he really was). It means that by nature he embodied the reasoning of reality, or the principle of naturalness.

Hōnen dōri or *hōni dōri* (*tao-li, yukti*) is the fourth reasoning among the four reasonings, which are as follows: (1) relation (*apekṣā*); (2) cause and effect (*kārya-kāraṇa*); (3) logical recognition (*upapatti-sādhana*); (4) ultimate reality or naturalness (*dharmatā-yukti*).

These reasonings were gradually formulated in the course of Abhidharmic studies. It was the idealistic scholars who put them into a system. But their systematization was incomplete, and their interpretations differed from each other.[14] And, again, it is worth while to notice the fact that, practically, in Japan only the fourth reasoning became very popular. Although Hōnen was named after this reasoning, as the founder of a new sect, he was much occupied with the practical promulgation of the new teaching of salvation by the *Nembutsu* (the repetition of *Namu Amida Butsu*), and left the task of theorizing to his disciples.

Shinran, one of his disciples and founder of the Shin sect, interpreted this *dharmatā-yukti* from three angles: (1) *dharmatā* as the altruistic necessity of Amida's vow (*praṇidhāna*); (2) *dharmatā* as the unconditioned and absolute *nirvāṇa;* (3) *dharmatā* as the view from the *nirvāṇa of* no-abode (*apratiṣṭhita-nirvāṇa*). Most people know that Shinran taught that the one all-important thing is faith in the vow of Amida, but there are few who know that, after deep studies of long standing throughout his life of adversity, he succeeded in recording his own words about *dharmatā-yukti* at the age of eighty-six. His work is generally known as an essay on naturalness (*jinen hōnishō* or *jinen hōni no koto*).[15] Therein Shinran developed a unique interpretation of *dharmatā-yukti*, synthesizing the Mādhyamika interpretation of Donran (T'an-lüan, 476–542) of China and the Buddhist idealist theory of Vasubandhu (*ca.* 400–480) of India.[16] He adeptly made the best use of both sides of reality, that is, the unconditioned nature and the altruistic intermediary nature.

Shinran's *Jinen hōni no koto* (Essay on *Dharmatā-yukti*) runs as follows:

"*Ji*" means "of itself" or "by itself." "*Nen*" means to cause to be as it is. It is not due to the devotee's designing but to Nyorai's vow (*Tathāgatāpraṇidhāna*) [that man is born in the Realm of *Dharmatā* to attain *nirvāṇa-satori*]. *Hōni*, or *dharmatā*, means that such *satori* is due wholly to the working of Nyorai's vow-power, without any devotee's contrivance. Being utterly devoid of the designing of man, all is caused by virtue of *dharma*-reality (*hō*). Therefore, you should know that "no meaning is meaning" [in faith in the Other Power].

"*Jinen*" is the term which means "to cause to be so because it is so." Amida vows and designs to make man trust in the expression "*Namu Amida Butsu*" and come to "his Realm of *satori*." There is nothing left at all for the devotee to design, but all is left to Amida. As far as the devotee is concerned, he does not know what is good or bad for him. Such spontaneity of Amida is called vow-power-*jinen*. This is what I have heard.

Amida's vow is meant to make us all achieve Supreme Buddhahood (*mujōbutsu*). The Supreme Buddha is formless, and, because of his formlessness, he is known as "all by itself." [This means "unconditioned *jinen*."] If he had a form to conform to, he would not be said to be abiding in the realm of "absolute *nirvāṇa*" (*mujōnehan*). It is because of his designing to let us know how formless he is that he can be called Amida. This is what I have learned.

Amida is the "means" (*ryō*) by which we come to know what reality by itself is like (*jinen no yō*). When you have once attained this "logic" (*dōri*, reasoning), you need not think further about *jinen*. Should you still think about *jinen*, then the very realm of "meaningless meaning" would assume a meaning again.

All this comes from the *butchi,* or the Buddha's wisdom, which is beyond thinking.

Shinran, at the age of eighty-six years old.

December 14th, 2nd year of Shōka (1258).[17]

Zonkaku (1290–1373), Shinran's great-grandson and the most authoritative commentator of Shinran's masterpiece, *Kyōgyōshinshō,* opined as follows: The principle of *nirvāṇa* and the Amida Buddha coincide with each other. *Nirvāṇa* is named from noumenon, and the *logos*-name of Amida from phenomenon. Phenomenon and noumenon differ from each other, but, non-dual in essence, they are one and the same. Amida is the *logos*-name of *nirvāṇa;* therefore, commentaries here and there reveal that *nirvāṇa* and Amida are nothing but the profundity of the Oneness." [18] It is obvious that Shinran and Zonkaku stood on the Mahāyāna idealist *advaya* theory of *nirvāṇa* of no-abode.[19] The theistic tendencies of the idealist *bodhi-sattvas* (beings whose essence is perfect wisdom),[20] and their artificial middle-way constructions admit this *nirvāṇa* of no-abode as the highest form of altruistic activity. *Bodhi-sattvas* neither abide in *saṁsāra,* because of wisdom (*jñāna*), nor abide in *nirvāṇa,* because of compassion (*karuṇā*), so as (because they wish) to devote themselves to a life of beneficent acitivity.

Shinran's view on *jinen-hōni* is based precisely on the old Abhidharmic definition, but his enlightened view marked a step in the progress of Buddhist philosophical thought. There are several idealist texts which supply different types of *dharmatā-yukti* definition: the *Saṁdhinirmocana-sūtra*, the *Yogācārabhūmi-śāstra*, the *Prakaraṇāryavāca-śāstra*, the *Mahāyāna-abhidharma-samuccaya*, its *Vyākhya* (Commentary), the *Mahāyāna-sūtrālaṁkāra*, etc. Among these, what largely coincides with Shinran's *jinen-hōni* is the *Sūtrālaṁkāra's* definition. It runs as follows: "*Dharmatā-yukti* means the realm beyond thinking. It is because *dharmatā*-reality, once attained, need not be thought about again: such as why does the right view arise from reasoned thinking? Why does the elimination of defilement as an effect arise from right view? etc." [21]

Although there are several vital points in Shinran's view of *jinen hōni*, I will mention here only two most important points which concern the matter at issue. First, the context: "Amida is the 'means' (*ryō*) by which we come to know 'what reality by itself is (*jinen no yō*).'" [22] Modern scholars generally lack definiteness [23] about this point. Besides there was once a certain historian of the Shin sect by the name of Ryōshō (1788–1842), of Mikawa province, who classed *jinen hōni shō* as unorthodox [24] from his personal point of view. But his seeming scholarship was not only far-fetched, but quite wrong from the present-day standard of Shinran study. On the basis of Donran tradition, Shinran held that Amida is the Buddha as altruistic means of salvation (*upāyakauśalya-dharmakāya*). This *upāya-dharmakāya* (*hōben hosshin,* or *fang-pien fa-shen*) corresponds to *sambhoga-kāya* (enjoyment body, *hōjin,* or *fa-shen*) of the idealist three-*kāya* (*sanshin,* or *san-shen*) theory: *dharma-kāya* (principle body), *sambhoga-kāya* (body of bliss), *nirmāṇa-kāya* (transformation body). And Shinran's view of Amida as "means" is firmly based on the Buddhist middle-way principle, which is the common cause for both the Mādhyamika (of Donran) and the idealist school (of Vasubandhu).

The rational process involved in reaching the principle of non-duality is strongly indicated by Shinran's enumeration of forty-eight pairs of opposites in the *Kyōgyōshinshō*: [25] abrupt and gradual, horizontal and vertical, superior and inferior, pure and mixed, straightway and roundabout, rational and non-rational, unbroken and broken, continuation and non-continuation, following one's own will and following another's will, transference and non-transference, self-power and other-power, etc. Thus describing the Original Saving Vow of Amida as non-duality, he means that the designing of Amida's vow is as boundless, unfathomable, and all-embracing as the sea. It is an interesting fact that it was only Zonkaku who inherited Shinran's philosophical culture and wisdom of non-duality.[26] But, by reason of his distinguished ability and his great fame and popularity Zonkaku was subjected to great pressure and remained all his life in exile from the Ōtani and Hongwanji (the eastern and western branches of the Pure Land sect) patriarchal succession.[27] It is stranger that his succession has not been restored. The situation was so peculiar that the person who suppressed him was his father, Kakunyo (1270–1351), the actual founder of the Hongwanji Order. In the cause of Hongwanji centralization,[28] what was needed was the creation of Shinshū prominence and distinctness: [29] for instance, the formulation of the new Shinshū catechism, by which Shin Hongwanji as a newly established Order could be distinctive from Jōdo and at the same time from other Shin Orders, such as Takada Senjuji, Bukkōji, Kinshokuji, etc.; the "idolization" of Shinran as the Hongwanji founder;[30] the ritualization of the Hongwanji cult; a movement and campaign for Hongwanji centralization; the suppressing of local Shinshū centers; the promulgation of the new dogma: "faith for salvation, *Nembutsu* with gratitude," that is to say, faith as heart-union; and daily life as thanksgiving, etc. After Kakunyo, for about seventy years under the successive patriarchs (Zennyo, Shakunyo, Gyōnyo, Zonnyo), Hongwanji was in a great depression. It was only when Rennyo (1415–1499) succeeded the eighth patriarch that Hongwanji extended its influence throughout the country through his evangelistic and propagandist personality. By such practical peculiarities as these—the prominence of the marriage system and blood lineage; the distinction of worshipping Amida only; regarding all one's activities in daily life as expressions of gratitude; whole-hearted worship of Amida consisting of nothing but thanksgiving with no room for prayers for health, temporal welfare, or any such petitions; mass communication through epistles and creed, etc.—Hongwanji was successful in creating quite a uniquely practical religion, and henceforth became one of the most influential sects in Japan.

Second, Shinran's definition of "*dharmatā*" coincides wholly with that of the *Sūtrālaṁkāra*: "When you have once attained this reasoning (*dōri*), you need no longer think about *jinen*." "*Dharmatā*-reality, once attained, need not be thought about again." While "*hōni*" expresses reality's positive side, revealing Amida's vow-power designing, "*jinen*" expresses its negative side, not only to shut out the devotee's designing, but also to exclude phenomenal forms.

Shinran was thus very faithful to the Buddhist cause, keeping the middle-way principle. Zonkaku also followed the old Buddhist way described above. But Kakunyo started to direct every possible effort to frame a new Pure Land. (Shin sect) doctrine conformable to the ideal of the greater Hongwanji. Through the efforts and abilities of Rennyo, Kennyo (1543–1592), etc., Hongwanji became a major power in Japanese society. And, practically speaking, the devotee's worshipping cult centers upon the idolized Shinran statue and Amida Nyorai of *hōben hosshin* as *honzon* (principal object of worship). Later, Shinshū survived two crises, the first at the Meiji Restoration (1868), and the second at the defeat in World War II (1945). Each time, Shinshū did not and could not recover the old Buddhist way to which Shinran and Zonkaku were faithful. This new situation is filled with new problems concerning the relation of philosophical theory to practical affairs in Japan, but these must await future consideration.

Notes

1. Miyamoto Shōson, *Chūdō shisō oyobi sono hattatsu* (Middle-Way Thought and Its Development) (Kyoto: Hozokan, 1944), pp. 854–911. The first part of this paper is re-constructed mostly from my article, "Kokka risō to kojin jinkaku," or "Taigi to Shiji" (Prince Shōtoku's Ideal of a National State and His Personal Individuality), which was originally published in *Nihon bukkyō no kenkyū* (Studies in Japanese Buddhism), a special issue of the Journal, *Bukkyō kenkyū*, II, No. 5 (September-October, 1938), 13–61.
2. Sir Charles Eliot, *Japanese Buddhism* (London: Edward Arnold & Co., 1935), pp. 198–199. S. Miyamoto, "Waga hō tōru (Eastern Flow of the Buddhist Dharma), in *Chūdo shinsō, op. cit.*, pp. 841–848.
3. See Masaharu Anesaki, *History of Japanese Religion* (London: Kegan Paul, Trench, Trübner & Co., 1930), p. 57, n.1. See translation of *"shōtoku"* as "sovereign moral power," in Wm. Theodore de Bary, ed., *Sources of Japanese Tradition* (New York: Columbia University Press, 1958), p. 37.
4. Anesaki, *Prince Shōtoku, the Sage-Statesman, and His Mahāsattva Ideal* (Tokyo: Shōtoku Taishi Hōsankai, 1948) (hereafter *Prince Shōtoku*), p. 17.
5. See Sir George Sansom, *A History of Japan to 1334* (Stanford: Stanford University Press, 1958), pp. 51–52: "It is an important document and one of considerable historical interest, but it is today not generally accepted by Japanese scholars as Shōtoku Taishi's

own work. It was most probably written as a tribute to his memory a generation or more after his death, when some of the reforms which he desired had at last been introduced; and this was a not unnatural act of piety, since he did beyond doubt play a leading part in the importation of ideas and things from China, thus leading the way towards an enrichment of Japanese life."

6. *Prince Shōtoku,* p. 28.

7. The tapestry is preserved in the nunnery, Chūgūji, in the precinct of Hōryūji. The statue of "Thinking Maitreya Bodhisattva" is very famous, together with the Maitreya statue of Kōryūji at Uzumasa, in Kyoto.

8. *Prince Shōtoku,* pp. 21–23.

9. In October, 1204, the priests of Mt. Hiei gathered for the purpose of petitioning for the suspension of the "single practice of the *Nembutsu*" (*senju Nembutsu*), that is, *Nembutsu*-absolutism. On hearing of this, in November, Hōnen wrote a "document in seven articles" (*shichikajō kishōmon*), as a solemn pledge and guarantee for the future generation, signed jointly by 190 disciples, and presented it to the Archbishop of Mt. Hiei: (1) to refrain from criticism of both Shingon and Tendai practices and to disregard other *buddhas* and *bodhi-sattvas;* (2) never to get into angry disputes with other Buddhists; (3) never to argue with people of a different faith and practice; and (4) in the name of the *Nembutsu,* which we say requires no *śīla* (discipline), not to encourage people to indulge in meat-eating, wine-drinking, or improper sexual intercourse. Never to say of people, by their sect, that they belong to the so-called "people of sundry practices," nor to say that those who trust in the Buddha's Original Vow need not be afraid of sin; (5, 6, and 7 are omitted here). Harper H. Coates and Ryūgaku Ishizuka, *Hōnen, the Buddhist Saint* (Kyoto: Chion-in, 1949), pp. 550–553.

In October, 1205, there came the [Nara]-Kōbukuji official petition for the suspension of the practice of *Nembutsu*-absolutism, listing nine faults: (1) establish a new sect without Imperial sanction; (2) promulgate salvation by a new *maṇḍala;* (3) disregard for Śākyamuni Buddha; (4) disturb good deeds and virtues; (5) revolt against the national deities; (6) obscure the realities of the Pure Realm; (7) misinterpret the *Nembutsu;* (8) corrupt public morals; (9) the partisanship of *Nembutsu*-absolutism ruins the harmony of state churches. Zennosuke Tsuji, *Nihon Bukkyō shi* (History of Japanese Buddhism), Medieval Period, Vol. I (Tokyo: Iwanami-shōten, 1947), pp. 319–324.

Two years later, in 1207, Hōnen, Shinran, and others were persecuted and exiled. In May, 1224, the priests of Mt. Hiei, in a petition of the same kind, enumerated six faults, repeating the old ones except the fourth, which attacked the socio-historical view of the age of degeneration (*mappō*). "*Mappō*" literally means decrease of destruction of the Truth (Law), but it was used as the "Law of the Latter Days," a dark age full of vices and strife. This petition is found in the MSS: *Teishi ikkō senjuki* (Suspension of the Practice of *Nembutsu*-absolutism). The text is reproduced in Kazuo Kasahara's *Shinran to tōgoku nōmin* (Shinran and Farmers of East Japan) (Tokyo: Yamakawa-shuppansha, 1957), pp. 229–235; Junkō Matsuno, *Shinran, sono shōgai to shisō no tenkai katei* (Shinran: Historical Studies of Life and Thought) (Tokyo: Sanseidō, 1959), pp. 81–96.

The doctrine of Three Periods (*shōzō matsu no sanji*) has been commonly used in China and Japan. See Eliot, *Japanese Buddhism*, pp. 279, 424; Anesaki, *History of Japanese Religion*, p. 150, and *Nichiren, The Buddhist Prophet* (Cambridge: Harvard University Press, 1949), p. 4. But among Sanskrit texts, for instance, the *Vajracchedikā-prajñāpāramitā-sūtra*, says only "in the future, in the latter age, in the latter time, five hundred years later, when the Good Law (Truth) becomes ruined." Further, the *Saddharma-puṇḍarīka-sūtra* says that "when his true law disappeared and the counterfeit of the true law (*saddharma-pratirūpaka*) was fading, when the reign (of the law) was being oppressed by proud monks, there was a monk, Bodhisattva Mahāsattva, called Sadāparibhūta." H. Kern, trans., *The Saddharma-puṇḍarīka or The Lotus of the True Law*, Sacred Books of the East, Vol. XXI (Oxford, Clarendon Press, 1909), pp. 355–356. Sanskrit "*saddharma*" and "*pratirūpaka*" correspond to Pāli "*saddhamma*" and "*patirūpaka*," but neither "*paścima-kāla*" nor "*paścima-samaya*" corresponds to "*mappō* as the third period." There is no Sanskrit or Pali word for *mappō*, and henceforth such an apocalyptic theory of *mappō* seems to have gained ground in Central Asia, China, and Japan. Especially Hōnen and Shinran, more particularly Nichiren, thought that this very *mappō* period was the right time to proclaim their own true doctrine.

10. Saburō Ienaga, *Nihon dōtoku shisōshi* (History of Japanese Moral Thought) (Tokyo: Iwanami-shōten, 1954), pp. 98–100; Junko Matsuno, "Shinran: Historical Studies of Life and Thought," pp. 108, 436–444.

11. Toshihide Akamatsu, *Kamakura Bukkyō no kenkyū* (Studies on Kamakura Buddhism) (Kyoto: Heirakuji-shōten, 1957, p. 71.

12. *Japanese Buddhism*, pp. 363–364.

13. *Hōnen, The Buddhist Saint*, p. 133. "*Hōnen*" means "Nature's saint" or "natural-born saint"; "*hōnenbō*," means "Nature's own priest."

14. *Nanjiō* 247, *Samdhinirmocana-sūtra*, *chüan* 5, *Taishō*, No. 676, Vol. 16, p. 709b; *Nanjiō*, 1170, *Yogācāra-bhūmi-śāstra*, *chüan* 25,

Taishō No. 579, Vol. 30, p. 419b; *Nanjiō*, 1177, *Prakaraṇāryavācā-śāstra*, *chüan* 20, *Taishō*, No. 1602, Vol. 31, p. 582b; *Nanjiō*, 1190, *Mahāyāna-sūtrālaṁkāra*, *chüan* 12, *Taishō*, No. 1604, Vol. 31, p. 653b; *Nanjiō*, 1100, *Mahāyāna-abhidharma-samuccaya*, *chüan* 6, *Taishō*, No. 1605, Vol. 31, p. 687a; *Nanjiō*, 1178, *Mahāyāna-abhidharma-samuccaya-vyākhya*, *chüan* 11, *Taishō*, No. 1606, Vol. 31, p. 745b. The references of the Tibetan equivalents are omitted here.

15. There are three sources: (1) *Jinen hōni no koto* or *Jinen hōni sho*: the fifth chapter of the *Mattōshō* (The Light to the Latter Days), *Taishō*, No. 2659, Vol. 83, p. 713. (2) *Kenchi kikigaki* (The Record by Kenchi). Kenchi (1226–1310) was Shinran's chief disciple and secretary—as Ānanda was to the Buddha. It says that Kenchi heard it from Shinran, who was eighty-six years old at the time, at the home of Shinran's bother in Kyoto in 1258. The manuscript is extant. *Shinran Shōnin zenshū*, (Collected Works of Saint Shiran) (Kyoto: Zenshu Kankokai, 1956), pp. 54–56. (3) Appendix to Shinran's *Sanjō wasan* (Hymns in Three Volumes), edited by Rennyo (1415–1495), the eighth patriarch, *Taishō*, No. 2652, Vol. 83, p. 668bc. The contents of the second and third are the same, but the first two lines are missing in the first text.

16. Shinran is a Japanese combination of the Chinese "*shin*" and "*ran*": "*shin*" of Tenjin (Ten-shin or T'ien-ch'in, Chinese name for Vasubandhu) and "*ran*" of Don-*ran*.

17. *Taishō*, No. 2659, Vol. 83, p. 713; *Shinshū shōgyō zensho*, Vol. II, pp. 663–664. See note 15.

18. Shinran, *Kyōgyōshinshō rokuyōshō ehon* (Collated Text of the Doctrine, Work, Faith, and Attainment) (Kyoto: Zeniya and Chōjiya, 1779), Vol. VII, p. 15b; Vol. V, p. 55a; Vol. VII, pp. 10b, 25a. There are several recent Otani editions of the above-mentioned by Kikuya, Chōjiya, Hōbunkan, Bukkyōtaikei, etc.; *Rokuyōshō* (Essentials of Six Volumes) (Kyoto: Shinshū-Shōgyō-Zensho, 1940), Vol. II, p. 148; Vol. III, p. 112; Vol. V, pp. 146, 149.

19. Louis de La Vallée-Poussin, *Vijñaptimātratā-siddhi*, Traduite et Annotée (Paris: Paul Geuthner, 1929), Vol. VII, p. 671; Chinese Text, *Taishō*, No. 1585, Vol. 31, p. 55b; Johannes Rahder, *Daśabhūmika-sūtra et Bodhisattvabhūmi* (Paris: Paul Geuthner, 1926), p. xxiv: "*Il n'est pas séparé du saṁsāra, ni ne se réjouit du nirvāṇa; il n'éprouve ni augmentation ni diminution.*"

20. There is a certain similarity between B. H. Streeter's interpretation of the identification of the Buddha and *Nirvāṇa* through the "Adoptionist view" of Christian theology and that of Zonkaku, which stood on the Mahāyāna idealist *advaya* (non-duality) theory of *apratiṣṭhita-nirvāṇa* (*nirvāṇa* without residue or *nirvāṇa* of no-

abode). B. H. Streeter, *The Buddha and the Christ* (London: Macmillan and Company, 1932), p. 85; Shōson Miyamoto, "Freedom, Independence, and Peace in Buddhism," *Philosophy East and West*, II, No. 3 (October, 1952), 223; Th. Stcherbatsky, *The Conception of Buddhist Nirvāṇa* (Leningrad: The Academy of Sciences of the USSR, 1927), p. 232: "Its seeming contradiction with strict Monism."

21. Sylvain Lévi, trans., *Mahāyāna-sūtrālaṁkāra*, Tome 1, *Texte* (Paris: Librairie Honoré Champion, 1907), p. 168; Tome II, *Traduction*, 1911, pp. 275–276. *"Le Raisonnement d'Idéalité, c'est le Lieu hors-réflexion; car l'Idéalité, une fois atteinte, échappe à la réflexion qui n'a plus à se demander: "De quel Acte mental à fond vient la Vue régulière? ou le rejet des Souillures ensuite comme fruit? . . ."* Chinese Text, *Taishō*, No. 1604, Vol. 31 (*Nanjiō*, 1190), p. 653.

22. Sōyō (1723–1783), *Mattōshō kankiroku* (6 vols.), Vol. III, in *Shinshū zensho* (Complete Collection of Shinshū Books) (74 vols.) (Kyoto: Jikiryō Tsumaki, 1913–1916), Vol. 17, pp. 326–327; Senmyō, *Mattōshō setsugi* (The Gist of Mattōshō) (3 vols.), Vol. I, in *Shinshū taikei* (A Great System of Shinshū Books) (37 vols.), (Tokyo: Shinshū Scriptures Publishing Society, 1916–1925; new series, 1953), Vol. 23, pp. 36–42; Hōkai (1768–1834), *Mattōshō jinshinki* (Notes of Mattōshō in the year of North Monkey [*jen-shen*, 1812]) (4 vols.); Vol. II, in *Shinshū taikei*, Vol. 23 (new series), pp. 189–206; Eken (?–1830), *Shōzōmatsu wasan kankiroku* (Views on Shōzōmatsu-Wasan) (6 vols.), Vol. VI, in *Shinshū taikei*, Vol. 20 (Tokyo: 1920), pp. 261, 296; Tokuryū (1772–1858), *Shōzōmatsu wasan kōgi* (Lectures on Shōzōmatsu wasan) (3 vols.), Vol. III, in *Shinshū zensho*, Vol. 43 (Kyoto, 1913–1916), pp. 59–64. All of them say that *"ryō"* means *"tame"* ("for the sake of"). Eken and Hōkai mention examples of *ryō* from the *Tales of Genji*. We can mention some more examples from Shinran's letters, *Shokanshū*, (Collected Letters), *op. cit.*, pp. 128 (second letter), 152–153 (eighth letter). But the true meaning of the context will not be clearly expressed unless *"ryō"* is translated as "means."

23. Kōshō Yamamoto, *Shinshū seiten* (Holy Scriptures of the Shin Sect) (Honolulu: The Honpa Hongwanji Mission, 1955), p. 254. "We hear of Amida Buddha. This is but to make us know of this *'jinen'* " (*Midabutsu wa jinen no yō wo shirasen "ryō" nari*); D. T. Suzuki, *Mysticism, Christian and Buddhist* (London: George Allen & Unwin Ltd., 1957), p. 155. We owe much to his fine English translation. But the line at issue is totally missing; Rev. Shinryū Umehara, "Jinen Hōni no Kaiken" (Shinran's Concept of *"Jinen honi"*), in Miyamoto Shōson, ed., *Bukkyō no kompon shinri* (The Fundamental Truth of Buddhism) (Tokyo: Sanseido, 1956), pp.

1113–1126. Notwithstanding his excellent scholarly contribution, there is no comment at all on the subject-matter.

Gesshō Sasaki, late President of Otani University, who invited D. T. Suzuki to Otani University, *Busshin to sono hyōgen* (Buddha mind and Its Revelation). (Originally, Kyoto: Gohōkan, 1919); now in *Busshin to bunka* (Buddha-mind and Culture), in *Gesshō Sasaki zenshū* (The Complete Works of Gesshō Sasaki) (Kyoto: Zenshū-kankōkai, 1928), Vol. V, pp. 105–190. In the passages on *"jinen hōni"* (p. 156), he says that *"ryō"* means "for the sake of," and that this very passage carries weight and could have been expressed only by Shinran among the disciples of Hōnen, but not by those disciples who understood Amida only as the external object of worhip or as the object for petitions; Daitō Shimaji (1875–1927), famous Buddhist scholar and authority on Shinshū, *"Jinen hōni,"* originally published in the journal, *Hōni*, 1918; now in his *Shisō to shinkō* (Thought and Faith) (Tokyo: Meiji-shoin, 1928), pp. 407–412. He harbored a doubt for a long time as to why the section on *jinen hōni shō* is of such rationalistic bias and so full of philosophical jargon. But, later, he discovered that his opinion was wrong, and realized that the whole passage accorded well with *dharmatā* as the altruistic necessity of Amida's vow-power.

24. *Igishū* (Collection of Dissentious Doctrines) in *Shinshū taikei*, Vol. 36, 1917, pp. 30–31.

25. *Kyōgyōshin shō* (Teachings, Practice, Faith, and Attainment) (Kyoto: Shinran Shōnin Zenshu Kankōkai, 1958), Vol. II, Section on Practice, p. 61.

26. "Freedom, Independence and Peace in Buddhism," *op. cit.*, p. 223; *Kyōgyōshinshō shōkan kōdoku* (Lectures on the chapter "Attainment" of *Kyōgyōshinshō*") (Kyoto: Hōzōkan, 1957), 27–28; *Fundamental Truths in Buddhism: The Middle Way and Nirvāṇa*, p. 62.

27. Senshō Murakami, *Shinshū zenshi* (The Complete History of the Shinshū Sect) (Tokyo: Heigo-shuppansha, 1916), pp. 380, 384–388, 391–396; Yūsetsu Fujiwara, *Kakushin Nikō gyōjitsu no kenkyū* (Life of Kakushin, the Youngest Daughter of Shinran) (Tokyo: Sankibo, 1932), pp. 107–135; Fujiwara, *Shinran Shōnin den'e no kenkyū* (Studies of the Illustrated Life of Shinran Shōnin) (Kyoto: Hōzōkan, 1943), pp. 171, 175; Bunshō Yamada, *Shinshūshi no kenkyū* (Studies on Shinshū History) (Nagoya: Hajinkaku, 1934), pp. 114–123. The article referred to was originally printed in the journal *Mujintō* (Unlimited Light), IX, No. 2 (19B). It was at this time that the historical studies of Shinshū by modern scientific methods gradually began; see, e.g., Ichimu Tanishita, *Zonkaku ichigoki no kenkyū narabini kaisetsu* (Study and Explanation of the Life of Zonkaku) (Kyoto: Shinshūgaku-Kenkyūjo, 1943), pp. 111–114.

28. Junkō Matsuno, *Shinran: Historical Studies of Life and Thought*, pp. 457–590; Genchi Sasaki, *Tannishō seiritsukō* (On the Formation of *Tannishō*) (Tokyo: Nihon Gakujutsu Shinkōkai, 1950), pp. 41–49; Kenmyō Nakazawa, *Shijō no Shinran* (Historical Life of Shinran) (Kyoto: Rakutōshoin, 1922), pp. 3–46; Fujiwara, *Kakushin nikō gyōjitsu no kenkyū*, 93–135; Yamada, *Shinshūshi no kenkyū*, pp. 24–113.

29. *Shinran: Historical Studies of Life and Thought*, pp. 457–490; *Tannishō seiritsukō*, pp. 41–49.

30. Kakunyo named Shinran's biography *Hongwanji Shōnin Shinran den'e* (Illustrated Life of Shinran the Saint), *Taishō*, No. 2664, Vol. 83, pp. 750, 753. The author, Kakunyo, idolized Shinran as the founder of Hongwanji in order to consolidate its authoritative tradition of their blood lineage. *Soshi Shinran Denjyu Sōjō* (The Founder Shinran's Transmitted Orthodoxy) in *Shinran Shōnin zenshū, op. cit.*, pp. 146–156, 160. "*Shōnin no Gohonbyō Hongwanji*" (Shinran's Hongwanji Mausoleum), *ibid.*, p. 173.

SAKAMAKI SHUNZŌ

Shintō: Japanese Ethnocentrism

AN ADEQUATE comprehension of the major ramifications of Japanese nationalist ideology postulates familiarity with the general outlines of the history and philosophy of the national cult, Shintō (The Way of the Gods). The history of Shintō is quite as old as that of institutional Christianity, and in this necessarily sketchy summary of its major movements attention is paid mainly to philosophical tenets propounded by its most articulate protagonists prior to the present period.

Before the arrival of Buddhism from the continent in the sixth century A.D., there was but little metaphysical speculation in Japan. There was no body of literature, no school of philosophy, no intellectual stimulus to encourage or maintain sustained inquiries into the invisible imponderables of the universe. Intellectual flights of fancy were closely circumscribed by the limits of the physical environment. There was no word for Nature, as something apart and distinct from man, something that might be contemplated by man, the "thinking reed." Man was treated as an integral part of a whole, closely associated and identified with the elements and forces of the world about him.

The physical universe was regarded as tripartite—the ethereal firmament above, the world on the surface of the earth, and the shadowy nether regions in the bowels of the earth. In this universe there were divinities beyond number, "8oo myriads" of them. They were indiscriminately denominated *kami*, which literally means "above" or "superior" in rank or position and which is a Japanese counterpart of the Melanesian *mana*. A classic definition of the term *kami* is that of Motoori Norinaga (1730–1801), renowned scholar of Japanese antiquity:

"The term *kami* is applied in the first place to the various deities of Heaven and Earth who are mentioned in the ancient records, as well as their spirits (*mitama*), which reside in the shrines where they are worshipped. Moreover, not only human beings, but birds, beasts, plants and trees, seas and mountains and all other things whatsoever which deserve to be dreaded and revered for the extraordinary and preeminent powers which they possess are called *kami*.

"They need not be eminent for surpassing nobleness, goodness, or serviceableness alone. Malignant and uncanny beings are also called *kami*, if only they are the objects of general dread.

"Among *kami* who are human beings I need hardly mention Mikados. . . . Among others there are the thunder, the dragon, the echo, and the fox, who are called *kami* by reason of their uncanny and fearful natures. The term *"kami"* is applied in the *Nihongi* (Chronicles of Japan) (720) and the *Manyōshū* (Collection of Myriad Leaves) (*ca.* 750), an anthology of ancient poetry, to the tiger and the wolf. Izanagi gave to the fruit of the peach, and to the jewels round his neck, names which implied that they were *kami*. . . . There are many cases of seas and mountains being called *kami*. It is not their spirits which are meant. The word was applied directly to the seas or mountains themselves, as being very awesome things." [1]

The more important of the *kami* were in greater or less degree affiliated with the natural phenomena of birth, growth, change, and death. Among these divinities were those populating the Plain of High Heaven (*Takamagahara*), these *kami* being both anthropomorphous and anthropopathic. They lived, moved, and had their being in quite the same manner as their human counterparts, with whom many of them also shared the attribute of mortality.

From the divine hosts inhabiting the Plain of High Heaven there eventually emerged two deities, Izanagi and Izanami, who are obviously personifications of the sky and the earth, respectively. This divine pair produced diverse other deities and, too, the islands of Japan. Izanagi, the sky-father, begot the Sun Goddess (Amaterasu Ōmikami) and the Moon God (Tsukiyomi) when he washed his eyes (which calls to mind other mythologies that picture the sun and the moon as the two eyes of heaven). Further, when Izanagi washed his nose, the Storm God (Susano-o) came into being, indicating that the concept was current that winds and storms were caused by the breathing or snorting of the sky-father.

The Sun Goddess came to dominate the divine scene, and is to this day the most important figure in the national pantheon. She dispatched a grandson, Ninigi-no-Mikoto, to Japan to possess and rule the islands, he and his descendants, in perpetuity, saying: "This Reed-plain-1500-autumns-fair-rice-ear-land is the region which my descendants shall be lords of. Do thou, my August Grandchild, proceed thither and govern it. Go! and may prosperity attend thy dynasty, and may it, like Heaven and Earth, endure forever!"[2] A great grandson of Ninigi-no-Mikoto, called Jinmu, was eventually enthroned as the first emperor of Japan, and the imperial sovereignty has to this day remained in the dynasty established by Jinmu some two thousand or more years ago.

The foregoing divine basis for the imperial sovereignty was carefully provided in the compilation of two official histories of Japan, the *Kojiki* (Records of Ancient Matters) (712) and the *Nihongi*. These two histories sought to make the imperial position inviolable and eternal by investing it with the attributes of divine destiny.

In the early centuries of the Christian era, no distinction was made between religious and governmental ceremonies. The chief of a community (*uji*) acted as its spokesman or intermediary in spiritual as well as temporal matters, and the "emperor" was virtually the "high priest" for the whole people.

The *kami* were invoked in prayers of thanksgiving or of supplication for some measure of material blessing, such as good harvests, protection from natural calamities and evil spirits or forces, freedom from sickness, and the like. Concepts of moral wrongdoing or sin were barely being adumbrated, so that prayers were not for forgiveness of sins or spiritual blessedness, but for physical well-being and temporal prosperity.

The people feared and abhorred physical contamination, such as might result from contact with blood, sickness, death, or any form of natural disaster. Purification was effected by various forms of exorcism, lustration, ablution, or abstention. Notions of extramundane existence beyond the grave, whether in some celestial realm or in the lower regions, were attenuated at best, and there were no prayers for the deceased or for happiness in a future life.

With the arrival of that vast conglomeration of cults and faiths that Buddhism had become by the sixth century A.D., the indigenous faith of Japan took on the appellation "Shintō," The Way of the Gods, to distinguish itself from "Butsudō," The Way of the Buddha. As a vehicle of the culture of the continent, Buddhism effected epochal changes in Japan, and in point of doctrinal content there was great disparity between it and Shintō. The former found in the latter, however, a worthy and formidable adversary, inasmuch as the latter was inextricably identified with Japanese ethnocentrism, and, too, its temporal power as possessor of land and guardian of the imperial domain could not readily be wrested from it.

Several centuries elapsed before a measure of doctrinal assimilation was achieved, principally through the efforts of priests of the Tendai and Shingon sects of Buddhism. The former evolved what is generally referred to as Ichijitsu Shintō, or Single-verity Shintō, an expression derived from a passage in the *Saddharma-puṇḍarīka-sūtra,* reading, "All the Buddhas that come into the world are merely this one reality (*ichijitsu*)." The Tendai tenet that the multiform phenomena of the universe are but manifestations of, or emanations from, the all-embracing Absolute, the one Reality, the primordial Buddha, was now adduced to support the pronouncement that the divinities of the Shintō pantheon were all traceable ultimately to the same transcendent source, the one Reality. The syncretism is also interpreted as being based on the idea of *honji suijaku,* or "source-manifest-traces," according to which every divine being of Shintō is an avatar of some Buddhist divinity, so that in the final analysis the two faiths can be equated, the one with the other.

The fusion movement was given great strength by Shingon thinkers who developed the *honji suijaku* theory and produced the system of thought known as Ryōbu Shintō, or Dual Shintō. According to the proponents of this system, Shintō could well be translated in terms of Shingon metaphysics, which divided the universe into two cycles, phenomenal and noumenal. The infinite forms of matter were all, without exception, either direct or indirect emanations from the Absolute, Mahāvairocana (Dainichi Nyorai) while, on the other hand, all thought in the universe was encompassed by, and each thought in its partial way was identical with, the transcendent thought of the ultimate reality, Mahāvairocana. Applied to Shintō, then, Shintō *kami* could be equated with "corresponding"

Buddhist divinities, and Shintō thought could be regarded as being part of the omniscience of the Shingon Absolute, so that there was no inherent conflict between Buddhism and Shintō, according to Ryōbu Shintōists.

In an effort to restore Shintō to its pristine purity, and wrest it from its incorporation within Buddhist schemes of thought, several Neo-Shintō movements were started in medieval times, of which two may be mentioned here. The first is generally called Yuiitsu Shintō or One-only Shintō, and is closely associated with Urabe Kanetomo (1435–1511). Urabe substituted the *kami* for Buddhist equivalents of the Absolute or the Single Verity and sought to turn the tables on the Ryōbu Shintōists by arguing that Buddhist deities were the avatars (the *suijaku*) of Shintō *kami* (the *honji*), rather than vice versa, as claimed by the Ryōbu Shintōists. And, under the sway of the ethnocentric imperatives of the indigenous faith, Urabe called attention to what he termed the peerless status of Japan as the Divine Country, and the matchless glory of the divinely descended Imperial Line.

Considerably more important as a movement than Yuiitsu Shintō was Fukkō Shintō, or Return-to-antiquity Shintō, which developed in the eighteenth century with a succession of three distinguished scholars as its leading exponents. First of these was Kamo-no-Mabuchi (1697–1769), scion of a long line of Shintō priests. He subscribed to Taoist naturalism in regarding careful observation of the processes of Nature as invaluable for the determination of proper principles of human conduct. On the other hand, he believed that the superior nature of the Japanese body politic was due to the intuitive apprehension and practice of natural principles of righteousness, on the part of both the divinely descended Emperors and their loyal subjects.

The amazing scholar Motoori Norinaga (1730–1801), who succeeded Mabuchi as leader of this movement for the renascence of so-called Pure Shintō, spurned Taoism as being merely a way of Nature, whereas Shintō was the way of the gods. Elaborating the ethnocentric presuppositions of his predecessor, Motoori lauded the unerring instinct for proper conduct which he claimed was possessed by the Japanese people by virtue of their direct genealogical kinship with the great divinities of the Shintō pantheon. He called on his compatriots to manifest unswerving and unquestioning fealty to their divinely descended imperial sovereigns. He wrote of Japan as "the native land of the Heaven-Shining Goddess [Amaterasu Ōmi-

kami] who casts her light over all countries in the four seas. Thus
our country is the source and fountainhead of all other countries,
and in all matters it excels all the others." [3]

Further elaboration of these ethnocentric doctrines was provided by Motoori's successor, Hirata Atsutane (1776–1843), according to whom the intimate divine connections of the Japanese people
invested them with qualities and attributes superior to those of all
other peoples. Hirata pointed with pride to the unbroken and
matchless continuity of the divinely descended Imperial Line,
which he believed was destined to extend its sway over the whole
world.

The contibution of such pronouncements to the final collapse
of the Shōgunate and the concomitant "restoration of the imperial
sovereignty" (1867–1868) was potent, if subtle. Moreover, leaders
of the reorganized imperial government, anxious to bolster the
imperial position and to effect national solidarity, were impressed
with the tremendous potentialities of the Neo-Shintō doctrines and
fostered the propagation of these doctrines through such organs of
modern nationalism at the school, the press, the armed forces, and
so on.

In January, 1868, a Department of Shintō (Jingika; presently
renamed Jingikan) was established as the most important of the
seven departments of the new imperial government. The hoary
slogan of "saisei itchi" (union of religion and government) was
revivified, as Shintō became the state religion. Many of the officials
appointed to the Jingikan were advocates of the Neo-Shintō pronouncements of Hirata Atsutane and Motoori Norinaga, and they
promptly took steps to reconstitute Shintō and Buddhism as dis-
parate entities. Shintō shrines were ordered to divest themselves of
all Buddhist elements, such as officials in Buddhist vestments serving as bettōsō (administrator priests) or shasō (shrine priests), also
of shrine names having Buddhistic terms such as gongen (avatar),
and of Buddhist images, bells, and altar equipment. Temples of
the Hokke sects were ordered to abolish their Sanjūbanjin (Thirty
Guardian Deities). Temple properties that had been conferred or
confirmed by the Shōgunate were expropriated. Buddhist images
and paraphernalia were removed from the Imperial Household,
Buddhist ceremonies at the Imperial Court were discontinued, and
sons of the court nobility were forbidden to enter the Buddhist
priesthood.

The slogan "haibutsu kishaku" (eradicate Buddhism; extirpate its teachings) spread like wildfire throughout the country, and severe anti-Buddhist violence and oppression flared in many regions, causing great turmoil and resentment among the people at large. The central government, anxious to promote national solidarity and tranquillity, disavowed any intention to destroy Buddhism, and adopted a new policy. On April 21, 1872, the Department of Shintō (then called Jingishō) was replaced with a Department of Religion (Kyōbushō), incorporating Buddhism with Shintō in a sort of dual state religion. However, rivalries and animosities between the two priesthoods and other factors led to the dissolution of this contrived union some three years later. In 1882, Shintō institutions were classified by law under two categories: State (Kokka) Shintō and Sect (Shūha) Shintō. State Shintō shrines were given exclusive right to the name *jinja* (shrine; literally, god house), while Sect Shintō institutions were called *kyōkai* (church) or *kyōha* (denomination). State Shintō was to be financed and managed by national, prefectural, or local governments, while Sect Shintō was privately supported.

Freedom of religious belief was vouchsafed in Article 28 of the Constitution that was promulgated on February 11, 1889, albeit with certain qualifications, to wit: "Japanese subjects shall, within limits not prejudicial to peace and order, and not antagonistic to their duties as subjects, enjoy freedom of religious belief." [4]

Japanese officialdom asseverated that State Shintō was not a religion, that Shintō shrines were national institutions of an ethical and historical character, and that all loyal Japanese should participate in State Shintō ceremonies as part of their patriotic duty. As a result of protests that requiring attendance at State Shintō rites violated the constitutional guarantee of freedom of religious belief, the government established, in 1900, a Bureau of Shrines (Jinja Kyoku) and a Bureau of Religions (Shūkyō Kyoku) in the Ministry of Home Affairs. The former was put in charge of State Shintō, while the latter supervised Sect Shintō, Buddhism, Christianity, and other religions. In 1913, the Bureau of Religions was transferred to the Ministry of Education, in a further effort to separate or distinguish State Shintō from Sect Shintō.

Despite the official protestations that State Shintō was not a religion, it was obvious that it did retain the mythological and ideological content of the earliest indigenous beliefs and the rituals of the ancient period, adding to all this the doctrinal legacy of the exponents of Shintō in the medieval period and more recent pronouncements on the nature of the official cult. In the words of Dr. Genchi Katō (1873-), a noted scholar of Shintō:

So far as State Shintō is concerned, it may be taken as a kind of national ceremony and teaching of Japanese morality, and to that extent it might be called secular and non-religious, but, as investigation proceeds, the truth will appear that even this State Shintō, which some Japanese go so far as to speak of as no religion at all, is in reality nothing short of evidence of a religion interwoven in the very texture of the original beliefs and national organization of the people, camouflaged though it may be as a mere code of national ethics and state rituals, and as such apparently entitled only to secular respect. [5]

State Shintō helped to suffuse the national mind with notions of a noble past rich in great traditions, a superior racial stock destined to endure as an eternal national family, and a matchless state headed by an unbroken, inviolable, divinely descended imperial dynasty. However, no distinction was drawn between mythology and authentic history, and the validity of State Shintō's doctrinal content was placed beyond the pale of public inquiry or dispute. In its role as a state cult, State Shintō fed the flames of ethnocentric chauvinism that finally led to the fiery holocaust of war and the utter defeat of Japan in 1945.

State Shintō was disestablished on December 15, 1945, under terms of a directive that stated, in part: "The sponsorship, support, perpetuation, control, and dissemination of Shinto by the Japanese national, prefectural, and local governments, or by public officials, subordinates, and employees acting in their official capacity are prohibited and will cease immediately." [6] The purpose of the directive was stated as being "to separate religion from the state, to prevent misuse of religion for political ends, and to put all religions, faiths, and creeds upon exactly the same legal basis, entitled to precisely the same opportunities and protection. It forbids affiliation with the government and the propagation and dissemination of militaristic and ultra-nationalistic ideology not only to Shinto but to the followers of all religions, faiths, sects, creeds, or philosophies." [7]

An Imperial Rescript promulgated on January 1, 1946, declared that "the bonds" between the Emperor and his people "have been tied together from first to last by mutual trust and affection. They do not originate in mere myth and legend. They do not have their basis in the fictititous ideas that the emperor is manifest god [*akitsu mikami*] and that the Japanese people are a race superior to other races and therefore destined to rule the world." [8]

Finally, definitive rejection of Shintō as the official cult of the government was provided in Article 20 of the new Constitution of Japan that was promulgated on November 3, 1946, as follows: "Freedom of religion is guaranteed to all. No religious organization shall receive any privileges from the State, nor exercise any political authority. No person shall be compelled to take part in any religious act, celebration, rite or practice. The State and its organs shall refrain from religious education or any other religious activity." [9]

All the while, Sect Shintō continued to exist, affording to the people a comforting sense of belonging to an eternal continuum of belief, unruffled by the hurly-burly of war and change.

Notes

1. W. G. Aston, *Shintō: The Way of the Gods* (London: Longmans, Green and Co., 1905), pp. 8–9.
2. W. G. Aston, trans., *Nihongi* (London: Kegan Paul, Trench, Trübner & Co., Ltd., 1924), reissue of original edition, Vol. I, p. 77.
3. Ryūsaku Tsunoda, Wm. Theodore de Bary, and Donald Keene, compilers, *Sources of Japanese Tradition* (5th printing; New York: Columbia University Press, 1960), p. 523.
4. George M. Beckman, *The Making of the Meiji Constitution: The Oligarchs and the Constitutional Development of Japan, 1868–1891* (Lawrence: University of Kansas Press, 1957), p. 152.
5. Genchi Katō, *A Study of Shintō, the Religion of the Japanese Nation* (Tokyo: Meiji-Japan Society, 1926), p. 2.
6. D. C. Holtom, *Modern Japan and Shintō Nationalism: A Study of Present-Day Trends in Japanese Religions* (rev. ed., 3rd impression; New York: Paragon Book Reprint Corp., 1963), p. 215.
7. *Ibid.*, p. 217.
8. *Ibid.*, p. 220.
9. Hugh Borton, *Japan's Modern Century* (New York: Ronald Press, 1955), p. 494.

HANAYAMA SHINSHŌ　　*Buddhism of the*

One Great Vehicle (Mahāyāna)

ŚĀKYAMUNI BUDDHA'S TEACHING was centered on our daily life.
Therefore, his thought was focused upon the welfare of human beings. He did not attempt to interpret or explain a cosmos or natural
world that was devoid of mankind, for he was chiefly interested in
mankind. Since he looked at our daily life with man at the center,
it was natural that he should begin by looking at himself. This
meant reflecting within himself and gaining insight into his being,
which led him to examine his environment. The conclusion he
reached was that all things are impermanent.[1]

This insight into the nature of all things as impermanent—which
produces emancipation from their tyrannical hold—is called *Nirvāṇa,* which literally means "quietude." The Buddha's death was
interpreted as his entering into *pari-nirvāṇa,* perfect quietude. This
was interpreted by his disciples as emancipation from pain, as entering into the absolute realm of spiritual freedom,[2] and as laying the
foundation for positive activities.[3] This is the highest truth, which
means becoming one with the *dharma,*[4] generally translated as
"law" or "principle." This is the realm of non-duality and identity,
where absolute reason and discriminating intellect become one.[5]

The Idea of Non-Being

The beginning of Mahāyāna thought is found in the *Mahā-
prajñā-pāramitā-sūtra.*[6] The principal idea expounded in this class

of Buddhist literature is that of non-being. This means that all things we perceive in our experiences have no self-nature (*sva-bhāva*), no substance. It means also that the truth exists in the realm transcending our thought. The truth is beyond speech and thought, and, therefore, it is *śūnyatā*, "nothingness" (no-thing-ness). In other words, all worldly phenomena are illusory.

In *śūnyatā* there is no one who sees, no object that is seen. The subject and the object become one; they are in a state of self-identity. No discrimination is possible between them; knowledge is no-knowledge. This is called undifferentiating knowledge (*nirvikalpa-jñāna*).

This *śūnyatā* knowledge affirms on the one hand and denies on the other; it does both at the same time. Since absolute no-thing-ness includes and unifies all oppositions and discriminations, it is also absolute existence. When we gain insight into the nature of *śūnyatā* and thus become free from dualistic attachments, all thoughts we cherish acquire a new aspect; they become true as they are. This is what is meant by the phrase "truly non-existent, mysteriously existent."

Theory of The "Middle Path"
(The Sanron [San-lun] or Mādhyamika)

Nāgārjuna's [7] (150–250) theory is founded upon the idea of *śūnyatā*, and, to make it more clearly understandable, he called it the "middle path." [8] By this he wished to purify the mind of one-sidedness, to show it the proper way of thinking, to lead it to the middle path, whereby the distinction of subject and object is abolished and the mind realizes the truth of non-duality. *Śūnyatā* thus comes to mean the clarification of the mind in order to restore its original purity.

Theory of "One-Mind"
(Idealism in Mahāyāna Buddhism)

The mind in our daily life is active as consciousness engaged in differentiating things. While this consciousness is what we ordinarily call mind, Buddhists conceive as active at its base another mind, which we may designate reason-mind, or reality-mind, in distinction from consciousness-mind. The reason-mind is the true mind, and the ordinary mind as consciousness is an illusion. Our temporal mind is stained owing to its defiled affections.

The reason-mind is the mind which is absolutely pure, one, true, and non-illusory. All the universe is included in this one-mind. The pure mind is not to be mistaken for our relatively conditioned individual minds. It is the One in which all things are contained. It is what makes our thinking possible, and therefore it transcends thought.

While transcending thought, this absolute mind is the principle of discrimination, and is present in every form of discrimination. It discriminates, and yet it does not discriminate; it thinks and yet it is above thinking. It expresses itself in words, but words fail to describe its nature as reality-mind.

This reality-mind is also called *bhūtatathatā* (suchness or thus-ness of things), *Nirvāṇa, dharmadhātu* (the domain of the *dharma*), the *dharma-kāya* (*dharma*-body), *tathāgata* (the one who is thus come).

But, since our ordinary minds think of this mind as absolutely pure in its nature, it must be said that this pure mind subjects itself to limitations and assumes a form of relativity. We thus have this world of distinctions coming out of purity. Impurities are our stained minds filled with all sorts of defiled affections. In Mahāyāna Buddhism, defilements as such are non-existent and are regarded as not belonging to the mind. The mind being absolutely pure, there is no room in it for the principle of impurity. Impurities in our ordinary minds are of our own making, resulting from our ignorance. When ignorance is cleared away, the true nature of the original mind is restored.

While absolutely pure in nature the mind allows itself to become impure as well as pure. Hence, this triple world [9] is said to be one-mind only. The triple world is: (1) the world of living beings; (2) the world of form; and (3) the world of no form.

That all the phenomena in the universe are of one-mind is taught in the Kegon *Sūtras*. What is true and real is this one-mind only, and things that are imagined to rise from it are mere phenomena and hence illusions. But we are apt to regard all illusory phenomena as permanently fixed realities; this is the work of our ordinary minds. When the real existence of these illusory phenomena is denied, the one-mind reveals itself. This doctrine of one-mind only is Buddhist idealism.[10]

The Tendai School [11]—Phenomenology
(The T'ien-t'ai or Saddharma-pundarīka)

The basic teaching of the Tendai school is "*sarva-dharmāṇāṁ dharmatā*," which means that all things are in reality the same as they are in appearance, that all phenomena are such as they are. According to the *Saddharma-puṇḍarīka-sūtra*, which is the text of the Tendai school, "It is *buddhas* only who can realize the true state of all *dharmas* as they are." This state of "suchness" or "thusness" is expressed in the following formula:

(1) All objects are of such form;
(2) All objects are of such nature;
(3) All objects are of such substance;
(4) All objects are of such power;
(5) All objects are of such activities;
(6) All objects come from such causes;
(7) All objects have such conditions;
(8) All objects come to such effects;
(9) All objects acquire such reward;
(10) All objects begin, end, and are completed in such ways.

These ten modes of suchness or thusness, in which all objects are conceived to manifest themselves, belong to the realm of relativity. "Thusness" itself remains unaffected by all these changing modes, and is beyond words. To explain the formula:

(1) Form is the form assumed by an object;
(2) Nature is that which underlies the form;
(3) Substance is the body sustaining the form;
(4) Power is a power not yet in manifestation;
(5) Activities are the power brought out in full evidence;
(6) Cause is the efficient cause;
(7) Conditions are that which helps the cause to work out in actuality;
(8) Effect is that which is produced by the combination of causes and conditions;
(9) Reward means an effect not directly issuing from them;
(10) Completion means the ultimate conclusion of all these events enumerated in succession; beginning refers to form (1) and ending to reward (9).

The first nine modes of "thusness" belong to what is known as relative knowledge (*saṁvṛti-satya*), while the last one is true knowledge (*paramārtha-satya*). The idea is to show thereby how all objects in the phenomenal world are of absolute reason even as they are in their various modes of actuality. Absolute reason is not something transcending objects; it is in them, with them; it is they such as they are.

According to the Buddhist view, the world of living beings is divided into ten realms. Reading upward from the lowest inhabitants, these are: (1) occupants of hell, (2) departed spirits, (3) beasts, (4) fighting demons, (5) human beings, (6) heavenly beings, (7) *śrāvakas* (Hīnayāna disciples of Śākyamuni Buddha), (8) *pratyeka-buddhas* (Hīnayāna saints), (9) *bodhi-sattvas* (Mahāyāna saints), and (10) *buddhas* (perfectly enlightened ones). These ten realms do not exist separately; each contains all the others. Man has in his nature something potentially beastly as well as potential *buddha*hood or *buddha*nature. It is because of this potentiality that all beings are able to become *buddhas* and thereby be saved. As each of the ten realms contains in it all the other realms, there are one hundred realms. As each of these realms has the ten modes of thusness, one hundred times ten makes one thousand modes of thusness. Further, each of the one thousand modes of thusness contains a threefold world: (1) the world of living beings, i.e., beings endowed with mind and body, (2) the world of spatial extension, and (3) the five aggregates (*skandhas* [11a]): form, perception, conception, volition, and consciousness. When the one thousand modes of thusness are multiplied by the threefold world, this makes three thousand worlds. And these three thousand worlds are contained in one thought. All the three thousand worlds are thus said to be immanent in one thought.[12] When a single thought-wave is stirred up in the ocean of consciousness all the three thousand worlds must be regarded as coming into existence. The All is the One and the One is the All. Ultimate reality is not a separate entity transcending the world of pluralities.

The Kegon School [13]—Totalism
(The Hua-yen or Avataṁsaka)

The principal teaching of the Kegon school is "the self-origination of the *dharma-dhātu*." [14] The *dharma-dhātu* is the world conceived spiritually, and all forms manifested here have their reason within themselves and are not controlled by an outside agent.

The Kegon doctrine distinguishes between *ri* (*li*) and *ji* (*shih*); *ri* is absolute reason, and *ji* is this world of plurality. *Ri* is not to be conceived, however, as an independent something residing in the multitudinous objects and moving them; it is they, and they are it.

All our experiences are experiences of an actual world of pluralities (*ji*), and reason (*ri*) is a logical postulate. Reason is not one of the pluralities we experience, but by this conception the mutual interpenetration, or mutual fusion, of the individual objects becomes intelligible.

The Kegon school thus teaches that the one is the many and the many are the one.[15] One particle of dust is said to contain in it the entire cosmos. This doctrine of perfect interfusion is apt to be conceived in terms of space only, but the Kegon theory applies it also to time.

From this it derives the formula known as "The Origination of the Ten Mysteries," [16] and another known as "The Interfusion of the Six Forms." [17]

Briefly, the philosophy of the Kegon school is based upon the following key-terms:

(1) *Sōsoku (hsiang-chi): Sō (hsiang)* means "mutual"; *soku (chi)* is a difficult term to translate—"identity" is the best approximation. *Sōsoku*, therefore, means "mutually identical."

(2) *Sōnyū (hsiang-ju): Nyū (ju)* means "to enter," and so *sōnyū* means "mutually entering" or "mutual fusion."

(3) *Yennyū (yüan-yung): Yen (yüan)* means "perfect," and *yū (yung)* or *nyū* means "fusion" or "dissolution" or "solution" or "thawing." *Yennyū*, therefore, means "in perfect solution."

(4) *Muge (wu-ai): Mu (wu)* means "not," and *ge (ai)* means "obstruction" or "hindrance." *Muge*, therefore, means "no obstruction."

The Shingon School [18]—Mysticism
(The Chen-yen or Mantra)

The teaching of the Shingon school is based on the conception of the Absolute Buddha as the *dharma-kāya*. It is called a mystical or secret doctrine because it is too profound and mystical for the common people to understand. The central point of the teaching is "attaining *buddha*hood in this body," which means one can attain *buddha*hood in one moment or in one life.

The *dharma-kāya*, or *Mahāvairocana* Buddha, has no beginning, no ending; he has been enlightened since the beginningless past. There is no time when, no place where he is not already in existence. To realize this originally enlightened Buddha in ourselves is the aim of the Shingon teaching. The other schools of Mahāyāna Buddhism teach that *buddha*hood is attained by religious practice, while the Shingon school emphasizes that *buddha*hood is immanent in us and is not something to be acquired or added to us from an external source.[19]

According to Mahāyāna Buddhism generally, the ways leading to enlightenment are teachable, but enlightenment itself is beyond description, for enlightenment is the ultimate truth, which transcends our thoughts and words. The Shingon school, however, claims that enlightenment itself is expressible in words, for this relative world of thoughts, words, and actions as such is the absolute truth itself. No distinction is to be made between phenomena and noumenon. Phenomenal facts are noumenal. When reality is referred to, the emphasis is to be placed on phenomenal facts rather than on that which is abstracted from them.[20]

It is generally taught in Buddhism that *buddha*hood is attained step by step and through long periods by morally disciplining oneself, but the Shingon school teaches that one can become a *buddha* in this very body and in this life here and now.

The ritualistic prescriptions,[21] so rich and elaborate in the Shingon school, are the rites symbolizing the mystical, abrupt enlightenment attained by the Tathāgata (the perfect one; literally, the one who has thus come or thus gone, that is, the Buddha). They richly describe the various forms of *buddhas* and *bodhi-sattvas*, methods of meditation, recitals and mass, *maṇḍala* (circle), *dhāraṇī* (mystic verse), and *mudrā* (the fingers intertwining).

The *sūtras* deal with the doctrines, while the ritualistic prescriptions, the Shingon *yogin* meditates on the Buddha as the without practice is empty. In conformity with the ritualistic prescriptions, the Shingon yogin meditates on the Buddha as the principal image in his mind, recites mystical verses silently, and makes forms of intertwining with the fingers. When the three mystical actions are harmonized with the three mystical actions of the Buddha or a *bodhi-sattva*,[22] the enlightened nature originally inherent in the devotee is realized. This is the unification of one with the Buddha or the realization of *buddha*hood in this very common body in one moment, in one thought, in one life, instead of going through immeasurable periods.

Mahavairocana Buddha is the Absolute. He is all-embracing; he is omnipotent; he can become any *buddha* at any moment. It does not matter what *buddha* is to be made the principal *buddha*. Thus, the realization of *buddha*hood in this very body has taken place through the three mystical actions, words, and mind in the Shingon school, though these are not absent in the Kegon and Tendai schools.

In the Shingon doctrine, earth, water, fire, air, space, and consciousness are called the six fundamental "Greats," because they prevail in all phenomena. All things are manifestations not of the ultimate reason but of these six fundamental "Greats." Of the six fundamental "Greats," the first five belong to "form," or body, and the last one is mind. The first five belong to reason, or principle, and the last one is wisdom. Consequently, *Mahāvairocana* Buddha is nothing but the six fundamental "Greats." Therefore, *dharma*-nature is the six fundamental "Greats," which pervade all phenomena at the same time. The six fundamental "Greats" are mutually identified and harmonize in making up our one great universe.

The teaching of the mutual penetration of the tenfold world in the Tendai school and the doctrine of the non-obstruction of all things and all events in the Kegon school are taken into the teaching of the *Mahāvairocana* Buddha or the *Dharma-kāya*. Both the Kegon and Tendai schools have a tendency to treat the noumenon as the source of all phenomena, but the Shingon school emphasizes the sameness of phenomena and noumenon by the "realization of *Mahāvairocana* Buddha in one's very body" and by the causation-theory based on the six fundamental "Greats."

The concept of noumenon (*ri*) is man's abstraction, the result of ratiocination, set up to explain the phenomena, which are actualities facing every one of us. Noumenon, taken by itself, has no real existence apart from the phenomenal world and cannot be regarded as an independent something out of which the world takes its rise. Noumenon is that which we finally reach when we continue our intellectual search for an underlying principle of all things. It is that which comes as the ultimate, and not the first thing from which we start. We are immediately conscious only of sense-objects made of the six "Greats," or elements. It is not necessary to go beyond these in order to discover their source. Things as they are, are realities.

This world of actualities is something quite definitely differentiated. It is this that is found confronting us, and we take it at its face value. Even the idea of the six "Greats" is an assumption placed at the back of sense actualities; they are the outcome of logical inference. The Shingon world is therefore the same as our sense world, i.e., where we have form, sound, smell, taste, touch, and the laws existing among sense-objects.

The Jōdo School [23]—Pure Land
(The Ch'ing-t'u or Sukhāvatī)

In the various schools of Pure-Land Buddhism, Amitābha ("infinite light") and Amitāyus ("infinite life") Buddha is worshipped as the object of faith. If a man reflects upon his own evil nature, he will find that it is impossible for him to become a *buddha* by his own efforts. All people become *buddhas* by believing in Amida Buddha as the savior of all beings. Therefore, Pure-Land Buddhism is the way for the common people to become *buddhas,* while all the other forms of Buddhism are for saints of highly gifted minds. The former is called "the easy path," in which there is no need for complicated philosophical discussions, and the latter is "the difficult path." [24] Pure-Land Buddhism is the teaching for people with limited mental abilities. Becoming deeply conscious of their sinfulness and stupidity,[25] they humbly believe in the absolute power of the Buddha as savior and pronounce the name, *"Namu Amida Butsu."* When this is done with the utmost sincerity of heart, they are surely led to final enlightenment. For Amida Buddha, as the object of faith and as the possessor of infinite all-embracing compassion, will take everyone unto himself. This "absorption" into Amida's boundless compassion is the climax of the Jōdo teaching.[26] The devotees are thereby freed from the grip of all egotistic impulses and pronounce in the most natural way the name of Amida Buddha.

When we reflect upon our daily life, we discover that it depends altogether on others. We are thus filled with the spirit of humility and gratitude.

In Buddhism, all phenomena are explained in terms of cause and effect. All things originate from the combination of direct and indirect causes. In indirect causes we distinguish two factors, positive and negative. For example, rice grows from the seed (direct cause) sown in the ground, is helped by water, sunshine, and fertilizer (positive indirect causes), and is not disturbed by birds or frost (negative indirect causes). These direct and indirect causes are due in their turn to other direct and indirect causes, and thus the process goes on *ad infinitum*. Understanding this, we realize that rice exists in infinite relations to other things making up the whole universe. The universe is a system of all things united and intimately related in causal chains, indeed to such an extent that even a single particle of dust can be said to contain the whole universe.

When rice ripens and is harvested, it becomes the staff of life, and we are thereby sustained. Similarly, our existence depends on others; we cannot be ourselves except for them. The whole universe conspires to our support. We ought to feel grateful for this.

When we understand our relation to the universe, we realize that we ought to be doing something for the welfare of our fellow beings, non-sentient as well as sentient.

While we live on earth, therefore, it goes without saying that our life must be one of repentance and gratitude: repentance for our sinfulness and gratitude for Amida's boundless compassion.

After being born in the Pure Land,[27] we are not to stay there; we must think of other fellow beings who are still deeply submerged in the mire of birth and death. This thought naturally leads to a life of work again on this earth.

Being born in the Pure Land should not be interpreted in its ordinary and relative sense. "Being born" really means "not being born"; it is a birth of no-birth.

Nor is the Pure Land to be interpreted dualistically. It is a world which transcends opposites, being free from the dualism of purity and non-purity. It is a world of absolute purity, beyond thoughts and words.

The Zen School [28]—*Pure Intuitionism* (*The Ch'an or Dhyāna*)

The Zen school is also called the Buddha-mind school. It claims that the enlightenment attained by Śākyamuni is not to be expressed in words. It is transmitted directly from one mind to another. It is called an abrupt attainment because it is attained

immediately in this life. According to Hīnayāna Buddhism, enlightenment requires sixty *kalpas* (aeons, very long periods of time) or
at least three lives for a man. Mahāyāna Buddhism, on the whole,
teaches that *buddha*hood is attained by passing through fifty-two
stages of hard religious practice during a period of innumerable
kalpas, which means endless time. In other words, the abrupt
realization of *buddha*hood is impossible for ordinary beings, and
yet all human beings can become *buddhas.*

Enlightenment means casting off the various forms of defilement such as covetousness, anger, infatuation, arrogance, doubt,
false views, etc. But our world of experience is that of good and
evil in all possible combinations, and it is impossible to do away
with defilement.

Personality is ever perfectible by incessant spiritual effort, but
an instantaneous realization of enlightenment is impossible.

The Zen school, however, claims that abrupt enlightenment is
possible by realizing the truth that "the mind is identical with the
Buddha." This may be considered a further elaboration on the
Shingon idea that "one becomes a *buddha* with this body in this
life." The mind referred to in the Zen teaching is not our everyday
mind; it is what may be termed the Buddha-mind. But these two,
the Buddha-mind and our minds, are not to be conceived as
separate and mutually negating entities, for they are really identical,
but this identity is to be achieved only by our own spiritual effort—
and that constitutes enlightenment.

The Zen school represents the extreme form of self-effort or
self-power, and even Amida Buddha is thought to be discoverable
in one's own mind.

The differentiation of self and not-self is not so clear as we
might desire. As one's viewpoint expands, one's self expands. If a
man lives for himself alone, his self is limited to himself. If he lives
for others, his self expands and includes others as well. In the Great
Self there is no difference between self and not-self. As the Great
Self includes others as well as its own self, it may be called the
other self. To see the "Great Other" is *ta-riki* (*t'a-li,* other-power),
and to see the "Great Self" is *ji-riki* (*tzu-li,* self-power). The former
represents the Jōdo school, and the latter the Zen school. Therefore,
the culminating point of these two schools is the same.

When the self becomes identical with the not-self, enlightenment is attained, and all our actions are the Buddha's actions.

The enlightenment supposed to be acquired is not something

imposed upon one from an outside source; it has been present from the beginning. Before this truth was discovered, one had all kinds of defilement, but after the discovery of the truth all these are changed to deeds of purity. Covetousness, anger, and ignorance are sublimated into the noble virtues of precept (*śīla*), meditation (*dhyāna*), and wisdom (*prajñā*). "Defilement is even enlightenment"; "this world is the Pure Land itself." [29]

Conclusion

In Buddhism generally, absolute reason (*ri, li*) is contrasted to individuals (*ji, shih*). Absolute reason is the outcome of postulation and cannot be considered as reality. We often forget this, and try to start from the absolute reason instead of beginning with individual objects. Absolute reason is what we finally reach after speculation, and must not be considered as the starting point of our study of reality. Especially, absolute reason is not to be understood in terms of time, in which case it is certain to be understood as a sort of actual entity.

Our active life is not the product of speculation but is real fact. It is something that has come out of absolute reason and, hence, is not an object standing in opposition to absolute reason. Individuals are not individualized absolute reason, as nations are not particularized mankind. Mankind is an abstraction and is therefore without content, and we cannot deduce from it the concrete facts of life which we individuals experience.

According to the Mahāyāna, which is the latest development of Buddhism, we are already *buddhas* just as we are; this fact is apprehended by some Mahāyānists as a conviction [30] and by others as a matter of faith.[31] Those who express the immediate apprehension of this fact in the form of a conviction have a doctrine known as "original attainment and mysterious disciplining," [32] whereby they explain this world of activities. Those who teach faith in Amida have the doctrine known as "deeds of gratitude" [33] "spontaneously and naturally" [34] surging from one's inmost heart.

Notes

1. The three traditional and characteristic tenets of Mahāyāna Buddhism are: (1) All things are impermanent (*sarva-saṁskāra-anityatā*), (2) All things are selfless (*sarva-dharma-anātmatā*), and

(3) *Nirvāṇa* is bliss (peace) (*Nirvāṇam sukham*). Sometimes a fourth is added: All is suffering (*sarvam duḥkham*).

In Theravāda Buddhism the first truth is always: "All is suffering"; and "*Nirvana* is bliss" is not mentioned. The traditional four Noble Truths of Buddhism are: (1) Life consists entirely of suffering; (2) Suffering has causes; (3) The causes of suffering can be extinguished; and (4) There exists a way (The Eightfold Path) to extinguish the causes.

2. In speaking about *Nirvāṇa*, two phases are usually to be observed: (1) the *u yo e ne han* (*sopādhiśeṣa-nirvāṇa*) (incomplete *nirvāṇa*) and (2) the *mu yo e ne han* (*nirupādhiśeṣa-nirvāṇa*) (no-remainder *nirvāṇa*, the *nirvāṇa* state in which *no remainder of the karma of suffering exists*). Even though all the roots of illusion and, thus, the cause of transmigration through many lives, are extirpated, so long as one has physical existence in the present life, which is but the fruit of the one preceding, the *nirvāṇa* of such a one is called incomplete, because, as long as one is subjected to a life of flesh and blood, it is but natural that one should suffer physical pains, even though one's soul is enlightened. When one's corporeal existence is nullified, however, and no more such pain is experienced, a person is perfectly emancipated. Such complete *nirvāṇa* is meant here.

3. *Nirvāṇa* is primarily a term to signify emancipation from pains arising from the life of the present after having totally nullified one's corporeal existence. But this would also mean, on the other hand, one's arrival at a wisdom of *bodhi* (enlightenment) itself, and an emancipation from the pains of the present life will at once lead to the experience of true knowledge, which will engender positive action to save others.

4. Gautama, a man, became a *buddha* by awakening to the *dharma*, the law governing the universe. When the *dharma* reigns over a man, he is called a *buddha*. In Buddhist terminology, this is called the mutual identity of man and *dharma*.

5. In Buddhist terminology, this is called a mutual and identical fusion of the objective and the subjective worlds.

6. The *Mahā-prajñā-pāramitā-sūtra*, which speaks about *śūnyatā* (nothingness), represents the thought of the early Mahāyāna school, laying thereby the foundation for all later Mahāyāna thought.

7. Nāgārjuna, who was born in South India, may well be called the progenitor of Mahāyāna thought. In India, he was the founder of the Mādhyamika school; in China, such schools as the San-lun Tsung (Sanron sect), the Shih-lun Tsung (Shiron shū), and the T'ien-t'ai Tsung (Tendai shū) drew their tenets from such works by him as: the *Mūla-madhyamaka-kārikā*, the *Dvādaśa-nikāya-śāstra*, and the *Mahā-prajñā-pāramitā-śāstra*.

8. The original aim of the *śūnyatā* theory was to extirpate the illusory conception which a man is likely to fall prey to, and, therefore, it does not intend to speak of reality as "nothingness" or "non-entity." Only when all illusory conceptions are removed can all phenomena be understood as they are. Both the negative and the positive are the guiding milestones in the path of truth. When it is accepted that both the "truly non-existent" and the "mysteriously existent" are one, we arrive at a plane of thought where both are true. This aspect is further synthesized and is called the middle way (*madhyamā-pratipad*).

9. The term "triple world" means the universe.

10. All the phenomena of the universe are of the eternal present that incessantly changes and differentiates in the course of time, and all are controlled by mind—that is to say, only what is conceived in the realm of mind can be regarded as having existence. This doctrine is therefore called "idealism." All Mahāyāna Buddhism upholds idealism in one form or another.

11. The Tendai is one of the Buddhist schools founded in China. It was organized and brought to perfection by T'ien-t'ai Ta-shih (Chih-i) (538–597). The school bases its tenets upon the *Saddharma-puṇḍarīka-sūtra* and the *Mūla-madhyamaka-kārikā* by Nāgārjuna. The *Hokke gengi* (The Profound Teachings of the Lotus Sutra), the *Hokke mongi* (The Profound Entrance to the Lotus Doctrine), and the *Makashikan* (Teachings on Calm and Insight in the Mahāyāna) are regarded as the three great representative works.

11a. The five *skandhas* (aggregates or groups), which are the elements of the "self"—there is no substantial self in Buddhism—are (1) form or matter, (2) perception, (3) conception, (4) volition, and (5) consciousness.

12. This means that everything in the world exists in a fraction of our own thought. Of course, there is no need of particularly restricting the application to a fraction of thought, since the purpose is to say that in all souls, in a particle of substance, or in one thought, all others co-exist. But, as a personal experience of one journeying toward enlightenment, it is both natural and reasonable that one should start from a fraction of one's own thought. Therefore, effort is purposely made to take up one thought, and say "one thought, three thousands." Philosophically, there is no need of particularly restricting it to a thought, but, from the standpoint of religious practice, stress needs to be placed on a fraction of thought. The case is a practical one in which the relation of all *versus* one is to be realized in one's own mind, particularly in a fraction of thought.

13. The Kegon is another Buddhist school that represents Chinese Bud-

dhism. It is a "One-Vehicle religion" (*Eka-yāna* Buddhism), organized and perfected by Hsien-shou Ta-shih (Genjyu Daishi), i.e., Fa-tsang (643–712). The Tendai and the Kegon are the two great representatives of Chinese Buddhist philosophy. Kegon bases its tenets upon the *Avataṁsaka-sūtra.* The representative works of the school are the *Kegon tangenki* (Notes on the Profound Teachings of the Kegon Sutra) and the *Kegon gokyōshō* (Chapters on the Five Teachings of the Kegon).

14. In Japanese, *hokkai engi: hok* or *hō, dharma* or law, principle; *kai,* world; *en,* conditions (abbreviation of *innen,* cause and conditions); *gi* or *ki* (arise—abbreviation of *shō-ki,* being born or arises).

15. The Kegon school speaks about the *shi hokkai,* a way of explaining this discriminatory world from the four angles of: (1) the discriminatory practical world; (2) the world of ultimate reality that rests upon the basis of equality; (3) the one-and-not-two relationship of the phenomenal and the noumenal; and (4) the world in which each phenomenon is freely related to and is identical with all other phenomena. The end at which the Kegon school aims is to heighten one's perspective up to the perspective of the fourth, the truest, aspect.

16. *Jūgen engi: jū,* ten; *gen,* profound; *en,* conditions; *gi* or *ki,* arise. This is the theory in which the phases of the above-mentioned *jiji muge hokkai* are approached from ten angles. Only when one becomes enlightened concerning this truth does he enter the profound depths of the Kegon philosophy. Hence the term *"genmon"* (profound gate) or, abbreviated, merely *"gen."* As each of these ten elements mutually works as a condition causing thereby the birth of the other nine, we say *"engi."* The ten Mysteries are: (1) when all things exist side by side, in the same category of time, in their full being, each fully exerting influence upon others and reflecting to each other; (2) when one and all do mutually fuse into each other, though each does not lose its own individuality; (3) when one and all are freely and mutually identical with each other and when one is all and all are one; (4) when one and all are mutually identical and interfuse, multifariously phenomenalizing and yet showing no end, like inter-reflection among all the jewel stones of the Indra-net; (5) when one includes all and all include one, yet all the phases of one and all show balance and stability; (6) when one and all, perceptibly or imperceptibly, originate each other, yet showing no precedential order of fore and aft; (7) when one and all mutually fuse into each other, comprising all in one; (8) when things that exist separated through time mutually fuse into each other. We say "ten worlds," since there are the past, the present, and the future, and each of these possesses again the

three worlds of the past, the present, and the future, which, combined, constitute the nine worlds, and, as the nine worlds mutually
fuse into each other and exist in fraction of thought, the separate
nine and the whole make up the number ten; (9) when all things
are conceived of, after all, as but the manifestation of a fraction of
thought; and (10) when one realizes and manifests that each fact
accords with the *dharma*.

17. *Rokusō ennyū: roku,* six; *sō,* form; *en,* perfect; *yū* or *nyū,* harmoni-
zation. This is a term in which an exposition is sought toward
showing that six forms are seen in everything, thus showing mutual
harmony: (1) as each phenomenon possesses in itself all the virtues
of the others, as, for example, a house contains rafters, tiles, etc.;
(2) as an existence in an aggregate of all things, as, for example, a
house is made up of rafters, tiles, etc.; (3) as all the conditions
conjoin, making up one entity of existence and not breaking down
each other, as, for example, rafters, tiles, etc., conjoin together,
constituting a house; (4) as all things are different in their own
constitution, as, for example, tiles, etc., differ from each other; (5)
as a thing comes into being by the joint actions of conditions, as,
for example, a house comes into being by the joint working of the
rafters, tiles, etc.; (6) as all conditions are different in nature, each
having its own immovable stand to hold, as, for example, the rafters, the tiles, etc., have their own manifestations of existence, being
in themselves the house itself of which they are parts.
For further details see J. Takakusu, *The Essentials of Buddhist
Philosophy* (Honolulu: University of Hawaii, 1947).

18. Historically speaking, the Shingon is an esoteric religion that came
into being in India, passing therefrom to China and then to Japan.
But the school is one that represents Japanese Buddhism, the theo-
logical system having been perfected by Kūkai, also called Kōbō
Daishi (774–835), who was sent to China by the then Japanese
government to study Buddhism. The school bases its tenets upon
the *Dainichikyō* (*Mahā-vairocanābhi-sambodhi-sūtra*) and the
Kongōchōkyo (*Vajra-śekhara-sūtra*). These *sūtras* of esoteric nature came into being in India around 600–800, having been brought
over to China by Śubhakarasiṁa (Zenmui, 637–735), Vajrabodhi
(Kongōchi, 671–741), Amoghavajra (Fukū, 705–774), and others.

19. As this school originally stressed the self-consciousness of the enlightening quality that one possesses, it reached the conclusion that
the moment one is conscious that he is none other than the Buddha
himself one may be said to have attained *buddha*hood.

20. As in the Kegon school the emphasis is shifted from the theory of
riji muge (no obstruction between absolute reason and individual
objects) to that of *jiji muge* (no obstruction among individual ob-

jects), so, in the Shingon school, which follows the Kegon, matters pertaining to the world of particulars (*ji*) are much more highly valued than those pertaining to the rational or universal (*ri*) aspect of things.

21. The Shingon school differs from others of Mahāyāna Buddhism in that it puts much more stress upon ritualistic prescriptions than upon Sūtras. These are sacred books in which the actual ways and means of becoming the Buddha are set down in words, corporeal forms, finger intertwinings, and thoughts.

22. This means that the body, words, and mind of the Buddha or a *bodhi-sattva* fuse with those of persons practicing the Shingon system. The Buddha and our own self fuse and become one and the same, when the three mysteries of the Buddha's body, speech, and thought are added to us and held by us.

23. The Jōdo school is one of the representatives of Japanese Buddhism. It was founded by Genkū (Hōnen, 1133–1212), who based his teaching on three *sūtras* and one *śāstra*, i.e., the *Daimuryōjukyō* (*The Larger Sukhāvatīvyūha-sūtra*), the *Kwanmuryōjukyō* (*Amitāyurdhyāna-sūtra*), the *Amidakyō* (*The Smaller Sukhāvatīvyūha-sūtra*), and *Jōdoron* (*Aparimitāyus-sūtra-śāstra*) by Vasubandhu. His main work is the *Senchaku hongwannenbutsushū* (A Collection of Lines Concerning the Nembutsu of the Best Selected Vow), which was followed by his disciples. Shinran (1173–1262), one of his disciples, organized the doctrine. Thereafter, the houses of Ben'a (1162–1238) and Shōkū (1177–1247), the other disciples of Genkū, came to be called the Jōdo shū, against which the school of Shinran was called the Jōdoshin shū, or merely Shin shū. The teachings of these two schools serve as guides for men to birth in the Pure Land in the West, they having been saved by Amida Buddha. Whereas in the former the pronouncing of the name of Amida Buddha, i.e., "Namu Amida Butsu," is regarded as the condition of salvation, in the latter it is regarded simply as the spontaneous flowing out of the inner feeling of happiness after acceptance of the faith, repetition of the name of Amida Buddha not being regarded as conditional in any way.

24. Traditionally, the proper course for the Mahāyāna *bodhi-sattvas* is to practice for the long period of the three great *asaṁkhyas* (innumerable eras) and to develop into a *buddha*. This is the "difficult path." It was Amida Buddha who took the vows and became a *buddha* to save all those who cannot become enlightened by their own power. It is extremely easy and simple to become a *buddha* by straightway believing in the vow of Amida Buddha (which will have all people of all times and lands saved) and thus to be saved by faith alone. Nāgārjuna distinguished the "easy path" from the

"difficult path" of the *bodhi-sattvas* for those who cannot stand the hardship of the difficult path.

25. Generally we are aware that man's power is limited, but it is not always so easy to reflect deeply into one's self and feel that one is ignorant and fully clad in evils and to repent. But so long as one does not think deeply into one's self of ignorance and evil, one cannot easily feel in oneself the salvation of Amida Buddha. This being the case, although the path may seem easy (to be guided by the other's power), it is not easy for everyone to follow the path purely and truthfully; believing may seem simple, but it is not easy. That is why Shinran says, "Nothing is more difficult than to have fully the faith of belief."

26. We find in the *Daimuryōjukyō* (*The Larger Sukhāvativyūha-sūtra*) that Amida Buddha takes vows to the effect that when he attains perfect enlightenment in the future he will save all people of all times and all lands.

27. According to the faith of the Jōdo school, death is a return from the temporal world to an eternal and true life. It is not death, therefore, but birth. Accordingly, this is called "going and being born." But going and being born in the Pure Land is not our final goal; instead, as it is not possible to save others in this world of limited life, the goal is to save others after being born in the Pure Land, becoming thereby the Buddha and reappearing in all worlds freely and unmolested, to perfect one's task to save others. And, as both going and coming back are conceived of as resulting from the other power of Amida Buddha, we call this *"ekō."* The term *"ekō,"* in the accepted terminology of Mahāyāna Buddhism, means turning one's good and all toward others. But in the Jōdo school, especially in the Shin school of Shinran, the term implies "being given by the great power of Amida Buddha." Therefore, it must be understood why it is said "by the absolute other power." Everything is accepted as arising from the grace of Amida Buddha.

28. The Zen (Ch'an) school is a practical school of Buddhism. It was brought to China by Bodhidharma (516), whence it was brought to Japan by Eisai (1141–1215), Dōgen (1200–1253), and others, flourishing in Japan as the Rinzai-shū and the Sōtō-shū. It is a school of Mahāyāna Buddhism which penetrates deeply into one's inner self and reveals the immanent nature of *buddha*hood, which we all possess in our own self, instead of expounding the precepts of the Sūtras or depending upon outside and material practices and rituals. Zen is one of the foremost advocates of *jiriki* Buddhism, i.e., "Buddhism of self-effort or power," standing quite opposite to the Jōdo school, which is *tariki* Buddhism, "Buddhism of other effort or power."

29. That is, an ideal land of tranquillity and wisdom.
30. This is *jiriki* Buddhism.
31. This is *tariki* Buddhism.
32. When one is conscious that one has already attained *buddha*hood, his subsequent action, as a natural course of events, will be like that of the Buddha. This is to say that everything could not but become positive and active.
33. This is to say that from the moment one has attained the conviction that one is already saved by the Buddha, the natural course of events will lead to a life in which our actions will be turned into gratefulness, to answer to the great grace of Amida Buddha and that our everyday life should consist of happy gratefulness, with the result that our life will become lively and positive, in every phase of social actions.
34. It is a life of gratefulness, naturally, being saved by Amida Buddha.
35. A term serving to speak of a state transcending the categories of time and space.
36. A term which does not conceive *tathāgata* as transcending, but as immanent in one's defiled self.
37. This means the original nature of the *dharma*.

YUKAWA HIDEKI   *Modern Trend of Western*

Civilization and Cultural Peculiarities in Japan

AS A THEORETICAL PHYSICIST, I shall first analyze, mainly from a scientific point of view, the general trend that seems now to be prevailing in the recent development of Western civilization. The peculiarities of Japanese culture will then be examined from a more general standpoint, and in this connection the possibility will be investigated for some of these peculiarities to contribute in mitigating the distortions that, as the result of the above development, will in the future become more and more serious in every stage of human activity.

Standing at the beginning of a new age of technology, we are confronted inevitably with a hitherto inexperienced change in every aspect of human civilization. This change is produced mainly by the liberation of a vast amount of energy and also by rapid development in the means of transmission and accumulation of information. This change is especially remarkable in the domain of physics. Dividing this branch of research into two parts, the experimental and the theoretical, it is already well known that the progress of the former has always been rendered possible by a corresponding progress on the technical side. But insofar as theoretical physics is concerned, our conviction has been that we are in a so-called safety zone avoiding the attack of technology. Of course, this attitude rests on the classical ideal that the rational, autonomous, and active power of human thinking discovers the fundamental laws in the chaos of natural phenomena. In the last analysis, theoretical physics is nothing but the endeavor to reconstruct this actual universe on the basis of the ensemble of possibilities. The process of postulation, succeeded by selection of the fit by means of trial and error, is the essence of the mental activities of all theoretical physicists. Experimental physics represents our outer activities, whereas theoretical physics represents our inner activities, to understand natural phenomena in a rational fashion.

But now we must take the possibility into account that, quite in the same way as human labor and skill have been almost completely replaced by mechanistic apparatus in the domain of experimental physics, most of the labor and skill of the human brain is to be replaced by electronic computers. Originally, these were devised for the purpose of numerical solution of various kinds of equations. But the essentially human process of creativity can be replaced, to a considerable extent, by mechanistic processes occurring in these computers. The validity or invalidity of any postulated fundamental physical law will, in many cases, be determined more easily by judging the outcome from the computers. The process of selection from among possible fundamental laws may well reduce to the level of mechanistic operations, shifting the real problem in theoretical physics to the stage of technology. The rational understanding of the physical data obtained by experimentation has long been conceived as being essentially a problem of the inner activity of the human power of thinking. It has become possible that many of the problems may be projected outside the realm of inner human activity.

The tendency discussed above will probably culminate in the following. The electronic computers can be thought of as a kind of experimental apparatus wherein any electro-mechanical input is designed to be transformed into a definite electro-mechanical output in quite the same way as any physical object reacts to external conditions in a definite fashion prescribed by fundamental laws. Then the task of theoretical physics may well be reduced to that of setting up a unique correspondence between two kinds of mechanistic processes, one occurring in experimental apparatus and the other in computers. In this branch of research not much room will be left for the autonomous power of human thinking. The human intellect and insight will in the future play less and less part in the act of theorization, and, accordingly, mankind will be able to be proud only of the human ability of devising complicated computing mechanisms. In short, we may characterize such a tendency as the prevailing of empiricism or positivism in a broad sense.

The above tendency is not peculiar to physical science only, but is common to all aspects of human civilization. Not only is the worship of the mystery of the physical universe in the process of decay, but, as for the dignity of human existence itself, the part properly played by activities of human origin seems to be less and less important. Now we wonder what will be left in the future for mankind to perform without the aid of mechanistic apparatus. Technocracy is now threatening the nucleus of the human spirit. This is a natural and at the same time necessary outcome of the European mode of rational thinking, which has so far been so effective in establishing the machine civilization. In the process of this development, the Eastern mode of thinking was evidently destined to exert a negative influence. But, now that the future of Western rationalism seems not to be a pleasant one, we notice the rise of the hope that the Eastern tradition will play a complementary part in the future development of world civilization.

It is certainly beyond my ability to make in detail a comparative study of the Eastern and the Western modes of thinking and, in addition to this, to point out the specialities of Japanese culture in the Oriental background. However, it may be said, at least, that the Western mode of human living is characterized, in a broad sense, by confrontation with external environments, whereas the Eastern mode is characterized by adaptation to them. According to the former attitude, human living is destined to be, in every respect, positive or adventurous both in action and in thought. This was the very origin of the rational and abstract mode of thinking, and, moreover, the active and dynamic approach to natural phenomena by experimentation gave rise to modern scientific civilization. Though Eastern culture is characterized as being passive and static in its essence, in contrast with Western culture, we may say, disregarding differences in many respects and the exceptional case of Japan, that rationalism is a common factor in both of the two contrasting civilizations. In short, rationalism is a pattern of thinking which inquires into everything in the background of an ensemble of complementary possibilities. The peculiarity of the Japanese mode of thinking lies in its complete neglect of complementary alternatives. This we may term Japanese irrationalism. Of course, this is completely foreign to any form of scientific spirit, but it is identical neither with absolutism nor with skepticism. Moreover, it is akin to an optimistic rather than a pessimistic point of view. Nevertheless, it is well known that Japanese mentality is very far from any kind of insensibility. The subject of the following analysis will therefore be the irrationalism of the Japanese way of thinking, which is so peculiar and contradictory that even a Japanese himself finds it hard to understand.

In the first place, we can distinguish Western culture from Eastern by the fact that the former is far more adventurous in nature than the latter. The tribes that settled in the Eastern zone preferred stability in life to drastic changes. In other words, they have long been satisfied with the existing conditions imposed on them from the outside. Of course, the Japanese cannot be an exception to this. Though it has experienced short periods of outward extension, its political history has been dominated by stability. In this sense, Japanese culture holds a conspicuous position, even among the cultures of the Orient.

Such a speciality of the culture of Japan may be attributed to its natural conditions, its geographical isolation, and its mild climate. The Japanese have escaped invasions from the outside and famines on a large scale. As has been pointed out, Western and Eastern modes of human life are characterized, roughly speaking, by conquest of natural conditions and adaptation to them, respectively. In other words, these attitudes are those of hostility to and reconciliation with Nature. But, in Japan, there was originally no such thing as alienation between man and Nature. Man's physical existence has been relatively easy in Japan because a small amount of compromise on man's part has sufficed for adaptation to physical conditions. In Japan, there has been little need for adventure either in action or in thought.

Under the severe circumstances of the Western zone, adventurous effort to secure survival leads to the establishment of artificial environments for human living and consequently gives rise to a dynamic idea of a non-directional progress. In order to compromise with Nature, man stands in need, not only of autonomous action to modify external conditions, but also of effort to modify himself. This implies that some existing conceptions are renounced, and then one is to conform to a new concept selected from an ensemble of alternative possibilities. This is the very origin of the rational mode of thinking, and, furthermore, of the scientific spirit to discover physical laws in natural phenomena. Science is the outcome of that rational contact of man with external Nature.

In Oriental culture, examples of adventures of human thought are seen in various systems of fantastic cosmology. Then among the main themes in the systems of Eastern philosophy we notice that of transmigration. In this, the recurrence of approximately the same pattern is essential. This tendency seems to be reflected in the Oriental speciality that after destruction reconstruction is made with little modification and no drastic change.

Now let us analyze the dominant pattern in the Japanese mentality. It has the tendency to sidestep as far as possible any kind of confrontation. This, in turn, leads to the tendency to retain the existing stability with the least amount of modification at the sacrifice of a thoroughgoing solution. It seems to avoid any form of rational compromise based on a selection from alternative possibilities. If a prejudice exists, it is therefore in danger of dashing into collapse. But it must be noted that this is not a simple renouncement of rationality. Originally speaking, rationality takes an interest in the permanent and universal order transcending the narrow scope of space and time. But Japanese thought is concerned mainly about the local and temporary order restricted in space and time. This may be termed, for convenience, Japanese rationality. As an illustration, we cite here the fact that among various forms of human association a conspicuous importance has so far been given to the one between father and son or to that among the members of a family. Even at present the morals of a human group are apt to be molded in conformity with this same pattern—the relationship between a boss and his henchmen. Generally speaking, the Japanese is out of his element in long-range and abstract thinking. This tendency is completely foreign to adventurous and drastic changes. The remarkable stagnation and the conservatism noticed in various stages of Japanese culture are explained by the fact that temporary neglect of a succession of difficulties ensures the stability of a once-established system.

The Japanese mentality is, in most cases, unfit for abstract thinking and takes interest merely in tangible things. This is the origin of the Japanese excellence in technical art and the fine arts. The unconscious recognition of their own defect in abstraction seems to drive the Japanese to the uncritical adoration and the unconditional adoption of the religious and philosophical systems brought in from the outside. Such a task is relatively easy for the high-level Japanese intellect. But, in these systems, only the elements familiar to the Japanese clime are assimilated, and the unfamiliar ones are left unappreciated. Thus, existing conditions remain untouched and unchanged, ensuring the conspicuous stability of traditional elements. The abstract mode of thinking will continue to be foreign to the Japanese. And to them any rational system of thought, generally speaking, will not be more than something mystical, satisfying their intellectual curiosity.

In the history of Japan, we can cite numerous examples of the above. As was seen in the instances of the introduction of Buddhism and Confucianism, the Japanese were very progressive in the assimilation of their high-level cultural assets. But, among these, only the ones were appreciated that were effective in regulating and maintaining the existing social and political order. Hence, a thoroughgoing rationalism, such as the philosophy of Lao Tzu and Chuang Tzu, escaped general comprehension and found sympathy in the intellectual minority alone. This indifferent mode of life, standing aloof from the world, is symbolized by the seven wise men in the bamboo grove. The elements of thought common to this have been found in the West from ancient times—especially in Greece and Rome. This higher form of epicureanism is still seen in Western Europe and, in particular, in France, but may be regarded as a kind of vice in America and Soviet Russia. Properly speaking, this element is also foreign to the Japanese mentality, and the minority's longing for it finds no chance of actualization, being hindered by the disposition of the majority. Furthermore, even in the Eastern zone, the trend of transmigrationism is more remarkable in India, and there we find fakirs instead of Chinese hermits.

In the philosophy of Lao Tzu and Chuang Tzu we notice an element of thought similar to that characterizing science. This recognizes the insensate aspect of Nature, as was symbolized by Lao Tzu's saying, "The law of the universe is insensate [without jen], for it regards all things as straw dogs," [1] and, moreover, contains an element of the negation of human existence itself. In contrast with this, the Japanese mentality has a regard for ideas having concrete applicability to human living. The indifferent pursuit of the truth, made independently of such implications, did not and cannot appeal to most of the Japanese. For example, at the time of the introduction of Western civilization in the Meiji era (1867–1945), the practical sciences of Anglo-American origin were dominant. In spite of this, it was curious that thereafter the philosophical systems of German origin became most popular in Japan, whereas the ones of Anglo-American origin lost ground. This is due to the fact that the German systems were looked upon as something like mysticism or as akin to religious thought, aiming at the salvation of the human being. We may say that their rational character, as systems of learning, escaped the general understanding of the Japanese. This is also true of the Nishida philosophy, the unique system of philosophy in Japan. In the last analysis, the introduction of alien culture has been characterized in Japan by a peculiar action of transmutation.

In Japanese thought, the most conspicuous part has been played by moral principles, which may be termed the Way. But this is somewhat different in meaning from the one seen in Confucius' saying, "If a man in the morning learns the Way, he may in the evening die without regret." [2] This is similar neither to the philosophy inquiring into absolute truth nor to the religious creed aiming at human salvation. This is, in a sense, a thoroughgoing passiveness that submits to the irrationalities omnipresent in the universe by regarding them as inevitable. Moreover, this represents a kind of enlightenment by subsuming in one's self all the irrational elements of the universe. This is of a purely individual nature and requires no universality. In Japan, this has been regarded as the ideal for character building, and the Japanese multitude has shown regard for followers of Stoic discipline who pursue the Way. The status of Buddhism and Confucianism in Japan must be estimated in connection with the Japanese Way. In this sense, the Zen school plays an essential part in Japanese thought.

In the region of science, the Japanese mentality discussed above is reflected in laying stress on applied science and correspondingly in the negligence of rationalistic, abstract, and fundamental study. The multitude pays due regard to the dignity and mystery of scientific research, but cannot appreciate the essence of academic freedom, which is primarily of European origin.

As was discussed in the beginning of this paper, European rationalism has led, of necessity, to the world-wide predicament of today. The Orient has hitherto been compelled to accept Western culture in a passive manner, has utilized it, and has reconstructed its own culture so as to conform to the Western pattern. Among the elements indigenous to Japan there have been many which have been inconvenient for such a purpose. But we must also note that the rationalistic and systematic aspects of European thinking cannot be the whole of the measure of value in human life. Elements of thought completely foreign to those in European culture, or complementary to them are abundantly preserved in the tradition of Eastern thought and especially Japanese thought. This state of affairs has hitherto escaped the attention of the Oriental himself, and, moreover, has not been of much importance, judging from the current of the world. But now, in the light of the present-day world predicament, close examination of the possibilities contained in Oriental thought is essential.

The Western mode of living is characterized by confrontation with external circumstances and by man's being armed against them. This isolation of an individual is the very origin of European individualism. But we find in Western civilization a note of stiffness and uneasiness. In contrast with this, the Oriental has the subtle wisdom to devise comfortable conditions of human living by adapting himself to natural conditions.

The spiritual predicament of Western civilization is certainly caused by its too great dependence on artificial conditions. Generally speaking, the happiness of human life is the less stable the more it depends on external conditions. Therefore, the Japanese mode of thinking is more closely allied to happiness, since it makes an ideal of attaining a complete union of man and Nature, and, accordingly, of resolving any kind of alienation between them. This Japanese peculiarity gave rise to no rationalistic systems of science and philosophy, to be sure, but has led to a high degree of excellence in the fine arts. By nature, the Japanese are interested in the fine arts, both new and old, and also are always ready to appreciate their value. The feeling of fineness is reflected in every aspect of human living in Japan.

Unique in world history is the fact that in a corner of the Orient a distinguishing form of culture has been cultivated which suffers the least amount of disturbance from the outside. But modern Japan is in the process of incessant transfiguration. At present, we note the dangerous tendency in Japan to disregard uncritically the peculiar elements of its own culture in order to conform to patterns of Western civilization. Instead, there would seem to be an urgent need of searching out the possible ways in which Japanese cultural elements may contribute to the dissolving of the world-wide predicament of today.

Comments by Miyamoto Shōson

I should like to add a few comments on Dr. Yukawa's paper. The first concerns his statement: "Japanese mentality is, in most cases, unfit for abstract thinking and takes interest only in tangible things. This is the origin of the Japanese excellence in technical art and the fine arts." Elsewhere, Yukawa speaks of "Japanese irrationality" and "defect in abstraction." In order to avoid any misconception among the non-Japanese members of the Conference, I want to point out the inadequacy of this presentation and show that the greatness of Japanese art does not lie merely in "irrationality." Any great art is based upon a balanced and exact observation of environment and a penetration into the depth of Nature. A certain amount of abstraction and rational thought-process is necessary for the conception and expression of art.

In Japanese art, the eye which penetrates the *dharma* (*dharma-cakṣu; hōgen* in Japanese) is considered to be essential to art. In fact, great artists, such as Kano Motonobu and his successors, used *dharma-caksu* as part of their names.

In Buddhism, *dharma-cakṣu* is the first stage of a *bhikkhu's* entering the stream of the Buddha's *satori*. It is to see and realize things in their true nature, just as they are. This is not mere irrationalism or intuition, but a balanced and exact observation of Nature. Art, which is universal, is based upon this, and in the deepest source of human culture there is neither East nor West, but only Truth, Goodness, and Beauty.

This universal basis of Japanese art must be taken into consideration for a balanced view of the subject. It was this universal element which attracted men like E. Fenollosa, the American professor of logic and latter aesthetics at the Imperial University of Tokyo in 1878, and Dr. W. S. Bigelow, the Western art-patron, to Japanese art. They saw the *universal* in Japanese art, and this aspect, beyond East and West, Japanese and non-Japanese, must not be overlooked in the enthusiasm to show what traits are peculiar to the Japanese mind.

Secondly, Yukawa states that the peculiarity of "Japanese irrationality" is "a complete neglect of complementary alternatives" and that, because of the utter lack of the abstract mode of thinking among the Japanese, "any rational system of thought, generally speaking, will not be more than something mystical, satisfying their intellectual curiosity."

Now, Buddhism in Japan took 300 years, after its introduction in A.D. 538, to produce the philosophical doctrines of Shingon and Tendai, and more than 600 years to produce original Japanese Buddhist thinkers such as Hōnen, Shinran, Dōgen, and Nichiren. But, since the modernization of Japan, which began in 1868, it took less than ninety years to master the ways of Western civilization and attain a level of rational, scientific thought which developed scientists, such as Noguchi, Yukawa, and others. What is the reason for this relatively swift accomplishment? It is because the Japanese mind has been trained and developed, consciously and unconsciously—we may say, existentially—by the streams of Buddhist rationalistic ways of thinking. Aside from Tendai and Shingon, Rinzai Zen greatly influenced the statesman, the warrior, and the intelligentsia; and Sōtō Zen, founded by Dōgen, and the Shin school, founded by Shinran, deeply affected the pattern of thought and life of the common people.

As an example of the fact that Buddhism cultivates rational thinking and does not rely merely upon intuition, I wish to discuss briefly one of the most important terms in Japanese Buddhist thought, namely, "dōri," [3] which may be translated as rational, reason, or principle.

Dōri is derived from the fourfold dōri (or yukti) of the Vijñānavāda school. ("Yukti" means "unity" or "way of union.") The fourfold dōri is:

1. The Mādhyamika's principle of relation (apekṣa);
2. The Buddhist causal principle of relation (kārya-kāraṇa), which stresses conditions of conditional functioning. This thought runs through the Abhidharma schools down to Vijñānavāda and the Hua-yen (Kegon) schools;
3. The Buddhist logical method of recognition (upapatti-sādhana); and
4. The search for the rationale of reality (dharmatā) (dharmatā yukti).

Although the fourfold dōri, or the four ways of philosophical thinking, influenced the Japanese way of life, it is the fourth, hōnidōri, which requires explanation.

Shinran, for example, wrote an essay on this subject, "Essay on *Dharmatā*" (Jinen hōni shō). He pointed out that "this *Dharmatā* is the Saving Vow of Amida itself," and that "Amida Buddha is the means by which we come to realize the principle (*dōri*) of *Dharmatā*." Shinran also describes the Original Saving Vow of Amida as non-duality.

The Middle Way is a practical principle of life which sees the living value of things themselves in their rightful place and at their opportune moment. Based upon an open point of view, it makes possible an infinite range of insight. The term "intuition" alone does not cover the insight which penetrates the vital fact in a balanced view of the whole, nor does it strike the truth of the thing itself by analysis. In order to grasp the changing, real moment, the rational analysis of the whole, an untiring activity of the will, continued with fortitude and perseverance is of absolute necessity. The Middle Way is such a practical principle of synthesis.

Non-duality (*advaya*) is the rejection of opposites and contradictory viewpoints, but it is also a rejection of nihilistic negation. This "no-position" is called "voidness" (*śūnyatā*), but this is not nihilism. It is a dynamic principle of life which permits a becoming of infinite progression. Non-duality is so called because it negates the pairs of opposites, but the opposites themselves are also in infinite progression; and, therefore, though it is a function of the process of negation, comparison, measurement, elimination, abstraction, postulation, and universalization are all involved.

Non-duality is not the name for mere intuition, because it is vital not to become attached to intuition itself. Since there is this comprehensive and total aspect to the Middle Way, non-duality, and voidness, they are sometimes termed "inexpressible," and yet none is absolutism. This is the most important point and the vital thing to remember. The rational process involved in reaching the principle of non-duality is indicated by Shinran's enumeration of forty-eight pairs of opposites; abrupt and gradual, horizontal and vertical, superior and inferior, pure and mixed, straightway and roundabout, rational and non-rational, unbroken and broken, continuation and non-continuation, one's own will and following another's will, transference and non-transference, self-power and other-power, etc. In *The Sūtra of Wei Lang*, thirty-six pairs of opposites are enumerated.[5] Thus, Shinran followed the basic stream of Buddhist thinking on *Dharmatā*, The Middle Way, and non-duality.

Dōgen speaks of the non-duality of practice and *satori*, and he dedicated his life to seeking the true philosophical meaning of *Dharmatā.*

Shinran, though he relentlessly sought the good, had a deep insight into the existential evil of man's nature. Consequently, his exposition of *dharmatā-yukti* has a strong tinge of religious practice and vow, whereas Dōgen pushed toward the living realization of *dharmatā,* the true nature of things, and engraved a philosophical poem in the realm of truth to be remembered as a poet-philosopher. The former is spiritual in its realistic faith; the latter is philosophical in its realized actuality. Both, however, are rational in their understanding of *dharmatā-yukti,* and both touch the aesthetic sense of reality.

Dr. Suzuki has expounded the intuition of Rinzai Zen for many years, but the philosophical, rational thought of Shinran and Dōgen await interpreters for the West.[6]

In conclusion, although there has not been a rational *system* of philosophy and science in Japan as in the West, nevertheless, the Japanese mind has been trained in rational thinking by Buddhism for many centuries.

The following excerpt from the paper presented by Dr. Suzuki at the 1959 Conference is such an excellent statement of the more or less typical difference between the Far East and the West in general method of thinking that it was felt almost mandatory to make it available to the reader of this volume. The statement is, of course, open to challenge; but it does seem to represent the way many Far Easterners think, on the one hand, and the way Westerners think, on the other. The passage is included *here* because the preceding material deals with the West, and this supplements that.

One, at least, of the most fundamental differences between East and West as far as their way of thinking is concerned is that the Western mind emphasizes the dualistic aspect of reality while the Eastern mind basically tends to be advaitist. Advaitism is not the same as monism; it simply asserts that reality is non-dualistic. Monism limits, whereas advaitism leaves the question open, and refuses to make any definite statement about reality. It is not-two, which is not the same as one. It is both yes and no, yet it is neither the one nor the other.

The West lives in a world separated into two terms: subject and object, self and not-self, yes and no, good and evil, right and wrong, true and false. It is therefore more logical or scientific, where yes cannot be no and not cannot be yes, where a square is not a triangle, where one is not two, where "I" and "thou" are eternally separated and can never be merged, where God creates and the creature forever remains created, where "our Father . . . art in heaven" and we mortals are groveling on earth. The Western mind abhors paradoxes, contradictions, absurdities, obscurantism, emptiness, in short, anything that is not clear, well-defined, and capable of determination.

Advaitism is not a very clear concept, however, and I should like to have another term to make my position better defined. When I say that reality is not dualistic, that a world of subject and object is not final, and that there is a something which is neither subjective nor objective, and further that this something is not to be subsumed under any category born of the dualistic concept of subject and object, I may be stamped as a mystic with all his scientifically unacceptable qualifications. Whatever this may mean, the mystic has a very concrete and therefore a very positive experience of ultimate reality which according to him cannot be conceptualized after the ordinary rules of logical thinking. Logic, as we understand it, has its limitation and cannot expect to catch every fish in its net.

All our sense-experiences are limited and definite, and the intellect based on them is also limited and definable. They all belong in the world of subject and object, seeing and seen, thinking and thought, that is, in the world of dualities. Here reality is always subjected to a separation; it is never grasped in its suchness or isness, or in its totality. Logicians and scientists deal with reality in its inevitably separated and therefore limited aspect. Therefore, there is always a something left over after their studies and measurements. They are not conscious of this something; in fact, they insist that there is nothing left behind, that they have everything they want to study. They go even so far as to declare that if there is anything left they have nothing to do with it, for it can never be scooped up with their logical shovel.

In fact, there are some minds that can never be satisfied with so-called logical accuracies and mathematical measurements, for they have the feeling or sense of a something which persistently claims their attention and which can never be "accurately" determined. This something is described by Baudelaire as "the steely barb of the infinite." They cannot rest until this disquieting something is actually held in their hands in the same way as we pick up a piece of stone or listen to a singing bird. Whatever name we may give to this mysterious something—God, or Ultimate Reality, or the Absolute, or the *Ātman,* or the Self, or *Brahman,* or *Tao,* or Heaven, or Reason, or the Infinite, or Emptiness, or Nothing—it is always bafflingly before us or behind the duality of "I and thou," or of the self and not-self, or subject and object, or God and creation.

Notes

1. *Tao-te ching,* V.
2. *Lun yü,* IV.8.
3. "*Do*" of "*dōri*" is the Chinese character *Tao,* and "*ri*" is the reason or law of things. Professor Wing-tsit Chan defines the character *ri* (read *li* in Chinese pronunciation) most aptly, as follows: "*Li* has come to mean the form, texture, quality, or nature of things, and acquires the meaning of the reason or the law of a thing or things" (*Philosophy East and West,* IV, No. 4 [January, 1955], 328). Chan is also in agreement with Joseph Needham's interpretation of *li* as "organization" and "principle of organization." In Japan, to give two illustrations: the famous historian, Kitabatake Chikafusa (1293–1354), author of *Jinnō shōtōki* (The Records of the Legitimate Succession of the Divine Sovereigns), used *dōri* as the basic concept in formulating his philosophy of history; and, in the contemporary age, Dr. Amano Teiyū, a colleague of Nishida at Kyoto University and one-time Minister of Education, used this as the main theme in the book entitled *Dōri no kankaku* (The Sense of Reason). "*Dōri*" was a word of common use among Buddhist scholars of those days, not to mention Hōnen, Shinran, Dōgen, Nichiren, etc.

SUZUKI DAISETZ TEITARŌ   *Reason and*

Intuition in Buddhist Philosophy

I

FOR "INTUITION," Buddhists generally use "*prajñā*" [1] and for reason, or discursive understanding, "*vijñāna*." [2] *Vijñāna* and *prajñā* are always contrasted.

The terminology usually accepted in philosophy does not seem to be sufficient to express what I have in mind, but I will try my best to explain what the Buddhist idea of "intuition" is and, in connection with it, that of reason.

Prajñā goes beyond *vijñāna*. We make use of *vijñāna* in our world of the senses and intellect, which is characterized by dualism in the sense that there is one who sees and there is the other that is seen—the two standing in opposition. In *prajñā*, this differentiation does not take place: what is seen and the one who sees are identical; the seer is the seen and the seen is the seer. *Prajñā* ceases to be *prajñā* when it is analyzed into two factors as is done in the case of *vijñāna*. *Prajñā* is content with itself. To divide is characteristic of *vijñāna*, while with *prajñā* it is just the opposite. *Prajñā* is the self-knowledge of the whole, in contrast to *vijñāna*, which busies itself with parts. *Prajñā* is an integrating principle, while *vijñāna* always analyzes. *Vijñāna* cannot work without having *prajñā* behind it; parts are parts of the whole; parts never exist by themselves, for, if they did, they would not be parts—they would even cease to exist. Mere aggregates have no significance, and this is why in Buddhist philosophy all *dharmas* (elements),[3] when they are regarded as individual existences, are declared to have no *ātman*.[4] The *ātman* is a unifying principle, and the idea is that, as long as all *dharmas* are conceived without any reference to that which unifies them, they are just disconnected parts, that is, they are non-existent. *Prajñā* is needed to make them coherent, articulate, and significant. The Buddhist conception of impermanence and suffering is not to be explained merely from the moral and phenomenological point of view. It has an epistemological background. *Vijñāna* without *prajñā* kills; it works for individualization, and, by making each individual disconnected with others, *vijñāna* makes them all impermanent and subject to the Law of *Karma*. It is by *prajñā* that all *dharmas* are observable from a unitive point of view and acquire a new life and significance.

Prajñā is ever seeking unity on the grandest possible scale, so that there could be no further unity in any sense; whatever expressions or statements it makes are thus naturally beyond the order of *vijñāna*. *Vijñāna* subjects them to intellectual analysis, trying to find something comprehensible according to its own measure. But *vijñāna* cannot do this for the obvious reason that *prajñā* starts from where *vijñāna* cannot penetrate. *Vijñāna*, being the principle of differentiation, can never see *prajñā* in its oneness, and it is because of the very nature of *vijñāna* that *prajñā* proves utterly baffling to it.

To illustrate this point let us see what kind of statements *prajñā* will make when it is left to itself without the interference of *vijñāna*. One statement which is very common is: "I am not I, therefore I am I." This is the thread of thought running through the Buddhist *Sūtras* known as the "Prajñā-pāramitā," [5] consisting of six hundred "volumes" in Chinese translation. In *The Diamond Sūtra*,[6] belonging to the Prajñā-pāramitā class, we have this: "What is known as *prajñā* is not *prajñā*, therefore it is known as *prajñā*." When this is rendered into popular language it takes this form: "I am empty-handed, and, behold, the spade is in my hands." [7] "When a man walks on the bridge, the bridge flows, while the water does not."

In still another way, "the logic of *prajñā*" may demand this of us: "Do not call this a staff; [8] if you do, it is an affirmation; if you do not, it is a negation. Apart from affirmation and negation say a word, quick, quick!" It is important to note here that *prajñā* wants to see its diction "quickly" apprehended, giving us no intervening moment for reflection or analysis or interpretation. *Prajñā* for this reason is frequently likened to a flash of lightning or to a spark from two striking pieces of flint. "Quickness" does not refer to progress of time; it means immediacy, absence of deliberation, no allowance for an intervening proposition, no passing from premises to conclusion.[9] *Prajñā* is pure act, pure experience. But we must remember that here is a distinctly noetic quality which really characterizes *prajñā*, and this is the sense in which *prajñā* is often regarded as an intuitive act—which interpretation, however, remains to be more fully examined.

Going back to the "staff" paradox, when the master of Buddhist philosophy produced the staff and demanded its definition, not by means of intellection, not by an objective method, the following happened: Someone came forward from the assembled group, took the staff, broke it in two, and without saying a word left the room. On another occasion, the answer came in this form: "I call it a staff." A third answer was possible: "I do not call it a staff." [10]

The staff is one of the things carried by the masters when they appear at the "*Dharma* Hall," and naturally they make use of it frequently while engaged in a discourse. Let me give some more examples in which the staff is very much in evidence.

When a monk asked a master as to the universality of *bodhi* [11] (enlightenment), the master took up his staff and chased him. The monk, surprised, ran away. The master said, "What is the use? When you see another master sometime later you may argue the point again." This story is not really to find a *prajñā* definition of the staff, but incidentally the staff comes out and gives its own definition. The same master had another occasion to refer to the staff. One day he produced it before the disciples and said, "For the last thirty years, while living in this mountain retreat, how much of my life I owe to this staff!" A monk asked, "What power could it be that you owe to it?" The master said, "While walking along the mountain trails, while crossing the mountain streams, it has supported me in every possible way."

When another master heard of this later, he said, "If I were he, I would not say that." A monk asked, "What would you say?" The master, without saying a word, came down from the seat and walked away with the staff supporting him.

Ummon (of the tenth century) was one of the great staff-wielders, and let me cite a few of his demonstrations.[12] His discourse once ran thus: "Vasubandhu, the *bodhi-sattva* [a being whose essence is perfect wisdom], was unexpectedly turned into a rough-hewn staff." Then he drew a line on the ground with his staff, and said, "*Buddhas* as numberless as the sands of the Ganges are here engaged in heated discussion over the Buddhist truth."

At another time, after the same gesture, the master said, "All is here!" Then, repeating the gesture, he said, "All is gone out of here! Take good care of yourselves!" At still another time he produced the staff before the congregation, and said, "The staff has transformed itself into a dragon, and the dragon has swallowed up the whole universe. Where are the mountains and rivers and the great earth?" Another master made this remark on the staff: "When you understand the staff, your study of Buddhist philosophy is completed."

The staff has been quite a useful and effective weapon in the hands of the masters. Though the following remark by Ummon has no direct reference to the staff itself, it may be found interesting to understand how the masters flourish it. Says Ummon, "Do you want to know how the ancient masters dealt with the matter for you? Tokusan chased a monk away with the staff the very moment the monk was approaching him. Bokujū, seeing a monk enter the gate, lost no time in saying, "Be gone, quick! Thirty blows are coming upon you!" [13]

"The matter" referred to here by Ummon is *prajñā*-intuition, and he has the following [14] to say about it, though his discourse is indirect from the rationalistic point of view. "O disciples, do not act like this: For instance, when you hear people talk about the teaching of *buddhas* and patriarchs, you ask what this teaching is. But do you know who the Buddha is, who the patriarch is? Can you tell me what makes them talk as they do? You ask again how to escape the bondage set by the triple world. But let me see what this so-called triple world is. Is there anything that will obstruct your way in any sense? Does your hearing do this? Does your sight do this? Where is the world of differentiation which you imagine to be obstructing your freedom? Where is the bondage you want to escape from?

"The wise men of old, seeing you so troubled with illusions and hypotheses, threw their whole being before you and exclaimed, 'Here is the whole truth! Here is the ultimate reality!' But I will say, 'Here! Is there anything you can mark as this or that? If you tarry even for a moment you have already lost its trail!'"

"Not to tarry even for a moment," "Say a word quick, quick!"

"Thirty blows on your head!"—all these admonitions on the part of the master point to the nature of *prajñā*-intuition, and, as this immediacy characterizes *prajñā*-intuition, it is mistakenly identified with ordinary intuition. This being the case, *prajñā should be classified as a very special form of intuition—that which may be termed "prajñā-intuition" in distinction from the kind of intuition we have generally in philosophical and religious discourses. In the latter case there is an object of intuition known as God or reality or truth or the Absolute,* and the act of intuition is considered complete when a state of identification takes place between the object and the subject.

But in the case of prajñā-intuition there is no definable object to be intuited. If there is one, it can be anything from an insignificant blade of grass growing on the roadside to the golden-colored *buddha*-body ten feet six in height.[15] In *prajñā*-intuition the object of intuition is never a concept postulated by an elaborate process of reasoning; it is never "this" or "that"; it does not want to attach itself to any one particular object. The master of Buddhist philosophy takes up the staff because it is always available, but he is ever ready to make use of anything that comes his way. If a dog is near, he does not hesitate to kick it and make it cry out, in order to demonstrate the universality of the *buddha*-nature.[16] He cuts off the fingertip of a little boy-monk to let him realize what is the meaning of finger-lifting—the favorite method used by a certain master in teaching his inquirers.[17] As for breaking a dish or a cup or a mirror,[18] or upsetting a fully prepared dinner table,[19] or refusing to feed a hungry traveling monk,[20] the masters think nothing of such incidents, since they help the truth-seekers come to an understanding of Buddhist philosophy.

As the methods of demonstrating *prajñā*-intuition permit of an infinite variety, so the answers given to a problem set by the master also vary infinitely; they are never stereotyped. This we have already seen in the case of the staff. To understand the staff in the *vijñāna* way of thinking will allow only one of the two, negation or affirmation, and not both at the same time. It is different with *prajñā*-intuition. It will declare the staff not to be a staff and at the same time declare it to be one, and the master's demand to go beyond affirmation and negation is, we can say, in one sense altogether ignored and in another not at all ignored. And yet, either answer is correct; it all depends upon whether you have an instance of *prajñā*-intuition or not. If you have it, you can establish your case in whatever way suits you best at the moment. You may even break the staff in two; you may take it away from the master and throw it down on the ground; you may walk away with it; you may swing it in the way of a skilled sword-player. There are many more ways to manifest the "mysteries" of the staff. *Vijñāna* cannot do this unless it is dissolved in *prajñā*-intuition. There is a key-point in all this and to comprehend it constitutes *prajñā*-intuition.

This key-point cannot be expressed as a concept, as something distinct to be placed before the mind. All is veiled in obscurity, as it were. Something seems to be hinted at, but it is impossible to put one's finger on it. It is alluring enough, but *vijñāna* finds it beyond its grasp. *Vijñāna* wants everything to be clear-cut and well defined, with no mixing of contradictory statements, which, however, *prajñā* nonchalantly overrides.

The difficulty in defining the "object" of *prajñā*-intuition can also be seen from the following *mondō* (questions and answers), in one of which it is disposed of as *acintya*, i.e., as beyond human understanding. As long as the understanding is based upon the principle of bifurcation, where "you" and "I" are to be set apart as standing against each other, there cannot be any *prajñā*-intuition. At the same time, if there were no bifurcation, such intuition could not take place. *Prajñā* and *vijñāna* may thus be said to be in a sense correlated from the point of view of *vijñāna* discrimination, but this is really where the root of misinterpreting the nature of *prajñā* grows.

Yikwan, the master of Kōzenji (Kozen temple), of the T'ang Dynasty (618–960), was asked by a monk, "Has the dog *buddha*-nature?" The master said, "Yes, it has." The monk asked, "Have you *buddha*-nature?" "No, I have not." "When it is said that all beings are endowed with the *buddha*-nature, how is it that you have it not?" "It is because I am not what you call 'all beings.'" "If you are not, are you a *buddha*?" "No, I am neither." "What are you then, after all?" "I am not a 'what.'" The monk finally said, "Can it be seen or thought of?" the Master replied, "It is beyond thought or argument, and therefore it is called the unthinkable (*acintya*)."

At another time, he asked, "What is the way (*tao*)?" The master answered, "It is right before you." "Why do I not see it?" Said the master, "Because you have an 'I,' you do not see it. So long as there are 'you' and 'I,' there is a mutual conditioning, and there can be no 'seeing' in the real sense." "This being the case, if there is neither 'you' nor 'I,' can there be any 'seeing'?" The master gave the final verdict, "If there is neither 'you' nor 'I,' who wants to 'see'?"

Thus we can see that *prajñā*-intuition is an intuition all by it-self and cannot be classified with other forms of intuition as we ordinarily understand the term. When we see a flower, we say it is a flower, and this is an act of intuition, for perception is a form of intuition. But, when *prajñā* takes the flower, it wants us to take, not only the flower, but at the same time what is not the flower, in other words, to see the flower before it came into existence—and this not by way of postulation but "immediately." To present this idea in a more metaphysical fashion: *Prajñā* will ask, "Even prior to the creation of the world, where is God?" Or, more personally, "When you are dead and cremated and the ashes scattered to the winds, where is your self?" To these questions, *prajñā* demands a "quick" answer or response, and will not allow a moment's delay for reflec-tion or ratiocination.

Philosophers will naturally try to solve these questions in some logically methodical manner worthy of their profession and may pronounce them absurd because they do not yield to intellectual treatment. Or they might say that they would have to write a book to give the subject an intelligent solution if there were any. But the *prajñā* method is different. If the demand is to see the flower be-fore it blooms, *prajñā* will respond without a moment of delay, saying, "What a beautiful flower it is!" If it is about God prior to the creation of the world, *prajñā* will, as it were, violently shake you up by taking hold of your collar and perhaps remarking, "This stupid, good-for-nothing fellow!" If it is about your cremation and the scattering of the ashes, the *prajñā* teacher may loudly call your name, and, when you reply, "Yes, what is it?" he may retort, "Where are you?" *Prajñā*-intuition settles such grave questions instantly, while philosophers, or dialecticians, spend hours, nay, years, search-ing for "objective evidence" of "experimental demonstration."

II

The fact is that *prajñā* methodology is diametrically opposed to that of *vijñāna*, or the intellect, and it is for this reason that what *prajñā* states always looks so absurd and nonsensical to the latter and is likely to be rejected without even being examined. *Vijñāna is the principle of bifurcation and conceptualization,* and for this reason it is the most efficient weapon in handling affairs of our daily life. We have thus come to regard it as the most essential means of dealing with the world of relativities, forgetting that this world is the creation of something that lies far deeper than the intellect—indeed, the intellect itself owes its existence and all-round utility to this mysterious something. While this way of *vijñāna* appraisal is a tragedy because it causes to our hearts or to our spirits unspeakable anguish and makes this life a burden full of miseries, we must remember that it is because of this tragedy that we are awakened to the truth of *prajñā* experience.

Prajñā thus is always tolerant toward *vijñāna*, though outwardly it may seem to be abusive and unreasonably harsh toward it. The idea is to recall it to its proper and original office whereby it can work in harmony with *prajñā*, thus giving to both the heart and the mind what each has been looking for ever since the awakening of human consciousness. When, therefore, *prajñā* violently breaks all the rules of ratiocination, we must take it as giving the intellect a sign of grave danger. When *vijñāna* sees this, *vijñāna* ought to heed it and try to examine itself thoroughly. It ought not go on with its "rationalistic" way.

That *prajñā* underlies *vijñāna*, that it is what enables *vijñāna* to function as the principle of differentiation, is not difficult to realize when we see that differentiation is impossible without something that works for integration or unification. The dichotomy of subject and object cannot obtain unless there is something that lies behind them, something that is neither subject nor object; this is a kind of field where they can operate, where subject can be separated from object, object from subject. If the two are not related in any way, we cannot even speak of their separation or antithesis. There must be something of subject in object and something of object in subject which make their separation as well as their relationship possible. And, as this something cannot be made the theme of intellectualization, there must be another method of reaching this most fundamental principle. The fact that it is so utterly fundamental excludes the application of the bifurcating instrument. We must appeal to *prajñā*-intuition.

When we state that *prajñā* underlies or permeates or penetrates *vijñāna* we are apt to think that there is a special faculty called *prajñā* and that this does all kinds of work of penetration or permeation in relation to *vijñāna*. This way of thinking is to make *prajñā* an aspect of *vijñāna*. *Prajñā*, however, is not the principle of judgment whereby subject becomes related to object. *Prajñā transcends all forms of judgment and is not at all predicable.*

Another mistake we often make about *prajñā* is that somehow it tends toward pantheism. For this reason, Buddhist philosophy is known among scholars as pantheistic. But that this is an incorrect view is evident from the fact that *prajñā* does not belong in the category of *vijñāna* and that whatever judgment we derive from the exercise of *vijñāna* cannot apply to *prajñā*. In pantheism there is still an antithesis of subject and object, and the idea of an all-permeating God in the world of plurality is the work of postulation. *Prajñā*-intuition precludes this. No distinction is allowed here between the one and the many, the whole and the parts. When a blade of grass is lifted the whole universe is revealed there; in every pore of the skin there pulsates the life of the triple world, and this is intuited by *prajñā*, not by way of reasoning but "immediately." The characteristic of prajñā is this "immediacy." If we have reasoning to do here, it comes too late; as the Zen masters would say, "a speck of white cloud ten thousand miles away."

Paradoxical statements are therefore characteristic of *prajñā*-intuition. As it transcends *vijñāna*, or logic, it does not mind contradicting itself; it knows that a contradiction is the outcome of differentiation, which is the work of *vijñāna*. *Prajñā* negates what it asserted before, and conversely; it has its own way of dealing with this world of dualities. The flower is red and not-red; the bridge flows and not the river; the wooden horse neighs; the stone maiden dances.

To speak more logically, if this is allowable with *prajñā*-intuition, everything connected with *vijñāna* also belongs to *prajñā*; *prajñā* is there in its wholeness; it is never divided even when it reveals itself in each assertion or negation made by *vijñāna*. *To be itself vijñāna polarizes itself, but prajñā never loses its unitive totality.* The Buddhist's favorite illustration of the nature of *prajñā*-intuition is given by the analogy of the moon reflecting in infinitely changing forms of water, from a mere drop of rain to the vast expanse of the ocean, and these with infinitely varied degrees of purity. The analogy is likely to be misunderstood, however. From the fact that the body of the moon is one in spite of its unlimited divisibilities, *prajñā*-intuition may be taken as suggesting oneness abstracted from the many. But to qualify *prajñā* in this way is to destroy it. The oneness or completeness or self-sufficiency of it, if it is necessary to picture it to our differentiating minds, is not, after all, to be logically or mathematically interpreted. But as our minds always demand an interpretation, we may say this: *not unity in multiplicity, nor multiplicity in unity; but unity is multiplicity and multiplicity is unity.* In other words, *prajñā* is *vijñāna,* and *vijñāna* is *prajñā;* only, this is to be "immediately" apprehended and not after a tedious and elaborate and complicated process of dialectic.

III

To illustrate the significance of *prajñā* in relation to *vijñāna,* let me cite some cases from the history of Zen (or Ch'an) Buddhism in China.

(1) When a Zen student called Shuzan shu (907–960) came to Hōgen, one of the great masters of the Five Dynasties era, Hōgen said, "There is a saying that an inch's difference makes it as widely apart as heaven from the earth. How do you understand this?" Shuzan shu merely repeated it, saying, "An inch's difference makes it as widely apart as heaven from the earth." Hōgen said, "If your understanding does not go any farther than that, you have not got the point." Shu then asked, "What, then, is your understanding?" Hōgen said, "An inch's difference makes it as widely apart as heaven from the earth." Shu then understood and bowed.[21]

Someone later added the comment: "Why was Shu wrong with his repetition? When he asked Hōgen for instruction, Hōgen merely repeated it and that made Shu realize his fault. Where was the trouble? If you understand the point, I will say you know a thing or two." (The Chinese original is terse and forceful but altogether loses its weight when translated. The original runs: "An inch's difference, heaven-and-earth's separation.")

(2) When Gensoku first saw Seiho,[22] Gensoku asked, "Who is the Buddha?" Seiho answered, "The god of fire comes and asks for fire." When Gensoku heard this, it touched his heart deeply. When later he came to see Jōye, and Jōye asked about his understanding, Gensoku answered, "The god of fire is fire itself and asks for fire, which is like my asking about the Buddha when I am he." Jōye said, "There! I thought you understood, but now I know you do not!"

This worried Gensoku greatly and he spent much time pondering Jōye's words. As he could not come to any conclusion, he finally came to Jōye again and asked for instruction. Jōye said, "You ask and I will answer." Thereupon Gensoku said, "Who is the Buddha?" Jōye replied: "The god of fire comes and asks for fire!" This at once opened Gensoku's spiritual eye.

(3) Tokushō (890–971),[23] one of the great masters of Kegon

(Hua-yen) philosophy and Zen Buddhism, before he came to a final understanding of the *prajñā* way, saw many teachers and thought he had thoroughly mastered it. When he saw Ryūge, he asked, "I am told that the greatest of the honored ones is unapproachable. Why is that so?" Ryūge said, "It is like fire against fire." Tokushō said, "When it suddenly meets with water, what happens?" Ryūge did not give him any further explanation but simply said, "You do not understand." At another time, he asked, "Heaven cannot cover it; the earth cannot hold it. What does this mean?" Said Ryūge, "That should be so." Tokushō failed to get the meaning and asked for further instruction. Ryūge said, "Sometime later you will come to understand it by yourself." When Tokushō interviewed Sozan, Tokushō said, "Tell me, please, that which transcends time." Sozan said, "No, I will not." "Why will you not?" Tokushō argued. "Because the category of being and non-being cannot be applied here." Tokushō said, "O master, how well you explain!"

After interviewing fifty-four masters, e.g., Sudhana, in *The Kegon Sūtra* (*Avataṁsaka-sūtra*), Tokushō thought he knew everything well that was to be known in Buddhist philosophy. When he came to Jōye, he simply attended his sermons but did not ask him anything. One day a monk appeared before Jōye and asked, "What is the one drop of water that has come down from the Sōkei source?" Now, Sōkei refers to the monastery where Enō (Hui-neng in Chinese) used to reside, and Enō is considered the real founder of the Chinese Zen school of Buddhism. To ask about the drop of water coming down from the Sōkei source is to be enlightened in the truth of *prajñā*-intuition. Jōye gave this answer, "The one drop of water that has come down from the Sōkei source." [24] The inquiring monk was nonplused and did not know what to make of it, Tokushō, who was merely present there without any desire to increase his own knowledge in Buddhist teaching, was thus most unexpectedly awakened to the truth of *prajñā*-intuition. He then felt as if everything that was accumulating in his mind in the way of intellectual acquisition had suddenly dissolved into nothingness.

After this experience, Tokushō was a thoroughly equipped master in the philosophy of *prajñā*-intuition, and the way he handled all the baffling problems of philosophy was truly remarkable. To cite a few instances: [25]

A monk asked, "Where does the dead one go?"
Tokushō: "After all, I will not tell you."

Monk: "Why not, master?"

Tokushō: "Because you may not understand."

Monk: "All these mountains and rivers and the great earth—where do they come from?"

Tokushō: "Where does this question of yours come from?"

Monk: "What does the eye of the great seer look like?"

Tokushō: "As black as lacquer."

Monk: "When no tidings are available, what about it?" [26]

Tokushō: "Thank you for your tidings."

Monk: "I am told that when one transcends the objective world,[27] one is identified with the Tathāgata. What does this mean?"

Tokushō: "What do you mean by the objective world?" [Is there any such thing?]

Monk: "If so, one is indeed identified with the Tathāgata."

Tokushō: "Do not whine like a *yakan*." [28]

Monk: "It is said that Prince Naṭa returns his flesh to the mother and his bones to the father, and then, showing himself on the lotus-seat, preaches for his parents. What is the body of the Prince?"

Tokushō: "All the brethren see you standing here."

Monk: If so, all the worlds partake equally of the nature of suchness."

Tokushō: "Appearances are deceptive."

This is perhaps enough to show Tokushō's attainment in *prajñā*-intuition. In one way, the Chinese language has a great advantage in demonstrating *prajñā*, because it can express much with its characteristic brevity and forcefulness. *Prajñā* does not elaborate, does not indulge in wordiness, does not go into details, for all these are features peculiar to *vijñāna*, or intellection. Reasoning requires many words; indeed, wordiness is the spirit of philosophy. The Chinese language, or, rather its use of ideographic signs, evokes concrete images full of undifferentiated implications—a very fitting tool for *prajñā*. *Prajñā* is never analytical and abhors abstraction. It lets one particle of dust reveal the whole truth underlying all existences. But this does not mean that the ideographs are suitable for discussing abstract subjects.

Tokushō's *mondō* were not always such short ones as cited above, and he often indulged in argumentation.

A monk asked, "According to the saying of an ancient sage, if a man sees *prajñā*, he is bound by it; if he does not, he is bound by it all the same. How is it that *prajñā* binds him?"

Tokushō said, "You tell me what *prajñā* sees."

Monk: "How is it that one's not seeing *prajñā* binds one?"

Tokushō: "You tell me if there is anything *prajñā* does not see." He then continued, "If a man sees *prajñā*, it is not *prajñā*; if he does not see *prajñā*, it is not *prajñā*. Tell me, if you can, how it is that there are seeing and not-seeing in *prajñā*. Therefore, it is said that, if one thing (*dharma*—concrete reality) is lacking, the *Dharma-kāya* (universal concrete) is not complete, that if one thing (*dharma*) is too much, it is not complete either.

"But I would say: 'If there is one *dharma*, the *Dharma-kāya* is not complete; if there is no *dharma*, the *Dharma-kāya* is not complete either. For here lies the whole truth of *prajñā* intuition.' " [29]

I have digressed somewhat, but as we are deeply concerned with *prajñā* let me quote another master.[30]

A monk asked, "What is *mahā-prajñā* (great or absolute *prajñā*)?"

Seishō, the master, said, "The snow is falling fast, and all is enveloped in mist."

The monk remained silent.

The master asked, "Do you understand?"

"No, master, I do not."

Thereupon the master composed a verse for him:

> "*Mahā-prajñā*—
> It is neither taking in nor giving up.
> If one understands it not,
> The wind is cold, the snow falling."

I have said enough already without going back to the three instances cited above to show what is the essential characteristic of *prajñā*-intuition. If it should appeal to the *vijñāna* point of view, or the intellect, the repetition of the statement that was quoted before would make no sense whatever. The one says, "An inch's difference and heaven-and-earth's separation," and the other repeats it; or the one says, "Sōgen's one-drop-water," and the other repeats, "Sōgen's one-drop-water." There is here no exchange of intellectually analyzable ideas. A parrot-like mechanical imitation of the one by the other is not what logically minded people expect of any intelligible demonstration of thought. It is evident, therefore, that *prajñā* does not belong to the same order as *vijñāna*. *Prajñā* must be a superior principle, going beyond the limits of *vijñāna*, when we see how Tokushō, master of Kegon philosophy, demonstrated his originality in handling problems of philosophy and religion. He could never get this originality and facility so long as he remained in the *vijñāna* way of thinking.

IV

Prajñā is the ultimate reality itself, and *prajñā*-intuition is its becoming conscious of itself. *Prajñā* is therefore dynamic and not static; it is not mere activity-feeling but activity itself; it is not a state of *samādhi* (concentration),[31] not a state of passivity, not just looking at an object; it knows no object; it is the activity itself. *Prajñā* has no premeditated methods; it creates them out of itself as they are needed. The idea of methodology is not applicable to it, nor is teleology, although this does not mean that it is erratic and recognizes no laws. In a sense, however, this disregarding of laws is true of *prajñā* because it is its own creator out of its own free will.

Thus *vijñāna* is evolved out of *prajñā*, and *prajñā* works its way through it. From the *vijñāna* point of view, *prajñā* is certainly teleological and methodological, but we must remember that *prajñā* is not governed by *vijñāna*, i.e., by something foreign to it, and that, being its own creator, *prajñā's* world is always new and fresh and never a repetition. The world was not created so many millions and millions of years ago, but it is being created every moment, and it is *prajñā's* work. Reality is not a corpse to be dissected by the surgical knife of *vijñāna*. If this were the case, when "the god of fire comes for fire" was repeated, the understanding would be said to have been final and conclusive, but the fact is that it was far from it, and "the god of fire" had to wait for *prajñā* to recognize himself in the most ultimate sense. Epistemologically interpreted, reality is *prajñā*; metaphysically interpreted, reality is *śūnyatā*. *Śunyatā*, then, is *prajñā*, and *prajñā* is *śūnyatā*.

Psychologically, *prajñā* is an experience, but it is not to be confused with other experiences of our daily life, which may be classified as intellectual, emotional, or sensuous. *Prajñā* is indeed the most fundamental experience. On it all other experiences are based, but we ought not regard it as something separate from the latter which can be picked out and pointed to as a specifically qualifiable experience. *Prajñā is pure experience, beyond differentiation*. It is the awakening of *śūnyatā* to self-consciousness, without which we can say that we cannot have any mental life and that whatever thoughts and feelings we may have are like a boat that has lost its moorings, for they do not have any co-ordinating center. *Prajñā* is the principle of unification and co-ordination. We must not think it is an abstract idea, for it is decidedly not, but most concrete in every sense of the term. Because of its concreteness, *prajñā* is the most dynamic thing we can have in the world. For this reason even the "one drop leaking out of the Sōkei spring" is enough to vivify not only one's whole life but the entire triple world filling the boundlessness of space.

This miracle-working power of *prajñā* is illustrated in almost all the Mahayana Sutras, and I give an instance from *The Kegon Sūtra*. When the Buddha attained enlightenment, the whole universe appeared in an entirely changed aspect.

It is evident that when *prajñā* asserts itself the whole aspect of the world undergoes change beyond the comprehension of *vijñāna*. This may be called performing a miracle on the grandest possible scale. But as long as the performance stays within the limits of *vijñāna*, however grand it may be, it cannot be anything more than a petty juggler's artifice, for it does not mean the revolution of our *vijñāna* point of view at its basis—called *parāvṛtti* (about-face). Some think that what is described in most of the Mahāyāna Sūtras is poetic imaginings or spiritual symbolizations, but this is to miss altogether the main issue in the activity and the significance of *prajñā*-intuition.

When *prajñā*-intuition takes place it annihilates space and time relationships, and all existence is reduced to a point-instant. It is like the action of a great fire at the end of the *kalpa* (aeon, a very long time) which razes everything to the ground and prepares a new world to evolve. In this new *prajñā* world there is no three-dimensional space, no time divisible into the past, present, and future. At the tip of my finger Mount Sumeru rises; before I utter a word and you hear it, the whole history of the universe is enacted. This is no play of poetic imagination, but the Primary Man manifesting himself in his spontaneous, free-creating, non-teleological activities. The Primary Man is Prince Naṭa, and, in fact, every one of us, when the flesh is returned to the mother and the bones to the father. This Man, now stripped of everything that he thought belonged to him, is engaged in his *anābhoga-caryā* (purposeless activity), which constitutes the *bodhi-sattva-caryā*—a life really constituting *bodhi-sattva*-hood.

It is interesting to note that the Primary Man (*gennin*) is everywhere the same but his expressions are not alike, showing marked differentiations in accordance with local limitations. In India, the

Primary Man acts dramatically, wonderfully rich in images and figures. But, in China, he is practical and in a sense prosaic and direct and matter-of-fact; there are no dialectical subtleties in his way of dealing with *prajñā*; he does not indulge in calling up brilliantly colored imageries. Let me give an example. To the monk who asks about Prince Naṭa's Primary Man, a Chinese master of Buddhist philosophy answers, "No mistaking about this robust existence six feet high." The monk now asks, "Is it up to the Primary Man, or not, to assume this form?" The master retorts, "What do you call the Primary Man?" Not understanding, the monk wishes to be instructed. The master, instead of giving him instructions as the monk probably desired, proposes the question "Who is to instruct you?" [32]

While the *mondō* (question and answer) selected here carries in it something of ratiocination, I am afraid it is still unintelligible to modern man. Keishō, the master alluded to here, was not so direct as some other masters might be, for they are sometimes apt to give a kick to such a questioner, or push him away with a remark such as, "I do not know," [33] or "He is right under your nose," [34] or "Carry this lunatic out of my sight!" [35] Let me try to make Keishō more intelligible by adding "legs to the snake."

By the Primary Man is meant ultimate reality or *prajñā*, as the case may be. The monk-questioner knew that his individual self was subject to disintegration sooner or later; he wanted to find, if possible, something which was untouchable by birth and death. Hence the question "What is the Primary Man?" Keishō was a past master in the art of teaching which developed in China side by side with the rationalistic interpretation of Buddhist thought. He knew full well how futile it was to resort to the latter method when the aspirant after the truth was really earnest in his endeavor to attain the final enlightenment. Such aspirants could never be satisfied with the logical handling of the subject. What they wanted was not a mere intellectual understanding, which would never give full satisfaction to the aspiring soul. The master, therefore, would not waste time and energy by entering into arguments with the monk who, he knew, would never be convinced by this method. The master was short in his remark, and the Chinese language is remarkably fitted to the purpose. He simply said, "There can be no doubt about this robust existence six feet high." He might easily have said "this body of yours," but he did not go into detail; he simply referred to "this robust existence," well built and of some height. As to the relationship between this physical body and the Primary Man, he gave no hints whatsoever. If there were any, the discovery was left to the monk's own devices, for the idea here, as everywhere else, is to come to an understanding by means of the inner light, by the awakening of *prajñā*.

The monk in question, however, did not come up to the master's expectation; he was still on the level of intellection. Hence his inquiry, "Is it up to the Primary Man, or not, to assume this form?" This is tantamount to saying, "Is this self, then, the Primary Man?" The monk's apparent inference was that the highest being, the Primary Man, incorporates himself in this bodily existence in order to make himself approachable to the human senses. The inference may not have been incorrect as far as ratiocination was concerned, but the master's idea was not to stop there. If he had, and had given his approval, the monk would never be enlightened, for the point of the whole discussion would have been utterly lost. The monk was not to be left with mere intellectualization.

The master fully knew where the monk's weakness lay. Hence the question "What do you call the Primary Man?" The Primary Man was not to be identified with this individual corporeal existence, nor was he to be regarded as a separate being outside of it, as if the Man were another entity like the monk or like the master. The Man and the individual could not be considered wholly one, nothing else remaining, but at the same time they were not to be looked upon as altogether separate and dualistic. The one was not to be merged into the other; they were two and at the same time one. This undifferentiated differentiation was the point to be grasped by *prajñā*-intuition.

The Primary Man is not a kind of general concept abstracted from individual existences. The Man is not an outcome of generalization. If he were, he would be a dead man, a corpse as cold as inorganic matter, and as contentless as mere negation. On the contrary, he is very much alive and full of vitality not only in the physical sense but intellectually, morally, aesthetically, and spiritually. He lives in the monk's robust body six feet high and also in the master's body, probably not so robust, not so high, but full of vitality and sensibility. The monk's task was to realize this and not to argue about it. The master then put the questions, "What do you call the Primary Man? Are you the Man himself? No, you are to all appearances and in full reality a monk miserably troubled with the question as to the whatness of the Man. If so, you cannot be he. Where, then, is he?" So long as no satisfactory answer was forthcoming from this exchange of questions, the monk's intelligence could not go beyond the limits of *vijñāna*, or sheer rationality.

The monk was helpless here and asked humbly for instruction. But from the master's point of view it was not a matter of just transmitting information. It was from the beginning beyond the sphere of possible instruction. If there could be any instruction, it was to evolve out of one's own *prajñā*. If the monk were at all able to ask a question about the Primary Man, something of his nature must reside in the monk, and the best way to know the Man would be to have an "interview" with him by awakening *prajñā* in the monk, for *prajñā* is the Man. The master's role could not go beyond pointing the way to it, and to awaken it was the monk's. Hence, "Who is to instruct you?"

In spite of all these interpretations of the *mondō*, we do not seem to be any wiser than we were at the beginning. To make the matter more intelligible to the Western mind, I shall add a few words before we proceed to more *mondō*.

The body is the expression of the will, and what unites the will and the body as an individual self is the inner creative life. The body, the will, and the individual self are concepts worked out by the analytical *vijñāna*, but the inner creative life as it creates all these concepts through *vijñāna* is immediately apprehended only by *prajñā*. When Prince Naṭa returns his body to his father and mother as its progenitors, he gives up his individual self, which, according to his *vijñāna*, he thinks he has, and which may be interpreted as reduced to total annihilation, but Buddhist philosophy tells us that it is then for the first time that he can reveal his Primary Man or Primary Body, in which he preaches to his parents, which means the whole world. This Primary Body seated on the lotus-seat is God's creative activity. The analyzing *vijñāna* stops here and cannot go any further; God is its postulate; it must wait for *prajñā*-intuition to transform this cold postulate-corpse into a creative life-principle.

Let me give a bit of logic here, hoping it will help clarify the nature of *prajñā* in this field. When we say that "A is A" and that this law of identity is fundamental, we forget that there is a living synthesizing activity whereby the subject "A" is linked to the object "A." It is *vijñāna* that analyzes the one "A" into the subject "A" and the object "A"; and without *prajñā* this bifurcation cannot be replaced by the original unity or identity; without *prajñā* the divided "A" remains isolated; however much the subject may desire to be united with the object, the desire can never be fulfilled without *prajñā*. It is *prajñā* that makes the law of identity work as an established self-evident truth requiring no objective evidence. The foundation of our thinking thus owes its functioning to *prajñā*. Buddhist philosophy is a system of self-evolving and self-identifying *prajñā*.

This consideration will shed light on the repetitive *mondō* cited above in regard to "The one drop of water streaming from the Sōkei spring" and "An inch's difference and heaven-and-earth's separation." In the case of "the god of fire seeks fire," Tokushō could not have an insight into its secret as long as his *vijñāna* kept the concept "the god of fire" disjoined from the concept "fire." He had to wait for his *prajñā* to come to its self-awakening in order to make the logically fundamental law of identity a living principle of experience. *Vijñāna* is always analytical and pays no attention to the underlying synthetic principle. The one "A" is divided into the subject "A" and the object "A," and by connecting the one with the other by a copula *vijñāna* establishes the law of identity, but it neglects to account for this connection. Hence *vijñāna's* utter incapacity for becoming a living experience. This is supplied by *prajñā*-intuition.

The problem of *prajñā*, which constitutes the essence of Buddhist philosophy, is really inexhaustible, and no amount of talk seems to suffice. I will give some more *mondō* here and indicate the trend of thought underlying them. Until the relation between *vijñāna* and *prajñā*, or that between *prajñā*-intuition and *vijñāna*-reasoning, is thoroughly understood, such ideas as *śūnyatā* (emptiness), *tathatā* (suchness), *mokṣa* (emancipation), *nirvāṇa*, and others will not be fully absorbed as living ideas.

One important thing to remember before we proceed is that, if we think that there is a thing denoted as *prajñā* and another denoted as *vijñāna* and that they are forever separated and not to be brought to a state of unification, we shall be completely on the wrong track. The fact is that this world of ours, as reflected in our senses and intellect, is that of *vijñāna*, and that this *vijñāna* cannot function in its full capacity until it is securely moored in *prajñā*, and, further, that though *prajñā* does not belong to the order of *vijñāna*, we have to denote *prajñā* in distinction from *vijñāna*, as if there were such an entity as *prajñā* which is to be subsumed under the category of *vijñāna*. Words are useful as the culminating point in the progress of thinking, but for that reason they are also misleading. We have to guide carefully our every step in this field.

In the following tabulation those items listed on the *prajñā* side must be understood as such only when *vijñāna* is enlightened by *prajñā; prajñā* in itself has nothing to be discriminated. For instance, *śūnyatā* (emptiness) or *tathatā* (suchness) is not to be taken as objectively denoted. They are the ideas whereby our consciousness locates its points of reference. Whenever *prajñā* expresses itself it has to share the limitations of *vijñāna* either in agreement with it or otherwise. Even when *prajñā* flatly denies what *vijñāna* asserts, it cannot go outside the *vijñāna* area. To think it does is also the doing of *vijñāna,* and in this sense *prajñā* cannot escape *vijñāna.* Even when the role of *prajñā* is emphatically upheld in the drama of human activities, it must be understood as ignoring the claims of *vijñāna. Prajñā*-intuition and *vijñāna*-discrimination are equally important and indispensable in the establishment of a synthetic philosophy. In the *mondō* to be cited later, this relationship of *prajñā* and *vijñāna* will be noticed.

On the *prajñā* side we list the following:	On the *vijñāna* side we may have these counterbalancing:
Śūnyatā (emptiness)	A world of beings and non-beings
Tathatā (suchness)	A world of clear-cut definitions
Prajñā-intuition	*Vijñāna*-discrimination
Nirvāṇa	*Saṁsāra* (birth and death)
Bodhi (enlightenment)	*Avidyā* (ignorance)
Purity	Defilement
The mind (*citta*)	The senses (*vijñāna*)
Dharma (ultimate reality)	*Sarva-dharma* (individual entities)
Pure experience	Experiences of multitudes
Pure act (*karma*)	A world of causation
Undifferentiated	Differentiated
Non-discrimination	Discrimination
No-mind, or no-thought	Individual consciousness
Eternal now, or absolute present	Time relations
Non-duality	Duality
Etc.	Etc.

V*

The reason so many *mondō* are given below is that by going over them one after another the reader is likely to feel something

---

* In this section so many cases of confusion would be involved if we sought verbal precision concerning such words as *ji, dera, in,* etc., that we have decided to leave the author's useage as it is.

glimmering between the questions and answers. Furthermore, in these *mondō*, the relationship of *vijñāna* to *prajñā* is brought out in a more practical way, whereby the reader may draw his own conclusions from the *mondō*. Besides, the literature recording these *mondō* is generally inaccessible to Western readers, and it seems appropriate to make use of this opportunity to quote them for the benefit of those who are interested in the subject. There is an almost inexhaustible mine of *mondō* in China and Japan, and there is no reason for it to remain unexplored.

The subjects of the *mondō* are varied; they appear sometimes not at all concerned with topics of Buddhist philosophy, because they deal with such subjects as "one standing at the head of a ridge ten thousand feet high," "the master of a monastery," "the place where a monk comes from," "a tombstone showing no seams," "the moon on a cloudless night," "playing on a stringless harp," and so on. As to the answers given even to the highest ideas of philosophy and religion, they seem to be treated with the utmost indifference. To those who have never been initiated into this mysterious world of Buddhist philosophy, the *mondō* will surely be a cache of absurdities. But from the Buddhist point of view there are no methods more effective than the *mondō* for demonstrating the specific character of *prajñā*-intuition.

Let us start, then, with the problem of the self.

Sekitō (700–790)[36] was one of the greatest figures in the Buddhism during the T'ang Dynasty. A monk called Shiri once asked him, "What is that which makes up this self?" To this the master answered, in the form of a counter question, "What do you want from me?"

The monk said, "If I do not ask you, where can I get the solution?"

"Did you ever lose it?" concluded the master.

Bunsui of Hōji monastery in Kinryo gave this discourse to his monks: "O monks, you have been here for some time, the winter session is over and the summer is come. Have you had an insight into your self, or not? If you have, let me be your witness, so that you will have a right view and not be led by wrong views."

A monk came forward and asked, "What is my self?"

The master answered, "What a fine specimen of manhood with a pair of bright eyes!" [37]

Entoku of Entsūin monastery: [38]

Q. "What is my self?"

A. "What makes you specifically ask this question?"

Ki of Unryūin monastery: [39]
Q. "What is my self?"
A. "It is like you and me."
Q. "In this case there is no duality."
A. "Eighteen thousand miles off!"

Yō of Kōri monastery: [40]
Q. "When I lack clear insight into my own self, what shall I do?"
A. "No clear insight."
Q. "Why not?"
A. "Don't you know that it's one's own business?"

Kaitotsu of Tōzen monastery: [41]
Q. "I have not yet clearly seen into my own nature. May I be instructed by you?"
A. "Why are you not thankful for it?"

Tokuichi of Ryūgeji monastery: [42]
Q. "What is my self?"
A. "You are putting frost on top of snow."

Various answers are given to this question, "What is the self?" They are so various, indeed, that one fails to find a common denominator whereby they yield a uniform solution. The answer requires certain insight into what constitutes the self, and this cannot be attained by merely thinking about it intellectually. While thinking is needed, what solves the question is not, after all, the intellect but the will power. It is solved by an existential method, and not by abstraction or by postulation. Buddhist philosophy is built upon the most fundamental, pre-rationalistic *prajñā*-intuition. When this is reached, such problems as the self, ultimate reality, *buddhadharma, Tao,* the source, the mind, etc., are all solved. However infinitely variable the masters' ways of handling them may be, there is always one line of approach whereby they become intelligible.

Tō of Kokutaiin monastery: [43]
Q. "When the old mirror is not yet polished, what would you say of it?"
A. "The old mirror."
Q. "When it is polished, what of it?"
A. "The old mirror."

The "old mirror" is another name for the self in a state of undifferentiation. "Polished" means differentiated. The "old mirror" remains the same whether or not it is differentiated.

A monk asked Chikaku of Yōmyōji monastery: [44]
"What is the great perfect mirror?"
"An old broken tray!" was the answer.

In this "the mirror" is not even an "old one"; it is an old broken tray, altogether useless. Zen philosophers of Buddhism often use this kind of expression when they wish to show the utter worthlessness of a concept where *prajñā*-intuition is concerned.

Dōke of Byakuryūin monastery: [45]
Q. "What is *Tao*?"
A. "The rider on the donkey seeks the donkey."

Ryōkū of Tōzenin monastery: [46]
Q. "What is *Tao*?"
A. "This, right here!"

Jūten of Hofukuin monastery: [47]
Q. "I am told that, when one wishes to attain the way of the Unborn, one must see into the source. What is the source?"
The master remained silent for a while, and then asked the attendant, "What did that monk ask me just now?" The monk thereupon repeated the question, which made the master scoff at him, saying, "I am not deaf!"

Jūten,[47] the master, once asked a monk, "Where do you come from?"
The monk answered, "I come from a monastery on the western side of the River where Kwannon is enshrined."
The master said, "Did you see Kwannon?"
"Yes, I did."
"Did you see it on the right side or the left side?"
The monk replied, "When seeing there is neither right nor left."

In a *mondō* like this, one can readily see that the question at issue is not Kwannon, which is used merely as a symbol for the self, or *tao*, or Ultimate Reality, and the seeing of it means *prajñā*-intuition. There is no differentiation in it of right and left; it is complete in itself; it is a unity itself; it is "pure" seeing. This monk apparently understood what *prajñā*-intuition was, and this form of question on the part of the master is known as a "trial" question.

Jūten,[47] the master, saw the head cook and asked, "How large is your cooking pan?"
The monk-cook said, "You measure it yourself and see."
The master assumed the position of measuring it with his hands.
The monk remarked, "Do not make a fool of me."
The master retorted, "It is you who are making a fool of me."

The master,[47] once seeing a monk, remarked, "How did you manage to be so tall as that?"

The monk answered, "How short are you?"

The master crouched as if making himself shorter.

The monk said, "Do not make a fool of me, O master!"

The master retorted, "It is you who are making a fool of me!"

Goshin of Saikōji monastery: [48]

Q. "What is the *mani*-jewel that takes colors?"

A. "Blue, yellow, red, and white."

Q. "What is the *mani*-jewel that does not take colors?"

A. "Blue, yellow, red, and white."

The *mani*-jewel is also symbolic, of course. The *mani*-jewel that takes colors refers to reality, or *śūnyatā*, conceived as subject to differentiation, while the *mani*-jewel that does not take colors is reality itself. The master's answers, however, are the same to both questions; apparently he makes no distinction between the two. Intellectually, or conceptually, there is decidedly a distinction, which is ignored by *prajñā*-intuition. Another master, who may wish to make his inquirers see another phase of *prajñā*-intuition, is likely to give his answers quite a different color. This is instanced by the *mondō* of the "old mirror."

Shutotsu of Jōran monastery: [49]

Q. "Who is the Buddha?"

A. "Whom are you asking?"

Fukusen: [50]

Q. "Who is the Buddha?"

A. "I do not know."

Reikan of Kōrai: [51]

Q. "Who is the Buddha?"

A. "Carry this lunatic away from here."

Kin of Koken monastery: [52]

Q. "Who is the Buddha?"

A. "Right under your nose."

Kyōyu of Hōju monastery: [53]

Q. "What is the ultimate principle of Buddhism?"

A. "Come nearer."

The monk moved forward, and the master said, "Do you understand?"

The monk said, "I do not, master."

The master remarked, "It is like a flash of lightning, and it went eons ago!"

Chikaku of Yōmyōji: [54]

A monk said, "I am told that all *buddhas* and all the *buddha-dharmas* issue from one *sūtra*. What could this *sūtra* be?"

The master replied, "Revolving on forever; no checking it, and no arguing, no talking can catch it." [55]

Q. "How then shall I receive and hold it?"

A. "If you wish to receive and hold it, you should hear it with your eyes."

Sōton of Dairinji monastery: [56]

A monk asked, "How do we discourse on the highest truth of Buddhist philosophy?"

To this, Gensha, the master, answered, "Few hear it."

The monk later came to Sōton and asked, "What did Gensha mean?"

Sōton said, "When you have finished removing Mt. Sekiji, I will tell you." [57]

Jyu of Kishū monastery later commented on this:

"Speak low, please."

This interjection of comment by later masters on a *mondō*, which took place between predecessors and questioners, is quite common. It is not necessarily a criticism, but is directed toward bringing out what is implied in the *mondō*. Gensha said, "Few hear it," and Jyu, referring to it, said, "Speak low!" The masters are generally off the track of "logic," and they frequently indulge in making fun of one another. They are witty and sportive. Followers of *prajñā*-intuition naturally avoid getting into a philosophical discussion of abstract ideas; they are partial to figures, imageries, facts of daily experience. The following, picked at random from numerous such examples, will show what I mean here.

A monk asked Zembi of Shurei monastery: [58]

"I understand that all the rivers, however different their sources, pour into the great ocean. How many drops of water could there be in the ocean?"

The master asked, "Have you ever been to the ocean?"

Monk: "What then, after we have been to the ocean?"

The master replied, "You come tomorrow, and I will tell you."

The monk who asked about the ocean evidently knew something about Buddhist philosophy; hence his second question, "What after having been there?" Seeing this, the master retorts, "Come tomorrow." They both understand, and the *mondō* serves to give us insight into the nature of *prajñā*-intuition. One may ask, "What has the ocean to do with *prajñā?*" But the ocean here referred to is the ocean of *śūnyatā,* in which all the phenomenal world is absorbed, and the counting of drops of water in it is to understand what becomes of the multiplicity absorbed therein. The monk wants to find out what the master will say concerning the relationship between the one and the many, between *prajñā* and *vijñāna.* To apprehend this no amount of philosophical argument helps, leading only to further confusion, and the expected "tomorrow" will never come. Instead of indulging in epistemological procedures, "I do not know" sums up the essence of *prajñā*-intuition.

> Seisho of Reiinzan monastery: [59]
> He once asked a monk: "Do you understand the *buddha-dharma* (the truth, or ultimate reality)?"
> The monk said, "No, I do not, master."
> "You honestly do not?"
> "That is right, master."
> "You leave me now and come tomorrow."
> The monk bowed saying, "Fare thee well."
> The master then said, "No, that is not the point."

This "come tomorrow" was taken by the monk in its literal or intellectual sense, and to remind him of his misunderstanding the master soft-heartedly states, "That is not the point." The point is to understand what is not understandable, to know what is unknowable, wherein *prajñā*-intuition really consists.

> A monk asked Yōmyō,[60] "I have been with you for a long time, and yet I am unable to understand your way. How is this?"
> The master said, "Where you do not understand, there is the point for your understanding."
> "How is any understanding possible where it is impossible?"
> The master said, "The cow gives birth to a baby elephant; clouds of dust rise over the ocean."

> When Seishu [61] was still in his novitiate stage under Jōye, the latter, pointing at the rain, remarked, "Every drop of it fills your eyes."
> Seishu at the time failed to understand this, but afterward, while studying the *Avataṁsaka-sūtra,* the meaning dawned upon him. Later, in one of his discourses, he said: "All the *buddhas* in the ten quarters of the world are ever facing you. Do you see them? If you say you see, do you see them with the mind or with the eye?"
> On another occasion this was his discourse: "It is said that when one sees form (*rūpa*) one sees mind (*citta*). Let me ask you, what do you call the mind? The mountains and rivers and the great earth extending before you—this world of pluralities—blue and yellow, red and white, men and

women, etc., infinitely varying in forms—are they mind, or are they not mind? If they are the mind, how does it transform itself into an infinite number of things? If they are not the mind, why is it said that when you see form you see the mind? Do you understand?

"Just because you fail to grasp this point and go on cherishing your confused views in manifold ways, you erroneously see differences and unities where there are really no differences and no unities.

"Just at this very moment your immediate apprehension of the mind is imperative, and then you will realize that it is vast emptiness and that there is nothing to see, nothing to hear. . . ."

This idea of "vast emptiness" is quite puzzling and baffling and always tends to be understood from the relativistic point of view. Buddhist philosophy has "*sat*" for "being," "*asat*" for "non-being," and "*śūnyatā*" for "emptiness," showing that "emptiness" has a positive connotation and is not a mere negation. Śūnyatā transcends being and non-being; that is, both presuppose the idea of *śūnyatā*. Therefore, when a Buddhist philosopher declares that there is nothing to see, nothing to hear, etc., we must not understand it as denying the experiences of our daily life but as indeed confirming them in every way. Hence the following:

Keijyū of Hannya monastery [62] came to the "*Dharma* Hall," and the monks congregated, hearing the board struck three times, which was the signal for them to come together. The master then recited an impromptu verse:

"Strange indeed—the board thrice struck,
And you monks are all gathered here.
As you already know well how to tell the time,
I need not repeat it over again."

He left the hall without saying anything further.

Buddhist philosophers, and every one of us ordinary sentient beings, not only hear sounds and see flowers, but also offer flowers to the Buddha, burn incense before him, and perform all kinds of acts of religious piety. We may not all claim to be Buddhists; we may even protest against being called religious; but the deeds here mentioned are what we are performing every day. It does not make any difference whether we are Buddhists or Christians or communists.

Mugaku of Suibi monastery [63] was a disciple of Tanka.[64] When he was found one day offering food to the *arhats* [ideal men, or worthy ones][65] a monk remarked, "Tanka burned the wooden image of the Buddha, and you offer food to the wooden *arhats*. How is that?"

Suibi said, "Let him burn the Buddha if he wants to, but he can never burn the Buddha to ashes. As for myself, I just offer this to the *arhats*."

There was another monk, who said this: "As to offering food to the *arhats*, do they come to partake it?"

Suibi said, "Do you eat every day, O monk?"

The monk made no answer. The master's comment was, "Few indeed are the intelligent!"

To conclude this section, let me add a word in regard to the distinction between *prajñā* and *vijñāna* in the understanding of the *mondō*. *Vijñāna* has a methodology, but *prajñā* has none, because it always demands immediacy and never allows hesitation or reflection in any form. When you see a flower, you know at once that it is a flower. When you dip your hand in cold water, you realize that it is cold, and this immediately, not after a moment of reflection. In this respect *prajñā*-intuition is like perception. The difference between the two is that perception does not go beyond the senses whereas intuition is far more deeply seated. When preception touches this foundation, it becomes *prajñā*-intuition. For perception to develop into *prajñā*, something must be added to it. This added something, however, is not something added from the outside; it is the perception itself, and to realize this is the function of *prajñā*-intuition. In other words, this is *prajñā* intuiting itself; *prajñā* is its own methodology.

When I draw a line on paper, it is not perfectly straight, but I can use it geometrically as such and demonstrate all the properties belonging to it. As far as visual perception is concerned, the line is limited, but, when our geometrical conception of a straight line is added to it, we can make it function as such. In a similar way, *prajñā*-intuition in one case makes the "rock nod even before the master uttered a word," [66] and in another case keeps the master very much alive even after he is cremated and his bones sound like copper. "How?" one may ask, in this second case. The master would say, "Does not the boy-attendant respond to my call, saying, 'Yes, master?'" One may still insist that the boy is not the master. If I were the master, I might strike you down, saying, "No such nonsense. O, this stupid fellow!" But, since I am not, I will say instead: "Your vision is still beclouded by *vijñāna*. You see the master on one side and the boy on the other, keeping them separate according to our so-called objective method of interpreting an experience. You do not see them living in each other, and you fail to perceive that death 'objectively' comes to the master but has no power over 'that' which makes the boy respond to the master's call. To see this 'that' is *prajñā*-intuition."

VI

This "that" is what is primarily and immediately given to our consciousness. It may be called "undifferentiated continuum," to use Professor F. S. C. Northrop's term. To the Western mind, "continuum" may be better than *śūnyatā*, though it is likely to be misinterpreted as something "objectively" existing and apprehensible by *vijñāna*. In the "continuum" immediately given, however, there is no differentiation of subject and object, of the seer and the seen. It is the "old mirror" that has not yet been polished, and therefore no world of multiplicities is reflected in "the mirror." It is the Primary Man, in whom neither flesh nor bones are left and yet who can reveal himself, not only to his parents, but to all his brothers, non-sentient as well as sentient. It is "the father" whose age is not calculable by means of numbers and therefore to whom everything is a "grandchild" of conceptualization. It lives with *prajñā* in the absolute state of quiescence, in which no polarization has taken place. It therefore eludes our efforts to bring it out to the discriminable surface of consciousness. We cannot speak of it as "being" or as "non-being." The categories created by ratiocination are not at all applicable here. If we attempt to wake it from the eternal silence of *"neti, neti"* (not this, not this), we "murder" it, and what *vijñāna* perceives is a most mercilessly mutilated corpse.

Prajñā abides here, but it is never awakened by itself. When it is awakened, it is always by *vijñāna*. *Vijñāna*, however, does not realize this fact, for *vijñāna* always imagines that without *vijñāna* there is no experienceable world, that if *prajñā* belongs in this world it must be of the same order as *vijñāna*, and therefore that *prajñā* can well be dispensed with. But the fact is that *vijñāna* is never *vijñāna* without *prajñā*; *prajñā* is the necessary postulate of *vijñāna*; it is what makes the law of identity workable, and this law is the foundation of *vijñāna*. *Vijñāna* is not the creator of the logical law, but it works by means of the law. *Vijñāna* takes it as something given and not provable by any means devised by *vijñāna*, for *vijñāna* itself is conditioned by it. The eye cannot see itself; to do this a mirror is needed, but what it sees is not itself, only its reflection. *Vijñāna* may devise some means to recognize itself, but the recognition turns out to be conceptual, as something postulated.

Prajñā, however, is the eye that can turn itself within and see itself, because it is the law of identity itself. It is due to *prajñā* that subject and object become identifiable, and this is done without mediation of any kind. *Vijñāna* always needs mediation as it moves on from one concept to another—this is in the very nature of *vijñāna.* But *prajñā,* being the law of identity itself, demands no transferring from subject to object. Therefore, it swings the staff; sometimes it asserts; sometimes it negates and declares that "A is not-A and therefore A is A." This is the "logic" of *prajñā*-intuition. The "undifferentiated continuum" is to be understood in this light.

When the "undifferentiated continuum" is the outcome of *vijñāna* dialectics, it remains a concept and never an experience. Buddhist philosophy, on the contrary, starts from pure experience, from self-identity, as self-evolving and self-discriminating activity, and *vijñāna* comes into existence. In *vijñāna,* therefore, there is always the potentiality of *prajñā*-intuition. When a flower is perceived as an object in the world of multiplicity, we recognize *vijñāna* functioning and along with it *prajñā*-intuition. But, as most of us stop at *vijñāna* and fail to reach *prajñā,* our vision becomes limited and does not penetrate deeply enough to reach ultimate reality or *śūnyatā.* So, it is declared that the unenlightened do not see the real flower in the light of suchness (*tathatā*).

From *vijñāna* to *prajñā* is not a continuous process or progress. If it were, *prajñā* would cease to be *prajñā*; it would become another form of *vijñāna.* There is a gap between the two; no transition is possible; hence there is a leap, "an existential leap." From *vijñāna*-thinking to *prajñā* seeing there is no mediating concept, no room for intellection, no time for deliberation. So, the Buddhist master urges us to "speak, quick, quick!" Immediacy, no interpretation, no explanatory apology—this is what constitutes *prajñā*-intuition.

I stated at the beginning that *prajñā* takes in the whole, while *vijñāna* is concerned with parts. This needs to be explained in more detail. If parts are mere aggregates, unconnected and incoherent masses, *vijñāna* cannot make them the subject of intellectual analysis. The reason *vijñāna* can deal with parts is that these parts are related to the whole, individually and collectively, and as such they present themselves to *vijñāna.* Each unit (or monad) is associated with another unit singly and with all other units collectively in a net-like fashion. When one is taken up, all the rest follow it. *Vijñāna* understands this and can trace the intricacy of relationship existing among them and state that there must be an integrating principle underlying them. Not only this, but *vijñāna* can also formulate what such principles are, as is done by philosophy and science. But *vijñāna* cannot do this over the entire field of realities; its vision is limited to limited areas, which cannot be extended indefinitely. They have to halt somewhere.

Prajñā's vision, however, knows no bounds; it includes the totality of things, not as a limited continuum, but as going beyond the boundlessness of space and the endlessness of time. *Prajñā* is a unifying principle. It does this, not by going over each individual unit as belonging to an integrated whole, but by apprehending the latter at one glance, as it were. While the whole is thus apprehended, the parts do not escape from entering into this vision by *prajñā*. We can better describe this experience as the self-evolution of *prajñā* whereby the whole is conceived dynamically and not statically.

The continuum is not to be interpreted as merely an accumulation of units or monads; it is not a notion reached by adding one unit to another and repeating this process indefinitely. It is a concrete, indivisible, indefinable whole. In it there is no differentiation of parts and whole. It is, as Zen Buddhist philosophers would say, "an iron bar of ten thousand miles"; it has no "hole" by which it can be grasped. It is "dark"; no colors are discernible here. It is like a bottomless abyss where there is nothing discriminable as subject and object. These statements, we may say, are figurative and do not give much information regarding *prajñā*-intuition. But to those who have gone through the actual experience of *prajñā*-intuition these figurative, symbolic descriptions are really significant. What is asked of the professional philosopher is that he translate them into his terminology according to the technique he uses.

It is evident that the continuum is not the whole attained by the accumulation of units; to be the whole, then, there must be something added to it, and this is what is done by *prajñā*-intuition. Therefore, *prajñā* must be considered a value-giving principle. When *prajñā* goes through the continuum, the whole thing acquires a value and every part of it becomes significant and pulsates with lifeblood. Each unit, even the most insignificant part, now appears in a new situation, full of meaning. A blade of grass is not something to be trodden under one's feet as standing in no relationship to the whole. A grain of rice inadvertently dropped off the washing pail is truly the root from which the ten thousand things germinate.

This is why it is said that *prajñā* vivifies, while *vijñāna* kills. Parts are to be united in the whole to become significant, and this kind of unification, not mechanical or arithmetical, is the doing of *prajñā*-intuition. *Vijñāna* realizes this only when it is infused with *prajñā*.

When we speak of the *prajñā* continuum as undifferentiated or differentiated, we must not think that this process of differentiation is a function given to the continuum from an outside source. The differentiation is evolved from within the continuum, for it is not the nature of the *prajñā* continuum to remain in a state of *śūnyatā*, absolutely motionless. It demands of itself that it differentiate itself unlimitedly, and at the same time it desires to remain itself. *Prajñā* is always trying to preserve its self-identity and yet subjects itself to infinite diversification. This is why *śūnyatā* is said to be a reservoir of infinite possibilities and not just a state of mere emptiness. Differentiating itself and yet remaining in itself undifferentiated, and thus to go on eternally engaged in the work of creation —this is *śūnyatā*, the *prajñā* continuum. It is not a concept reached by intellection, but what is given as pure act, as pure experience; it is a point fully charged with creative *élan vital*, which can transform itself into a straight line, into a plane, into a tridimensional body.

Now we can understand what is meant by this saying: Creation is contemplation, and contemplation is creation. When *śūnyatā* remains in itself and with itself, it is contemplation; when it subjects itself to differentiation it creates. As this act of differentiation is not something imposed upon it but an act of self-generation, it is creation; we can say it is a creation out of nothing. *Śūnyatā* is not to be conceived statically but dynamically, or, better, as at once static and dynamic. The *prajñā* continuum thus creates through contemplation and contemplates through creation.

In *prajñā*, therefore, there is an eternal progression and at the same time a never-changing state of unification. Eternally evolving, endlessly limiting itself, *prajñā* never loses its identity in *vijñāna*. Logically speaking, *prajñā* creativity involves an interminable series of contradictions: *prajñā* in *vijñāna* and *vijñāna* in *prajñā* in every possible form and in every possible manner. There thus takes place a state of infinitely complicated interpenetration of *prajñā* and *vijñāna*. But we must not understand this spatially. For this most thoroughgoing interpretation, indefinably complicated and yet subject to systematization, is the self-weaving net of *prajñā*, and *vijñāna* takes no active part in it. When, therefore, there is *prajñā*-intuition, all this "mystery" yields its secrets, whereas, as long as our vision does not go beyond *vijñāna*, we cannot penetrate to its very foundation and will naturally fail to perceive how *prajñā* works into *vijñāna*.

The following is a short and final part of Dr. Takakusu Junjirō's chapter entitled "Buddhism as a Philosophy of Thusness," most of which is included in the Indian volume of this series, since it deals primarily with Indian Buddhism. The following few pages are not indispensable to this volume, but they add material on Buddhism's Method of Meditation to supplement the material offered by Dr. Suzuki.

Method of Meditation

All the basic principles of Buddhism at once melt into the way-of-life-culture, which, in reality, is the application of the life-view to the practical life. As to the realization of the life-ideal, the theory of perfect freedom (*nirvāṇa*) speaks for itself. It is a state that is spaceless, timeless, of no condition, of no abode, of no limitation whatever. Negatively, *nirvāṇa* is "extinction," "total negation," "undifferentiated indetermination"; but, positively, it is perfect freedom. It is identical with perfect enlightenment (*bodhi*). *Nirvāṇa* may be attained by meditation and contemplation, if the negation theory of the method of dialectic proves unsatisfactory to anyone.

If Buddhism as rationalism is negative and as intuitionism is passive, it may seem to some to have nothing to do with actual life. On the contrary, it is a philosophy of self-creation and teaches the way-of-life-view, the way-of-life-culture, and the way of realization of the life-ideal. Since Buddhism takes the integration of consciousness seriously, its method ought to be exhaustive and negative to wipe out all possibilities of errors and perplexities. If the fullness of insight, that is, the perfection of knowledge and wisdom, is aimed at, one should not linger in the world of transitoriness or be entangled in the wire of attachment. For without self-discipline there will be no equipoised mental activities; without poise, no insight. The Buddha, therefore, teaches the three-fold learning: higher discipline, higher thought or meditation, and higher insight. These three are inseparable. The ideal of the *bodhi-sattva* is the sixfold perfection: charity (for others), discipline (for oneself), resignation (in toil), bravery (in effort), contemplation (meditation), and wisdom (insight). Insight cannot be attained without the preceding five, especially meditation.

The Buddha contemplated under the *bodhi* tree on the twelve stages of causation, first in order, then in reverse, "this is, therefore that is; this is not, therefore that is not," all being interdependent. When he became perfectly enlightened, and was about to preach his ideal, he further meditated 49 days as to how, where, and whom, to teach his ideal. When he began to teach, he taught about the actual life of suffering which was easy to demonstrate or intuit. "Aging, ailing, and dying are suffering. Birth is not joy, because it ends in death; union is not joy, if it ends in separation." When people began to realize the hardship of life, he taught them not to be deceived by the guise of joy but to face suffering as suffering. His Four Noble Truths to be believed by the noble are: 1. Suffering; 2. Cause of suffering; 3. Extinction of suffering; 4. The way to the extinction of suffering. Truths 1 and 2 are real, and 3 and 4 are ideal. What these are should be known by the first round of learning (investigation) according to the way-of-life-view. Next, the Truth of suffering should be fully realized. The cause of suffering should be cut off. The extinction of suffering fully experienced (or intuited) and the way leading to extinction of suffering should be cultivated (or practiced). These should be pursued by the second round of learning (realization) according to the way-of-life-culture. Thirdly, the Truth of suffering has been known, the cause has been cut off, the extinction has been attained, and the way leading to the extinction of suffering has been cultivated. These constitute the third round of learning (perfection), the stage of no-more-learning.

The way to extinction of suffering is the well-known Eightfold Path of the noble (*ārya*), i.e., right view; right thought; right speech; right action; right remembrance; right effort; right livelihood; right contemplation. These are principles of ethics, but at the same time a religion by which perfection of personality is attained and self-creation is fulfilled.

Though the highest principle is reached chiefly and ultimately by meditation, we must realize that Buddhists use other methods of self-culture in order to attain the ideal end. The Buddhist schools which use chiefly the method of meditation (*dhyāna*) can be called the schools of intuitionism, in which Thusness is intuited in differentiations, noumenon and phenomenon being inseparable.

The method of meditation is twofold: (1) *Tathāgata* meditation
and (2) Patriarchal meditation. The former was taught by the
Buddha along with the other teachings, while the latter was transmitted only in Japan, the founder patriarch being Bodhidharma, an
Indian who came to China in A.D. 520. What we call Zen at present is this second method.

(1) TATHĀGATA MEDITATION (*Nyorai Zen*)

As we have seen, the existence of the higher meditation of the
Three Learnings, the contemplation of the Six Perfections, and the
right meditation of the Eightfold Path of life-view show that
meditation is one of the most important factors in the teaching of
Buddhism. Meditation is the "basis of action." The object of meditation with the Buddha seems to have been to attain, first, tranquillity or calmness of mind and, then, activity of insight.

a. *Calmness* (Samatha)

A fivefold restraint of mind is to be practiced:
1. Meditation on impurity of the worldly life, to adjust the
   mind with regard to passion and avarice (individual).
2. Meditation on mercy, to cultivate the idea of sympathy
   to others and to stop the tendency to anger (universal).
3. Meditation on causation, to get rid of ignorance (individual).
4. Meditation on diversity of realms, to see the difference of
   standpoints and to get rid of a selfish view (universal).
5. Meditation on breaths, to aid concentration and to cure the
   tendency of mental dispersion (individual).
   When one's faulty mind has been adjusted and calmness
   has been obtained, one proceeds to the method of insight.

b. *Insight* (Vipaśyanā)

Fourfold retention of mind
1. The impurity of body is meditated upon and fully realized.
2. The evils of sensations are meditated upon and fully realized.
3. The evanescence or impermanence of mind and thoughts
   is meditated upon and fully realized.
4. The transiency of all elements of selflessness is meditated
   upon and fully realized.

These practices are called "bases of action," which is one of the modes of analytical meditation. Forty such meditations, with the corresponding subjects of meditation, are given in the *Visuddhi-magga*. They are: the ten universals, the ten impurities, the ten reflections (reflection on the Buddha, on the Doctrine, etc.), the four sublime states (friendliness, compassion, etc.), the four formless states (the infinity of space, of consciousness, etc.), the one perception (of the loathsomeness of nutriment), and the one analysis (into the four elements).

The ordinary way of meditation is as follows:

Arrange your seat properly, sitting erect, legs crossed, having your eyes not quite closed, not quite open, looking 10 to 20 feet ahead.

You may sit properly, but your body may move on account of your breaths. Count your in-breath and out-breath as one, and slowly count as far as 10, never beyond.

Now your body may seem upright and calm, but your thought may move about. You have to meditate on the impurity of the human being in illness, in death, and after death.

When you are well prepared to contemplate, you will begin to train yourself in concentration by meditating upon the ten universals.

It is a meditative unification of diverse phenomena into one of the ten universals, that is, blue, yellow, red, white, earth, water, fire, air, space, and consciousness. In this you will meditate on the universe until it becomes to your eyes one wash of a color or one aspect of an element. If you meditate on water, the world around you will become only running water.

Such a process of meditation is common to Hīnayāna as well as Mahāyāna, and is the feature of *Tathāgata* meditation.

(2) PATRIARCHAL MEDITATION (*Soshi Zen*)

The history of the Zen is mythical. It is said that, one day, Brahmā came to the Buddha, who was living at the Vulture peak, offered a *kumbhalā* flower, and requested him to preach the law. The Buddha ascended the Lion (supreme) seat, and, taking the flower, touched it with his fingers without saying a word. No one in the assembly could understand his meaning. The venerable Mahākāśyapa alone smiled with joy. The world-honored One said: "The *pitaka* [collection of writings] of the Eye of the True Law is hereby entrusted to you, oh Mahākāśyapa! Accept it, and hand it down to posterity." Once Ānanda asked him what the Buddha's transmission was. Mahākāśyapa said: "Go and take the Banner-stick down!" or Ānanda understood him at once. Thus the mind-sign was handed down successively. The 28th patriarch from the Buddha was Bodhidharma.

Later Bodhidharma went to Mount Wut'ai, where he remained nine years, and, facing a cliff behind the edifice, meditated in silence. Bodhidharma transmitted his idea to Hui-k'o (Eka), who in turn transmitted it to later Zen teachers in China and Japan.

Zen has much philosophy in it, but is not a philosophy in the ordinary sense. It is the most religious school of all, yet is not a religion in the ordinary sense of the word. It has no scripture of the Buddha, nor does it follow any discipline set forth by the Buddha.

Unless it has a *sūtra* or a *vinaya* (discipline) text, no school or sect would seem to be Buddhistic. According to the ideas of Zen, however, those who stick to words, letters, or rules that have been set forth can never get into the speaker's true idea. The ideal or truth conceived by the Buddha should be different from that preached by him, because the preaching is necessarily conditioned by the language he uses, by the hearers whom he is addressing, and by the environment in which the speaker and hearers are placed. What Zen aims at is the Buddha's ideal, pure and unconditioned. The school is otherwise called "the school of the Buddha's mind" (*Busshin-shū*). The Buddha's mind is, after all, a human mind. An introspection of the human mind alone can bring an aspirant to perfect enlightenment. But how?

The general purport of Buddhism is to let one see rightly and to walk rightly. The way of viewing is different from the way of walking. People walk often without seeing the way. Religions generally lay importance on practice, that is, how to walk, but neglect intellectual activity to find the right way, that is, how to see. To judge whether the path we are going to take is right or not, first of all, science is important, and all branches of science are welcomed by Buddhism. But, as we go on, we shall discover that philosophy is much more important than anything else. Buddhism is a philosophy in the widest sense of the word. In case science and philosophy do not give a satisfactory result, we have to resort to the meditative method of Zen to get insight into any given problem. First, find your way and begin to walk in it. Steps acquired by meditation can carry you across the wave-flux of human life, or over and above the airy region of the heavenly world (Form and Formless) and can finally make you perfect and enlightened like the Buddha. Contemplation is the eye to give insight and, at the same time, feet to provide a proper walk. Zen (meditation and concentration) is the lens on which diverse objects outside will be concentrated and again dispersed and impressed on the surface of the negative plates inside. The concentration on the lines itself is *samādhi* (concentration), and the deeper the concentration is, the quicker the awakening of intuitive intellect and wisdom. The further impression on the negative film is *prajñā* (wisdom), and this is the basis of intellectual activity. Through the light of "insight" or wisdom, we see in review the outer world of diversity once again so as to function or act appropriately toward actual life.

The meditation of Patriarchal Zen, therefore, is not an analytical method like science, nor is it a synthetic method like philosophy. It is a method of thinking without ordinary thinking, transcending all methods of logical argument. To think without any method of thinking is to provide an opportunity for the awakening of intuitional intellect or wisdom. Other methods of meditation, as taught by the Hīnayāna, by the Yogācāra of pseudo-Mahāyāna, by the abrupt method of "calm and insight" of the Tendai school, or by the mystical Yogācāra of the Shingon school can be used if an aspirant likes, but are in no way necessary.

A summary of the ideas peculiar to Zen is as follows: "from mind to mind it was transmitted"; "not expressed in words or written in letters"; "it was a special transmission apart from the sacred teaching"; "look directly into the human mind, comprehend its nature and become an enlightened *buddha*"; and "the very body or the very mind is the Buddha." The idea was very well expressed in Hakuin's hymn on sitting and meditating (*zazen*): "All beings are originally *buddhas;* it is like ice and water: without water there will be no ice. This very earth is the lotus-land, and this body is the Buddha."

Generally, Zen expressions and statements are very witty and often paradoxical, but the basic idea is the identity of *ens* and *non-ens.* For example, the "true state is no [special] state"; "the gate of *Dharma* is no gate"; "holy knowledge is no knowledge." The mutual identification of two opposed ideas, such as black and white, good and evil, pure and impure, or the like, results from deep meditation. "The ideal body has no form, yet any form may come out of it." "The golden mouth has no word, yet any word may come out of it." Many ideas of like nature are often encountered.

There is, however, a peculiar process in Zen. To concentrate one's mind in silent meditation, a *kōan* (public theme) is given to an aspirant to test his qualification for enlightenment. On receiving a *kōan*, one sits in silence in the Zen hall. One has to sit at ease, cross-legged and well-poised with upright body, with his hands in the meditating sign, and with his eyes neither quite open nor quite closed. It is called *zazen* (sitting and meditating), which may go on for several days and nights. The daily life, lodging, eating, sleeping, swimming, or bathing, should be regulated properly. First of all, the threefold silence is strictly required and kept, that is, while meditating, dining, or bathing, no word should be uttered and no noise should be made. In the Zen hall a superintending priest with a large flat stick strolls around now and then, and, if any sleep, yawn, or show a neglectful attitude, he is rewarded with a number of blows. Sometimes a public dialogue called a *mondō* (question and answer) takes place, and the traveling students ask questions of the teacher, who gives answers, hints, or scoldings. When a student or an aspirant thinks that he is prepared in the problem, he pays a private visit to the teacher's retreat and explains what he understands, and proposes to resolve the question. When the teacher is satisfied, he will give sanction; if not, the candidate must continue to meditate.

Zen, which is generally practiced in a forest retreat, seems to be far from the real world, but the general trend of mind of Zen people is toward a strict observance of rules and a minute accomplishment of discipline. Their ideals are immediately expressed in their daily life and in personal experiences. They are generally very practical. The famous words of the Zen patriarchs, such as "no work, no food," "one day without work, one day without food," "every day, good day," "daily mind the way," "the living, the teaching," "going, staying, sitting, or lying are the sacred teaching," exemplify their practical application of ideals. It requires training to hear a voice in silence, to find action in inaction, motion in immotion, or to have preparedness in peace and fearlessness in death. Such a tendency must have appealed to the warrior class, thus eventually producing the way of knightly behavior (*bushidō*).

Besides, when we see Zen influence so conspicuously discernible in Japan, in literature, drama, painting, architecture, industrial arts, and the social life (tea ceremony, vegetable cookery, flower arrangement, decorations of rooms), and, at present, in the educational training of Japan, Zen ideas can be regarded as almost inseparable from the national life of Japan. Probably the national ideal of simplicity, purity, and sincerity can find its expression most appropriately in the Zen practice of Buddhism. (1939 Conference)

Notes

1. *Prajñā, pra-jñā,* is the fundamental noetic principle whereby a synthetic apprehension of the whole becomes possible.
2. *Vijñāna, vi-jñā-na,* is the principle of differentiation.
3. *Dharma* is derived from the root "*dhṛ*," to "subsist," to "endure," and is used for a variety of meanings: "substance," "existence," "object," "teaching," "doctrine," "principle," "truth," "law," "relation," "norm," etc.
4. *Ātman* is "self," "the free will," "one who is master of self." When Buddhist philosophy denies the existence of the self it means that there is no self-governing free-willing agent in the individual as long as it is a conditioned being, for the individual owes its birth to a combination of conditions which are always subject to dissolution, and anything liable to birth and death cannot be thought of as a free-willing, self-governing agent. A free-willing agent means a unifying principle.
5. *Prajñā-pāramitā* is one of the six perfections (*pāramitās*): giving (*dāna*), moral precepts (*śīla*), humility (*kṣānti*), diligence (*vīrya*), meditation (*dhyāna*), and transcendental wisdom or absolute knowledge (*prajñā*). *Pāramitā*" is generally translated "going over to the other shore"—meaning that when these items are practiced one will finally cross the stream of birth-and-death. The Sūtras classified under the general title of "Prajñāpāramitā" expound the philosophy of *prajñā*-intuition or *śūnyatā*.
6. *The Diamond Sūtra (Vajracchadikā-sūtra)* is one of the "Prajñā-pāramitā" *Sūtras* and contains the gist of *prajñā* philosophy. Being short, it is quite popularly read by Buddhists. There are several translations in English.
7. The verse is by Zenne Daishi, popularly known as Fu Daishi (497–569), a contemporary of Bodhidharma. The verse in full runs thus:

> *Empty-handed, I hold the spade;*
> *Walking, I ride on an ox;*
> *A man passes over the bridge;*
> *The bridge flows and the water does not.*

8. Masters of *prajñā* philosophy make use of any object near their person to demonstrate the logic of *prajñā*-intuition. The staff, or *shippe* (a stick shorter than the staff), is frequently used for the purpose. Sometimes the question takes this form: "I do not call this a staff; what do you call it?"

9. The idea of being quick is well illustrated by Tokusan (790–865), who displayed his staff lavishly and refused to listen to any talk. Once he announced that "you commit a fault when you ask a question; you also commit a fault when you do not ask." A monk came forward and bowed to him, preparing to say something. Tokusan struck him. The monk protested, "I have just been bowing to you, and why do you strike me?" The master said, "If I wait for you to open your mouth, nothing avails!" *Records of the Transmission of the Lamp (Keitoku dentō roku)* (Tokyo: Kōkyō-shoin, 1881), xv, 122a. This edition (hereafter *RTL*) is used throughout this paper.

10. Ummon (?–949) once raised his staff forward and said, "When you see the staff call it a staff; when you see the post call it a post; and what fault could there be?" At another time he said, "What do you call this? If you say it is a staff, you go to hell; if it is not, what is it?" At still another time he brought the staff forward and said, "Common people would call this a reality; the Hīnayāna Buddhists would analyze it and declare that it is non-existent; the *pratyeka-buddhas* would call it a visionary existence; the *bodhi-sattvas* would say that the staff is *śūnya* (empty), as it is. As for Zen monks, they just call the staff a staff; if they want to walk they walk, if they want to sit they sit; no wavering in any circumstances!" *Sayings of Ummon (Ummon sokudo-zenji goroku)* (Goto-yegen, 1861), fasc. xv, pp. 1–7.

11. *RTL*, xxi, 38b.

12. *RTL*, xix, 23a; *Sayings of Ummon.*

13. *RTL*, xix, 22b.

14. *RTL*, xix, 23a.

15. *RTL*, v, 80.

16. *RTL*, xix, 25a.

17. *Hekiganshū* (Blue Cliff Records) (Ning-po, 1876), case xix.

18. *RTL*, xi, 86b. Isan sent a mirror to his disciple Kyōzan. Kyōzan, producing it before the congregation, said, "Is this Isan's mirror or is it Kyōzan's? If you can say a word about it, I will not break it." The whole brotherhood did not say a word, and Kyōzan smashed it.

19. *Sayings of Rinzai (Rinzai roku)* (Kyoto, 1648). Once when Fuké and Rinzai were invited out to dinner, Rinzai remarked, "A hair swallows the great ocean, and the seed of a poppy holds Mt. Sumeru in it. What does this mean?" Fuké, without saying a word, upset the whole table. The following day they were again invited out. Rinzai

said, "How much is today's dinner like yesterday's?" Fuké again upset the table. Rinzai said, "What a rude fellow you are!" Fuké retorted at once, "In Buddhism there is neither rudeness nor politeness. What a blind fellow you are!"

20. Tokusan, on his way to Taisan, felt hungry and tired and stopped at a roadside teahouse and asked for refreshments. The old woman who kept the house, finding that Tokusan was a great student of *The Diamond Sūtra*, said, "I have a question to ask you. If you can answer it, I will serve you refreshments for nothing, but, if you fail, you will have to go somewhere else for them." As Tokusan agreed, the woman proposed this: "In *The Diamond Sūtra* we read that 'The past mind is unattainable'; the present mind is unattainable; the future mind is unattainable; and so, with what mind do you wish to punctuate?" (Refreshments are known in Chinese as *t'ien-hsin* [*tenjin*], meaning "punctuating the mind," hence the question.) Tokusan was altogether nonplused, and did not know how to answer. He had to go without anything to eat. "The past mind" and so on require a somewhat detailed explanation which I omit here.

21. *RTL*, xxiv, 65b.

22. *RTL*, xxv, 78b.

23. *RTL*, xxv, 73b.

24. As in the case of "an inch's difference and heaven-and-earth's separation," the original Chinese for this quotation is also extremely terse and loses a great deal of its force in translation. The original runs like this: "Sōgen's one-drop-water." The question: "What is Sōgen's one-drop-water?" The answer: "Sōgen's one-drop-water." (Sōgen means "Sōkei source.")

25. *RTL*, xxv, under "Tokushō."

26. This refers to the Absolute (*Śūnyatā*).

27. Literally, "to turn things," or "to transform things."

28. When a lion roars the *yakan's* head splits. The *yakan* is an insignificant creature.

29. *RTL*, xxv, 74b.

30. *RTL*, xxv, 78b.

31. *Samādhi* means a state of intense concentration, in which the subject becomes identified with the object. This is often mistaken for *prajñā*-intuition. So long as there is no *prajñā* awakening, *samādhi* is merely a psychological phenomenon.

32. *RTL*, xxvi, 93a.

33. *RTL*, xxvi, 85b.

34. *Ibid.*

35. *Ibid.*

36. *RTL*, xxiv, 114b.

37. *RTL*, xxv, 77b.

38. *RTL*, xxvi, 86b.
39. *RTL*, xxii, 45b.
40. *RTL*, xx, 30a.
41. *RTL*, xxi, 41a.
42. *RTL*, xxi, 40a.
43. *RTL*, xxi, 38a.
44. *RTL*, xxvi, 87b.
45. *RTL*, xxi, 38b.
46. *RTL*, xxi, 41b.
47. *RTL*, xix, 21a.
48. *RTL*, xviii, 16b.
49. *RTL*, xxvi, 85b.
50. *Ibid.*
51. *Ibid.*
52. *Ibid.*
53. *RTL*, xxiv, 72a.
54. *RTL*, xxvi, 87b.
55. "Revolving" refers to the reading of the *Sūtra*. When certain *Sūtras* are read they are simply unrolled and folded back, and this is repeated several times. The *Sūtras* being too long for a regular reading, the priests resort to this simplified method. Thus *Sūtra*-reading came to be known as "*Sūtra*-revolving," though in this case the actual *Sūtra*-revolving has nothing to do with the master's enigmatic statement.
56. *RTL*, xxvi, 86b.
57. As is already well known to the reader, the masters frequently make such factually impossible statements. The idea is to make the questioners, that is, all objectively minded people, reverse their way of thinking. Ultimately, this means to re-examine our ordinary "logical" way of reasoning.
58. *RTL*, xxvi, 86b.
59. *RTL*, xxv, 78b.
60. *RTL*, xxvi, 87b.
61. *RTL*, xxv, 78a.
62. *RTL*, xxiii, 55a.
63. *RTL*, xiv, 117b.
64. *RTL*, xiv, 115a. Tanka was a great master of Zen philosophy during the T'ang Dynasty. One winter night when he was staying at a certain monastery, he felt very cold, and so he took down the wooden image of the Buddha from the shrine and burned it to make a fire. When he was blamed for this sacrilegious deed, he simply said that he just wanted to collect the *śarīra* of the Buddha-image. When he was told that no *śarīra* could be obtained from the wood,

he said, "Why, then, do you blame me?" (The *śarīra* is some mineral matter which is sometimes found in the ashes when the body is cremated. The holier the man, the more and brighter the *śarīra*, it is said.) I may add an encounter Tanka had with the daughter of his friend Hōkoji. Both Hōkoji and his daughter were advanced in their understanding of Zen. When Tanka called on Hōkoji one day, he met his daughter picking vegetables in the garden. Asked Tanka, "Is your father home"? The girl did not say anything in answer, but, throwing down the basket she carried, she stood up with her hands folded over her chest. Tanka asked again, "Is he home?" The girl took up the basket and walked away.

65. In Buddhism food and other offerings, such as flowers, incense, and candles, are placed before the Buddha-image and other holy images as tokens of gratitude for what they have done.

66. This refers to the story of an old Buddhist philosopher. He made the stones nod when he talked earnestly about *dharma* to the stones since he had no human audience.

67. A banner-stick is a sign to indicate that preaching is going on at that place.

KISHIMOTO HIDEO *Some Japanese Cultural*

Traits and Religions

I

SUPPOSE A MAN is taking a walk in the countryside of Japan. He is surrounded by quiet autumnal scenery. Some sentiment comes to his mind. He feels it and wants to express the sentiment. He would say, "*samishii*" (lonesome).

What he says, on such an occasion, can be simply one word, as above. This single word can well be regarded as a complete statement in the Japanese language. For the Japanese language, a full sentence in the Western grammatical sense is not ordinarily called for. The nature or structure of its syntax has its own peculiarity. A complete statement can be made just by saying "lonesome," and nothing else.

It is not necessary in Japanese to specify the subject by explicitly stating whether "I" am feeling lonesome, or "the scenery" is lonesome. Without such analysis, one's sentiment can be projected there in its immediate form. Analytically, the sentiment is the result of the collaboration of the subject and the object. No doubt, both are taking part in it. But, what is actually coming up in his mind is the sentiment of lonesomeness, working in the domain of an immediate experience. It is in-between. One of the characteristics of the Japanese language is to be able to project man's experience in its immediate and unanalyzed form.

No doubt, in modern Western languages, also, people can say things in short abbreviated form. But, when they use such a simple form, they are always conscious of the fact that what is being said is only the abbreviated part of the more complete full statement.

The syntax of Western languages requests, in their construction, more distinct and full indication of the subject-object relation than does the Japanese. So, a full statement of the subject-object relation is expected in English, while the Japanese language is more closely connected with man's immediate experience.

This peculiarity is not limited to the language alone. It is rooted more deeply in Japanese culture. It seems to be reflected in the way the Japanese people think. This is a more fundamental problem. A subtle but significant difference between the Japanese mind and that of Western people seems to be betrayed here.

To the Japanese, the Western mind seems to be making a sharper distinction between subject and object. The first reaction of Western people to any given situation seems to be in contrast to the Japanese, more inclined in the direction of analysis, analyzing the situation into a subject-object-predicate relation. To the Western mind, these composite elements of experience arise immediately. Based on them, the instinctive reaction of the Westerner is to achieve an analytical grasp. They use many more "I's," "you's," and "it's" than would Japanese. Of course, on similar occasions, the Japanese are also aware of the subject-object relation. But the Japanese seem to direct their interest more to the domain of immediate experience.

This cultural trait seems to have some bearing on the nature of Japanese thought. It is often said that the general trend of Japanese thinking is idealistic. It certainly is strongly tinged with introspective tendencies. The Japanese usually do not show too much interest in the exact details of factual events and objects. In this sense it seems idealistic. But, in spite of that, it could be asked whether it is really idealistic in the Western sense of the term.

In the West, the distinction between the two types of thought, realism and idealism, is more distinct. Realism is factual. It puts its focus on objective facts. Idealism is conceptual. It puts its emphasis on subjective ideas. Japanese thinking may seem idealistic because it is introspective and takes less interest in factual objects. But it has seldom taken the form of conceptual idealism. It should be noticed that, in the course of cultural history, the Japanese have never shown strength in speculative thinking. The system of formal logic or abstract concepts has made little progress in Japan. Outstanding thinkers are rather few in Japan. Buddhism has been equipped with deep and complicated philosophical systems, such as Tendai and Hossō. But they had developed in India and China.

Japanese Buddhism, in turn, has grown more as a practical religion. Confucianism also prevailed in Japan. But no leader like Chu Hsi (1130–1200) or Wang Yang-ming (1473–1529) appeared in Japan. To repeat, the Japanese have been more interested in the domain of immediate experience. So, if one wants to call Japanese thinking idealistic, it might be better to call its empirical idealism. It should be distinguished from conceptual idealism of the Western type.

Immediate experience plays a very important role in Japanese life. The Japanese people introspectively ponder and explore the domain of immediate experience. This is a very concrete domain for a Japanese. If conceptual speculation goes too far into abstract thinking, a Japanese quickly loses interest. And he wants to be less abstract and more concrete and realistic. But to be realistic does not necessarily mean, for a Japanese, to go back to factual realism, but to be realistic to the reality of immediate experience.

In the philosophical trends of the West, there is a third general trend which may not be as influential as the other two. It is the trend which is more concerned with immediate experience, such as Bergsonian intuitionism, the radical empiricism of William James, and recent existentialism. It is not unnatural that such trends in philosophy should have a strong appeal to the Japanese mind.

The characteristic mentioned above may be called the "radically empirical trait" of the Japanese, in contrast to the "analytical trait" of the Western mind. Why has this peculiarity developed in Japanese culture? The indigenous intuitive nature of the Japanese people, as well as the cultural influence of the Buddhists, must be credited with that. In the long course of history, the introvert nature of Buddhism must have accelerated this tendency a good deal. This is a subtle trait. But it seems to have fundamental importance. It is so basic that various features of Japanese culture may be interpreted from this point of view. Taking this as a clue, I shall offer here a brief observation on some features of religions and other spiritual values in Japanese culture.

II

There are many religions in Japan. Various different religions are flourishing side by side, such as Shintō, Buddhism, Christianity, and others.

Among them, Shintō is an age-old native religion of the Japanese people. It originated in Japan and has grown along with the development of her culture. Buddhism came from India by way of China. The transmission of Buddhism to Japan was in the middle of the sixth century. It spread all over Japan, and also penetrated Japanese culture. Christianity entered Japan once, briefly, in the fifteenth century. Present-day Christianity, including both Catholic and Protestant, is the second entrance, which was about one hundred years ago. Besides these, there are many independent religions which have been founded by individual spiritual leaders. Some of them are Sectarian Shintō, and there are still other new religions. New religions are abundant. Within the span of a decade of post-war Japan, statistics say about six hundred religions came into being.

The variety of religions is broad and extensive in Japan. But, excepting Christianity, most of them share a common general characteristic. This seems to be rooted in the basic empirical trait of Japanese culture.

The common concern of all these religions is the internal problems of man. Their main focus is on immediate experience. How to remove worries and anxieties from man's mind is their main task. Various devices are suggested for that purpose. They generally try to remold man's mind. This constitutes the central part of the religious activities. Mental training is the indispensable element in these religions. Religious experience of a mystical nature is also cherished by them. But those religions do not show too much interest in the social life of the people. They do not put special emphasis on the ethical problems of man. Such religions present a fairly different picture as compared to those of the Western religious tradition.

For instance, Shintō has a strong tinge of Nature mysticism. Shintō has long maintained that there should not be a rational interpretation of it. It has no sacred scripture corresponding to the Bible of Christianity or the holy Sūtras of Buddhism. A faithful believer would come to the simple hall of a Shintō sanctuary, which is located in a grove with a quiet and holy atmosphere. He may stand still quite a while in front of the sanctuary, clap his hands, bow deeply, and try to feel the deity in his heart. He would not try to build up rational proof for the existence of an invisible deity. For him, the proof of divine existence depends on whether or not he can feel the deity directly in his heart. Shintō being a polytheistic religion, each sanctuary has its own particular deity. But seldom do the believers know the individual name of the deity whom they are worshipping. They do not care about that. It is not a matter of importance for them. The more important point for them is whether or not they feel the existence of the deity directly in their hearts.

In the case of Japanese Buddhism, its supreme aim is to emancipate man from the miseries of life. Most of the miseries of life are undoubtedly caused by the difficulties of environmental situations. But such environmental difficulties themselves are not the direct cause of the real miseries of life. They become real miseries of life only if the mind is affected and disturbed by such difficulties. In the disturbed mind, conflicting desires arise, and they combat each other in the mind. Such a state of mind causes worries and anxieties, and man is tormented by agonies. Therefore, the key to the real miseries of life is how a man accepts a given situation. Thus, this key point is closely connected with immediate experience. Buddhism can check the miseries of life. In such a way, Buddhism focuses its interest on the internal problem of man. Worries and anxieties in the domain of immediate experience have become its main concern.

To discover the ultimate means for overcoming the miseries of life, the Buddha made introspective inquiries, deep into the psychology of man. What is the main cause of worries and anxieties in man's mind? According to Buddhist teachings, it is the basic desire within man. Stimulated by environmental situations, conflicting desires flare up in the mind. Unfulfilled desires become the further cause of disorder in the mind. This is the main cause of worries and anxieties. So, the task of emancipating man from them develops in Buddhism into the problem of how to handle basic desire in man.

Indian Buddhism, reflecting the extremely speculative mind of the Indian people, went far. It carried the solution of the problem to the goal of logical conclusions. If the basic desire in man is the cause of the miseries of life, the most effective means to check them is to exterminate such basic desire. Then worries and anxieties should disappear. But utter extermination of desires would mean no life at all. The metaphysical theory of Indian Buddhism logically puts its ultimate goal on the disappearance of man from this worldly life (*saṁsāra*). Such an ideal of life-negation, however, was too much for the Japanese people. The Japanese are apparently life-enjoying people. They want to take a more affirmative attitude toward life.

Buddhism in Japan shows radical differences from such life-negating Buddhism. It is Mahāyāna Buddhism. It also aims at re-molding man's mind, but there is an important shift in the purpose of such remolding. It does not try to exterminate basic desire, but it tries to correct the desire-structure of man. Conflicting desires are the cause of worries and anxieties. Desires as such are not only the cause of worries and anxieties, but are also the cause for all life-activities. Only the wrong desire-structure becomes the cause of worries and anxieties. So, desires as such should not be exterminated. But desires should be given a right structure. Following the teaching of the Buddha, Japanese Buddhists believe man can re-mold his mind to give his desire-system a right structure. Enlightenment means that a man has a right structure of mind. The stimulations of environmental situations will no longer make conflicting desires arise. His worries and anxieties disappear. He suffers from no miseries of life. The environmental world may re-main the same, but, for him, the life of miseries changes into the life of happiness. After having achieved enlightenment, a man will still enjoy earthly life. Buddhism, for the Japanese people, is thus a life-affirming religion.

Buddhism, with its influence penetrating very deeply into Japanese culture, has made the Japanese mind more and more introverted. Turning inward, the radically empirical trait of the Japanese people was further strengthened. But Japanese philos-ophy did not develop into abstract conceptual idealism.

In this way, both Shintō and Buddhism focus their main con-cern on the domain of immediate experience. The role of religions in Japan is to teach people how to accept the given environmental situation. If man's mental state is well adjusted, his grasp of situa-tions will be well balanced and conflicting desires will not rise. Thus, the radically empirical trait of Japanese culture seems to be effective as the basic factor of Japanese religions.

III

The peculiar nature of Japanese religions has brought forth two conspicuous cultural features. One is a distinct separation in the sphere of activities between the religious system and the ethical system. The other is the close relation between religious value and aesthetic value.

All through the history of Japan, Japanese religions have been steeped in the inner problem of man. The inner problem has exclusively occupied the interest of Japanese religions. They were not active in providing ethical principles for man's social conduct. What should man's respectable social conduct be? How should a man endeavor to reform society according to his religious ideal? Such a problem did not develop within the domain of religion. The problem whether a man's conduct is good or bad is different by nature from the problem of how to emancipate man from worries and anxieties. In Japan, religion has concentrated upon the latter problem. Neither Buddhism nor Shintō has had much concern for the ethical problem. In the well-known words of Shinran (1173–1262), "Even a righteous man can be saved, why not a sinner."

Because of the peculiar nature of Japanese religions, they have tried to deal with the sphere of man's problem which is beyond the sphere of good and evil conduct.

But the fact that Japanese religions had not supplied any ethical principles to Japanese society does not mean that Japanese society was not in need of ethical principles. In earlier days, because of the homogeneous social structure of Japan, the need for an established system of ethical principles might not have been as serious as in other nations. But the society grew and became more complicated. It could not do without some kind of ethical system. Confucianism, transmitted from China, came to fulfill this need. From the beginning of the seventeenth century, by the time of the Tokugawa government, the Confucian system was taken over as the ethical code of Japan. This has been the social role of Confucianism in Japan. As a result of this, a kind of division of labor was developed. For principles of moral conduct, people rely on the Confucian code. The domain of inner problems is left to Shintō and Buddhism. In other words, Confucianism functions for ethics, and Shintō and Buddhism for religion.

This dualism of religion and ethics in Japanese culture is often misunderstood by Western people. It is not too easy for them to grasp. Western visitors to Japan often ask the Buddhist or Shintōist what is his moral code. The answer is often weak and negative. Interpreting the weakness of such an answer in Western fashion, they draw the conclusion that these religions in Japan are either half dead or out of date. They take the moral code of religion as the index of its vitality. The Japanese religions may well be getting out of date, but the judgment of their vitality should not be based upon this. A religion of the Japanese type can be vitally active without being equipped with a full-fledged moral code. In fact, this is the characteristic nature of Japanese religions.

The introduction of Christianity into Japan is particularly interesting in this connection. Christianity is new to Japanese culture, not only in its monotheistic structure, but in its tight integration of religious principles with its ethical principles. It is for the Japanese people a religion with a new structure.

Professor Friedrick Heiler and Professor Gustav Mensching say that there are two different types of religion. They would say that Buddhism and Shintō are religions of the mystical type, and that Christianity is the prophetic type. It is not that Buddhism and Shintō are out of date, or undeveloped, or do not have an effective moral code, but that they are a different kind of religion.

While the ethical system and the religious system are divided, the aesthetic value and religious value, on the other hand, are regarded as having a close relationship in the Japanese cultural tradition. In their achievements, religious values and aesthetic values are not two different things. Ultimately, they are one for the Japanese.

This close relationship between religion and the arts does not simply mean that Japanese religions specifically base their expression upon an abundant use of artistic representations. It goes more deeply into the basic problem.

As has been mentioned above, the main concern of Japanese religions, especially Buddhism, has not been so much with the good and evil of man's conduct as with the attitude of man, that is, how he accepts the given environment. In other words, they put stronger emphasis on the mental aspect of man than on the behavioral aspect. They instruct man how to reach a tranquil and balanced state of mind. Then man can see things just as they are, without any disturbance or bias in his mind. Such mental emphasis on the part of religion makes its relationship to aesthetic value very close.

When we turn to aesthetic value, we find that the general attitude of Japanese artists also reflects the basic empirical trait of Japanese culture. They believe that the artist's mind must be calm and tranquil. A polished mirror can reflect things as they are. Only when the artist's mind is as calm as the surface of a mirror can the real nature of the outside object be grasped.

In the mind of the artist, nothing but an exact image of the object should exist. In this sense, the mind of the artist must become one with the object. To achieve this, the artist must practice mental training along with his technical training in art. This will explain why so many artists practice Zen training. And, also, why many Zen monks became master artists.

Religion tries to emancipate man from worries and anxieties. Art tries to grasp beauty and represent it. But both religion and art try to achieve tranquillity of mind and to grasp objects as they are. On this point, religious value and aesthic value become one.

IV

In Japanese society, also, among the people as a matter of social custom, it has been regarded as a high virtue to be able to keep the mind tranquil and calm. This was mainly the influence of Buddhism. Confucianism also helped to encourage people to subdue their emotional excitement. Anger and sorrow should not appear on the countenance. Tears should be suppressed with full effort. For the Japanese, tears cannot be seen by others without some feeling of embarrassment. Generally speaking, the more subdued in emotion a man is, the more he is respected.

There is a prevailing interest among the people in practicing mental training. "*Shugyō*" is the Japanese term for mental training. Various kinds of systematic training—such as waterfall ablution, mountain climbing, fasting, and others—have been offered by religions and other systems of culture. Zen, which is distinctly Buddhist, may be taken as the typical example of these. Flower arrangement and calligraphy are also taught for that purpose.

Naturally, in such circumstances, the Japanese have developed a complicated emotional structure of personality—probably to the degree that it is not easy for the outsider to understand it fully. The so-called Japanese "poker face" typically symbolizes it. The Japanese "poker face" is not due to any lack of emotion. Strong and powerful emotional feelings are hidden behind it. The long cultural tradition has given the people the mental power to control the expression of their emotions.

This complexity of the Japanese mind often brings forth a peculiar form of emotional reaction. It is a familiar scene in which a Japanese champion at the Olympic Games stands on the victor's platform with a golden trophy in his hand, and, although he is expected to laugh happily, tears are in his eyes, as if he has just come away from a Greek tragedy. It is not that he is unhappy. In actuality, a feeling of joy is welling up within him, but he tries rigorously to suppress it. As the result, a complicated combination of emotions brings happy, warm tears.

Suppose a Japanese woman makes a small commotion by falling down on the street. As she struggles to get up, one may notice a faint smile on her face. In spite of her inner disturbance, she instinctively tries to keep her mind calm and balanced, and to observe the situation objectively. With great effort she tries to say to herself: "What a blunder you are making," and tries to smile at herself. This whole reaction can occur in an instant, because of long cultural tradition.

The emphasis on balanced tranquillity of mind has cultivated among the Japanese a peculiar ability to meet difficult situations; the attitude of accepting any difficulty quietly and courageously is regarded as a high virtue.

The most difficult problem of all for man to face is the oncoming of death. The problem as to how to face death has developed in Japan as a peculiar pattern of culture. It makes the Japanese feel that they must meet death squarely, rather than avoid it. The cultural tradition encourages them to be prepared to accept death with courage and with tranquillity. So how one faces death has come to be regarded as an important feature of life. Death is not a mere end of life for the Japanese. It has been given a positive place in life. Facing death properly is one of the most important features of life. In that sense, it may well be said that for the Japanese death is within life.

Thus, cultural tradition has developed to the extent of establishing an etiquette for committing suicide. The ceremonial performance of *seppuku* (often called *harakiri* by Westerners), which has aroused the curiosity of Western people, is a very interesting cultural phenomenon. It was officially observed until the end of feudalistic days in the middle of the last century. It was not a blind admiration of suicide. It was the last honor given to a *samurai* whose conduct deserved death.

In Japanese society, committing suicide has never been regarded as a sin, or a shame. The point of concern was the manner of committing it. If one could commit suicide in a fine self-composed manner, it could be taken as a respectable achievement. This will explain the *banzai* attacks and the *kamikaze* attacks during the recent war. The Japanese could do such daring acts, not because the Japanese have emotionally less fear of death, but as a result of cultural tradition. From childhood, consciously and unconsciously, they have been trained to meet death courageously.

Emphasis on tranquillity and a balanced state of mind may thus be taken as another expression of the empirical trait of Japanese culture.

V

During the last one hundred years, modern Western culture has been penetrating Japan. No other country on the globe has ever met Western culture and Eastern culture in such an overwhelming way. Japanese culture is changing rapidly. A new Japanese culture, modernized and Westernized, is coming into being. But, in the case of Japanese religions, it is still too early to make any appraisal of these changes. The traditional religions are not affected. In spite of the vigorous trend of modernization and actual changes of other aspects of culture, they remain little changed.

Modern Western culture came into Japan as an integral whole. But it consisted of two different elements. These were Western culture and modern culture. These two have had very different effects upon Japanese culture. One has Westernized Japanese culture, and the other has modernized it. But, the Japanese accepted them as an integral whole. The Japanese could not clearly distinguish the difference between these two elements. The problem as to whether a Japanese should learn English in addition to the indigenous Japanese language involves Westernization. To learn how to use the modern equipment of technology is modernization. The Japanese could not distinguish the difference between these two. This indiscriminate acceptance has caused deep confusion.

For the Japanese religions, it was fatal to become Westernized. Buddhism and Shintō could not take monotheistic form without losing their fundamental trait. Confucianism could not easily abandon its theory of benevolence. The empirical trait of Japanese culture could not change suddenly into a rational trait. They therefore resisted Westernization. But they could not resist Westernization alone. Modernization and Westernization were thought of as one. Resisting Westernization, they were unconsciously resisting modernization at the same time. As a result of this, while all other aspects of culture in Japan were making rapid progress toward modernization, Japanese religions and other indigenous cultural institutions lagged behind. The lag in the steps of modernizing religions is one aspect of present-day confusion.

But, now, Japan seems to be coming to the turning point. As the result of one hundred years' effort, though it was a difficult struggle, Japan has been modernized rather successfully. Having achieved this, the Japanese people are now, for the first time, realizing the distinction between Westernization and modernization. Japanese culture can be modernized without being Westernized. Now the Japanese people are able to see that their religions can be safely modernized, and that there is no need for infringement upon their intrinsic nature by Westernization. This turning point means the starting point for the modernization of Japanese religions and other indigenous institutions. We must watch their course of development.

SUZUKI DAISETZ TEITARŌ

An Interpretation of Zen Experience

I

THE PHILOSOPHY of Zen Buddhism is that of Mahāyāna Buddhism, for it is no more than a development of the latter. But the development took place among a people whose psychology or mentality widely varies from the Indian mind, whose product Buddhism is. Buddhism, after Nāgārjuna and Vasubandhu and their immediate followers, could not continue its healthy growth any longer in its original soil; it had to be transplanted if it were to develop a most important aspect which had hitherto been altogether neglected—and because of this neglect its vitality was steadily being impaired. The most important aspect of Mahāyāna Buddhism which unfolded itself in the mental climate of China was Ch'an (Zen). While China failed to perfect the Hua-yen (Kegon) (or Avataṁsaka) or the T'ien-tai (Tendai) system of Mahāyāna thought, she produced Ch'an. This was really a unique contribution of the Chinese genius to the history of mental culture generally, but it has been due to the Japanese that the true spirit of Zen has been scrupulously kept alive and that its technique has been completed.

When it is asked what Zen is, it is very difficult to give an answer satisfactory to the ordinary questioner. For instance, when you ask whether Zen is a philosophy or a religious faith, we cannot say it is either, as long as we understand these two terms in their usual sense. Zen has no thought-system of its own; it uses Mahāyāna terminology liberally; it refuses to commit itself to any specified pattern of thinking. Nor is it a faith, for it does not urge us to accept any dogma or creed or an object of worship. It is true that it has temples and monasteries where images of the *buddhas* and *bodhi-sattvas* (would-be *buddhas;* technically, beings whose essence is perfect wisdom) are enshrined in some specially sanctified quarters, but they do not hesitate to treat them unceremoniously when they find it more useful for the elucidation of their subject-matter. What the Zen masters stress most is a certain kind of experience, and this experience is to express itself in ways most characteristic of Zen. Those ways, they consider, constitute the essential features of Zen as differentiated from the other schools of Buddhism, as well as from all other religious or philosophical thought-systems of the world. What modern students of Zen have to do is to make a thorough examination of Zen experience itself and of the ways in which the experience has expressed itself in history.

II

To study Zen means to have Zen experience, for without the experience there is no Zen one can study. But mere experience is not enough; to experience means to be able to communicate it to others; the experience ceases to be vital unless it is adequately expressible. A dumb experience is not human. To experience is to be self-conscious. Zen experience is complete only when it is backed by Zen consciousness and finds expression in one way or another. In the following I will attempt to give a clue to the understanding of Zen consciousness.

Daian (died 883), the Zen master of Dai-i San, once gave this to his congregation: "[The conception of] being and non-being is like the wistaria winding around the tree."

Sozan, hearing this, lost no time in undertaking a long journey, for he wished to find out the meaning of Daian's most enigmatic statement. Seeing the master engaged in making a mud wall, he approached and asked, " [The conception of] being and non-being is like the wistaria winding around the tree; did you really say that?"

The master said, "Yes, my friend."

Sozan queried, "When the tree is suddenly broken down and the wistaria withers, what happens?"

The master threw up his mud-carrying board and laughing loudly walked away toward his living quarters. Sozan followed and protested: "O Master, I come from a remote district three thousand *li* [one *li* is about two and a half miles] away, I have sold my clothing to pay for the traveling expenses, and this for no other purpose than to get enlightened on this subject. Why do you make fun of me?"

The master felt pity for the poor monk and told his attendant to gather up enough money for his return trip. He then turned toward Sozan, saying, "Some day you may happen to see a master who is known as the 'One-eyed Dragon,' and he will make you see into the matter."

Later, Sozan came to Myōshō and told him about the interview he had had with Daian of Dai-i San. Myōshō said, "Daian is all right through and through; only, he misses one who really understands his mind." Sozan now proposed the same question to Myōshō, saying, "What happens when the tree is broken down and the wistaria withers?" Myōshō said, "You make Daian renew his laughter!" This made Sozan at once comprehend the meaning of the whole affair, and he exclaimed, "After all, there is a dagger in Daian's laughter." He reverentially bowed in the direction of Dai-i San.

III

In this citation, what strikes one most is the disparity between the question and the answer, for, as far as our common sense or logic allows us to see, no connection whatever exists between the statement concerning being and non-being and the master's laughter or, as is given later on, Yengo's repetition of his own master. The question in regard to being and non-being is a philosophical one dealing with abstract ideas. All our thoughts start from the opposition between being and non-being; without this antithesis no reasoning can be carried on, and therefore the question is a fundamental one: "What will become of our thought-system when the conception of being and non-being is wiped out?" When the tree dies, naturally the wistaria withers. Being is possible only with non-being, and conversely. This world of particulars is comprehensible only when we recognize the fundamental antithesis of being and non-being. Where shall we be when this is no more? An absolute nothingness? This, too, is inconceivable. Is it an error then to speak at all of the antithesis? But it faces us; we cannot get rid of this world of birth and death, which, however, in its present state, is quite unsatisfactory to our moral and spiritual nature. We always have the craving to go beyond the antithesis, which somehow does not seem to be final; it points to something higher and deeper, and this we wish to take hold of. The mutual conditioning of antitheses must be transcended, but how? This is in fact the question raised by Sozan.

As long as we stay with the mutual conditioning of opposites, i.e., in the world of antitheses, we never feel complete; we are always haunted with a feeling of uneasiness. Sozan must have been deeply stirred with the question of being and non-being, of birth and death, or, speaking more like a Christian, with the problem of immortality. When he heard of Daian of Dai-i San's making the statement about it, he thought that here was the master who could solve the riddle and give him spiritual rest. He sold his scanty possessions and with what little he had realized he managed to travel a long way up to Dai-i San. Seeing the master engaged in making the mud wall, he approached him precipitously and wished to be enlightened on the subject: "What will become of us, of human souls, of their immortality, when the world with all its multitudinous contents is reduced to ashes at the end of the present *kalpa* [an aeon or very great length of time]?"

The question is metaphysical as well as religious. It is religious as long as it does not attempt to develop its significance along the purely intellectual line; it is metaphysical inasmuch as its approach is by means of abstract concepts. This is a feature peculiar to Zen Buddhism. If we choose, we can call it a kind of practical philosophy, and this practicalness may well be illustrated by the laughter given by Daian of Dai-i San as an answer to Sozan's question. Sozan was metaphysically minded enough to resort to such an abstraction as being and non-being, while his practical mindedness is shown by transforming this abstraction into the relation between concrete objects such as the wistaria and the pine tree. Even this practical mindedness of Sozan was thoroughly upset by Daian's ultrapracticalness: the throwing up of the mud carrier, and the laughter, and the hurried departure for his room. Daian was all action while Sozan was still on the plane of word symbolism; that is, he was still on the conceptual level, away from life itself.

IV

As long as we are gregarious animals and therefore social and rational, everything we experience, be it an idea, an event, or a feeling, we desire to communicate to one another, and this is possible only through a medium. We have developed various mediums of communication, and those who can command them at will are leaders of humankind: philosophers, poets, artists of all kinds, writers, orators, religionists, and others. But these mediums must be substantiated, that is, must be backed by real personal experiences. Without such experiences, mediums are merely utilized and will never vibrate with vitality.

Some mediums are more readily counterfeited than others, being subject to all devices of ingenious simulation. Language as one such medium lends itself most easily to misrepresentation, intentional or otherwise. The highest and most fundamental experiences are best communicated without words; in the face of such experiences we become speechless and stand almost aghast.

Another consideration to note about means of communication is that, however eloquent a medium may be, it will not have the desired effect on the one who never had an experience somewhat similar in kind or one fainter in intensity. Like a pearl thrown before swine, the eloquence is wasted. On the other hand, if two people have had an experience of the same nature, the lifting of a finger will set the whole spiritual mechanism in vibration, and each can read the other's inner thought.

The Zen master is adept in the use of a medium, either verbal or actional, which directly points to his Zen experience and by which the questioner, if he is mentally ripe, will at once grasp the master's intention. The medium of this kind functions "directly" and "at once," as if it were the experience itself—as when deep calls to deep. This direct functioning is compared to one brightly burnished mirror reflecting another brightly burnished one which stands facing the first with nothing between them.

V

In the case of Daian and Sozan, the latter was still a captive in the prison of words and concepts, and was not capable of grasping reality at first hand. His mind was filled with ideas of being and non-being, of trees and wistarias, of birth and death, of the absolute and the conditioned, of cause and effect, of *karma* and *nirvāṇa;* he had no direct, non-mediated understanding of reality; and this was indeed the reason why he brought himself before the amateur mason, after traveling over a distance of several thousand *li.* The mason master was a master indeed, in every sense of the word. He never argued with the logician, who was entangled like the wistaria around the problem of being and non-being. He did not talk about the Absolute; he never resorted to a dialectic of contradiction; he never referred to a fundamental assumption lying behind the antithesis of being and non-being. What he did was simply throw down his mud carrier, give a hearty laugh, and hurry to his private quarters.

Now let us ask: Was there anything peculiar about Sozan's question? We human beings are always worried over the disruption of things we see, especially about the dissolution of this carnal existence, and about the life to come after it, if there should be one. This seems to be quite a natural feeling with us all, and so, why should it excite the Zen master's laughter? Merely laughing was not enough, he even threw down his instrument of work, stopped his wall making, and made for his quiet retreat. Does he mean by this that it is far better to ask nothing, to enjoy life as it goes on, to take things as they display themselves before us, to laugh when laughable objects are presented, to weep when events excite this feeling, in short, to accept all things and be cheerful about them? Or did he mean that when the world should come to an end, he wanted to enjoy the ending with the world? Or did he mean that there is no such thing as the ending of anything—things are eternal as they are; a world of relativity is mere appearance—and, therefore, that there is in reality no breaking down, no withering, thus barring all conceptual guessings based on the notion of relativity and appearance? Or did he laugh at the questioner's stupidity, which showed that the latter had failed to realize the working of something in himself quite apart from—or, rather, along with—his deep concern for the breaking down of the tree and the withering of the wistaria? Such a variety of meaning may be read into Daian's behavior. But what is desired here from the Zen point of view is to experience the meaning itself and to leave its intellectual interpretation to a later elaboration of your Zen consciousness, which inevitably rises out of the experience.

In any event, Sozan could not take in Daian's laughter, or, as we can say, he could not grasp the idea that was behind it or in it. He next visited Myōshō, the "One-eyed Dragon," wishing to be enlightened about the whole situation, in which he found himself all the more involved. Myōshō, however, did not give him any plausible intellectual explanation which might satisfy a philosophical inquirer; he simply remarked that this questioning on the part

of Sozan would end in renewing Daian's laughter. This was really
an enigmatical confirmation of his predecessor, but, miraculously
enough, it helped Sozan to dive into the significance of Daian's
puzzle. The whole thing was clarified now, and the only step he
could take was to bow reverentially in the direction where Daian
was and to express his heartfelt appreciation.

VI

Through the whole course of this incident, there are no metaphysical discussions of any kind; nor are there any devotional pro-
ceedings such as confession, repentance, or mortification; again,
there are no references to sin, God, prayer, shrinking from an everlasting fire, or asking for forgiveness. It starts with a kind of philosophical inquiry concerning being and non-being, which is likened
to the wistaria winding itself around the tree; but the solution given
is not at all along the line suggested by the question—it is absolutely beyond what ordinary-minded people would expect on such
occasions. In the whole history of human thought there is really
nothing comparable to this extraordinary Zen transaction. And what
is still more extraordinary and incomprehensible is the fact that
Sozan, the inquirer, finally grasps the meaning of the strange behavior of the master, which evidently solves the antithetical en-
tanglements of being and non-being.

VII

Somewhat similar to this Zen incident was the experience of
Rinzai (Lin-chi), whose case is given in one of my *Essays in Zen
Buddhism,* and I quote it:[1]
Rinzai (died 867) was a disciple of Ōbaku and the founder of
the school that bears his name. His Zen experience shows some in-
teresting features which may be considered in a way typically ortho-
dox in those days when the *kōan* system of Zen discipline was
not yet in vogue. He had been studying Zen for some years under
Ōbaku when the head monk asked:
"How long have you been here?"
"Three years, sir."
"Have you ever seen the master?"
"No, sir."
"Why don't you?"

"Because I do not know what question to ask."

The head monk then told Rinzai: "You go and see the master and ask: 'What is the principle of Buddhism?'"

Rinzai saw the master as he was told and asked, "What is the principle of Buddhism?" Even before he could finish the question, Ōbaku gave him several blows.

When the head monk saw him coming back from the master, he inquired about the result of the interview. Said Rinzai sorrowfully, "I asked as you told me and he struck me several times." The monk told him not to be discouraged but to go again to the master. Rinzai saw Ōbaku three times and each time the same treatment was accorded him, and poor Rinzai was not any the wiser.

Finally, Rinzai thought it best to see another master, and the head monk agreed. The master directed him to go to Daigu. When Rinzai came to Daigu, the latter asked, "Where do you come from?"

"From Ōbaku."

"What instruction did he give you?"

"I asked him three times about the ultimate principle of Buddhism and each time he gave me several blows without any instruction. I wish you would tell me what fault I committed."

Daigu said: "No one could be more thoroughly kindhearted than that dotard master, and yet you want to know where you were faulty."

Thus reprimanded, Rinzai's eye was opened to the meaning of Ōbaku's apparently unkind treatment. He exclaimed: "After all, there is not much in Ōbaku's Buddhism!"

Daigu at once seized Rinzai's collar and said: "A while ago you said you could not understand and now you declare that there is not much in Ōbaku's Buddhism. What do you mean by that?"

Rinzai without saying a word probed Daigu's ribs three times with his fist. Daigu loosened his hold on Rinzai and remarked, "Your teacher is Ōbaku; I am not at all concerned with your business."

Rinzai returned to Ōbaku who asked him, "How is it that you are back so soon?"

"Because your kindness is much too grandmotherly!"

Ōbaku said, "When I see that fellow Daigu, I will give him twenty blows."

"Don't wait for that," said Rinzai, "have them now!" So saying he gave the old master a hearty slap.

The old master laughed a hearty laugh.

VIII

In Rinzai's case the answer was given, not in the form of laughter, but in a more forbidding manner, for he was given so many blows by the master. In fact, however, whether it is a blow or a laugh or a kick or a slap, it makes little difference so long as it comes directly from an experience on the part of the master. Rinzai, too, failed to comprehend Ōbaku and had to run to Daigu for elucidation. And the elucidation came in the form of a good-natured comment: "Ōbaku was indeed grandmotherly!" The dealing of the hard blows was a kindhearted treatment to wake up the spirit-weary Rinzai.

From these citations we can readily see what a remarkable experience Zen is. Is it a philosophy? Or is it a religion? What kind of spiritual discipline is it, after all? Zen experience is an absolutely unique one in the whole history of human culture.

To make this point clearer, I will add another Zen incident in relation to the antithesis of being and non-being.

The same problem came up later between Engo and Daiye, of the Sung Dynasty (960–1279). Engo wanted Daiye, a disciple, to give his view on the aforementioned statement regarding the tree and the wistaria. Whenever Daiye tried to express himself, the master invariably interrupted him, saying, "Not that, not that." About half a year passed, when Daiye one day asked Engo, "When you were with your master, Goso Hōyen, I understand you approached him with the same problem, and I wish to know what Goso's response was." When Engo hesitated, Daiye insisted, "Your asking at the time took place before an open congregation, and I do not think there is any harm in your giving me Goso's answer now." Engo could no longer refuse him and said, "When I asked my teacher, Goso, about the statement concerning the conception of being and non-being, his answer was, 'No paintings, no delineations can do justice to it!' When I further asked, 'What happens when the tree is suddenly broken down and the wistaria withers?' Goso said, 'You are caught in your own trap!' "

This reiteration on the part of Engo revealed at once the whole secret before his disciple's mind, for Daiye now thoroughly understood what it was, and this fact made Engo say, "You now see by yourself that I have never deceived you."

IX

The statement that "[this antithetical world of] being and non-being is like the wistaria winding around the tree," in fact aptly describes the state of affairs about us. Intellectually speaking, we cannot go beyond this. Philosophers attempt to make it logically comprehensible—this fundamental contradiction lying at the bottom of this life—and they succeed in varied degrees, only to be superseded by those who follow. Some day they may develop perfect logic or a dialectic which will be the final word to our ratiocination. But people not so intellectually gifted as professional philosophers, yes, even the philosophers themselves as human beings endowed with feelings for the most fundamental experience, have an insatiable longing for a spiritual rest which may not necessarily yield to logical treatment. In other words, we cannot wait for a perfect thought-system which will solve most satisfactorily all the mysteries of life and the world; we impatiently aspire for something more practical and of immediate utility. Religion talks of faith, teaching that God somehow takes care of us, all the intellectual difficulties notwithstanding. Let the antithesis of being and non-being remain as it is; for what is beyond our intellectual comprehension may best be left in the hands of God. The faith that things are all well somehow or other with God, in whom we have our being, delivers us from doubts and worries.

The Zen way of deliverance, however, is not that of religion; to be free from doubts and worries, Zen appeals to a certain inner experience and not to a blind acceptance of dogmas. Zen expects us to experience within ourselves that the suchness of things—the antithesis of being and non-being—is beyond the ken of intellectual painting or dialectical delineation, and that no number of words can succeed in describing, that is, reasoning out, the what and why of life and the world. This may sound negative and may not be of positive use to our spiritual life. But the real trouble with us whenever we try to talk about things beyond intellection is that we always make our start from intellection itself, although this may be natural and inevitable; therefore, when Zen experience and other such things are talked about they sound empty as if they had no positive value. But Zen proposes that we effect a complete *volte-face* and take our stand first on Zen experience itself and then observe things—the world of being and non-being—from the point of view of the experience itself. This is what may be designated as an absolute standpoint. The usual order of things is hereby reversed: what was positive becomes negative, and what was negative becomes positive. "Emptiness" is reality, and "reality" is emptiness. Flowers are no longer red, and the willow leaves are no longer green. We are no longer a plaything of *karma*, of "cause and effect," of birth and death; the values of the changing world are no longer permanent ones; what we consider good or bad from the worldly point of view is neither good nor bad, for it has only a relative value. Logically, too, the antithesis of being and non-being holds good only for our relative knowledge, for our discursive understanding. After the Zen experience, an entirely new order of things takes place, a complete change of front is effected, and the result is that a relative world of changes and multiplicities is contemplated *sub specie æternitatis*. This in a way may be considered the meaning of "No paintings, no delineations can do justice to it."

X

Can we say, then, that Zen teaches a kind of mystical contemplation of life and the world? Before this is answered, let me make a further remark about Engo and Goso, who also had a great deal to do, as we saw, with the problem of being and non-being.

When Engo asked Goso concerning the breaking down of the tree and the withering of the wistaria, Goso emphatically declared, "You are caught in your own trap." The truth is that Zen experience by itself is not enough; it must be elaborated by means of Zen consciousness or Zen dialectic if it is to be articulate and communicable, not only to others, but to oneself. The experience needs to be rationalized, as it were; it wants to speak out. It wants to assert itself, to be conscious of itself; and, to do this, Zen has its own way, has opened up quite a unique one—absolutely unique, we may say. Where no paintings, no drawings, can portray a perfect world of Zen experience, how can we speak of being and non-being, of tree and wistaria, of birth and death, of synthesis and antithesis, of immanence and transcendence, of destruction and construction, of breaking down and withering and being reduced to nothingness? All these ideas and categories are so many instruments we have devised for our own convenience in this world of action and work; but, unless we know how to make use of them as occasion requires, they turn against us and trap us; that is, we are ensnared and enslaved by them. When the Zen experience is not properly made articulate it becomes an instrument of mischief. The experience is a double-edged sword, requiring careful handling, and in this handling Zen follows its own tradition, which first originated in the philosophy of Mahāyāna Buddhism and later managed to be fitted into the stream of Chinese psychology.

XI

It is not clear whether Zen can be identified with mysticism. Mysticism, as it is understood in the West, starts generally with an antithesis and ends with unification or identification. But in Zen there is no antithesis, therefore no synthesis or unification. If there is an antithesis, Zen accepts it as it is, and makes no attempts to unify it. Instead of starting with dualism or pluralism, Zen wants us to have a Zen experience, and with this experience it surveys a world of suchness. It has adopted Mahāyāna terminology, it is true, but it has the tendency to resort to concrete objects and happenings. It does not reduce them to oneness—which is an abstraction. When all things are reduced to oneness, it asks to what this One is reducible. If all comes from God, lives in God, and returns to God, Zen wants to know where this God is or lives. If the whole world, with all its multiplicities is absorbed into *Brahman,* Zen asks us to point out the whereabouts of *Brahman.* If the soul survives the body, Zen demands that you locate the soul or bring it out before us.

A master was asked where he might be found after his death, and he said, "Lying on my back in the wilderness, my limbs pointing straight up to the sky!" When another master was asked about the immutability of *nirvāṇa,* he replied, "The fallen leaves follow the running stream while the autumnal moon rises above the solitary peak." Another appeared in the pulpit apparently ready to give a sermon, but, as soon as he had mounted the pulpit, he declared that his discourse was over, saying, "Farewell!" After a while he resumed, "If there is any who has no understanding yet, let him come out." A monk made an advance toward the master and bowed down reverentially, whereupon the master, raising his voice, said, "How painful!" The monk stood up and was about to

propose a question, but the master cried, "Ho!" and drove him out.
When another monk approached, saying, "What is the most wonderful word (expressing the highest truth)?" the master merely remarked, "What say you?" Going carefully over all these *mondō*
(dialogues), where do we find traces of mysticism in Zen? The
masters give no hints whatever as to the annihilation or absorption
of the self in an Absolute, or the casting of the world into the
abyss of *nirvāṇa*.

XII

Mystics, generally agree with this characterization of God:
"God is not an 'object' for human understanding. He utterly transcends knowledge, and everything one says of Him is untrue. 'Be
still,' Eckhart says in a sermon, 'and prate not of God (i.e., the
Godhead), for whatever you prate in words about Him is a lie
and is sinful.' 'If I say God is good, it is not true; for what is good
can grow better; what can grow better can grow best. Now these
three things (good, better, best) are far from God, for He is above
all,' i.e., all such distinctions. No word that voices distinctions or
characteristics, then, may be spoken of the Godhead. Eckhart's
favorite names are: 'the Wordless Godhead'; 'the Nameless Nothing'; 'the Naked Godhead'; 'the Immovable Rest'; 'the Still Wilderness, where no one is at home.'" [2]

However mystical one may be, he cannot avoid using the term
"God" or "Godhead" or some similar concept corresponding to it.
But this is not so with Zen. Zen avoids abstract terms, not necessarily deliberately but unavoidably. When the question arises concerning such terms, the Zen master turns them down, making the
questioner realize that they have no direct hold on life. Zuigan
Shigen asked Ganto (829-887), "What is the original eternal reason?"

Ganto: "Moving!"

Zuigan: "What about it when moving?"

Ganto: "It is no longer the original eternal reason."

This made Zuigan reflect for some time over the matter.

Ganto continued, "When you assert, you are still in the world
of senses; when you do not assert, you sink into the ocean of birth
and death!"

Ganto does not wish to see his disciple stay with the original eternal reason, nor does he want him to lose sight of it. He knows that Zen is neither to assert nor to deny, that Zen is the suchness of things. Zen masters are not mystics and their philosophy is not mysticism.

XIII

In this respect, Kwasan's answer, which he gave uniformly to the various questions regarding the Buddha, mind, and truth, is significant.

Kwasan (died 960) used to quote the passage from Sōjō's work, *The Sacred Treasure* (*Hōzōron*): "Learning-and-disciplining is called [the stage of] hearing; non-learning, [the stage of] approximation; and when these two [stages] are transcended, we pass on to [the stage of] truth."

A monk came up and asked: "What is the stage of truth?"

The master said, "I know how to beat the drum."

Another time a monk asked, "What is the first principle?"

"I know how to beat the drum."

The master's response was the same when he was asked by still another monk: "I do not ask you about 'Mind is the Buddha,' but I wish to know what is meant by 'Not Mind, Not the Buddha.'"

"I know how to beat the drum," quickly came from the master.

On another occasion, a monk asked, "How would you treat him if a man of the highest attainment should come?"

Still the master would not give up his favorite expression: "I know how to beat the drum."

Kwasan was probably once a drum beater in his career as a monk, and it is likely not only that he said "I know how to beat the drum," but also that, so saying, he actually beat the drum, or at least went through the whole process, keeping time, "Do-ko-dong, do-ko-dong!"

When you say "this" or "that," however abstract and universal it may be, you are singling the particular "that" or "this" out of multiplicities, thus making it one of them. We cannot help this as long as we are what we are, so many "that's" or so many "this's." The only way to escape this infinite regression is actually to beat the drum, or to dance up and down with a rice-bowl, or to sing out loudly "La-la-la!"

XIV

A nun named Ryūtetsuma one day came to see Isan (died 853), the veteran master. ("Isan" is believed to be the posthumous name of Reiyū, who founded a Chinese subsect of Zen at Dai-i-San or Isan.) The master, seeing her approach, said, "Old Cow, are you come?" This is as if to say, "It is best for an old lady like you to stay home comfortably and enjoy these long spring days. What makes you leave your quiet peaceful hut? An altogether unnecessary tottering out!" The nun, however, announced: "Tomorrow they are going to have a great religious function at Taisan; I wonder if you are going to attend it." This is a mere story, for Taisan in the north is many thousand *li* away from Isan, which is situated in South China, and so, how could the nun know of the event and how could Isan fly to such distance? The nun seems to mean that she herself was going to be present at the function even across the great continent and that her coming over here was nothing. However old and doddering, she is mistress of herself, just as the sun rises in the east at dawn or as the cat leaps up in the garden to catch a butterfly. Can you, too, perform this miracle? But Isan had his own way of asserting his mastership. He threw himself down on the floor. What did he mean by this? Did he prefer a quiet nap to the active exercise of traveling so many miles? Did he mean that lying quiet is just as much a miracle as to be busily engaged in the practical affairs of life? Did he mean that the Absolute is active in lying down as well as in being up and doing? What was the nun's response to this? Without saying anything or doing anything, she just left Isan alone, and made for her own retreat.

What is the significance of the whole proceeding? Probably I have read too much of Zen-like thought into it. Instead of that, we may take it just as an episode in our daily life. A visitor appeared; she was welcomed, and they—visitor and host—had a pleasant conversation about various things of life, among them a big feast given at a certain monastery. The old master enjoyed the visit, but, getting tired, he fell asleep, and she left without further ceremony— this is what takes place between old friends. When the event is over, we have a pleasant memory of friendship, and the matter happily comes to an end.

To make a more general statement of this Isan-and-Ryūtetsuma incident: We are born to this world of many incidents and accidents, we go through them doing our best, and when the time comes, we say good-by to them all. If we are bound for the Pure Land, very well; if otherwise, also very well. We are perfectly passive in this respect, or perfectly active—all depends on the point of view we like to take. Zen has added nothing to the sum total of reality, nor has it subtracted an iota of it. Zen is radical realism rather than mysticism.

We must remember here, however, that Zen does not mean to ignore our moral thoughts, aspirations, and feelings which determine the value of life while on earth. Zen is essentially concerned with the thing most fundamental and most primary, and as to what relates to our worldly lives, it leaves that where it properly belongs. Everything that exclusively belongs to the dualistic sphere of existence is taken up by moral philosophy, religion, political science, and other fields of human consciousness, while Zen aims at taking hold of what underlies all phenomenological activities of the mind.

XV

Rudolf Otto, while referring to Fichte's mysticism together with Eckhart's, which he differentiates from Śaṁkara's, writes: "Thus the true relationship of the man who is saved is for Fichte, as it was for Eckhart: To know that he is one with the One, life with the Life, not united but absolutely unified, and *at the same time,* to stand in this world of multiplicity and division, not straining after its dissolution, but, with Eckhart, working righteousness in it, and, with Fichte, completing in it the living deed of ethical culture, and thus with both teachers bringing into this very world of non-being and of death, Being and Life. He must do this in such a way that his transcendental possession is itself the very source of power and the impelling force to moral and cultural activity." [3]

Even with Eckhart and Fichte, we observe that the basis of their philosophy lies in the dualism of being and non-being, of life and death, oneness and multiplicity. At times, it is true, they seem to go beyond the antithesis, but, as their thought revolves primarily around the dualistic axis, they always return to it after they have made a so-called mystical excursion into the field of identity. Zen, on the other hand, always keeps itself in the suchness of things, where this world of multiplicity and discrimination is at once the transcendental world of emptiness (*śūnyatā*) and non-discrimination (*avikalpa*). Zen, therefore, tries to guard most jealously against our consciousness getting tipped to one side or to the other. This is not a deliberate balancing. In the beginning of Zen life there may be something of the sort, but the object of its discipline is to transcend all such artificialities and to have the principle of suchness work out its own activity.

XVI

Once, when Hofuku (died 928) and Chōkei (853–932) took a walk in the mountain, Hofuku pointed at it and said, "Look here, this is no other than the Holy Peak itself!" Chōkei replied, "Fine, just as you say, but what a pity!" Zen is loath to see its experience lopsided, for it is sure to end in a lame Zen consciousness. Chōkei's remark points to this.

Hyakujō (720–814) was asked, "What is the most wonderful fact in the world?" He answered, "I sit here all by myself on the top of Mount Daiyu." The monk bowed to him, and Hyakujō struck the monk. This striking is significant, betraying the spirit of Zen, for Zen aspires to independence, self-mastery, freedom from every form of one-sidedness which means restraint and conditionality.

When Baso (died 788) was asked, "What is the first principle of Buddhism?" he struck the monk, saying, "If I did not strike you thus, all the world would be laughing at me." When another monk came to him with this: "What is the idea of Bodhidharma coming from the West?" Baso told him to come forward and he would let him know. The monk, as he was told, stepped forward. Baso lost no time in giving him a slap over his ear, and said, "The secret's already out."

When these Zen incidents are observed from the point of view of relativity and dualism, they appear to have no sense whatever; but, when looked at from the inside, as it were, there looms up the big character, "Zen," which is the key to all the "mysteries" so far cited. What Zen dislikes most is mediation, deliberation, wordiness, and the weighing of advantages. Immediacy is impossible as long as we are onlookers, contemplators, critics, idea-mongers, word-manipulators, dualists, or monists. All these faults are corrected and Zen is revealed when we abandon our so-called common-sense or logical attitude and effect a complete about-face, when we plunge right into the workings of things as they move on before and behind our senses. It is only when this experience takes place that we can talk intelligently about Zen consciousness from which the Zen incidents or Zen dialogues making up the annals of Zen are produced.

XVII

Zen is not mysticism, therefore, although there may be something in it reminding one of the latter. Zen does not teach absorption, identification, or union, for all these ideas are derived from a dualistic conception of life and the world. In Zen there is a wholeness of things, which refuses to be analyzed or separated into antitheses of all kinds. As they say, it is like an iron bar with no holes or handles to swing it about. You have no way to take hold of it; in other words, it cannot be subsumed under any categories. Thus, Zen must be said to be a unique discipline in the history of human culture, religious and philosophical.

Zen often speaks of a flash of lightning as if it valued an instantaneous or instinctive action in dealing with the fundamental problems of life. When somebody asks you about *buddha*hood or Godhead, you strike the questioner, saying, "What a blockheaded fellow of a monk!" There is no time lost between asking and striking, and you may think this is an immediacy, which is Zen. But the fact is far from it. Zen has nothing to do with rapidity or immediacy in the sense of being quick. A flash of lightning refers to the non-mediating nature of Zen experience.

Zen experience, one may say, is a kind of intuition which is the basis of mysticism. We have to be careful, however, about the use of the term "intuition." If we make it presuppose the existence of an antithesis of some form, Zen is not this kind of intuition, which we may designate as static or contemplative. If Zen experience is an act of intuition, it must be distinguished from the static form, and let us call it dynamic or actional. The following Zen incidents may help one to understand what is meant by dynamic intuition, which is Zen experience.

XVIII

So, some more Zen incidents are given here, in order to indicate which way Zen consciousness tends. They are culled at random from a Zen work known as *The Transmission of the Lamp (Keitoku dentō roku;* Chinese, *Ch'ing-te ch'üan-teng lu).* When these incidents are perused thoughtfully and without bias, one may be able to come in touch with an invisible thread running through them.

1. An officer once visited Gensha (836–908), who treated him to a dish of cake. The officer asked, "They speak of our not knowing it while using it all the time. What is this 'it'?" Gensha looked as if he were not paying attention to the questioner, for he innocently picked up a piece of cake and offered it to the officer. The latter ate it and repeated the question. The master said, "There you are! It is daily made use of, and yet they know it not!"

2. One day, Chōsa had all his monks work in the field to gather wood. The master said, "You all partake of my power." "If so, why do we all have to work in the field?"—This came from the monks at work. Chōsa reprimanded them, saying, "If you did not all work, how could we gather enough wood for our kitchen?"

3. When Nansai visited Seppō (822-908), the latter made him see Gensha. Gensha said, "Says an ancient master: 'This is the matter I alone have knowledge of.' What do you say to that?" Nansai replied, "You should know that there is one who does not seek being known." Gensha concluded, "What is the use of your going through so many hardships, then?"

4. A monk asked Gensha, "What is my self?" Replied Gensha, "What do you want to do with your self?"

5. A monk came to Gensha and wished to know how he was discoursing on the principle of Zen. Said Gensha, "I have very few listeners." Monk: "I wish to have your direct instruction." "You are not deaf?" came straightway from the master.

6. When Seppō, with all his monks, was working on the farm, he happened to notice a snake. Lifting it up with a stick, the master called the attention of the whole gathering, "Look, look!" He then slashed it in two with a knife. Gensha came forward, and picking up the slain snake threw it away behind them. He then went on working as if nothing had happened. The whole party was taken aback. Said Seppō, "How brisk!"

7. One day Gensha entered the pulpit, and for a while he sat quietly without saying a word. He then began, "All the kindheartedness I have is given out to you without reserve. Do you understand?" A monk ventured the question: "What is the meaning of a perfect silence?" The master said, "No talking in sleep!" Monk:

"Please tell, O master, about what concerns us most in Zen." "No use dreaming!" "I may be dreaming, but how about you?" Said the master, "How could you be so senseless as not to know what's what?"

XIX

Any reader who goes carefully over all the Zen incidents cited in this chapter will see that there is something in Zen which we never meet anywhere else in the history of human thought and culture. It certainly begins with enough rationalism since it deals, as we have noticed, with such religio-philosophical concepts as being and non-being, truth and falsehood, the Buddha and *nirvāṇa*; but after the beginning is once made, the matter is strangely switched off in a most unexpected direction, ending sometimes in what seems to be a comedy or farce or even a quarrel. Indeed, the history of Zen is filled with such records. To judge them by the ordinary standard of reasoning is altogether out of place, for that standard is simply inapplicable here. Superficial people, however, are likely to insist upon trying what ought not to be tried here; their world of vision is very limited, and they fail to realize that there is a much wider world than theirs which is beyond their mentality. The fact alone that Zen has been thriving in the Far East ever since the days of Bodhidharma and Enō (Hui-neng) and Rinzai, and that those masters and their followers, monks and otherwise, have contributed considerably to the widening of the spiritual horizon and to the enhancement of human ideals, is enough to prove the practical value and usefulness, not to say anything about the validity, of Zen-experience.

The only thing we can state here about Zen is that it is an altogether unique product of the Oriental mind, refusing to be classified under any known heading, as either a philosophy, or a religion, or a form of mysticism as it is generally understood in the West. Zen must be studied and analyzed from a point of view which is still unknown among Western philosophers. The study will give us a rich yield, not only in philosophy and the science of religion, but also in psychology and allied studies.

Notes

1. *Essays in Zen Buddhism,* II (London: Luzak & Co., 1933), pp. 33–35.
2. Rufus Jones, *Studies in Mystical Religion* (London: Macmillan and Co., 1909), pp. 225–226.
3. *Mysticism, East and West,* Bertah L. Bracey and Richarda C. Payne, trans. (New York: The Macmillan Co., 1932), p. 230.

NAKAMURA HAJIME   *Basic Features of the*

Legal, Political, and Economic Thought of Japan

I. Introduction

THE LEGAL, POLITICAL, AND ECONOMIC THOUGHT of a people cannot be discussed without taking their chief philosophical concepts into consideration.

As the main features of the Japanese ways of thinking we must note the following three major characteristics and other subordinate factors:

1. *The acceptance of actuality:* (a) apprehension of the Absolute in the phenomenal world; (b) this-worldliness; (c) acceptance of natural human qualities; (d) the spirit of tolerance; (e) cultural stratification; and (f) weakness of the spirit of direct criticism.

2. *The tendency to emphasize a particular social nexus:* (a) emphasis on human relations; (b) human relationships as of greater importance than the individual; (c) absolute view of limited social organization; (d) reverence for family morality; (e) emphasis upon hierarchical relations of status; (f) the supremacy of the state; (g) absolute obedience to some particular person; (h) emperor worship; (i) closed character of sects and cliques; (j) protection of the particular social nexus by force; (k) emphasis on activity in society; (l) sensitivity to moral introspection; and (m) lack of self-consciousness in religious reverence.

3. *Non-rational tendencies:* (a) non-logical tendencies; (b) weakness in ability to think in terms of logical consequences; (c) intuitional and emotional tendencies; (d) lack of ability to form

complex representations; (e) fondness for simple, symbolic representations; (f) weakness in knowledge of objective processes.[1]

With regard to such legal, political, and economic thought, which is the problem under consideration, the first and the second of these sets of basic attitudes are especially important.

II.   Esteem of Human Nature in Society

The Japanese in general are inclined to search for the Absolute within the phenomenal world or in what is actual. Among all the natures that are given and real, the most immediate to man is the nature of man. Hence, the Japanese tend to esteem highly man's natural disposition. So, as one of the most prominent features of traditional Japanese ways of thinking, we may point to an emphasis on the love of human beings. This may be described as the naturalistic view of life.[2] This tendency has been conspicuous among Shintōists. Even Buddhist ideas have been taught with close reference to matters of love, and even sexual love is considered not to be incompatible with religious principles. The tendency to esteem man's nature gives rise to the love of human beings in actual life.

The tendency toward humanitarianism has been traditional among the Japanese. The love of others in its purified form is named "benevolence" or "compassion" (Sanskrit, *maitrī, karuṇā*). This idea was introduced into Japan with the advent of Buddhism, and special emphasis has been put on it in Japanese Buddhism. The attempt to apply universal religions in politics caused rulers to deal with the people with affection and compassion, as in the case of Aśoka in India (third century B.C.). The Constitution of Prince Shōtoku (574–622) esteems the welfare of the people and is sympathetic with them. In this Constitution, the common people have a significant place in the consciousness of the ruling class. This role could not be destroyed in later history, and this trend might be regarded as the first step of gradual development toward democracy.

The spirit of benevolence was not preached by the Buddhists. It made its way into Shintōism and was associated with one of the three divine symbols of the Japanese Imperial Family, which claimed to rule on the spiritual basis of benevolence. The Tokugawa Shōgunate (government) (1571–1867) inherited this attitude. Benevolence also came to be regarded as one of the principle virtues of the *samurai* (knights), who asserted that it was not sufficient for them to be physically brave and strong, but that they should also be compassionate toward the common people.[3] Japanese Confucian scholars of politics also lay special emphasis upon the love of others. Kumazawa Banzan, a famous Confucian of the Tokugawa period, called Japan "the land of benevolence." [4] These facts give ample testimony to the assumption that the ruling class of Japan aimed at benevolence as its principal ideal.

In pre-Buddhist Japan, cruel punishments were not lacking. Emperors killed their subjects arbitrarily.[5] On the occasions of the internment of emperors, their retainers were buried alive around their graves.[6] Such customs were abolished, and after the advent of Buddhism there existed in Japan hardly any punishment that was cruel. In the Heian period (794–1192), capital punishment was not practiced for about three hundred and fifty years. Since crucifixion appeared for the first time in Japanese history during the Age of Civil Wars (1138–1560), it was probably introduced after the advent of Christianity and suggested by it.

The love of human beings seems to be closely connected with the love of the beauties of Nature, which is as old as the Japanese people themselves.

These tendencies give some clues to the basic concepts of the legal, political, and economic thought of the Japanese.

III. The Spirit of Harmony or Concord

The unanimous moral solidarity of a community has been sought as the social ideal, on an island scale, of Japan. This was felt intuitively in the spiritual atmosphere of the primitive society of Japan. Later, when the centralized state was established after the conflicts among various tribes had ended, "concord" was stressed as the most important principle of the community. Prince Shōtoku emphasized "harmony" or "concord" in human relations. With deep self-reflection, he advocated such concord in the first Article of his Constitution: "Above all else esteem concord; make it your first duty to avoid discord. People are prone to form partisanships, for few persons are really enlightened. Hence, there are those who do not obey their lords and parents, and who come in conflict with their neighbors. But, when those above are harmonious, and those below are friendly, there is concord in the discussion of affairs, and right views of things spontaneously gain acceptance.

Then what would there be that could not be accomplished?" Some scholars say that this conception of concord (*wa*) was adopted from Confusianism, for the word "*wa*" was used in *The Analects* of Confucius.[7] But the term "*wa*" was used in connection with propriety or decorum in that work,[8] and concord was not the subject being discussed. Prince Shōtoku, on the other hand, advocated concord as the principle of human behavior.[9] His attitude seems to have been derived from the Buddhist concept of benevolence, or compassion, which should be distinguished from the Confucian concept. Men are apt to be bigoted and partial. Within a community or between communities conflicts are sure to occur. One should overcome such conflicts, and concord should be realized, so that a harmonious community may be formed in an ideal way. The spirit of concord was stressed throughout all the Articles of the Constitution. Concord between lord and subject, between superior and inferior, among people in general, and among individuals was taught repeatedly. Prince Shōtoku did not teach that the people shall merely follow or obey but that discussion should be carried on in the atmosphere of concord or harmony, so that one might attain right views. Earnest discussion was most desirable. If we discuss affairs with the feeling of harmony, desisting from anger, difficult problems will be settled spontaneously in the right way. In this way alone is it possible that decisions may be reached at conferences.[10]

The democratic way of managing a conference was achieved in the remote past. In the mythology which reflects the primitive society of Japan, deities gathered in a divine assembly in the bed of a river. This tradition was followed and developed by later monarchs. Prince Shōtoku denounced dictatorship and stressed the necessity of discussing things with others: "Decisions on important matters should generally not be made by one person alone. They should be discussed with many others. But small matters are of less importance, and it is unnecessary to consult many persons concerning them. In the case of weighty matters, you must be fearful lest there be faults. You should arrange matters in consultation with many persons, so as to arrive at the right conclusion." [11]

This trend developed into the edict after the Taika Reformation (A.D. 645), which denounced the dictatorship of a sovereign by saying that things should not be instituted by a single ruler. The ancient way of ruling represented in Japanese mythology is not dictatorship by a monarch or by the Lord of All, but a conference of gods in the bed of a river. Where public opinion was not esteemed, a conference could not have been held successfully. So, the spirit of primitive Shintōism must have been inherited and developed by later rulers. This ideal was preserved in the days when the emperors were in power. Japanese monarchy or the Emperor Institution developed as something different from dictatorship.

Professor Northrop holds that when a dispute arises among Asians one does not settle it by recourse to determine legal principles, but pursues the "middle way" or mediation between the determinate theses of the disputants, by fostering the all-embracing intuitively felt formlessness common to all men and things.[12] Chiang Mon-lin writes: "Modern legal sense as the West understands it is not developed in China. Avoid the courts if you can. Let us settle our disputes without going to law. Let's compromise. Let's have a cup of tea and sip together with friends and talk things over."[13] This is exactly the situation we find among the Japanese also. There is a well-known Japanese proverb which is understood by everybody in practice: "In a quarrel both parties are to blame."

But this is not due to lack of esteem for law on the part of the Japanese people, but due to financial and other considerations. If they should go to court, they would lose much time; sometimes it would take several years to settle even one case. They would have to employ lawyers and spend much money. Even if they should win at court, they would get very little. So, taking everything into account, to resort to legal measures very often impairs the happiness and welfare of the people concerned and others around them. Barristers-at-law are not always respected, but very often abhorred, by the common people of Japan, who fear that they may take advantage of the people's lack of legal knowledge in order to make money for themselves. The writer personally knows some Japanese intellectuals who claim to be businessmen at home, but to be lawyers when they go abroad. They want to conceal their status as lawyer while they work with the Japanese.

But this does not mean that Japanese laws are applied partially. The Japanese meanings for the expressions of definite laws or codes are the same for all men and occasions. There is no difference at all. Yet, they do not always want to resort to legal measures.

As the objective causes which brought about such a tendency in the Japanese people, we may cite the social life peculiar to their land and climate.

The primitive Indo-Europeans, being nomadic and living chiefly by hunting, were in contact with alien peoples. Here human relations were marked by fierce rivalry. Peoples were in great migration; one race conquered another, only to be conquered by still another. In such a situation, struggles for existence were based, not on mutual trust, but on rational plan and strategem. This mental feature seems to have been preserved even in modern times in the West.

Japanese society, on the other hand, developed from small localized farming communities. The Japanese did away with no-madic life early, and settled down to cultivate rice fields. People living on rice must inevitably settle permanently in one place. In such a society families continue generation after generation. Genealogies and kinships of families through long years become so well known by their members that the society as a whole takes on the appearance of a single family. In such a society, individuals are closely bound to each other, and they form an exclusive human nexus. Here, an individual who asserts himself will hurt the feelings of others and thereby do harm to himself. The Japanese learned to adjust themselves to this type of familial society, and created forms of expression suitable to life in such a society. And here grew the worship of tutelary gods and local deities. Even today, there is a strong tendency in Japanese social structure to settle closely around such tutelary gods and local deities. This tendency is deeply rooted in the people, and it has led to their stressing of human relations, especially the spirit of harmony or concord in society. The Japanese have learned to attach unduly heavy importance to their human nexus in disregard of the individual.

IV. The Concept of Law

Law-giving was not lacking even in the genuinely Shintōist, pre-Buddhist age. To illustrate, it is said that Emperor Seimu determined the frontiers and civilized the country, and that he issued laws. He held sway, reforming the surnames and selecting the gentle names.[14] The laws of the primitive Japanese, as of all ancient peoples, were those of custom. Though their details have been lost, it is likely that the two fundamental principles—imperial sovereignty and the family system—were firmly established even in those days. But no positive law of those days is now known to us.

It is with Prince Shōtoku that we first come to know something of laws in the modern sense.

Prince Shōtoku, the real founder of the centralized State of Japan, proclaimed the Seventeen-Article Constitution in A.D. 604. This was the first legislation in Japan—the characteristic expression of the original and creative development of the Japanese in those days—adopting the civilizations and thought of China and India sufficiently for their purposes, based chiefly upon the spirit of Buddhism. This is, so to speak, the *Magna Charta* of Japan. The Constitution prescribed the rules of conduct which the officials of the imperial government should obey, thereby, perchance, revealing how badly needed such rules were. It has been confirmed by scholars that there is a close connection between the spirit of Shōtoku's Constitution and the political regime established at the Taika Reformation, which brought about the unified state of Japan.

In contrast to Prince Shōtoku and his Seventeen-Article Constitution, King Srongtsan-Gampo, the founder of the centralized state of Tibet, in the seventh century, proclaimed his Sixteen-Article Law of similar purport at nearly the same time, and, looking back to antiquity, we find that King Aśoka commissioned many Rock and Pillar Edicts which proclaimed various precepts whose number was not fixed. The characteristic common to all of these is that they approximate to moral precepts in the form of representation, and that they were different from positive laws in practice.

Positive laws were officially promulgated later. In A.D. 671, a code of laws, said to have consisted of twenty-two volumes, was formed; but the entire code was lost, and its contents are unknown. The work of codification was completed in A.D. 701. This entire code, consisting of eleven volumes of general law concerning government organization, administration, and private relations, and six volumes of criminal laws, was promulgated and enforced; this is known as the *Taihō Code*. This was revised in A.D. 718. These Taihō laws, with many revisions and supplements, governed the nation for about five hundred years, until 1190. With the establishment of the feudal regime, the individual shōguns issued laws; and, as the authority of the shōguns increased, the territory within which the Taihō laws were enforced decreased. In the Age of Civil Wars, many feudal lords issued their own regulations or family laws. The Tokugawa Shōgunate government (1615-1867) tried to govern the country according to already existing customs, and, as far as possible, avoided the making of written laws. Contact with Western nations and a study of their civilization after the Meiji Restoration (1868) showed the necessity of laws in harmony with the modern world. In 1882, the criminal code was promulgated. This was followed in 1889 by the proclamation of the Constitution, and, in 1900, by the civil code. Up to the end of World War II, Japanese laws were characterized by two fundamental principles: the sovereignty of the emperor and the patriarchal family system. In 1946, after the surrender of Japan, the new constitution was promulgated, and these two characteristics were legally abolished, although they are still virtually in effect.

The move to conceptualize human affairs in terms of laws and concepts, which are universals, has been effected by the Japanese to some extent. The concept of universal law came into existence very early in the time of Prince Shōtoku, when he said: "Sincerely revere the Three Treasures. The Three Treasures, viz., the Buddha, the Law (*Dharma*), and the Congregation (*Saṅgha*), constitute the final ideal of all living beings and the ultimate foundation of all countries. Should any age or any people fail to esteem this truth? There are few men who are really vicious. They will all follow it if adequately instructed. How can the crooked ways of men be made straight unless we take refuge in the Three Treasures?" [15] Here we find the concept of a universal law which is something beyond laws based on the inductively given status of the individual in the joint family and of the family in its respective tribe or caste. According to the Prince, the "Law" is the "norm" of all the living creatures, the "Buddha" is the fact "the Law embodied," which, "being united with reason," becomes the *Saṅgha*. So, according to his teaching, everything converges in the one fundamental principle called the "Law."

It is likely that other Asian kings who adopted Buddhism thought in the same way. Aśoka, however, resorted to *dharma*, which is valid for various religions, and not necessarily Buddhism alone. Things being so, it may seem that there was a fundamental difference between Aśoka and other Asian monarchs, including Prince Shōtoku. Investigating the fundamental ideas which brought these historical facts to reality, however, we find there was not much difference. In the case of Prince Shōtoku, there was only one philosophical system which taught univeral laws, Buddhism. It was natural that he termed Buddhism "the final ideal of all living beings and the ultimate foundation of all countries." In the case of Aśoka, however, many religious systems had already become highly developed, and there were many other religions which claimed to be universal philosophical systems. So, he had to consider many religions. When we examine the situation more deeply, we find that the quintessence of Buddhism consists in acknowledging the universal laws taught by all religions and philosophies, as is evidenced in both early and Mahāyāna Buddhism. So, we are led to the conclusion that there is no fundamental difference in ideology between King Aśoka and Prince Shōtoku. In this respect they had this in common, that they wanted to found their kingdoms on the basis of universal laws or the truth of the universe.

Due to this characteristic of Buddhism, neither Prince Shōtoku nor King Śrongtsan-Gampo, not to mention Aśoka, suppressed indigenous faiths native to their respective peoples, although they both esteemed and revered Buddhism. That is why Shintōism in Japan and the Bon religion in Tibet have been preserved, as their respective religions, up to the present time. In Burma, the faith of Nats is prevalent even now among the common people. Taking this attitude into consideration, we shall be able to understand why such an edict was proclaimed in the reign of Prince Shōtoku as the following: "In my reign, why shall we be negligent of practicing the worship of Shintoist gods. All my officials should worship them sincerely."

When we compare these facts with the situation in the West, we find a fundamental difference. Some Western intellectuals say that Eastern peoples hold no distinction between good and bad, right and wrong. But Prince Shōtoku taught that the spirit of esteeming good and hating bad should be cherished: "Punish the vicious and reward the virtuous. This is the excellent rule of antiquity. Do not, therefore, let the good deeds of any person go concealed, nor the bad deeds of any go uncorrected, when you see them. Flatterers and deceivers are like the fatal missile which will overthrow the state, or the sharp sword which will destroy the people." [16] This spirit can be found also in the case of King Aśoka. He deplored the fact that good is difficult to perform, whereas to do bad is easy.[17] Moreover, the Prince wrote: "Light crimes should be embraced by our power of reforming influence, and grave crimes should be surrendered to our power of strong force." He did not avoid resorting to force in order to punish the severely wicked.

In "Bushidō" (the way of knights), which developed in later times as the peculiarly Japanese "way," and which was regarded as the actual political philosophy of the Japanese, the distinction of good and bad was extremely stressed and strictly observed. *"Bushi"* (knights) should do nothing mean or despicable even at the cost of their lives.

Considering these historical facts, the assertion made by some scholars that Westerners are keen to the rigid distinction between good and bad, whereas Eastern peoples are not, is untenable.

V. *Nationalism and the Prestige of the Emperor*

It has often been pointed out that the basic social and moral principles of Asian peoples consist essentially of filial piety. With regard to the Japanese, this feature holds true to some extent, but not wholly. In Japan, loyalty to lords in the feudal age and loyalty to the emperor in the days since the Meiji Restoration have been much stronger than filial piety.

The peculiarly Japanese conception of the prestige of the emperor and the Emperor Institution have close relation to the traditionally fundamental conception of harmony. The atmosphere of "harmony" which has prevailed between the emperor and his subjects has enabled the Emperor Institution to last so long as the institution which has been characteristic of the political history of Japan. In other countries dynasties have changed. But in Japan there has been only one ruling dynasty or royal family; it has no specific family name, thus evidencing the remote antiquity of its rulership. This dynasty has never been abolished during a long history of more than two thousand years. In the past, the emperor was looked upon as a child of the Sun Goddess,[18] but not with awe. In the olden days, the prestige of a deity was superior to that of an emperor.[19] In the genuinely Shintōist, pre-Buddhist Japan, an emperor who was compassionate with the people was respected with affection as an ideal monarch, as is illustrated in the person of Nintoku (973–1053).[20] In later days, the prestige of the emperor came to be closely connected with the hierarchical order of Japanese society.

What was stressed by Prince Shōtoku was the relation between lord (emperor), officials, and the common people in the centralized state. The principle of governing the state is propriety, morale or morality in a wider sense. The relationship between the emperor, the officials, and the common people was fashioned after the model of ancient China, which was formulated by State Confucianism, but was implanted in the soil of Japan. It seems that this conception was closely connected with the abolition of ownership of land and people by big clans on the occasion of the Taika Reformation. And this firmly established the basis for the Emperor Institution.

The thought of esteeming the prestige of the emperor is especially conspicuous in the Prince Shōtoku Constitution. "In a country there should not be two lords; the people should not have two masters. The people of the whole country have the sovereign as their sole master. The officials appointed to administer the local affairs are all his subjects." [21] This phase harbingers the absolutism of the later Emperor Institution, which was characteristic of Japan. Such a way of esteeming the prestige of the emperor can hardly be illustrated in the abundant classical literature of India and China. In the West, where Christianity has been the predominant factor, it is also difficult to find a counterpart.

The ultimate form in which the Japanese concept of emphasis upon a specific limited human nexus manifested itself was nationalism, which appeared after the Meiji Restoration. But Japanese nationalism did not suddenly appear in the post-Meiji period. Its beginning can be traced to the very remote past.

The notion of Japanese superiority is most boldly expressed in the concept of the Divine Nation. We find the following statement by Kitabatake Chikafusa (1293–1354), a Shintōist writer: "Our Great Nippon is a Divine Nation. Our Divine Ancestors founded it; the Sun Goddess let her descendants reign over it for a long time. This is unique to Our Nation; no other nation has the like of it. This is the reason why Our Nation is called 'Divine Nation!' " [22] This concept of "Divine Nation" was adopted by some Buddhists, such as Nichiren and Zen masters.

Confucianism, however, was the best system to provide a theoretical basis for the theory of nationalism. It will be remembered that Confucianism, which the Chinese had earlier adopted as their official theory of the state, was accepted by the Japanese with hardly any trouble. The only controversial point was the problem of changing unsuitable emperors; even this, however, caused no special friction. When Confucianism was introduced into Japan, the ruling class studied it so that they could "become government officials and Confucians and serve the country." [23]

This attitude toward Confucianism was to persist among the

ruling classes, and, in the Tokugawa period, Confucianism was taught with special reference to the concept of the state (*kokutai*) by almost all the schools and individual scholars of Confucianism including Itō Jinsai, Yamaga Sokō, Yamazaki Ansai, and the Mito school. Japanese Confucianism, associated with the nationalism or the authority-consciousness of the Japanese people, asserted its superiority over foreign systems of thought.

But, since the Confucian concept of the state was formulated in accordance with the needs of Chinese society, it naturally contained a number of principles with which the more thoroughgoing Japanese nationalists could not agree. The state conceived by Chinese philosophers was an idealistic model state; on the other hand, the state that the Japanese nationalists had in mind was the actual Japanese state. This was the reason Japanese nationalism, nurtured, so to speak, by Confucianism, had ultimately to deny the authority of Confucianism. Yoshida Shōin, the most influential leader of the movement to establish the modern state of Japan, declared in his criticism of Confucius and Mencius: "It was wrong of Confucius and Mencius to have left their native states and to have served other countries, for a sovereign and a father are essentially the same. To call one's sovereign unwise and dull and to forsake one's native state in order to find another sovereign in another state are like calling one's father foolish and moving from one's house to the next house to become the son of a neighbor. That Confucius and Mencius lost sight of this truth can never be justified." [24]

A similar tendency can easily be discerned in the process of the assimilation of Buddhism. Japanese Buddhists carefully picked out such doctrines as would be convenient for, or not inconsistent with, their nationalism.

The *Suvarṇa-prabhāsa-sūtra* and some later texts of Mahāyāna Buddhism, unlike those of early Buddhism, advance the theory that a monarch is a son of divine beings (*tenshi, deva-putra*) to whom has been given a Mandate of Heaven, and whom Heaven would protect. This theory, which became greatly cherished in Japan, had its origin in the Brāhmaṇistic lawbooks, which regulated the feudal society of medieval India. Later, Indian Buddhists came to mention this theory merely as a prevailing notion of society. It was not characteristic of Buddhism. However, this idea came to be especially stressed by the Japanese.

The attitude which Indian Buddhism assumed toward the state

was, from the time of its origination, one of cautiousness. For instance, it placed monarchs in the same category with robbers; both were thought to endanger the people's welfare. According to the Buddhist legend, the people in remote antiquity elected a common leader who would see to it that the people were protected, good people rewarded, evil people punished. The sovereign originated from this (social contract). Buddha Śākyamuni is said to have praised the republic of the Vajjians as the ideal form of the state.

But the Japanese, who accepted Buddhism on a large scale, refused, nevertheless, to adopt its concept of the state, which to them seemed to run counter to the native idea of "state structure" (*kokutai*). One writer, Kitabatake Chikafusa, was ready, on the one hand, to accept Buddhism in general but, on the other hand, was eager to emphasize the importance of the Japanese Imperial Family in the following way: "The Buddhist theory [of the state] is merely an Indian theory; Indian monarchs may have been the descendants of a monarch selected for the people's welfare, but Our Imperial Family is the only continuous and unending line of family descending from its Heavenly Ancestors." [25] Hirata Atsutane (1776–1843), a fanatic Shintōist leader, discredits the whole Indian theory of the origin of the state as a mere explanation of the origin of "Indian chieftains." [26]

It is evident from the references in historical documents to the purpose of the adoption of Buddhism that considerations for the protection of the state by means of prayers and religious rites constituted a dominant factor in Japanese Buddhism from the very beginning. Most Japanese monasteries in those early days were state-operated places of worship. The protection of the state, one of the most dominant concerns in the Japanese mind, was thus firmly established in religion. It became the slogan of nearly all the Buddhist schools.

So far we have dealt with the problem from the viewpoint of philosophy and religion. The outstanding features of Japanese nationalism, however, may be summed up as follows:

The Japanese people of the past dedicated a large and important part of their individual life to their state. In this respect, the Japanese went to an extent to which no other Eastern people has ever gone. The extent of such dedication is itself the first feature of Japanese nationalism.

The second feature is that Japanese nationalism was developed from concern for the particular state of Japan. Now, there are different ways in which nationalism is applied to practice. We know that nationalism has a number of times been expounded by thinkers in India and China, as well as in the West. But their nationalism was theoretically concerned with the state in general, not with their particular state. Now, nationalism tends, from its very nature, to be applied to a state in particular. In India and China, nationalism was theoretical. In Japanese nationalism, on the other hand, the particular State of Japan came to be the sole standard upon which all judgments were based. This, without doubt, has a close relationship with the general tendency in Japanese thinking, especially in the past, to overlook the universal and to lay stress upon an exclusive human nexus. The natural basis for Japan's exclusive concern for herself is the insular position of Japan, isolated from the continent by water. The Japanese have only rarely experienced a real fear of alien peoples; they have known the existence of foreign nations only indirectly, except in the case of World War II.

The dominance of the state over individual life was, in a sense, a condition extremely favorable for Japan's making a start as a modern state, if only in form, in the Meiji era. One imagines that it would have been difficult for her to become the modern state that she is today so quickly had it not been for the strong consciousness its people had of the state. As the modern history of the West has shown, the formation of the state is a necessary condition for the active progress of peoples. Japan, in this sense, may be said to have been more favorably conditioned for modernization than other nations of the East which were not so unified.

Certain apprehension may be felt here by some. They may ask: Is not Japanese state-consciousness already a thing of the past? Has not the experience of defeat in World War II brought the Japanese people to consider themselves as individuals who make up their society and who participate in the sovereignty of the state, rather than as "subjects" of the emperor? We are inclined to give only a tentative "yes" to these questions. We must remember that the country is overflowing with people. The network of tightly formed village communities covers the land. The nation's economy is such that the state must still exercise controls over a large portion of individual life. Above all, from great antiquity the nation's progress has always had its motivation in the Imperial Family, although it is now not so powerful as before. Furthermore, the Japanese sentiment toward the Imperial House has been friendly rather than hostile, as in some foreign countries, and the ruling class was often quite benevolent in their dealings with the people. All in all, an atmosphere of family-like intimacy has always pervaded the country. Such a term as "family state," for instance, would have been rejected by Westerners, and even by Indians, or Chinese, as self-contradictory. The Japanese, however, felt no inconsistency in the term, but found it good and valid. Just as religion was the basis of the ethical thinking of the Indians, family the basis of the practical morals of the Chinese, so the state was the basis of all thought of the Japanese. The Japanese way of thinking is undergoing a change, but their thinking is an inheritance, a tradition. It is important for the Japanese to see to it that this tradition never again gives rise to an inhuman ultra-nationalism, but to a worldwide solidarity in the future.

VI.   Economic Activities in This-Worldly Life

It is a problem worthy of study why several decades ago the Japanese alone among the many Asian countries came to be most advanced in adopting modern civilization. In respect to this, it is necessary to point out the emphasis upon social activities as one of the features of the Japanese way of thinking.

The phenomenalistic way of thinking that asserts reality itself to be emergent and in flux has been traditionally conspicuous among the Japanese. This emergent and fluid way of thinking is compatible with the inclination of thinking that emphasizes a particular human nexus, which is another way of thinking that is traditionally conspicuous among the Japanese. These two factors are combined to bring about emphasis upon activities within a concrete human nexus.

It is a well-known fact that primitive Shintōism was closely connected with agricultural rituals in agrarian villages, and that Shintōist gods have been symbolized, and still are, as gods of production.

Coming into contact with foreign cultures and becoming acquainted with Chinese philosophies and religions, the Japanese adopted and absorbed Confucianism in particular, which teaches the way of conduct appropriate to a concrete human nexus. The views of Lao Tzu and Chuang Tzu are inclined to a life of seclusion in which one escapes from a particular human nexus and seeks tranquillity for oneself in solitude. Such was not to the taste of the Japanese at large. In contrast, Confucianism, and not Taoism, principally determines the rules of conduct according to a system of human relationship.

In the case of Buddhism, however, certain problems arose. Buddhism declared itself to be a teaching of otherworldliness. The central figures in Buddhist orders were monks and nuns, who were not allowed to be involved in any economic or worldly activities.

Meanwhile, the topographical characteristics of Japan, vastly different from India, required men to serve humanity within a specific human nexus. The doctrine of early Buddhism is not compatible with such requirements. So, it came about that early Buddhism and traditional conservative Buddhism, which inherited the former teachings, were despised and rejected under the name of "Hīnayāna" (literally, Lesser Vehicle), whereas Mahāyāna Buddhism was particularly favored and adopted. Some schools of Mahāyāna Buddhism, if not all, advocated the finding of the absolute truth within secular life. In accepting Buddhism, the Japanese selected in particular that form which had such characteristics. And even in accepting those doctrines which were originally devoid of this nature, they deliberately bestowed such a character upon them.

Such an attitude in accepting Buddhism is clearly shown in the case of Prince Shōtoku. His "Commentaries upon Three *Sūtras*" are those upon the *Shōmankyō* (*Śrīmālā-devīsiṁhānada*)-*sūtra*," the *Yuimakyō* (*Vimalakīrti-nirdeśa*)-*sūtra* and the *Hokkekyō* (*Saddharma-puṇḍarīka*)-*sūtra*. In the first two *Sūtras*, laymen give sermons to priests and ascetics, reversing the usual order. They commend the idea of grasping the truth in secular life. And, according to the third, all laymen who faithfully follow any of the teachings of the Buddha are expected to be redeemed. The intention of Prince Shōtoku was to put emphasis upon the realization of Buddhist ideals within the concrete human nexus of the people while they remain in secular life. He sought absolute significance within the practical conduct of everyday life. He put special emphasis upon altruistic deeds and considered that *buddhas* and *bodhisattvas* should serve all living beings.

A similar idea underlies the later teachings of Japanese Buddhism. According to Saichō (Dengyō Daishi, 767–822), both priests and laymen attain the same ideal. According to Kūkai (Kōbō Daishi, 774–835), the founder of Japanese Vajarayāna (i.e., esoteric) Buddhism, absolute reason should be realized through actuality. Pure Land Buddhism also developed along that line. According to the Jōdo-Shin sect, it is emphasized, not only that all living creatures are saved through their religious faith (the turning toward the Pure Realm), but also that the Great Benevolence saves all those who are lost (those returning from the Pure Realm). During the Tokugawa period, the most famous itinerant merchants of Ōmi, who peddled assiduously all around the country, were mostly devoted followers of the Jōdo-Shin sect and traveled around in the spirit of service to others.

The emphasis upon the human nexus ran parallel to the stress upon all the productive services of men.

In a country like India, where the intensity of heat, the abundance of seasonal rainfall, and the fertility of the soil, together, bring forth a rich harvest, without much human labor being exerted on the land, the ethics of distribution rather than that of production is naturally emphasized. That is why alms-giving comes to be considered most important. In a country like Japan, by contrast, production is of vital importance; hence, stress is placed upon the ethics of labor in the various professions. Government and production, therefore, could not be in contradiction with the True Aspect of Reality. Some Japanese Buddhists were thus led to recognize the particularly sacred significance of physical labor. It is a historically well-known fact that Buddhists endeavored to go directly to the people through various welfare activities.

This feature can be noticed even in Japanese Zen literature. Dōgen, the founder of the Sōtō Zen sect, thought that Buddhism could be realized within the professional lives of secular society. Suzuki Shōsan, a Zen master, found absolute significance in the pursuit of one's own profession, be one a warrior, a farmer, a craftsman, a merchant, a doctor, an actor, a hunter, or a priest. Since it is the essence of Buddhism, according to him, to rely upon the original self or upon "the true Buddha of one's own," and because every profession is the function of this "One Buddha," to pursue one's own profession is to obey the Absolute One. So, he teaches farmers: "Farming is nothing but the doings of the Buddha." To merchants he teaches: "Renounce desires and pursue profit single-heartedly. But you should never enjoy profits. You should, instead, work for the good of all the others." [27] Since the afflictions of this world, it is said, are predetermined in former lives, one should torture oneself by working hard in one's own profession, in order to redeem the sins of his past.[28] It is noteworthy that immediately after the death of Calvin, an idea similar to his happened to appear almost contemporaneously in Japan. The fact, however, that it never grew into a capitalistic movement of great consequence ought to be studied in relation to the underdevelopment of the modern bourgeois society in Japan.

Such a theory of religion also lends itself to religious movements outside of Buddhism in Japan. To illustrate, Ninomiya Sontoku's movement inclines to be practical and activistic. Sectarian Shintōism assumes a similar tendency. The founder of the Tenrikyō teaches: "Keep your heart pure, busy yourself with your profession, and be true to the mind of God." [29] The other newly arisen sects of Shintōism mostly fall into a similar pattern.

Respect for labor in professional life resulted in high esteem for things produced as the fruits of labor. Reverence for foodstuff is especially manifest.

The teaching that we should take good care of economic products, the fruit of human labor, is not necessarily confined to Japanese religions; it seems common to most of the universal religions. In India or South Asian countries, however, where men are not required to labor too hard in order to produce daily necessities, relatively little has been said against waste. The fact that the preservation of economic products is particularly emphasized should be considered in the light of the topological peculiarity of Japan.

The form in which Chinese thought was accepted was also tinged with the activist tendency in interpreting the way of human beings. Itō Jinsai (1627–1705), in particular, understands what is called the Way as being active and as representing the principle of growth and development. On that basis, he rejects the nihilism of Lao Tzu. Ogyū Sorai (1666–1728), a peculiarly Japanese Confucianist, positively advocated activism, rejecting the static tendency of the Confucians of the Sung period of China (960–1279). Quiet sitting and having reverential love in one's heart are the methods of mental training made most of by the Confucians of the Sung, which was ridiculed by Ogyū: "As I look at them, even gambling appears superior to the quiet sitting and having reverential love in one's heart." [30] A necessary conclusion drawn from such an attitude was Ogyū's recommendation of practical learning, useful in practical life. And such was the mental climate which nurtured the economic theory of Dazai Shundai (1680–1747) and the legal philosophy of Miura Chikkei (1688–1755). Whereas the Chinese Confucianism of the Sung period surpassed the Japanese Confucianism which followed it in thinking of metaphysical problems, Japanese Confucianism directed its attention to politics, economics, and law, the practical aspects of human life.

The fact that Japan alone was rapid in the progress of modernization in the years just before World War II, while the other Asian countries were generally slow in this process, may be attributed partly to the emphasis laid by the Japanese upon practical activities within the human nexus.

A great danger lies in the fact that the religious views of the Japanese may easily degenerate into a sheer utilitarianism of profit-seeking activities, if they lose sight of the significance of the Absolute, which underlies the productive life of the professions. But, at the same time, credit should be given to the tendency to esteem the human nexus. If the religions of Japan are enhanced to such a height that religious truth may be realized in accordance with the human nexus, which is at once universal and particular, transcending every specific nexus and embracing all of them, then and only then will it achieve universal significance.

QUESTION 1: Dr. Yukawa stressed the irrational character of Japanese thinking. But, even in the feudal days of Japan, there appeared some forerunners of modern sciences, although they are little known to the West. How do you evaluate the results of their studies?

QUESTION 2: The sciences cannot develop as sciences as such, i.e., in the framework of science alone. Do you find any social hindrances which prevented sciences from developing in Japan?

ANSWER: On the whole, I agree with Dr. Yukawa, insofar as the field of my studies is concerned. However, I am not completely disappointed with regard to logical thinking by the Japanese. Studies of Buddhist logic were introduced into Japan in antiquity, approximately thirteen hundred years ago. Buddhist logicians largely occupied themselves only in making glosses on the basic works by Śaṁkarasvāmin and Chinese expounders. But they made slight progress beyond Indian and Chinese Buddhist logic. For example, they came to distinguish between M and P in the syllogism, both of which were occasionally called by the same word (*pakṣa-dhar-matā*) in Indian and Chinese logic. In that context, M was called *shūbō*, whereas P was called *shūhō*, in Japanese.

Notes

1. These features were discussed in my *Tōyōjin no shii hōhō* (The Ways of Thinking of Eastern Peoples), 2 vols. (Tokyo: Misuzu-shobo, 1949), Vol. I, pp. 1–378. This was translated under the supervision of the author and published as *The Ways of Thinking of Eastern Peoples*, under the auspices of UNESCO (Tokyo: The Japanese Commission for UNESCO, 1960). A revised, one-volume edition was published by the East-West Center Press, Honolulu in 1964.
2. Hajime Nakamura, "Some Features of the Japanese Way of Thinking," *Monumenta Nipponica*, XIV, Nos. 3–4 (1958–1959), 31–72.
3. The details are set forth in my work *Jihi* (Compassion) (Kyoto: Heirakuji-shoten, 1956), pp. 258–271.
4. Kumazawa Banzan, *Shūgi washo* (Collection of Discourses), Vol. X, p. 1a. (An old printed text, with neither date nor publisher mentioned, preserved in the library of the University of Tokyo.)
5. For example, the stories of *"Mie no Uneme"* (Court Waitress of Mie) and of Emperors Kensō and Keitai, in Basil Hall Chamberlain, trans., *Kojiki, Record of Ancient Matters*. Transactions of the Asiatic Society of Japan, Vol. X (Tokyo: The Asiatic Society of Japan, 1906), Supplement, pp. 402, 419, 424 etc.
6. *Ibid.*, pp. 213, 215.
7. Confucius *Analects*, I.12: "In practising the rules of propriety a natural ease is to be prized." Here "a natural ease" is the translation of the Chinese word "*wa*." In James Legge's version, edited with notes by Yoshio Ogaeri (Tokyo: Bunki-shoten, 1950), p. 4.
8. In the Chinese versions of Buddhist texts, such technical words as "*wakyō*" (reverential compliance) and "*wagō*" (concord) are frequently used.
9. Prince Shōtoku's Constitution, Article 10.
10. Chamberlain, *op. cit.*, p. 112.
11. Prince Shōtoku's Constitution, Article 17.
12. F. S. C. Northrop, *The Taming of the Nations* (New York: The Macmillan Co., 1953), p. 62.
13. Cited by Northrop, *ibid.*, p. 126.
14. Chamberlain, *op. cit.*, p. 2.
15. Prince Shōtoku's Constitution, Article 2.
16. *Ibid.*, Article VI.

17. Pillar Edict V.
18. Prince Shōtoku, *Shōmangyō gishu* (Exposition of the *Śrīmāla-devīsiṁhānada-sūtra*), Shinshō Hanayama, ed. (Tokyo: Iwanami-shōten, 1948), p. 34.
19. Chamberlain, *op. cit.*, pp. 161–399.
20. *Ibid.*, p. 336.
21. Prince Shōtoku's Constitution, Article 12.
22. In the introductory manifesto of Kitabatake Chikafusa, *Jinnō shō-tōki* (Discourses on the Genealogy of the Imperial Family). Kōchu Nippon Bungaku Taikei, Vol. XVIII (Tokyo: Kokumin Tosho Kabushiki Kaisha, 1925), p. 585.
23. (Ascribed to) Sugawara Michizane, *Kanke bunsō* (Ancient Collection of Works), Vol. III. Also in *Kitano bunsō* (Collected Works of Kitano Shrine), Vol. II, p. 24; and in *Kitanoshi* (The History of the Kitano Shrine), edited and published by Kitano Shrine, Kyoto, no date given.
24. Yoshida Shōin, *Kōmō tōki* (Exposition of the Teachings of Confucius and Mencius), Vol. I, in Yoshida Shōin, *Yoshida Shōin zenshū* (Collected Works of Yoshida Shōin), Vol. II, edited by Yamaguchiken Kyōikukai (Educational Committee of Yamaguchi Prefecture) (Tokyo: Iwanami-shoten, 1934), p. 263.
25. *Jinnō shōtōki*, p. 592.
26. Hirata Atsutane, *Shutsujō shōgo* (Ridicule of the Teachings of the Buddha), Makoto Nagai, ed. (Tokyo: Kōbundō, 1936), p. 41.
27. Suzuki Shōsan, *Roankyō* (Crossing the Bridge on a Donkey), in *Zenmon hōgo shū*, Vol. III, Kōdō Yamada and Daikyō Mori, eds. (Tokyo: Kōyukan, 1921), p. 237.
28. Suzuki Shōsan, *Banmin tokuyō* (The Significance of all Vocations), in *ibid.*, pp. 536 f.
29. Yasusada Hiyane, *Nippon shūkyōshi* (History of Japanese Religions) (Tokyo: Sankyo Shuppansha, 1925), p. 825.
30. Ogyū Sorai, *Rongo chō* (Critical Comments on the Analects of Confucius), cited in Junsei Iwahashi, *Sorai kenkyū* (Studies on Ogyū Sorai) (Tokyo: Seki-shoin, 1934), p. 300.

UEDA YOSHIFUMI   *The Status of the Individual*
in Mahāyāna Buddhist Philosophy

I.   The Fundamental Way of Thinking in Buddhist Philosophy

There is a unique way of thinking in Buddhist philosophy which is not found in any other philosophy. Since in early Buddhism this unique way of thinking existed in an immature, naïve form [1] whose special characteristic was not clearly distinguishable, it was open to several differing interpretations. Consequently, it was difficult to determine which among the various interpretations was the correct one. It was in Mahāyāna Buddhism that this way of thinking appeared in a form clear enough not to allow differing interpretations. From the Prajñā-pāramitā Sūtras, through the Mādhyamika, the Yogācāra, and Zen, to the Shin Buddhism of Shinran, who expounded faith in Amida Buddha, all Mahāyāna Buddhist philosophies, with the exception of a few,[2] have followed this way of thinking. Since they follow this way of thinking, they belong to the Mahāyāna tradition. If one should take away this way of thinking, it would not be an overstatement to say that, basically, the whole point of view had thereby lost its essence as Mahāyāna Buddhist philosophy. To say that almost all Mahāyāna Buddhist philosophies follow this way of thinking means that they have all originated in or have been derived from one and the same concept of ultimate reality *(dharma-kāya,*[3] literally, reality-body).

If Aristotelian logic is meant by the word "logic," this Buddhist way of thinking will probably not be considered logical. However, this is clearly one way of thinking, and, if we should wish to include in the broad meaning of "philosophy" a way of thinking that is unique to many Asian peoples, then we must recognize a type of logic that is non-Aristotelian. Perhaps we need not necessarily call it "logic." It is simply that, should we not recognize that we have here a unique way of thinking and should we immediately decide that its propositions are not valid simply because they go against Aristotelian logic, it would be impossible to understand Buddhist philosophy. This way of thinking is truly difficult to understand for those who have been trained in philosophies which base their thinking upon Aristotelian logic. And, since we shall follow this way of thinking in our consideration of the problem, "The Status of the Individual," we must consider here why Buddhist philosophers had to develop this way of thinking.

The focus of the problems pursued by Buddhist philosophers has been the true self. They pursued the true self to its limits and were finally able to realize it through a unique experience. This way of thinking was born within that experience. It goes without saying that most people and many philosophers think it is possible to know ourselves—through self-reflection. However, if we consider this very carefully, we will see that the self grasped through reflection is a conceptualized self and that our true selves, i.e., the self as it really is, can never be grasped through reflection. Those philosophies which think it is possible to cognize the self through reflection establish self-cognition on an assumption. The problem is whether or not that assumption may be permitted. One of the leading philosophers of Japan during the first half of this century, Hatano Seiichi, had the following to say concerning self-cognition.[4]

Parallel to the recognition of the objective world, the subject also knows itself. As is stated above, objects are expressions of the subject and contain the factor of selfhood which is disclosed in them. The subject does not express itself except as object or in objects. This is the reason why the subject can know its own self. When the objects, that is, the expressions of the subject, become the symbols of the subject: that is, when the subject gets acquainted with its own self, and the hidden self or the center of the knowing act and the disclosed self or the known self are separated and opposed and, at the same time, maintain or realize their identity, the subject knows itself. . . .

Of course, while we talk and think in this manner, we are obliged to stand at the level of reflection. And while distinguishing the factor of life of experience, i.e., of real existence, from that of reflection, i.e., of ideal content, we establish a relationship of the two. So the former, i.e., the real existence, may also be introduced into the content of conceptual cognition. This is, however, the very difficulty one must face when he seeks for the source of experience. But it is a problem which one can no longer solve at the level of reflection. It is the very basic fact of life, and there is no other way than to be in it and to live through it. A closer observation will show us that, as we have seen in the cognition of the self, all the difficulties in identifying the hidden, really existing subject with the disclosed, ideal subject belong, after all, to the same category. They may all equally be reduced to what we call the transcendental identity of the subject. It is the identity of the subject of basic experience and that of reflection, in other words, the identity of the really existing subject and the subject which is expressed in reference to concepts in their objective phase. That is, it is the identity of the cognizing subject (the really existing subject) and the subject which is cognized (the ideal, conceptual subject). Thus, as this identity is primarily assumed as a prerequisite of reflection, it is not a matter of comprehension, but is a basic fact of life that should be experienced as we live through it.

The attitude expressed in Hatano's consideration of the problem is sound, and a penetrating insight faithful to the facts is advanced. As long as we take the standpoint of reflection, we cannot help but agree with Hatano. However, if we look at the problem from the standpoint of Buddhist philosophy, we can ascertain whether or not "this identity . . . assumed as a prerequisite of reflection" can be established. The reason we can do so is that Buddhist philosophers have succeeded in "knowing" the really existing subject without transforming it into an ideal, conceptual content, and, since they were able to cognize the true self, they were able to know just what constituted the identity between the subject which knows and the subject which is known in the self-cognition of the true self.

What is the nature of this identity between the subject which knows and the subject which is known in the self-cognition of the true self? In the self-cognition of the true self, since the really existing subject knows itself, what knows and what is known are both the same real self—they are completely one and the same. Nevertheless, since the act of knowing is thereby established, the differentiation of the knower and the known must be established within this one and the same self. The fact that there is one and the same self and at the same time that there is the differentiation of the knower and the known is a logical contradiction, but, in order to establish the self-cognition of the true self, such a contradictory relationship must be capable of establishment. Buddhist philosophers put their greatest effort and endeavor into establishing in reality this kind of experience, and into finding a way of thinking through which this experience can be expressed. When Asaṅga and Vasubandhu spoke of differentiation of non-differentiation, i.e., the subsequently realized wisdom (*tat-pṛṣṭha-labdha-jñāna*), and when Pai-chang Huai-hai said, "Awaking to the Here-Now," it was of the experience of the realization of the true, real self. Nāgārjuna's "highest wisdom" (*prajñā-pāramitā*) is nothing other than this experience. This experience is established when there is no differentiation of subject and object, i.e., when one has gone through the experience of non-differentiation (*nirvikalpa*). What is realized in this non-differentiated experience is called "fundamental wisdom" (*mūla-jñāna*).[5] When this fundamental wisdom develops further and the differentiation of the knower and the known arises, though without losing its non-differentiation, the realization of the true self is established. This is what Asaṅga called "the subsequently realized wisdom."

Since this simultaneous relationship between the non-differentiation and the differentiation of the knower and the known is logically contradictory, it is completely different in nature from that identity which had to be assumed as a prerequisite of self-cognition from the standpoint of reflection. When it is seen that this non-differentiation must be a complex structure which includes contradiction, it can be seen that the identity necessarily assumed as a prerequisite of self-cognition from the standpoint of reflection is not a true one. In other words, the identity between the ideal, conceptual subject and the really existing subject (known through reflection) cannot be established, and it is clear that the former (the ideal, conceptual subject) does not manifest the latter (the really existing subject).

"*Prajñā*" (the term Nāgārjuna uses), or "the subsequently realized wisdom" (Asaṅga's and Vasubandhu's expression), is the wisdom established upon pursuing and realizing the true self. In this wisdom, one can know, not only the really existing self as it is, but also each thing in the world as it really is. This is because, when one realizes the real self, one at the same time touches reality itself; to know the real self means, at the same time, to know reality. A thing known as it really exists is nothing other than reality known as it is. To know reality can be nothing other than to know ourselves and all the things in the world as they really exist and become. In this manner, the wisdom that can know the real self can also know everything in the world as it really exists and really becomes, i.e., it can know things completely objectively. We shall consider this more in detail in the following.

In the self-cognition of the self, the knower and the known are the same self, i.e., the same subject. Herein there is only the subject; there is no object. With this meaning, it is subject-only (*vijñāna-mātra*).[6] This subject-only has a twofold structure. That is, it has the aspect of the differentiation of the knower and the known, i.e., the affirmation of the subject and the negation of the object, and it has the aspect of the non-differentiation or identity of the knower and the known. Although subject-only shows that it is not an object, i.e., the known, if it were simply a subject, there would not be the least meaning of "the known." If this were the case, there would be the meaning of a knowing subject only and no meaning of a known subject. It could not be said that the self knows the self. How can the meaning of a known subject be included in subject-only? It is the other aspect of subject-only, i.e., it is nothing other than the known which is included in the non-differentiation of the knower and the known. However, since this known is identified with the knower, its meaning is not completely manifest. In order to manifest completely the meaning of this known, it must be made clear that it is not the knower—in other words, there must be the negation of the knower. Accordingly, since the knower is truly the self, or the subject, the negation of the knower is non-self, or non-subject, i.e., the object. In this manner, in order that the meaning of the known, which is included in subject-only, may be completely manifest, the object must be affirmed and the subject negated. That is, object-only must be established. Only in this manner can the true self first be known as it is really exists, i.e., become the known. This is why Vasubandhu said subject-only (*vijñāna-mātra*) is non-subject (=no-mind=*acitta*).[7] That subject-only is object-only he expressed as "subject seen as things in the world" (*arthaprati-bhāsaṁ-vijñānam*).[8] No-mind has the same meaning as non-self (*anātman*).

As to the meaning of object-only, although it means that the true self is known, it is nothing other than reality being known. And reality is not merely the self; it is all things in the world. Object-only means that, besides all things in the world, there is no subject opposed to them. And yet, the fact that this thing is an object shows that this is that which is known. Accordingly, that the subject knows all things reveals the relation of all things (reality) as they are known by themselves. Here, the identity of the knower with the known is included. It is not that the subject is existent outside the object and sees it as an object. Rather, the subject, being non-existent other than as an object, knows all things. The subject, being non-existent, as it were, sees the object. This is nothing other than being free of all subjective and partial views and seeing things just as they are. Seeing the self as it is is not different from seeing things as they are; neither is it anything other than seeing reality as it is. It is only because the self is the knower and things are not the knower that knowing the self as it is is called "subject-only" and that things known as they are are called "object-only." However, since the self as reality is no different from things, subject-only simultaneously includes the meaning of object-only. And, since the self as reality is the knower, the identity of the knower and the known is included in the fact of things' being known. Accordingly, if there is no subject-only, object-only cannot be established, either.

Subject-only, i.e., non-self, is nothing other than the true self, which has cognized itself. At the same time, it cognizes the world just as it is (object-only). And, on the other hand, in order that things in the world can be known just as each is or becomes (object-only), subject-only, i.e., the non-existence of the object, must be established, too. This is the meaning of Seng-chao's "All things in the world, though real, are formless," and Zen's "To see the form of the formless." [9] The true self is non-self, and things as they really are are formless forms. The so-called fourfold consideration of Rinzai (Linchi, died 867), a famous Zen Master, shows this subject-only and object-only in four phrases:

(1) Object only
(2) Subject only
(3) Both subject and object negated
(4) Both subject and object affirmed

The true self is this kind of subject, and really existing things are this kind of object. When one knows the self and the things in the world in this unique way, one knows *tathatā* (suchness). *Tathatā* has many synonyms: *śūnyatā* (emptiness), *animittam* (the formless), *dharmatā* (things as they really are), *bhūta-koṭi* (extent of reality), *paramārthatā* (objects as known in supreme wisdom), *dharma-dhātu* (realm of things as they really are).[10] In addition to these, the following, which were previously given, are also synonyms: *vijñāna* (=*vijñapti*)*-mātratā* or =*citta-mātratā* (subject-only or mind-only) and *acitta* (no-mind).

One of the greatest Buddhist philosophers of Japan, Dōgen, had the following to say. "To study Buddhism is to study oneself. To study oneself is to forget oneself. To forget oneself is to realize oneself as all things [in the world]. To realize oneself as all things is to strip off both one's own mind and body and the mind and body of others." [11] Here, what was said before—that Buddhist philosophy began with the problem of knowing one's true self, that the self-cognition of one's true self (subject-only) is non-self, that this is object-only, and that this is freedom—is expounded in a way different from that of Rinzai and in a clearer manner. The first original philosopher to be respected as such after the transplantation of Western philosophy into Japan and whose name is known even in other countries, is Nishida Kitarō. That his thought has something in common with the foregoing thought of Buddhist philosophy can be seen in his words: "Our true self is the basic substance of the universe, and, when we know the true self, we not only unite with the good of mankind, but we merge with the basic substance of the universe and spiritually unite with the divine mind." [12]

That an individual knows his true self means that the universe awakens to itself from itself. The individual's self-cognition is not simply a phenomenon in the consciousness of an individual, but indeed a fact of the universe. When he knows things in the world, it is not merely the individual himself who knows, but the universe; and, when things are known by him, the universe knows itself from within itself. When he knows things, this brings about the self-awakening of the universe from within itself, and this is nothing other than the development and growth of the universe. It is the becoming of the universe.

We have pursued in the foregoing the fundamental way of thinking in Buddhist philosophy. All the problems of Mahāyāna Buddhist philosophy are considered on this base, so that one cannot consider other problems without touching upon it. As we have seen in the foregoing, the relationship between the knower and the known is not simply an epistemological problem but is fundamentally a metaphysical one. "To be" and "to know" cannot be discussed apart from each other. (And, as hinted at the end of the last paragraph, "to be" and "to become" cannot be considered apart from each other.) Next, let us consider the relationship of the individual and the world from the aspect of the relationship between the one and the many.

II. The One and the Many

In Buddhist philosophy, the logic of the relationship between the individual and the world is grasped as the relationship in which "the one enters the many and the many enter the one" (one is one and not many, many are many and not one, and yet, at the same time, the one is identical with the many, and the many are identical with the one [13]). The one and the many are in a mutually negating opposition at the same time as they are one and the same. This is a case of differentiation of non-differentiation. But why is the relationship between the individual and the world like this? First, the individual, because he is born, lives and dies in the world, is completely within the world. That the individual is established within the world as a historical product is because the one enters into the world as the many. Second, however, at the same time, the historical world is being built by the creative power emanating from the individual. The world exists, not only as an object seen by the individual, but, at the same time, as something being created by each individual it is in the process of becoming. The individual is not simply a seer, but also an actor. As something being created by this actor, the many are included in the one. This is stated as "the many enter into the one." The individual and the world are mutually created by each other.

That this relationship is established is due to the fact that the individual is not simply one among many but is also the one as a negation of the many, and that the many are not simply a collection of ones but are the many as a negation of the one. To say that the individual is not simply one among many but is the negation of the many means that the individual is the subject. An individual viewed as a speck in society is an objectified individual. A man can survey a society which is made up of many people as an object. In what respect is this man different from the others in this situation? It is due, of course, to the fact that he is a subject who is seeing and creating the society. When he is subject, all the other persons are object; he alone is affirmed as subject, and all the others are negated. This is the aspect in which the many enter into the one, or it is the one as a negation of the many. This one is an affirmed self or the aspect of the existence of the subject, and the aspect of the non-existence of society or the historical world.

To say that the many are not simply a collection of ones but are the many as a negation of the one means that society is established with the negation of the individual. Each individual has to give up his own welfare when the welfare of his whole society requires it. This is the aspect in which the one enters the many, or it is the many as a negation of the one. This one is a negated self or the aspect of the non-existence of the subject (*anātman*, non-self), and the aspect of the existence of society or the historical world.

The Buddhist philosopher who made the framework of this mutual relationship of the one and the many clearest is Fa-tsang (643–712) of the Hua-yen school. He calls this the relationship of mutually becoming a lord and vassals.[14] In the aspect in which the many enter the one, each individual is, respectively, the center of the universe. When individual A is the lord, all other individuals and Nature, or the whole world, are the vassals. At the same time, A, with respect to B or C, is a vassal. All individuals are at the same time lords and vassals. In this situation, the world of the many does not refer only to the assembly of men, with Nature unconsidered. There is no thought of a realm of matter severed from spirit or life. The concept of a body separated from mind, or of matter separated from spirit or life, was unknown to the Buddhist philosopher. Material things, too, are grasped as things inseparable from spirit or life. All things are considered as sentient beings.

When the relationship between the individual and the world is grasped as the relationship in which the many are negated in the one and the one is negated in the many, it is probably the most radical manner of grasping that relationship. The individual does not refer to each respective human being, but to the *subject*. And the very subject is the true life. That the life observed from the outside is not true life is seen in the fact that our own death can never be the same to us as is that of others. In the respect that the one enters the many, this is not monism; and in the respect that the many enter the one, this is not pluralism in the usual sense. Since the establishment at the same time of the mutual negation and identity of the one and the many, in other words, of the relationship of differentiation of non-differentiation between the one and the many, as seen previously, is nothing other than the other aspect of the establishment at the same time of the mutual negation and identity of the subject and object, the opposition of monism and pluralism in the history of Western philosophy is based on a way of thought quite different from that of Buddhist philosophy. In Buddhist philosophy, since subjectivism is transcended due to the concept of the non-existence of the subject, i.e., non-self or no-mind, idealism was not established; and, because of the negation of the concept of a real existence transcending the subject due to the concept of the non-existence of the object, realism was not established.

The following table shows a detailed analysis of the logical structure of the "differentiation of non-differentiation" stated in Part II.

Reality has realized itself

A. Self that is awakened to itself—*prajñā*

B. Things which have been known as they are—*tathatā* (suchness)

I	II
Differentiation of	Identity (non-differentiation) of
i) known from knower	i) Knower with known
ii) being from non-being	ii) being with non-being

A	A
Subject only (pure subjectivity) There is only subject, no object; that is, self knows itself. (Subject is affirmed, object is negated. This is united with II-a, i.e., identity of subject with subject.)	Identity of subject with object (emptiness=*śūnyatā*) (a) Self knows itself; that is, subject (the knower) is identical with subject (the knower). (This is united with I-a, i.e., subject is affirmed, object is negated.)
B Object only (pure objectivity) There is only object, no subject; that is, things are known from within. (Object is affirmed, subject is negated. This is united with II-b, i.e., identity of object with object.)	(b) Things are known from itself; that is, object (the known) is identical with object (the known). (This is united with I-B, i.e., object is affirmed, subject is negated.) **B** Identity of being of subject of object with non-being of both subject and object (emptiness=*śūnyatā*)

The delineation given above of the framework of the establishment at the same time of the mutual negation and identity between the subject and object follows the interpretation of men belonging to the early Yogācāra, i.e., Maitreya, Asaṅga, Vasubandhu, Sthiramati, and Paramārtha,[15] while the delineation of the framework of the one entering the many and the many entering the one follows the interpretation of Fa-tsang. The reason for this is that these men have best clarified the logic of these relationships. Neither of the two concepts can be established without the other. Fundamentally they are one. This single thought in its naïve form is Nāgārjuna's idea "Form (*rūpa*) is emptiness (*śūnyatā*), and the very emptiness is form." Form and emptiness are identical, yet, at the same time, they stand in mutually negating opposition.

If we desire to delve deeper than this into the logic of the relationship of the individual and the world, or the one and the many, we must enter into a consideration of Buddhist philosophy's most difficult problem, "time and eternity." With a consideration of this problem, the place of the individual as the center of the world of becoming would become even clearer; but, since it would be impossible to give an elucidation of this problem in the time available, I should like to leave it for a later occasion.

QUESTION: I would like to raise two elementary points. First, a point in regard to reflexive relations. In Western logic the notion of a reflexive relation is not regarded as involving a contradiction; at least, by most people it is not regarded as contradictory. The fact that A has a relation to A is not an absurd situation. You appear to be using an argument to the effect that, if A assumes two functions, if the relation were asymmetrical and something assumes two functions in the relation, two places in the relation, it would, as it were, become directed to two distinct entities. Now, this does not follow, any more than it follows that, if I love you and you love me, I assume both the loving and loved position, but it does not follow for that reason that I am two persons. I am one and the same person. If, now, I love myself or know myself, it does not for that reason follow that I am two persons. I am one and the same person. I would be very far from regarding self-knowledge as a very lucid thing and very far from saying that it might not involve very profound difficulties that would lead to contradictory formulae. But the very fact that it is a reflexive relation does not appear to be one of these. That is one point. I would like to raise a second.

The second is: I am profoundly confused as to how, granted that, in knowing the self as object, the self assumes these two positions, both as subject and as object. I am confused as to how the object gets differentiated. The self as object gets differentiated into a great number of distinct objects. Once these distinct objects are there, I can understand the rest of the paper perfectly. But this differentiation appears unclear. Now, there have been other philosophers who have held similar views. St. Thomas thought that God, in knowing himself, knew everything else. But he gave reasons why—because God was in an eminent manner everything else, and so on. And, similarly, people like Hegel have said that all knowledge of things is knowing them in the form of self, in the form of universals. But, again, this depends on a particular view of the self. Now, there does not appear to be any sort of mechanism which differentiates the self *qua* object in this system.

Re-phrased: the questions are: What is contradictory about the same thing being both subject and object? How can the knower be known? You say that the Buddhist way of thinking is a unique way of thinking which is not found in any philosophy. I do not see why this is so. What is the meaning of the expression "to know" when you say "to know the true self"?

ANSWER: These question will be answered en bloc because of the nature of the problem.

Some of the questions seem to be asked from the standpoint of reflective thinking without paying careful attention to the distinction between that standpoint and the standpoint of Buddhist philosophy. As long as we are standing on the level of reflection, there is no contradiction about the same thing being a subject and an object. The proposition that I can know myself is established without any contradiction. In this case, however, "I" is divided into two parts, the really existing I, or the center of the knowing act, and the conceptual I, or the known I, and, besides, it is only the latter that is known; the former remains unknown. It is in this sense that we say we cannot "know" our really existing self by means of reflection.

Buddhist philosophy, however, does not stand on the level of reflection. It has gone far beyond reflective thinking and stands where it is possible for the really existing self to know itself.

In order to get to this level of thinking, a Buddhist philosopher or a *bodhi-sattva* (one whose essence is perfect knowledge) passes through two stages. Starting from the level of reflective thinking, he goes into the first stage, where ordinary reflective thinking gradually dies away in his consciousness by being replaced by the thinking which acts in accordance with the way of thinking which belongs to the third stage, that is, the standpoint of Buddhist philosophy. Going through this first stage with strenuous discipline for many years, he reaches *samādhi* (intense contemplation), where there are no thoughts; there is neither the consciousness of the conceptual self nor any concept of the objects, nor consciousness of the really existing self or of the subject; there is no subject-object dichotomy. His mind at this stage becomes completely identified with reality, or suchness (*tathatā*). This is called literally "reality-body" (*dharma-kāya*). This is explained by Asaṅga as non-differentiation of that which is originated in time (*saṁskṛta*) and that which is not originated and timeless (*asaṁskṛta*). This is the second stage.

From this stage, i.e., *samādhi,* he suddenly becomes awakened to the here-now, that is, reality becomes conscious, and the differentiation of *saṁskṛta* from *asaṁskṛta* appears. He sees colors and shapes and hears voices and sounds; he thinks and speaks of anything. This is the third stage. The standpoint of Buddhist philosophy is established here.

These three stages were called by Asaṅga, in sequence, wisdom leading to wisdom-without-differentiation (*prāyogika-nirvikalpa-jñāna*), wisdom-without-differentiation (*nirvikalpa-jñāna*), and subsequently-realized-wisdom (*tat-pṛṣṭha-labdha-jñāna*), whereas Nāgārjuna called all these stages with only one name *"prajñā-pāramitā"* (perfect wisdom).

Though a Buddhist philosopher sees or thinks everything at this stage, he no longer sees or thinks of anything as an object which confronts him; in other words, there is no subject which sees anything as an object, and, accordingly, there is no object which stands *vis-à-vis* the subject. There is no subject except object (non-self, *anātman,* or no-mind, *acitta*), on the one hand. A thing, as it were, is seen from itself, from within. There is seen here an identity of the seer with the seen. This identity means not only that there is no seer or subject except the seen or object (non-self or no-mind) but also that the seer or subject sees his own self: this latter sense shows the other aspect of non-self or no-mind, namely, that there is no object except subject (mind-only, *vijñāna-mātratā*).

The reason why he is non-self is the reason why he "knows" his true self without conceptualizing it, and, at the same time, it is the reason why he can "know" everything as it is (suchness, *tathatā*).

In order to understand the uniqueness of Buddhist philosophy, it would be helpful for us to notice the uniqueness of the philosophy of Martin Heidegger in the history of Western philosophy. He calls that thinking "*vorstellendes Denken*" (object-thinking) which sets being before oneself and observes it as an object (*Gegenstand*). He says, "The thinking, strictly speaking, is the thinking of being. The genitive 'of' has a twofold meaning: (1) The thinking belongs to being; the genitive 'of,' in this case, means that being is an agent of thinking, and (2) The thinking listens to being; the genitive 'of,' in this case, expresses an objective case."

Here is implied a sense of identity of that which thinks with that which is thought of. We shall be able to see in this idea of Heidegger a logic through which we are able to grasp our really existing self without setting it up as an object before us. If there is no sense of the identity of that which thinks with that which is thought of, he may be said not yet to have transcended his so-called "*vorstellendes Denken*," because, when or if there is no sense of identity, there is nothing other than that there is fundamentally the dichotomy of subject and object. If we suppose that he could make his consideration deeper to that extent where he could state clearly the identity of that which thinks with that which is thought of and, at the same time, the differentiation between the two, we would be able to know or understand the standpoint of Buddhist philosophy. This is why I emphasized the uniqueness of Buddhist philosophy in my paper.

Notes

1. For example, see Pali Text Society's *Pāli-English Dictionary*, edited by T. W. Rhys Davids and William Stede, on the term, "*sankhāra*" as ". . . one of the most difficult terms in Buddhist metaphysics, in which the blending of the subjective-objective view of the world and of happening, peculiar to the East, is so complete that it is almost impossible for Occidental terminology to get at the root of its meaning in a translation."

2. There are a few in later Indian Mahāyāna Buddhism who are not in accord with this way of thinking.

3. The *Mahāyāna-saṃgraha* (*Taishō*, Vol. 31, No. 1595, p. 1736) states: "The correct teaching of the Mahāyāna is that which has been streamed out of the pure world of reality (*dharma-dhātu*)."

4. Hatano Seiichi, *Time and Eternity*, Suzuki Ichirō, trans. (Tokyo: Japanese National Commission for UNESCO, 1963), pp. 29, 35–36. Although the lines quoted here are the same as those quoted in my Thinking in Buddhist Philosophy," in *Philosophical Studies of Japan* (Tokyo: Japanese National Commission for UNESCO, 1964), Vol. 5, I have cited them again since the latter is still in press.

5. The substance of fundamental wisdom is the *dharma-kāya*. The *dharma-kāya's* characteristic is "the non-duality of the conditioned" (*Asaṅga, Mahāyāna-saṁgraha, Taishō*, Vol. 31, No. 1595, p. 225b).

6. This is a term used by Yogācāra philosophers. D. T. Suzuki (Suzuki Daisetz Teitarō) calls it "pure subjectivity." See my above-quoted article, "Thinking in Buddhist Philosophy."

7. *Triṁśikā-vijñaptimātratāsiddhi,* ed. by S. Lévi, verse 29. See my article, "What Is Idealism in Buddhist Philosophy," in C. A. Moore, ed., "Idealism in World Perspective" (in preparation) for a more detailed exposition of the theory of *vijñapti-mātratā*.

8. See my "Thinking in Buddhist Philosophy" for more concerning the meaning of "*artha-pratibhāsaṁ-jñānam.*"

9. *Taishō*, Vol. 45, No. 1859, p. 154c. Although the phrase quoted here is the same as that quoted in my "Thinking in Buddhist Philosophy" (see note 4), I have cited it again since the article is still in press.

10. Maitreya, *Madhyānta-vibhāga,* ed. by Yamaguchi Susumu, p. 49; Asaṅga, *Mahāyāna-saṁgraha, Taishō*, Vol. 31, No. 1595, p. 191c.

11. Dōgen, *Shōbōgenzo,* (Repository of True Buddhist Teachings) chapter on *Genjō kōan; Taishō*, Vol. 82, No. 2582, p. 23c. Although the lines quoted here are the same as those quoted in my "Thinking in Buddhist Philosophy" (see note 4), I have cited them again since the article is still in press.

12. Nishida Kitarō, *Zen no kenkyū* (A Study of Good) (2nd ed.; Tokyo: Iwanami-shōten, 1924), p. 261.

13. Fa-tsang, *Hua-yen i-ch'eng-chiao I-fen-chi-cheng* (*Kegon ichijō kyōgi bunzai shō*) (A System of Kegon Philosophy), *Taishō*, Vol. 45, No. 1866, p. 503b.

14. *Ibid.*, p. 505c, and also, Fa-tsang, *Hua-yen-ching T'an-hsüan-chi* (*Kegongyō tangenki*) (A Commentary on the *Avataṁsaka-sūtra*), *Taishō*, Vol. 35, No. 1733, pp. 123b, 124a.

15. For details see my article, "What is Idealism in Buddhist Philosophy?" *op. cit.*

NAKAMURA HAJIME   *Consciousness of the*

Individual and the Universal

Among the Japanese

ANY ADEQUATE DISCUSSION of the status of the individual and of the
relationship between the individual and the universal in Japanese
thought and culture, in terms of methodological tendencies, requires an examination of two major aspects of the problem—the
philological or linguistic and the logical,* that is, the tendency
toward an absence of theoretical or systematic thinking, along with
an emphasis upon an aesthetic and intuitive and concrete, rather
than a strictly logical, orientation. The status of the individual tends
to be determined for the Japanese mind by both of these somewhat
unique tendencies of thought.

I. The Consciousness of the Individual in Daily Life

The logical problem of the relationship between the universal,
the particular, and the individual was not discussed with full
awareness by Japanese scholars before the introduction of Western
scholarship, except by some Buddhist monastic scholars who elaborated on Chinese versions of Indian Buddhist logical texts.

The concept of "the individual" can be expressed with the
singular in daily usages of speech, but the singular and the plural
have always been expressed in the Japanese language in terms of
human relationships.

* Both of these aspects of the problem are treated at some length in my
Ways of Thinking of Eastern Peoples, Philip P. Wiener, ed. (Honolulu: East-
West Center Press, 1964), from which some of the material here is taken.

Number is not always made explicit in the grammar of Japanese sentences. A distinction is not always made between the singular and the plural. And reduplication in the Japanese language (e.g., "*yama-yama*," i.e., mountains; "*kami-gami*," i.e., gods) cannot be said strictly to indicate plurality, as reduplication requires the individuality of signification. Furthermore, not all nouns can be put into plural forms. Plurals become better indicated as we proceed higher from domestic animals to servants. Several kinds of plural suffixes are variously used to suit different occasions: "*domo*" and "*tachi*" are used for persons of equal or inferior status or for intimates, as, for example, *funa-bito-domo* (boatman), *hito-tachi* (people), *tomo-dachi* (friends).[1] When respect must be shown, the suffix "*kata*," which originally meant place or direction is used, as, for example, *anatagata* (you) and *sensei-gata* (teachers). In short, the use of plural suffixes is determined by the relationship of social ranks and the feeling (intimacy, hate, respect, disrespect, etc.) which the speaker entertains for the persons of whom he is speaking, just as in the cases of "*tu*" and "*vous*" in French, and "*du*" and "*Sie*" in German. This clearly evidences the Japanese trait to think of things in terms of human relationships rather than as separately existing facts in the objective world. The various plural forms are therefore not strict equivalents of Western plural forms, though in modern times, owing to the influence of Western languages, number has come to be expressed in nearly the same way as in Western languages. (An affix, "*moro-morono*," can be added to any word to denote the plural.)

It sometimes happens that a plural suffix attached to a noun loses its own meaning, becoming simply a blank, meaningless component of a compound, and the compound may indicate the singular number, as in the case of the word "*wakai-shū*,"[2] which is made up of "*wakai*" (young) plus "*shū*" (plural suffix, people). This word may mean both youngsters and a youngster.

The Japanese do not think it necessary to represent the individual as objectively existing, but, when two people are conversing, they are clearly aware of the distinction between singular and plural. One of the most distinguishing features of the Japanese language is the lack of clear indication of number. This is not so, however, with regard to personal pronouns, particularly the first and second person. The singular and plural in the first and the second persons are clearly distinguished. This phenomenon in their language indicates that the Japanese, who are disinclined to measure the objective world with a certain established unit, are quire sensitive to the distinction between "I" and "you" in human relations. In this case, the consciousness of the individual appears conspicuously.

This does not mean that conceptualization in universals was lacking among the Japanese of the past. The move to conceptualize human affairs in terms of laws and concepts, which are universals, was effected by the Japanese to some extent. The concept of universal law came into existence very early, in the time of Prince Shōtoku, when he said, "Sincerely revere the Three Treasures. The Three Treasures, viz., the Buddha, the Law (*Dharma*), and the Brotherhood (*Saṅgha*), constitute the final ideal of all living beings and the ultimate foundation of all countries. Should any age or any people fail to esteem this truth? There are few men who are really vicious. They will all follow it if adequately instructed. How can the crooked ways of men be made straight unless we take refuge in the Three Treasures?" [3] Here we find the concept of a universal law, which is something beyond laws based on the inductively given status of the individual in the joint family and of the family in its respective tribe or caste. This is merely one example. The concept of natural law was most conspicuously expressed by Master Jiun (1718–1804) in the modern period. But the Japanese seem not to have had the inclination to express things in an abstract way. Logic was nothing but a transplantation of Buddhist logic from India, and it did not develop from among the Japanese.

Among Japanese thinkers, a tendency to respect the natural feelings of man justifies the great importance attached in Japan to the rules of propriety based upon human relationships.

The recent trend in philosophical writings in Japan to assign individuality only to man might have come from this humanistic tendency of thinking among the Japanese. The habit of attaching importance to human relationships is manifested outwardly in their practice of the rules of propriety. Generally speaking, exchange of greetings in the West is simple. Japanese greetings are, on the contrary, highly elaborate, although they differ greatly from area to area.

Due to the stress on social proprieties in Japan another characteristic of its culture appears, viz., the tendency of human relationships to supersede or take precedence over the individual. To lay stress upon human relationships is to place heavy regard upon the relations of many individuals rather than upon the individual as an independent entity.

Personal pronouns are much more complicated in Japanese than in other languages. The choice of the proper pronoun to fit the particular situation is an ever-recurring problem in speaking Japanese. Special pronouns are required for superiors, equals, inferiors, intimates, and strangers. If one should confuse them, difficulties would ensue. A Japanese, therefore, must bear in mind such human relationships as rank and intimacy every time he uses a personal pronoun. Such restricted uses of personal pronouns are related to the use of nouns and verbs as well. A distinction is made, for example, between words used in addressing persons of superior rank and those used in addressing persons of inferior rank.

When this type of thinking is predominant, consciousness of the individual as an entity appears less explicit, i.e., always in the wider sphere of a consciousness of personal relationships, although the significance of the individual as an entity is still recognized; the recognition of the equal value of all individuals is lessened, of course, when he is placed in a class, but it means that it represents the tendency to pay more attention to each individual as the subject to which various virtues belong, not as an object like an inanimate thing.

The first person or the second person is often omitted as the subject in a Japanese sentence. Generally, in such a case the subject is implied in the whole sentence-structure, but frequently a sentence may completely lack the subject. The subject can be determined according to the context. The Japanese do not want to express explicitly the subject of an action, unless necessary. This indicates that the Japanese do not think it always necessary to mention the individual or an independent performer of actions as an objective being.

The Japanese in general did not develop a clear-cut concept of the human individual *qua* individual as an objective unit like an inanimate thing, but the individual is always found existing in a network of human relationships. It means that the Japanese wanted to locate the individual in experience, not in the abstract. Largely because of the Japanese emphasis on concrete immediacy in experience, the individual was grasped as a living thing, and not as a bloodless, inanimate thing in the realm of the abstract. The living individual is always located in various kinds of human relationships.

II. Awareness of the Relation Between the Individual and the Universal

In terms of logical thinking, the forms of expression of the Japanese language are more sensitive and emotive than directed toward logical exactness. This reflects the traditional attitude of the Japanese of laying more emphasis on the aesthetic and artistic aspect of human life.

The relation between the individual and the universal was not thought of with full awareness by the Japanese in the past. The concept of "the individual" in the logical sense was expressed by Buddhist logicians of Japan with the word "*jisō*," a Japanese equivalent of the Sanskrit word "*sva-lakṣaṇa*," but it was not used by intellectuals at large.

The word "*kobutsu*," meaning the individual, was coined after the introduction of Western logic. The Japanese language does not tend to express precisely and accurately the various modes of being, but tends to be satisfied with vague, topological expressions. As for nouns, the Japanese have no clear distinction between singular and plural, nor is there a distinction between genders, and no articles are used. For verbs, also, there are no distinctions of person and number. In these respects, Japanese resembles Chinese. Genders and articles may not have anything to do with the logical character of a language. The absence of these may make it better for logical thinking. This problem needs further investigation.

The original Japanese language, as clearly revealed in Japanese classical literature, had a rich vocabulary of words denoting aesthetic and emotional states of mind. On the other hand, words denoting intellectual, inferential processes of active thought are notably lacking. In the original Japanese language, in which words were for the most part concrete and intuitive, the construction of abstract nouns was deficient. Hence, it is extremely difficult to express abstract concepts solely in words of the original Japanese. When Buddhism and Confucianism were later introduced into Japan and philosophical thinking developed, the vocabulary which was the means of expressing these philosophical thoughts was entirely Chinese, simply taken over. Although Buddhism was very widely propagated among the people, its scriptures were never translated into the Japanese language. "In our country, there is no attempt to translate [Chinese versions of Buddhist scriptures]," [4] said Kōkan Shiren (1287–1346), in his *Genkō-shakusho* (A History of Japanese Buddhism), and he cited this fact as a characteristic of Japanese Buddhism. Western philosophical ideas now prevail widely in Japan, but the linguistic means by which they are expressed are, in most cases, words coined by properly connecting two Chinese characters which are, by convention, made to correspond to the traditional Occidental concepts. The words *"gainen"* and *"risei,"* for instance, are the present-day Japanese terms for "concept" (*Begriff*) and "reason" (*Vernunft*), respectively. Sometimes such words are constructions of three or four characters. The pure, original Japanese had difficulty in serving as a means of expressing philosophical concepts.

The greatest obstacle in this respect seems to lie in the fact that the Japanese language does not have any fully established method of composing abstract nouns. The language does not have the infinitive form of the verb, the special character of which is to express an indefinite situation, a relation itself rather than a thing. Although the Japanese do have what is called the "nominal use" corresponding to the infinitive, this is completely identical in form with a verbal form which, in conjunction with temporal verb-endings or an adjective, forms a compound word. For example, the so-called nominal form *"warai,"* which is completely identical in form with the form of the verb *"warau"* (to laugh) appearing in *"warai-tari"* (laughed), *"waraite"* (laughed and . . .), *"warai-goto"* (laughing matter), etc., signifies the act or fact of laughing. Moreover, this verb-form in time has tended to lose its special significance as an expression with a compounding function, and has also come to be used as a noun. For instance, *"warai"* has the senses both of *"waraukoto"* (the individual act or the fact of laughing) and of *"warai to yūmono"* (the universal concept of laughter); consequently, the distinction between *"die Lache"* and *"das Lachen"* is not made.

Furthermore, the Japanese have no established method of turning adjectives into corresponding abstract nouns. As may be seen in such examples as *fukasa* (depth), or *fukami* (deepness), the suffixes *-sa* and *-mi* make abstract nouns out of adjectives to some extent. But this manner of transformation or noun-building is available for only a limited range of adjectives.

Things being so, present-day Japanese intellectuals have come to add the Chinese character *"sei"* to any word to form any abstract noun. This is the Japanese substitute method for the original lack of an ending to form an abstract noun.[5]

In short, the Japanese language, so far, has had a structure rather unfit for expressing logical conceptions. The fact that it is difficult to make derivatives representing abstract nouns means that it has not been habitual for the Japanese to be aware of the relations between the universal and the individual in terms of logical thinking. Consequently, when the Japanese adopted the already highly advanced conceptual knowledge of Buddhism and Confucianism, they made no attempt to express it in the original Japanese language, but used Chinese technical terms without modification. Again, in translating the concepts of Western learning, the Japanese used Chinese characters and did not render these concepts into pure, original Japanese directly.

When we step into the realm of syntax from that of word-construction, the Japanese language manifests its non-logical character all the more clearly. The language lacks the relative pronoun "which," standing for the antecedent, that helps develop the process of thought. We find it inconvenient, therefore, to advance closely knit thinking in a succinct form in Japanese.[6] If we repeat nouns and adjectives unsparingly, their logical exactness can be attained. In scientific works this way of expression has been carefully adopted. However, in literature it is often difficult to determine what modifies what, when several adjectives or adverbs are juxtaposed. Because of these defects, Japanese presents difficulties for logical expression, which has to be exact, and, as is generally pointed out, its non-logical character naturally handicaps the development of ability in logical thinking among the Japanese people, and has actually brought about grave inconveniences in their practical lives. Indian books of Buddhist philosophy were originally written with logical accuracy, but Chinese versions of them and Chinese commentaries upon them became remarkably non-logical. Thereafter, the Japanese continued their ambiguous and obscure interpretations of the Chinese texts without change, and, as a result, they did not attempt to analyze them logically.

Although special phraseologies have been worked out in legal jargon, etc., for technical considerations, to avoid ambiguity, such a practice is by no means universal.

In the same way, Japanese frequently omits the subject, and this, too, has something to do with the non-logical character of the Japanese people. In such a case, even though the subject is omitted, we usually find it naturally suggested or can easily infer what it is by referring to linguistic context, or by looking at the situation in which the utterance is made. But it cannot be denied that at times, when the situation is not completely clear, the omission of the subject makes the meaning ambiguous and causes misunderstanding. Very often it is not clear whether the subject is an individual or a group of individuals.

In connection with the omission of the subject, we must note that anacoluthon very frequently occurs in Japanese sentences. While it is to be found also in Indo-European languages, examples there are rare,[7] whereas Japanese not only has abundant examples of it, but also even the fact that the subject has changed within a single sentence is not clearly noticed. For example, in literary works of the Heian period (794–1186), instances of anacoluthon are very frequent. And this characteristic of the Japanese way of thinking appears also in the annotations to Chinese Buddhist texts.[8] That the Japanese people can dispense with the subject in their linguistic expression is due to the fact that the intuitive understanding of the scene referred to in their discourse is usually attained beforehand by their close bonds and nexus with others. Therefore, the necessity of clearly indicating the subject occurs only in those cases in which some doubt about the intuitive understanding of the subject arises. (In other words, a logically correct assertion of the "obvious" sounds harsh to the Japanese people.)

Generally speaking, logical consciousness begins with consciousness of the relation between the individual or the particular and the universal; and the Japanese on the whole have not been fully aware of this relation, or have been poor in understanding a concept apart from particular or individual instances. This exactly corresponds to the tendency, characteristic in the Japanese way of thinking, not to make a sharp contrast between subject and predicate in the expression of judgment.

Hio Keizan (1789–1859), in his two-volume work, *Kuntenbukko* (Restoration of Kunten), criticized the usages of *kunten* (marks used in paraphrasing Chinese into Japanese) prevalent in the Tokugawa period (1615–1867). According to his view, for example, scholars at that time misread the Chinese phrase *"yen-hui-che,"* which means "a man called Yen Hui (i.e., Gankai)" as *"Gankai naru mono,"* which is an abridged form of *"Gankai ni aru mono"* (strictly, "the man exemplified in Gankai"). In so doing, he argued, they committed an error in the indication of the meaning. However this may be, such a distinction is generally not recognized by Japanese scholars, and this confusion continues to the present time. Whether or not Hio's theory is right is a question to be entrusted to experts, but in any case one can say that there was no method fully established in Japanese for expressing universals by a universal concept, in contrast to individual cases.

Therefore, the Japanese people are not inclined to present the universal concept as a predicate in a judgment, so as to make its expression concise. They are not usually content until they have presented a set of particular instances or individual cases pertaining to universal propositions.

Dōgen (1200–1253) has been called one of the greatest philosophers Japan ever had. When an Indian philosopher formulated an idea simply and definitely in a universal proposition, e.g., "The Three Worlds are but one mind," [9] Dogen explained the thought by enumerating various particulars. Thus:

> The mind is neither one nor two. It is neither in the Three Worlds nor beyond the Three Worlds. It is infallible. It is an enlightenment through contemplation, and it is an enlightenment without contemplation. It is walls and pebbles; it is mountains, rivers, and the earth. The mind is but the skin, flesh, bones, and marrow; the mind is but the communication of enlightenment through the Buddha's smile. There is a mind, and there is no mind. There is a mind with a body; there is a mind without a body. There is a mind before a body; there is a mind after a body. A body is generated from the womb, the egg, moisture, or fermentation. The mind is generated from the womb, the egg, moisture, or fermentation. Blue, yellow, red, and white are nothing but the mind. Long, short, square, and round are nothing but the mind. Life and death are nothing but the mind. Years, months, days, and hours are nothing but the mind. Dreams, illusions and mirages are nothing but the mind. The bubbles of water and the flames of fire are nothing but the mind. The flowers of the spring and the moon of the autumn are nothing but the mind. Confusions and dangers are nothing but the mind. [10]

A similar way of thinking may be noticed in Japanese Confucianists. Ogyū Sorai (1666–1728), for example, did not like the sort of abstract speculation found in the Sung school; he made more of particular or individual "things" (*wu*) than of universal "principles" (*li*):

> The great sage kings of the past taught by means of "things" and not by means of "principles." Those who teach by means of "things" always have work to which they devote themselves; those who teach by means of "principles" merely expatiate with words. In "things," all "prin-

ciples" are brought together; hence, all who have long devoted themselves to work come to have a genuine intuitive understanding of them. Why should they appeal to words? [11]

Words are relevant to universals. Therefore, learning consists, to Ogyū, in knowing as many particular or individual things as possible: "Learning consists in widening one's information, absorbing extensively anything and everything one comes upon." This reflects his attitude that scholarship should be based upon empirical facts. But, since Ogyū ignored the science of Nature, learning, which is to amass a knowledge of particular or individual facts, culminates, for him, in the study of history—a preference which is closely related to the empiricistic character of his "learning": "Since learning is to have wide information and to have experience with realities, it culminates in history." [12] Here individual cases were emphasized.

Even the scholars of the Japanese classics, who tried to repudiate Buddhism and Confucianism, exhibited the same way of thinking. Hirata Atsutane (1776–1843), for example, rejected the concept of abstract, universal "principles," and declared that we only had to know "actual things," i.e., concrete particulars or individual cases.

In fact, that which is called the "true way" is given in actual things, whereas conventional scholars are erroneously inclined to think that the "way" cannot be found out except by reading doctrinal books. For, if we can appreciate actual things, doctrines are dispensed with; and it is only when actual things, in which the "way" is given, are lacking that doctrines arise. Therefore, doctrines are far less valuable than actual things, (i.e., individual cases). Lao Tzu fully recognized this fact when he said, "When the Way decays, the doctrines of humanity and justice arise." [13]

As is shown by the historical development of Japanese thought —although, so far, only a few representative thinkers have been considered—the ability to think in terms of abstract universals has not fully developed among the Japanese. They have been rather poor in ordering various phenomena on the basis of universal patterns.

Japanese expressions are for the most part abundant in aesthetic and emotional feelings. A special kind of logic may be found, but it is quite different from that generally called "logic." Japanese, rather, emphasized the aesthetic way of expression and the artistic way of life, and, with regard to scientific thinking, they tended to base their studies upon individual facts.

(Nowadays there might be a question as to how to reconcile this alleged Japanese preference for the particular with the commonly observed modern preference of Japanese scholarship for theoretical learning rather than the pragmatic approach. Among present-day Japanese intellectuals there is a conspicuous tendency toward German abstract philosophy. Why the change? We would answer: This is not a real change. Such a tendency among intellectuals is due not so much to fondness for theoretical thinking as for things abstruse and productive of imaginative impressions upon them. Their alleged fondness for theoretical thinking is not always based upon the process of induction and deduction in the logical sense.)

III. Weakness in Logical Thinking in the Past

The non-logical character of the Japanese people naturally tended to prevent them from thinking with logical coherence or consistency.

Even in ancient times, Kakinomoto-no-Hitomaro composed a famous poem in which he said, "In our land covered with reed and rice-ears, they have not argued since the time of the gods." Out of such a point of view, the technique of constructive universal laws reducing individuals to order is not likely to develop. Motoori Norinaga (1730–1801), a scholar who claimed to have made clear the spirit of ancient Japan, said:

In ancient times, we had no talk at all even about the Way. The classic [of Kakinomoto] declares that in our land covered with reed and rice-ears, they have not argued since the time of the gods. Not to argue means not to expatiate or have much talk, as is the custom in foreign countries.[14]

In ancient times in our land, even the "Way" was not talked about at all, and we had only ways directly leading to things themselves, while in foreign countries it is the custom to entertain and to talk about many different doctrines, about principles of things, this "Way" or that "Way." The Emperors' land in ancient times has no such theories or doctrines whatever, but we enjoyed peace and order then, and the descendants of the Sun Goddess have consecutively succeeded to the throne.[15]

"To things themselves" has been the motto of many Japanese scholars.

The way of thinking on the part of the Japanese in general could not easily be changed by the introduction and dissemination of Buddhism.

It is commonly said that Japanese Buddhism reached its maturity in the Kamakura period (1186–1392). "Kamakura Buddhism," however, did not develop systematic philosophical thinking on a large scale. Such prominent figures as Hōnen, Shinran, and Nichiren concentrated their efforts chiefly upon demonstrating the orthodoxy or validity of their own interpretations of Buddhist sacred texts. To cite an extreme instance, Genshin (Sage Ippen) (1239–1289) declared on his deathbed that the people of this world should be content with the one phrase, "Pay homage to Amitābha Buddha" (*Namu Amida Butsu*), and ordered his books destroyed by fire.

On the other hand, some contemporary philosophers in Japan have tried to see in Dōgen, who continued to write philosophical works throughout his lifetime, the pioneer of Japanese philosophy. Though it is doubtless true that Dōgen was a distinguished thinker, as well as a high-minded spiritual leader, he was not the sort of thinker who developed a logically coherent system of thought. In spite of the fact that he cherished deep philosophical ideas which were gem-like in character, he was not inclined to elaborate the ethical thoughts he apprehended in a purely logical system. Probably he thought that a philosophical system set forth in a systematic way was useless and unnecessary.

Dōgen opined as follows, referring to the problem of life and death: "Life and death matter little, because the Buddha exists therein. And one is not perplexed by life and death, because the Buddha does not exist therein." [16] As far as the expression is concerned, we have here two formally contradictory propositions. But the gist of what he meant by the two sentences was quite the same.

The teacher Musō (Soseki) (1275–1351) declared, very clearly, that he does not aim at fixed logical coherency:

Clear-sighted masters of the Zen sect do not have a fixed doctrine as something to be cherished for all time. They present any doctrine as the occasion demands, and preach as their tongues happen to dictate. They do not have a fixed source to rely upon. If one asks them what Zen is, they sometimes answer in terms of the sayings of Confucius, Mencius, Lao Tzu, Chuang Tzu, and non-Zen Buddhist teachers, and sometimes in forms of popular proverbs, and sometimes they explain what Zen teaches, point out a particular situation, or simply swing their mace in front of them or shout in a loud voice. Or they simply raise their fingers or fists. All these are means used by the masters, and called "the vivacious ways of the Zen sect."[17]

In this state, no universal proposition which is logically coherent is mentioned, but esteem of the individual situation in each case is emphasized.

Ever since the Tokugawa period (1615–1867), the schools of Chu Hsi and Wang Yang-ming have been energetically studied in Japan, but it is a question how far Japanese scholars were virtually sympathetic with them. It is likely that Japanese Confucianists did not like metaphysical speculation.

Absence of theoretical and systematic thinking is equally characteristic of former scholars of Japanese classics. Motoori, for example, did not want to express any concrete conception of method in his learning: "In final conclusion, to make strenuous efforts consecutively for long years is most essential to those who are engaged in learning, and it does not matter how they learn." [18] Motoori exhorted his disciples just to be diligent in their study, and did not develop any constructive thinking as to the learning itself.[19]

Of course, one cannot deny the possibility that one actually can express oneself as clearly in Japanese as in any other language. It is said that there is one school of thought which stresses the cultural conditioning of thought-patterns more than the limitation of a language concerned. At least, the Japanese *esprit* should not be overlooked. However, the value of ways of Japanese expression lies more in aesthetic and intuitive aspects than in exactly logical ones.

Moreover, there is no intention here to advocate any sort of linguistic determinism. We admit the working influences of other factors. We just point out, with regard to logical aspects, some features of the manner of expressing thoughts by the Japanese in earlier days, for these features are quite irrelevant to those in contemporary times with regard to the concepts of the universal and the individual.

On the other hand, Japanese expressions focus the thought and expression of the person on immediate, concrete details of life. This tendency is quite unique to the Japanese. That is why the Japanese way of thinking habitually avoids summations of separate facts into broad statements about whole categories of things, although such abstraction is necessary for logical and scientific thinking.

IV. The Development of Logic in Japan Beyond Indian and Chinese Buddhist Logic

We need not despair completely, however, of the capacity of the Japanese people for logical thinking. The way of thinking of a people is simply a tendency and is capable of being reformed. There is evidence for this in the fact that modes of expression in the Japanese language have gradually been growing more and more strict and precise in recent years. Although it is true that Japanese heretofore has not tended to be fit for exact thinking, it will surely improve in this respect.

The fact that Buddhist logic did not fully develop in the past can be ascribed to the non-logical character of its immediate source, the Chinese *inmyō* (Buddhist logic). In spite of this limitation, there were Japanese scholars who tried at several points to initiate a development beyond Chinese logic in Japan. We mention an interesting, if rather trivial, example. In Chinese logic, the word *"shūhō" (tsung-fa, paksa-dharma)* represents the predicate of an assertive proposition (*tsung*, major term, *sādhya*) as well as the predicate of a causal proposition (*yin*, middle term, *sādhana*). Chinese technical terminology did not distinguish between the two. Even if a distinction was made at first between the two uses through pronunciation, this distinction could not be preserved for a long time in a country using the Chinese language, in which pronunciation rather frequently changed. The Japanese, distinguishing the two terms in pronunciation, read in voiceless sound *shūhō*, in one case, where it means the predicate (P) of an assertive proposition, and in voiced sound (*shūbō*), in the other case, where it means the predicate (M) of a causal proposition.[20] Moreover, before the Meiji era (1867–1911), there were several scholars who had mastered Indian formal logic and had actually applied it to the study of Buddhist ideas. As examples we can mention the name of Rinjō (1751–1810) and Kaijō (?–1805), of the Buzan school of the New Shingon sect. Surely, logic can be disseminated and developed among the Japanese people, if they endeavor seriously to study it.

There were some Japanese in the past who were willing to

use terms of Buddhist logic, even with changed meanings. For example, it has been asserted that the word *"rippa"* (magnificent, splendid) is a phonetic equivalent to *"ryūha"* (assertion and refutation in a debate) and that, *"mutai"* (unreasonable), also is due to Buddhist logic.[21] Although it is doubtful whether or not this assertion or conjecture is right, it is an established fact that there were some men of letters who took it that way. This means that some ideas related to logic were not alien to the common people, although they may not have been fully aware of the exact meaning of them.

It is an object of interest how far Japanese logicians developed their thought beyond the Chinese scholarship of Buddhist logic, which originated in India. Saṁkarasvāmin (at the end of the sixth century) asserted that perception (*pratyakṣa*) is caused by the individual object.[22] The traditional definition of perception in Indian and Chinese Buddhist logic was interpreted by Zenju, a Japanese logician (723–797), as implying individuality.[23] An ancient Japanese logician said, "That which cannot be described with any word is called the thing-in-itself (*jisō, sva-lakṣaṇa*), i.e., that which should be predicated (*uhō, dharmin*). That which should be described with a word is called 'characteristic' or 'quality" (*hō, dharma*)." [24]

Hōtan (1654–1738), a modern Buddhist logician, went still further. He said, "The thing-in-itself is apprehended by direct perception. Any characteristic which can be found in common throughout various things is an object of inference." [25] "The reality of things is called the thing-in-itself. It is an individual and cannot be in common with others. Genus is found throughout various things, just like a thread piercing flowers. This characteristic can be set up as an object of the mind in an ordinary situation (not in meditation). Genus in Buddhist logic is an object of inference." [26]

What characterized his concept of the individual was that he thought that the thing-in-itself is something substantial. He said, "Fire burns the body. Therefore, this fire can be regarded as an individual object. Only the fire that can burn the body is named the thing-in-itself." [27] This definition of the thing-in-itself is conspicuously empiricistic, and makes quite a contrast to the idealistic concept of the thing-in-itself held by Indian Buddhist logicians, such as Dharmakīrti, etc., who belonged to the tradition of Buddhist idealism (Vijñāna-vāda).

Dialectical thinking was not clear in Eastern countries before the introduction of Western civilization. The Tendai and Sanron philosophies of ancient China and Japan had conspicuously dialectical thinking, but it did not develop in the line of dialectics. In modern Japan there have been some individual thinkers who held some dialectical ideas. Ishida Baigan set forth the thought that negative and positive are two things and yet they cannot be separated. But, even if they seem to be one they are the two aspects of motion and quiescence.[28] Miura Baien expressed a theory of dialectics of his own. "The way to understand Nature (or the universe) is dialectics (*jōri*). The secret (*ketsu*) of dialectics is to see synthesis (*gōitsu*) in antithesis (*han*). It is to give up one-sided preoccupation and to correct marks (*chōhyō*)—*yin* and *yang* are antithetic to each other and constitute opposition. As they are antithetic to each other, they can be brought to synthesis." [29] Here we find the thought of dialectics in its incipient stage.

V. Conclusion

We have discussed the reflection on, or the awareness of, the concept of the individual by the Japanese in terms of the daily use of the common people and in language in terms of the logical thinking by thinkers. Throughout various phenomena we may safely notice the following four features:

(1) Conflation, rather than confrontation, of different individuals was esteemed, at least in the realm of subjective reflection, reflecting the social concept in which each individual is situated.

(2) When the Japanese have discussed the significance of the individual as against the universal in terms of linguistic use, the significance of the individual has tended to be minimized, but now it is going to be emphasized as something contrasted with the universal when necessary.

(3) When any proposition was made in terms of logical and philosophical thinking, individual cases relevant to the proposition were mentioned emphatically in detail.

(4) Japanese thinkers have tended to lay more emphasis upon, and have paid more attention to, empirical facts, which should be mentioned individually. This reflects the traditional empiricistic attitude of the Japanese.

The focus of the Japanese on the facts of life did not allow for the abstraction from experience of a concept of the individual "as such," in isolation.

The above discussions lead us to an important corollary. Heretofore, it has often been said in the West as a cliché that Westerners tend to be individualistic and diremptive, whereas Easterners tend to be monistic or all-embracing. But it has been made clear that this is wrong. Insofar as Japanese thought is concerned, we can say with certainty that the Japanese have tended to be individualistic, due to the attitude of focusing on immediate experience directly.

Concerning logical thinking, we can say that, although the mass of Japanese people have been limited to a language that was rather deficient as a tool of logical exactness, philosophic thinking did develop among Japan's educated classes through the use of Chinese.

Logic can be disseminated and developed among the Japanese people, if they endeavor seriously in a right way. Logical improvement will not be impossible in the future, although it is fraught with many difficulties. This will entail a greatly increased awareness of the relation between the universal and the individual on the part of the Japanese.

It is important for the Japanese people as a nation to develop the habits and language tools of logically exact thinking. We cannot foresee the developments in the future, but industrialization, which is going on very rapidly in contemporary Japan, does not seem to change the above-mentioned features very much or easily, but to develop along the lines which have been long established and practiced among the people. It is natural that the Japanese do not want to lose their traditional aesthetic and empirical attitude.

QUESTION: There is a theory in Western philosophy that Greek concepts of reality (which still influence modern Western concepts) derived from the subject-predicate structure of the Greek language. But it is also held that it was the other way around. The Greek language-structure grew out of early Greek concepts of reality. The non-abstracting characteristics of the Japanese language might have derived from a natural temperament of concrete concerns among the Japanese people.

ANSWER: There is probably a reciprocal influence between a people's language and their way of thinking, as well as other influences bearing upon both of them, such as climate, social structure, ways of production, human relationships, and so on.

QUESTION: You mentioned the ideas of Motoori and Hirata. I understand that the so-called Kokugaku school they belonged to had been led by their teacher Kamo-no-Mabuchi, who strongly insisted on the historico-linguistic approach to the Japanese classics in order to clarify the pure and real meanings of the Japanese way of thinking as well as their way of life. Motoori and Hirata and other scholars of Kokugaku also pursued their studies in strict conformity with this principle. Though their achievements and interpretations were sometimes farfetched and might not be comparable with Indian or Western philosophy and logic of language, they were neither simple linguists nor grammarians but scholars who ardently wanted to discover the metaphysical meanings of the ancient Japanese language and words. They probably had some non-logical logic as the results of their researches.

ANSWER: The Kokugaku school had the command of a sort of logic of its own. They advocated what might be called "empiricism of language," but they did not develop a system of methodology, as did Indian and Chinese scholars. It is necessary to determine what the Kokugaku scholar had in mind concerning methodology. This calls for further study.

QUESTION: You mentioned that there were some Buddhist monastic scholars who elaborated Buddhist logic, though this school did not develop from among the Japanese. However, I understand that from the ninth to the fourteenth century the annual examination systems for officially authorized monks and for the promoting of the scholarly monks' ranks in the Tendai, Hossō, Kegon, and Shingon sects, were institutionalized. And, in these examinations, two or three among ten to twelve questions necessarily came from the field of Buddhist logic. Therefore, many Buddhist scholarly monks necessarily had to study and learn Buddhist logic thoroughly. These currents—or training—cannot be overlooked when we observe the history of Japanese metaphysics and sciences which gradually develop from medieval to modern times.

ANSWER: It is true that Buddhist logic was enthusiastically studied by monks in the ancient and medieval periods of Japan. But few studies have been launched so far with regard to how far Japanese scholars have made progress in logical investigation beyond Indian and Chinese Buddhist logic. That is up to the scholars in the future.

QUESTION: In medieval and modern Japan we find many original and unique thinkers who have left a tremendous volume of work in which deep philosophical thinking was expressed. Do you not admit the historical significance of these thinkers?

ANSWER: I admit the historical fact that the Japan of the past produced a great number of thinkers whose speculation was very deep. But most of them wrote down their philosophical thought only in classical-style Chinese, and did not write in Japanese. I have mentioned in this paper chiefly those thinkers (except some logicians) who have expressed their thought in Japanese, and not in Chinese.

QUESTION: It occurred to me that your paper has wider implications than you claimed. It not only called attention to the Japanese preference for the: "individual" over the general-categorical. It really pointed out that the present Japanese tendency is that of wishing to move toward the Western (Continental: German, French, and earlier scholastic) tendency to connect individuals, i.e., thing-words in relational-categorical-general words.

ANSWER: My paper points toward *no* structure—either universal or otherwise.

What I find interesting is that Japanese thought is moving in the direction of several structures, whereas the "West" is trying so to move in the opposite direction: away from the abstract, away from the general, toward the concrete, immediate perception, non-connective, "instant-by-instant" perception and experience. It could be said that the English started out with this in modern philosophy—for example, Francis Bacon. He advocated it for scientific method. (i.e., empiricism versus scholasticism). But from the nineteenth century on we got away many times from "system-building" in philosophy, mostly by way of reaction again Hegel. Existentialism had its roots in that (Kierkegaard versus Kant), too.

At present, the trend toward immediate experience and the search for a "language" of immediacy is especially strong in the arts —away from "general truths," from "ideas," and toward unique forms, form that includes spiritual qualities, unique spiritual qualities, not "general" spiritual (or emotional) qualities. The most extreme trend in this respect is the so-called "aleatoric" or "aleatory" art (alea=dice, i.e., random choice). It defies "composition" in the familiar sense of the term, and, of course, it defies "intentionality" in art. Aleatory experiment is a dead-end; but there are some good artists who take it seriously (in music, poetry, and dance). Conclusion: The "East" (i.e., Japan) and the "West" (i.e., the United States and some European cultures) are not "meeting" but passing each other, the West turning where the East is leaving.

There are some evidences that the East is going in the direction opposite to the one in which it went previously, i.e., in the direction in which the West advanced in the past, and vice versa. For example, activity was exceedingly cherished in the West of the past, but now the West is going in the direction of cherishing receptivity or passivity. The East, on the other hand, is going to emphasize activity, forsaking the previous attitude of esteeming receptivity or passivity. The phenomenon which you have pointed out may belong to this same movement.

Notes

1. I mention these linguistic expressions as current in contemporary daily life. They represent the present-day usage of these words. Historically speaking, "*domo*" was used for persons of inferior status, such as "*midomo*" (me). "*Tachi,*" which seems to have derived from "*doshi,*" was used for persons of superior rank in such cases as "*kindachi*" (courtiers). From around the Muromachi period (1138–1568), it came to be used for persons of equal rank also. I owe this historical information to Professor Hori Ichirō.

2. Originally it meant "a group of youngsters of the same age grade."

3. Prince Shōtoku's Seventeen-Article Constitution, Article 2.

4. *Genkō shakusho*, Vol. 30.

5. Watsuji Tetsurō, *Zoku Nihon seishinshi kenkyū* (Supplement to Studies in Japanese Intellectual [Spiritual] History) (Tokyo: Iwanami-shōten, 1935), p. 397.

6. Sakuma Kanae, on the other hand, maintains that the Japanese language contains words performing the function of the relative pronoun, by the suitable manipulation of which the lack of the relative pronoun may be compensated for. "*Kyūchakugo no mondai,*" (The Problem of Agglutinative Languages), in *Kokugo kokubun* (Japanese Language and Literature), VIII (October, 1938).

7. In the sentence, "All beings who hear his name, blissfully trust in him, and think even once—which all is the directing of their minds toward him with the sincerest effort—and who desire to be born in his country will at once be born, attaining thereby the Unretrogressive State," in the *Daimuryōjukyō* (The Great *Sūtra* of the Pure Land), it is obvious that the object of "the directing of their minds"

is living beings; cf. *Sukhāvatīvyūha-sūtra*, 26: *ye kecit sattvās tasya bhagavato 'mitābhasya nāmadheyaṃ śṛṇvanti śrutvā cāntaśa ekacittotpadam apy adhyāśayena prasādasahagatena cittam utpādayanti te sarve vaivartikatāyām santy anuttarāyāh samyakṣam bodheh*, but Shinran took the subject of the phrase "the directing of their minds" for Amitābha Buddha (!); cf. his works, *Jōdo monrui jushō* (Anthology of Scriptural Passages on the Pure Land), *Ichinen tanen shōmon* (Scriptural Passages on Immediate and Mediate Attainment), and *Kyōgyō shinshō* (The Book on the Teaching, Practice, Faith, and Attainment); see Rev. Kusaka Murin, ed., *Bantō shimpon kyōgyō shinshō* (An Authentic Text of the *Kyōgyō shinshō*) (Kyoto: Chojiya-shōten, 1923), p. 103.

8. Hiroike Chikurō, *Shina bunten* (Grammar of Chinese) (Tokyo: privately published, 1905), p. 67.

9. *"Cittamātram idam yad idaṃ traidhātukam"* (the universe is nothing but our presentation), *Daśabhūmika-sūtra*, J. Rahder, ed. (Paris: Paul Geunther, 1926), p. 49; *ci vijñaptimātram evedam* (the universe is nothing but our ideation), *Trimśikā*, S. Lévi, ed., (Paris: Libraire Ancienne Honore-champion, 1932), 27, p. 42.

10. *Shōbōgenzō* (Repository of True Buddhist Teachings), chap. "Sangai yuishin" (The Universe is Nothing but Our Presentation).

11. *Tōmonsho* (Questions and Answers), Book I, in *Nihon rinri ihen* (Collected Japanese Ethical Texts), Tetsujirō and Kanie Yoshi, eds. (Tokyo: Ikuseikai, 1902), Vol. VI, p. 157.

12. *Ibid.*, p. 156.

13. *Nyūgaku mondō* (Elements of Study) in *Hirata Atsutane zenshū* (Collected Works of Hirata Atsutane), Hirata Moritane and Miki Ioe, eds. (Tokyo: Hirata Atsutane Zenshū Kiseikai, 1918), Vol. 15, p. 1. (In discussion, Professor Mei expressed the idea that Atsutane's citation is a twisted interpretation).

14. *Naobi no mitama* (The Honest Spirit), in *Motoori Norinaga zenshū* (Collected Works of Motoori Norinaga), Motoori Seizō, ed. (Tokyo: Yoshikawa-kōbunkan, 1926), Vol. I, p. 53.

15. *Ibid.*

16. *Shōji* (Life and Death) in *Shōbōgenzō*, in *Taishō shinshū daizōkyō* (Sacred Buddhist Texts edited in Taishō Period) (Tokyo: The Taishō Issaikyō Kankō Kwai, 1931), Vol. 82, p. 305.

17. *Muchū mondō roku* (Questions and Answers in Dreams).

18. *Uiyamabumi* (Introduction for Beginners), in *Motoori Norinaga zenshū*, Motoori Seizō, ed., Vol. IV, p. 601.

19. *Ibid.*

20. Ui Hakuju, *Bukkyō ronrigaku* (Buddhist Logic) (Tokyo: Daito-shuppansha, 1944), p. 168.

21. Yamada Yoshio, *Geirin* (Arts), Vol. 3 (1952), Nos. 1, 2. As for *"mutai"* (non-entity), see Chikū, *Inmyō inu sanshi* (Introduction to Buddhist Logic) (1854), p. 19b. But this term seems not to have been so important in original Indian Buddhist logic.

22. *pratyakṣam kalpanāpoḍham yaj jñānam arthe rūpādau nāmajātyā-dikalpanārahitam/tad akṣam akṣam prati vartata iti pratyak-sam kalpanājñānam arthāntare pratyakṣābhasam/yaj jāñam gha-ṭaḥ paṭa iti vā vikalpayataḥ samutpadyate tad arthasvalakṣaṇaviṣ-ayatvāt pratyakṣābhāsam.*

The *Nyāya-praveśa*, Anandshankar B. Dhruva, ed. (Baroda: Oriental Institute, 1930) (Gaekwad's Oriental Series, No. XXXVIII), p. 7.

23. *Gengen betten shoryō shikyō* (Objects of Perception), in *Inmyō nisshō riron myōtōshō* (Gloss on the Commentary on the Intro-duction to [Buddhist] Logic) (Traditional edition, Vol. 6b, p. 454b). See p. 461b: "It is not called 'perception' because it par-takes in universals."

24. See also: "With regard to the fact that it cannot be described, it is called 'thing in itself'; if it can be described, then it is called 'universal,'" in *Myōhon shō* (Clarification of Rules), Bussho-kankōkai, ed., in *Dai-Nippon Bukkyō zensho* (Tokyo: Bussho-kan-kōkai, 1911), Vol. 4, p. 47.

25. *Inmyō zuigenki* (Sources of Buddhist Logic), Vol. 8, published in 1711, p. 16a.

26. *Ibid.*, pp. 9b–10a.

27. *Ibid.*, p. 13a.

28. *Seiri mondō* (Questions and Answers on Nature), translated into English by Paulo Beanio-Brocchieri (Rome: Instituto peril Medio ed Estremo Oriente, 1961), pp. 19–20.

29. Saigusa Hiroto, *Miura Baien no tetsugaku* (The Philosophy of Miura Baien) (Tokyo: Daiichi-shobō, 1941), p. 132; also his *Nihon no yuibutsuronsha* (Japanese Materialists) (Tokyo: Eihōsha, 1928), p. 93.

HORI ICHIRŌ   *The Appearance of Individual*

Self-consciousness in Japanese Religion

and Its Historical Transformations

I.   Introduction

I WOULD LIKE, on this occasion, to discuss the problem of self-consciousness and the ultimate destiny of individuals as seen in the history of Japanese religion. However, I must confine myself to pointing out only a few main historical currents, especially within the early stages of Japanese religious history, when those conceptions so pervasive to the present-day Japanese people seem to have been founded. Emphasis, therefore, will be placed primarily on the first stage or the appearance of these conceptions, and, secondarily, on the following stages of the historical transformations, which were brought about by the introduction into Japan of the Tendai sect (T'ien-t'ai in Chinese), the Shingon sect (Chen-yen in Chinese), and the Amidist movement of the Pure Land school.

II.   Primitive Religious Foundation—Shintō in Pre-Buddhist Japan

Primitive Shintō, or primitive religious forms, in ancient Japan, should be classified into two categories. The first category may be defined as the *ujigami* type (tutelary or guardian shrine system), which was based on the particular family or clan system. Each family had its own shrine as a central symbol of its solidarity as dedicated to the ancestral spirit (*kami* [1] or *kamis*), those who had been worshipped and enshrined successively by their descendants. This type of belief system is characterized by particularism and exclusiveness from other families, so that the main function is to integrate all the members of the family into the patriarchal hierarchy of the family system. The maintenance of the good name of a hereditary family, continuing their ancestors' glorious work from generation to generation, was the most important respon- sibility, not only for the patriarch, but also for all the family members.[2] Heavy emphasis on ancestor-worship and filial piety (kō) in almost all Japanese religious groups has been connected closely with the ancient family system and the ujigami system founded on the cultivation of rice fields. Strictly speaking, there are no means for the salvation of individuals within the ujigami system. Rather, the ultimate destiny of individuals was conceived in terms of their loss of identity and joining with a vague community of ancestral spirits after death,[3] although there existed distinctions ac- cording to their social, political, and also magico-religious status.

The second category may be called the hitogami type (man- god system), which was based on the close relationship of an individual kami with a religious specialist such as a shaman or a medicine man. More integrative state-systems, such as village states or small-scale united kingdoms which appeared in ancient Japan, supposedly were ruled by charismatic or shamanic leaders such as Pi-mi-ko of the Yamatai Kingdom in the third century A.D.[4] This type of belief is characterized by the strong individuality both of the individual kami and of its transmitter, who lived for a long time in the memory of the believers, and their functions came to influence ordinary individuals. With this type of kami, sincere reverence and obedience were the only conditions to gain the kami's favor, regardless of the believers' origins. Charismatic per- sonages and their descendants entered into a special relationship with their hitogami and created a kind of ujigami system independ- ently, playing an important role in the politics of ancient theocratic ages by utilizing their divine power for blessing or curses. However, this belief in the hitogami seems not to have provided for any salva- tion or afterlife for individuals, even though only the charismatic personages could be easily deified by their relationship with the hitogami.[5]

Under the rigidity of the ancient Japanese social structure and value system that apparently was characterized by the primacy of political values, the emphasis on on (blessings or favors handed down, not only by invisible beings, but also by social and political superiors) and on hōon (obligation of the recipient to return something for these blessings) had increased.[6] As Watsuji Tetsurō has pointed out, the Japanese social structure and value system took the shape of a human relationship which is strictly controlled and regulated by the patriarch according to the status of each member of the family.[7] However, the patriarch, in turn, must be responsible to the higher authorities of the nation at large as well as to his ancestors. Even the emperor himself is responsible to his ancestors for his behavior and must account to them. In the Japanese way of thinking which emerged from the context of such a value system, there could be no room to develop the concept of an "Almighty God," as in the traditions of Judaism, Christianity, and Islam. On the contrary, Japanese *kami*, as well as men, are not considered as independent personalities, but as lowly figures dependent on their superior in either the divine or the social hierarchy, and in need of salvation and help. In this context, the superiors, including human beings and ancestors, were believed to be semi-*kami* (demi-gods) or even low-ranking *kami* or *buddhas*. Being linked with ancestor-worship and dependence upon superiors, the belief in spirits of the dead and also the idea of the intimate connections between men and *kami* (in other words, ease in deification of human beings) were and even today are quite widespread and important.[8] The dead are commonly called *hotokesama* (*buddhas*), a fact which surprised Sir Charles Eliot. He says that this bold language is peculiar to Japan and is an imitation of Shintō teaching, according to which the dead become *kami*, superhuman beings. It could hardly be admitted that the Buddhist dead had a status inferior to *kami*, and therefore in popular speech they were termed *buddhas*, *buddhas* and *kami* being much the same.[9]

III. Introduction of Confucianism and Buddhism to Japan and Their Influence, Especially on Prince Shōtoku's Way of Thinking

The introduction of Confucianism in the fourth century and of Buddhism in the middle of the sixth century from China via Korea to Japan greatly influenced the attitudes of the ruling-class people and intelligentsia from the outset. The idea and belief in *T'ien* or *Ten* (Heaven) and *T'ien-ti* (Lord of Heaven), as well as social ethics and moral codes, were introduced by the Confucian teachers, and some ideas of the philosophy of Lao Tzu and Chuang Tzu were accepted. Several instances of Chinese influences are clearly seen in ancient historical documents.[10] On the other hand, universalistic metaphysics and principles, such as the law of causality, the Three Seals of Law (impermanence, non-self, and *nirvāṇa*), and the equality of all human beings, were introduced by the Buddhist priests. These kinds of religious and moral codes were rather contrary to the exclusiveness and discrimination of original Shintō. The aim of Shintō prayer was never individual salvation, but only group salvation or unification with the spirits of ancestors. However, Buddhist influence gradually penetrated into Shintō beliefs, introducing the element of individual salvation, so that it promoted the tendency for some Shintō *kami* to have a particular divine favor according to their own functions.

Confucian and Buddhist universalism and rationalism had a great influence on the spiritual attitude of Prince Shōtoku (593–622) and his adherents. He was venerated by all Japanese Buddhist scholars and monks as the real founder of Japanese Buddhism, since he promoted Confucian ethics and Buddhist teachings in various ways. Prince Shōtoku actually declared these to be a proper basis for the state. He prepared in person the Seventeen-Article Constitution (*Jūshichijō kempō*) with the purpose of establishing an ideal harmonious state in the land. Evidently his ideas and thoughts were revolutionary and much beyond his time. The first clause pleads that harmony is to be valued and avoidance of wanton opposition to be honored, according to the spirit of the Confucian *Analects* and Buddhist teachings. In order to realize his utopian society, Prince Shōtoku recommended three major principles to his peoples: sincere reverence of Buddhism (Second Article), sincere obedience and loyalty to the Holy Sovereign (Third Article), and appropriate behavior (Chinese *li;* Japanese *rei*) for their leading principle (Fourth Article).[11]

Prince Shōtoku's understanding of Buddhism and especially his viewpoint regarding individuality are to be seen in the Second Article and also the Tenth Article. He said, "Since [the Three Treasures of] Buddhism, viz., the Buddha, the Law (*Dharma*) and the Order (*Saṅgha*), are the final refuge of all beings, and are the supreme objects of faith in all countries, what man in any age can fail to reverence this doctrine? Few men are utterly bad; they may be taught to follow the doctrine, but, if they do not betake themselves to the Three Treasures, wherewithal shall their crookedness be made straight?" Again, in the Tenth Article, he declares, "Let us cease from wrath, and refrain from angry looks. Nor let us be resentful when others differ from us. For all men have hearts, and each heart has its own leanings. Their right is our wrong, and our right is their wrong. We are not unquestionably sages, nor are they unquestionably fools. Both of us are simply ordinary men (*bompu*). How can any one lay down a rule by which to distinguish right from wrong? For we are all, one with another, wise and foolish, like a ring which has no end. . . ."[12]

According to the *Nihongi* and other documents, Prince Shōtoku usually instructed his consorts and descendants with the sayings: "This world should be empty and evanescent, while the Buddha himself alone should be real and true"[13] and "Avoid wickedness of every kind, practice good of every kind."[14] Being strongly impressed by these teachings, his eldest son, Prince Yamashiro-no-Ōye, refrained from military defense against his enemy's attack, saying, "For the sake of myself, I was unwilling to destroy the people; therefore, I deliver myself up to my enemy." Finally, he and all members of his family strangled themselves and died together at their family temple, Hōryūji. Their tragic death marked the beginning of the Taika Reformation, which put into effect their ancestor's principles.[15] Prince Shōtoku especially brought all his mind to bear upon *The Lotus Sūtra* (*Saddharma-puṇḍarīka-sutra*),[16] which taught a social consciousness that encompassed all classes. *The Lotus Sūtra's* promise of salvation for all mankind was in sharp contrast with pre-Buddhistic religious conceptions in Japan.

Buddhism was also conceived as a religion which gave security in this life and salvation for the individual in the afterlife. After Prince Shōtoku's death, his survivors with heartfelt prayers made two kinds of *maṇḍalas* and a life-size image of Śākyamuni Buddha for the sake of the departed Prince's spirit. The two *maṇḍalas* were called *Tenju-koku mandara* (*Maṇḍala* of the Heavenly-Life Paradise)[17] where they believed that Shōtoku's spirit must have been reborn. After this time, we find many written copies of Buddhist Sūtras, statues of the Buddha, paintings, and *maṇḍalas*, as well as temples, *buddha* halls, and pagodas, all of which were dedicated to the spirits of the dead with their relatives' prayers for the salvation of the deceased.[18]

IV. State Buddhism and Individual or Personal Buddhism

On the other hand, as pointed out in the previous section, the universalism and rationalism of Confucianism and Buddhism were not necessarily fully appreciated in the beginning, except by Prince Shōtoku and his followers, but were accepted on a traditionalistic level. At first, the *ujidera* system (the tutelary temple system) became institutionalized, manifesting almost the same character as the *ujigami* system.[19] For in the initial acceptance of Buddhism the Buddha had been called a *hotokegami* (a *kami* named a *buddha*) and recognized as a kind of *kami* from abroad, and the Buddhist temple was called *hotokegami no miya* (a shrine dedicated to the *kami* called *hotoke* [a *buddha*]).[20] When in 594 Empress Suiko instructed Prince Shōtoku and all of her subjects to promote the prosperity of Buddhism, the *Nihongi* says that all the princes, princesses, and subjects vied with one another in erecting Buddhist shrines for the benefit of their lords and parents (or ancestors).[21]

Also, State Buddhism flourished mainly after the Taika Reformation in 645, modeled after the state-shrine system under the Chinese influence of the unified empire system of the Sui and T'ang dynasties. *Ninnō gokoku hannya haramittakyō* (*Prajñā-pāramitā-sūtra on a king who protects his country*)[22] and the *Konkōmyō-saishō-ōkyō* (*Suvarna-prabhāsottan-arāja-sūtra*)[23] were selected from the Tripiṭaka by Emperor Temmu (622–686) and distributed all over Japan to be recited and interpreted for the benefit of public security and the prosperity and welfare of the nation.[24]

However, the harmonious connection between state Buddhism and individual Buddhism may be seen in the spirit of the erection of the Great Vairocana at Tōdaiji in Nara under Emperor Shōmu (701–756) and his consort Kōmyō, with the explanation that this Buddha (the Great Sun Buddha—Dainichi Nyorai) and the mythical ancestress of the Imperial Family, Amaterasu Ōmikami (Sun Goddess), are one and the same. That is to say, the emperor wanted to make manifest his pious belief in Buddhism as well as his own sovereignty, and, again, he eagerly desired to be reborn in the Great Vairocana's lotus realm (*padma-garbha-loka-dhātu*)[25] following the *Avataṁsaka-sūtra*'s cosmological theories of the Kegon sect (Chinese Hua-yen). This is the first historical indication of the commingling of Buddhism with Shintō, which afterwards developed the theories of the blending of Shintō *kami* and *buddhas* (or *bodhi-sattvas*, beings whose essense is perfect wisdom) named *honji suijaku* (manifestation of the prime noumenon).[26] However, Emperor Shōmu adopted the *chishikiji* system when he erected the Great Sun Buddha, which had just appeared among common believers in local communities in the eighth century. *"Chishiki"* means a fraternity of the Buddhist believers in the same *buddha, bodhisattva,* or *Sūtra,* and *"chishikiji"* means a Buddhist temple built with the alms and help of a *chishiki* fraternity.[27] Emperor Shōmu wanted to let all districts make contributions toward the erection of the Great Sun Buddha, even a token gift such as a handful of soil or a spray of a tree. Having been deeply impressed by the emperor's edict, a Buddhist saint, Gyōgi (670?–749), traveled through the country to ask the common people for offerings so that they would be saved by the Great Sun Buddha along with the emperor himself as the members of the *chishiki* fraternity.[28] Here we can see the historical subsumption of individual or personal Buddhism to state Buddhism.[29] Gyōgi also endeavored to distribute to the common people the Buddha's teachings centering around the law of causality, and engaged in public welfare services based on the way of the *bodhi-sattva* (*bosatsudō*).[30]

Saichō (Dainichi Nyorai), who aspired to develop an indigenous form of Buddhism, favored belief in Amida (*Amitābha* or *Amitāyus* in Sanskrit) Butsu concerning ultimate destiny, as well as concerning meditation on the mystery of existence which leads to enlightenment. He regarded prayer and the contemplation of Amida (*Nembutsu*) as a means of clearing the mind and enabling it to concentrate on the presence of Amida and also as a means for the spirit to be saved after death by Amida's merciful hand.

Belief in Amida Buddha and the practice of *jōgyō zammai,* especially in reference to the ultimate destiny of individuals, was strongly promoted by an eminent disciple and successor of Saichō whose name was Ennin or Jikaku Daishi (794–864).[31] Ennin studied about nine years in T'ang (618–906) China, mainly at Mount Wu-t'ai and in Chang-an. He brought back to Japan many *maṇḍalas,* religious paraphernalia, and Sūtras of both Mantrayāna and T'ien-t'ai Buddhism, as well as the belief and practice of Amida, influenced by Hui-yüan (334–416) of Mount Lu and Fa-chao (about the eighth century) of Mount Wu-t'ai in the Chinese Pure Land school. After he became the third patriarch of the Tendai sect, Ennin built the Jōgyō Zammaidō Seminary in the precincts of Enryakuji on Mount Hiei. Thereafter, the *Nembutsu* practice at the Jōgyōdō Seminary became, not only an important practice of meditation for Tendai monks, but also an important annual function for the salvation of the spirits of the dead.[32]

V.   Kūkai's Approach to the Concept of Salvation and Enlightenment

Kukai, the founder of the Shingon sect (at Mount Kōya) incorporated the insight of other sects, but his central focus was *The Great Sun Sutra*,[33] which teaches that the phenomenal world is a manifestation of the ultimate reality known as the Great Sun Buddha.

In contrast to Saichō, Kūkai preferred, on the one hand, the belief in the Great Sun Buddha representing two aspects of *vajra-dhātu* (diamond element) and *garbhā-dhātu* (womb element),[34] and, on the other hand, he entrusted his ultimate destiny to the future Buddha Maitreya (Miroku) in the Tuṣita Heaven (Tosotsuten), who would come down to this world in order to save human beings 5,670,000,000 years after Buddha Śākyamuni's death.[35]

From the former belief, Kūkai insisted on the theory of "becoming a *buddha* in one's body" (*sokushin jōbutsu*), following the cosmological and metaphysical theories of the *Vairocana-sūtra* and the *Avataṁsaka-sūtra*. Kūkai wrote several outstanding books,[36] in which he criticized and classified all the spiritual and religious stages of mankind from the lowest to the highest (or Shingon) level, proceeding through the lower stages of natural religion and ethics, Confucianism, Taoism, Theravāda, and, finally, Mahāyāna Buddhism. The highest (or Shingon) stage is not a mere system of doctrine, but the actual embodiment of the life and idea of the Great Vairocana, especially by means of the performance of mystic rites. This condition of spiritual development is called "the soul filled with the glories of mystery," which expression is explained by the analogy that the *buddhas* in the innumerable *buddha*-lands are naught but the *buddha* within our own soul, the Golden Lotus, as manifold as drops of water in the ocean, is living in our body. These words remind us of the Advaita Vedānta, but there is a difference in that Shingon theology insists that the phenomenal world is a manifestation of the only ultimate reality known as the Great Sun Buddha. This theory of becoming a *buddha* in one's body does not mean that the individual is annihilated but that he embodies absolute reality in his body itself.[37]

These theories and beliefs, together with those of *The Lotus Sūtra* and Amida Buddha of the Tendai sect, were widely accepted, not only by all the branches of the Tendai and Shingon sects, but also by various other Buddhists. Even in the Tendai sect, the theory of *sokushin jōbutsu* was accepted by the end of the ninth century,[38] and also by Nichiren, the reformer of *The Lotus Sūtra*'s school, in the thirteenth century,[39] while in the Shingon sect the belief in Amida was accepted for the purpose of the securing of the afterlife of individuals.

Kūkai was believed to have become a *buddha* in his own body while still absorbed in meditation and awaiting the advent of Maitreya in the cave sanctuary at Mount Kōya. There were several mountaineering ascetics (Yamabushi or Shugenja) of *shugen-dō*[40] of the Shingon tradition who became self-mummified *buddhas* following their great master's legendary model.[41]

VI. The Awareness of the Arrival of the Latter Age of the Buddha's Law and the Emergence of the Amidist Movement

Prince Shōtoku, Saichō, and Kūkai are the most remarkable personages in the early stages of Japanese religion to emphasize the dignity of individuals, as well as the ultimate destiny of individuals. However, after the two great masters' deaths, the Tendai and Shingon sects gradually declined into occult mysticism and ritualism and became secularized in conspiracy with the Imperial Family and the nobility. The high ideals and the metaphysics of the two great masters' intentions were thus degraded into superstitious performances and abused in justifying this degeneration. Consequently, if a person awakening to real religious conviction wanted to live a life of seeking after the Buddha's truth and distributing the Buddha's teachings, he had to deny the ecclesiastical organizations and escape from them anew.[42]

Having been strongly influenced by this work and resisting the extremely secularized and formalized Buddhist institutions, the new religious movement, called the *hijiri* (holy man) movement,[43] stressed the essential importance of individual faith and anti-secularism. This should be described as the movement "from magico-religious and secular restrictions to the spiritual freedom of individuals." This movement suddenly appeared in the latter part of the tenth and the early part of the eleventh centuries. Kyōshin,[44] Kōya, Jakushin,[45] Genshin (known as Eshin Sōzu), and Ryōnin,[46] may be pointed out as *hijiri* representatives of the Amidists. Zōga,[47] Shōkū,[48] and others were *hijiris* from *The Lotus Sūtra* school, though some different attitudes should be recognized between the

two groups of *hijiris*. The *hijiris* of *The Lotus Sūtra* school, for example, were characterized by strict seclusion from both the secular
and the ecclesiastical worlds, while the Amidist *hijiris* were characterized by the distribution of Amida's gospel among the masses;
the Lotus school *hijiris* should be defined as individualistic or self-
perfectionistic, the Amidist *hijiris* as evangelistic.

Since the fear and awareness of entering the fateful Age of the
Latter Law had penetrated, not only the orthodox Buddhist priests
and upper-class peoples, but also even the lower classes and
country people, we should point out the two reactions or adjustments to this consciousness of crisis: (1) helpless despair and anx-
iety which largely overwhelmed orthodox Buddhist priests and
the sophisticated upper class; [49] and (2) the forerunners of the new
movement mentioned above endeavored to find ways of self-
enlightenment to cope with this hopeless and depraved age as a
given reality, as well as striving for the salvation of the common
people in their everyday life. Genkū and Shinran (the followers of
the Amidist group and its organizers), Eisai and Dōgen, Zen
masters, and Nichiren (the successor of the Lotus school *hijiri* and
the founder of the Nichiren sect) appeared in the twelfth and
thirteenth centuries under the direct influence of the new movement and the consciousness of the arrival of the Latter Age.

VII.   Religious Reformation—from Genshin to Genkū

Among the several Amidists in the tenth century, Kōya should
be considered as a pioneer. Kōya hid himself among the citizens of
Kyoto, strongly encouraging them in the belief in Amida and recom-
mending the *Nembutsu* practice for the sake of their individual
salvation.[50] Then Genshin (942–1017) advanced the Amidist movement in a different way. Genshin devoted himself to writing his
well-known work entitled *Ōjō yōshū* (Birth in Amida's Paradise),[62]
as well as to organizing the fraternity of *Nijūgo zammai kesshū*
(assurance of rebirth in Amida's paradise).[52] In the preface to the
Ōjō yōshu written in 948, he said that the teachings and practices
for rebirth in the Amida's paradise were the best suited for the corrupt world of the Latter Age. Everyone, priest and layman, high and
low, must be converted to faith in Amida's paradise; however, the
Buddha's teachings were divided into apparent doctrines (*kengyō*)
and secret doctrines (*mikkyō*) consisting of various theories and

austerities. Although for the wise and diligent man it would not be difficult to understand and practice these several doctrines, the stupid and obstinate man "like Genshin" could be saved only by invoking the name of Amida Buddha.[53]

This idea expressed by Genshin struck a response in nearly every heart and gave a great incentive to simple faith in the grace of Amida, who had opened the gateway of his paradise to all without distinction of training or knowledge. The original vow taken by Amida was believed to have the mysterious power to save those unable to undergo vigorous training in spiritual exercise or disciplinary life. Emphasis was put on pious devotion to Amida's mercy and his original vow.

Genkū (known as Hōnen Shōnin, 1133–1212), after having searched in the Tripiṭaka to find the best way to salvation in the Latter Age, discovered and was converted to the works of Shan-tao of the Chinese Pure Land school, as well as to the works of Genshin. Genkū abandoned and criticized the "way for the wise" (*shōdōmon*) through severe training, intricate ritualism, and methodic contemplation, as well as belief in "salvation by one's own power" (*jiriki*) and belief in the Buddhist and Shintō pantheons (*zōgyō*). He taught that the way to the Pure Land is necessarily through simple faith in Amida's grace, which is called the "easy way" (*igyō*) of salvation. This is in contrast to the "difficult way" (*nangyō*) of perfection. The "easy way" is also called "salvation by another's, i.e., Amida's, power" (*tariki*). Genkū inevitably alienated himself from the complicated teachings and practices of the prevailing forms of Buddhism and finally came to declare his independence and to achieve thereby a religious reformation.[54]

His major work establishing the independence of his sect, named Jōdoshu, is the *Senjaku hongan nembutsu shū* (On the Nembutsu of the Original Vow),[55] written in 1198 (or 1204). But the most intense statement of his belief and teaching is to be seen in his last handwritten essay, entitled *Ichimai kishō mon* (On Genkū's Final Enlightenment): [56]

What I teach is neither a sort of meditation such as has been talked of by many priests both in China and in our own country nor an invocation such as is possible only to those who have grasped by thought its real meaning. No, all that is needed to secure birth in the Paradise of perfect bliss is merely to repeat the "*Namu Amida Butsu*" without a doubt that one will certainly arrive there. Such details as the three states of mind and the fourfold practice [57] are all included in the repetition of the words "*Namu Amida Butsu*" with perfect faith. Had I any other profound doctrine besides this, I should miss the mercy of the two Holy Ones [58] and have no share in the vow of Amida. But those who believe in the power of calling on the Buddha's name, though they may have thoroughly studied all the doctrines which Shaka taught in the course of his whole life, should behave like a simple man of the people who cannot read a word or like an ignorant nun, and without giving themselves airs of wisdom should simply fervently call on the name of the Buddha.

Here we can clearly see Genkū's intentions: rationalization and simplification of religious theory and form; concentration of religious piety—pure and simple faith; emphasis on the rejection of over-speculation or ritualism; and emphasis on salvation of the lowest level of the people.

VIII.　Triumph of Religious Simplicity and Rationality— Shinran and Rennyo

Genkū's principle had strong influence on the reformative movements of Buddhism, as well as on Shintō in the Kamakura period (1185–1333). Among them, Shinran, (1173–1262) advanced Genkū's theory several steps, though he had been a pious pupil of Genkū and intended sincerely to succeed him and to distribute his gospel. He said that as far as Shinran was concerned his sole reason for repeating the *Nembutsu* lay in the teaching of the good man (Genkū) who made him understand that the only condition of salvation is to say the *Nembutsu*.[59]

According to Shinran, human nature is originally so sinful and hopeless and the situation of the times and of society so absolutely confused that no one could attain spiritual enlightenment and peace by his own power unless he threw himself for support on the Other's mysterious power. Therefore, the original vow of Amida, expressing the desire to save without exception even the lowest and most wicked person, should be the one and only foundation for salvation of individuals in the Latter Age. His famous ironical expression that "even a good man will be received in to the Buddha's Land, how much more a bad man!" played upon a saying of the regular Amidaists that "even a bad man will be received into the Buddha's Land, how much more a good man!" Neither virtue nor wisdom, but faith, was his fundamental tenet, and faith itself has nothing to do with our own intention or attainment but is solely the Buddha's free gift.[60] "Calling the Buddha's name" in pious devotion and absolute trust in Amida is the way to salvation, but there is no value whatsoever in theorizing about the actual process of invocation.

Shinran carried the idea of Genkū to extreme simplicity in his doctrine of "once calling" (*ichinen'gi*), though Kōsai and others among Genkū's disciples also advocated *ichinen'gi*.[61] Shinran was far from objecting to the repetition of the *Nembutsu*, but he held that the essential thing was to say that prayer with full faith and confidence in the Buddha; furthermore, that one such believing utterance is sufficient to secure birth in Amida's Land, and that all subsequent repetitions are to be regarded simply as expressions of joy and gratitude. Shinran strictly denied the formal temple-and-priest system of his time, following his teacher Genkū's principle, as well as the tradition of the Amidist movement in former times. He never lived in a temple but in huts or small hermitages, mainly in the East Province far from Kyoto, and preached his doctrine among the country people. He married, reared a family, and in every way lived like a normal citizen or farmer. Shinran severely criticized ritualism, magic or divination, and the worship of the old pantheon. The worship offered to Amida does not consist of prayers for health or temporal welfare or any such petitions. After a man has once obtained faith in Amida, he commits all to his power, and his worship consists of nothing but thanksgiving.[62]

The rationalizing tendencies in the Jōdo-Shin sect were promoted by Rennyo (1415–1499). Rennyo was Shinran's direct descendant, and is often called the second founder of the Shin sect because of his great influence on its development and theoretical formulation. Rennyo opposed the practice of austerities and meditation, insisting on the practice of Confucian virtues in daily life and on obedience to state authorities, while, at the same time, one's inner life was to be given up wholly to Amida Buddha. Rennyo opposed any worship of Shintō deities. Until recent times, almost all Shin sect families had no shelf for the family *kami*, as well as no charms, talismans, or amulets in their house; there is merely a huge decorative Buddhist altar dedicated to Amida alone. There are no mortuary tablets in the Shin sect Buddhist altar as in those of other Buddhist families. He made an important advance with respect to the ethico-religious regulation of everyday life. He wrote his main work, entitled *Ofumi* (Collected Writings) [63] completely in colloquial Japanese (as contrasted to the formal Chinese style of writing) for the sake of the common, uneducated people's understanding. Rennyo's remark that "if we engage in business, we must realize that it is in the service of Buddhism," indicates his view of the occupational life as integrated with the religious life. He also stressed the obligation of bestowing blessings on the people, and this-worldly asceticism, as well as returning for Amida's blessings.

Here we see the most radically rationalizing Buddhist sect in Japan, together with Zen Buddhism, which was introduced from China at the time of Genkū and Shinran. Though the Shin sect gradually declined into an institutionalized religious order and became secularized in the course of its history, the principles established by Shinran and Rennyo should be recognized as a close Japanese analogy to Western Protestantism, and its ethics as quite similar to the Protestant ethics described in Max Weber's famous work.[64] This should be called the beginning of the spiritual modernization in Japanese religion.

IX. Conclusion

By way of conclusion, I would like to point out some common tendencies manifested in the major Japanese religions as well as in the folk-beliefs which several scholars have mentioned with some validity in speaking of Japanese religion as an entity, in spite of the variety of its manifestations: (1) emphasis on filial piety ($k\bar{o}$) and ancestor-worship connected with the Japanese family system and agriculture from ancient times; (2) deep-seated and common beliefs in spirits of the dead in connection with ancestor-worship, as well as with more animistic conceptions of malevolent or benevolent spirit-activities; (3) emphasis on *on* (debts or favors given by superiors, human or superhuman) and *hōon* (the return of *on*); (4) continuity between man and deity, or ease in deification of human beings; (5) mutual borrowing and mixing of different religious traditions, in other words, a syncretistic character; (6) co-existence of heterogeneous religions in one family or in one person.

Because the gap between the religious élites and the masses in Japan is so broad and deep even today, consciousness of individuality among the people, in the Western sense, seems to have been undeveloped. Also, because of the supremacy of group-consciousness and the political value system seemingly based on the ancient sociocultural religious system, individualism and universalism did not necessarily develop completely among the common people. However, certain particularistic tendencies still survive even in modern industrial Japan.

In the first stage of the history of Japanese religion, from the earliest times to the Medieval Age, we see that, especially on the intellectual level, the vague formless conceptions of individual self-consciousness and the ultimate destiny of the individuals in the primitive Shintō age gradually became more explicit with the introduction and influences of Chinese philosophy and ethics (Confucianism and Taoism) and of Indian religion (Buddhism) as the turning points. Though there were a few exceptional intelligentsia in the pre-Buddhist age in Japan, the great role played by Prince Shōtoku at the first stage of the ethico-religious enlightenment, depending mainly upon the introduction of Confucian ethics and the Mahāyāna Buddhist spirit, was important.

The second stage was opened under the leadership of Saichō and Kūkai. Having been deeply influenced by Shōtoku's idealism, principally *The Lotus Sūtra*, Saichō insisted on and spoke out for the dignity of the individual. His idealistic theories on the equality of human nature and *buddha*hood penetrated and dominated Japanese intellectuals. Among Kūkai's doctrines, the idea and practice of becoming a *buddha* in one's *body* (*sokushin jōbutsu*) enjoyed great esteem and acceptance, not only by Buddhist priests, but also by many of the intelligentsia and common people. Even the Tendai and Nichiren sects inclined to accept this teaching. Zen Buddhists were also under the influence of this idea, though they transformed it into the idea of becoming a *buddha* in one's *mind* (*sokushin jōbutsu*). Saichō and Kūkai are presupposed to have been the theoretical pioneers of the amalgamation between Shintō and Buddhism. For the first time, they and their followers established Shintō theologies and metaphysics, respectively, and thus Shintō *kami* became personalized and functionalized. The prevalence of Shintō theologies based on Tendai and Shingon doctrines was considered to have had a deep influence on the common people in the development of the self-consciousness of individuals even at the popular level.

The third stage of the history of Japanese religion is the Kamakura period (1186–1392), twelfth and thirteenth centuries, when several religious reforms flourished simultaneously, both in Buddhist and in Shintō circles. Kamakura Buddhism might be evaluated as the establishment of a truly Japanized Buddhism for the first time, because of the following features: (1) rationalization and simplification of religious theory and form; (2) concentration of religious piety—pure and simple faith and devotion; (3) emphasis on religious practice in connection with the daily life of the believers and rejection of over-speculation as well as of complicated magico-religious ritualism—all of which were symbolized by the special term of the "easy way" of salvation.

Nevertheless, we should not overlook the factors that became the direct causes of religious reforms in the early Kamakura period: (1) the rise and prevalence of the critical consciousness of the arrival of the Age of the Latter Law, and (2) the religious movements of the *hijiri* (saintly men) groups. These emerged mainly on the basis of the self-consciousness of individuality and the ultimate destiny of individuals, and in turn stimulated that critical consciousness.

Generally speaking, Tendai, Shingon, and Zen Buddhism exerted strong influence on the religious élite and intellectuals, as is symbolized by Dōgen's famous saying that he wanted to cultivate only one disciple or even a half in his life. On the other hand, Shugendō, the Amidist sects, and the Nichiren sect have been a main basis of the formation of the self-consciousness of individuality and of the ultimate destiny of individuals among the common people. Zen Buddhism on the intellectual level and the Shin sect on the popular level have played more important roles than any other movements from the viewpoint of our present problem. Indeed, a major factor in Japanese spiritual modernization that historically prepared the basis for the Meiji Restoration and the industrialization of modern Japan was the role played by Shin and Zen believers. Their rationalistic faith and practices, together with rationalistic Confucian ethics, established the religious and moral codes of warriors (*Bushidō* [1868]) in the Kamakura period, and then their influence reached to the self-awareness of the way of the merchant or the tradesman's spirit (*shōnindō*) as well as on the formation of the craftsman's spirit (*shokunindō*) in the Tokugawa period, (1615–1867).

On the other hand, the individual self-consciousness of the peasantry was enlightened and promoted by Rennyo and his followers, as witnessed, for example, in the peasant revolts in the sixteenth century waged by those who had ardent faith in Amida.

Although the Meiji Restoration and the industrialization of

modern Japan were brought about directly by the new movements of Neo-Confucianism and the revival of pure or nationalistic Shintō, as well as by Western colonialism, we should not overlook the great part played in the development of individual consciousness in the history of Japanese religion and ethics, especially by Shin and Zen believers from medieval to modern times.

QUESTION: You use the terms "rationalization" and "simplification" several times. I have some difficulty in seeing the meaning of "rationalization" in these connections. I wonder whether you do not have in mind "anti-supernaturalism" or some such idea. Please consider whether you really mean "rationalization" at these points.

ANSWER: By the term "rationalization" I mean the tendency of what we call "from magic to metaphysic" or "freeing the world of magic." In the primitive or "magical" religions, the concept of the divine tends to be extremely diffuse, and permeates daily life. In this way, religion undoubtedly functions toward the stereotyping of life in traditionalistic societies.

The new conception of the sacred and of religious action I mentioned which mark the emergence of universalistic religions out of primitive traditionalism are characterized by a relatively high degree of "rationalization." These original rationalizing directions had a determining effect on the subsequent development of these traditions. The concept of the divine is usually more abstract and more simple, and less diffuse, than that of the primitive religions. Concomitantly, religious action is simplified, is made less situational, and is concerned with a more direct relation with the divine. The important point of these rationalizing tendencies lies in the changes in attitudes and actions of the individuals, which lead to important effects far beyond the sphere of religion—modernization and industrialization.[65]

QUESTION: I am interested chiefly in your idea of faith. This concept has been so essential to Christianity that I am anxious to understand it in other traditions. What is the basic connotation of the term "faith" in Shinran? Does it mean committing the self to a discipline, to a belief?

I was particularly interested in why it is called "the easy way." Is that because it is opposed to self-discipline or "works"? Is it because it involves trust in a power beyond the individual self? Another way of approaching the problem is to ask what the easy way is contrasted with, i.e., what is the "difficult way"?

ANSWER: The expression "easy way" was first used by Nāgārjuna, but it was Shan-tao who elaborated this term as the most important way to attain enlightenment, because, according to Shan-tao, the essential quality of the utterance of the name of Amida is nothing but the Vow of Amida, that is, the meaning of the utterance began to change from human practice to the Buddha's practice.

The man who consummated this development of devotional piety was Genkū (Hōnen Shōnin). He said, "There may be millions of people who would practice Buddhist discipline and train themselves in the way of perfection, and yet in these Latter Days of the Law there will be none who will attain the ideal perfection. The only way available is the Gateway to the Pure Land." In this respect, Genkū represented the heritage from the culture of the preceding age, while he was a typical pioneer of the new age in his aspiration for the salvation of all. In fact, he demonstrated his zeal by abandoning all his former attainments and devoting himself exclusively to faith in the grace of the Buddha. Hōnen's religion was a simplified form of Amida Buddhism, purged of mystic elements and tempered to pious devotion.

Then Shinran carried the idea of the Buddha's grace to extreme conclusions, because no sin was an obstacle to salvation through grace. He never protested against the idea of purifying oneself from sin, yet strongly denounced it as an impediment to real faith. Any scruple about sins or depravities was, in Shinran's faith, reliance on "one's own power," and therefore a menace to absolute faith in "another's power," in the Buddha's grace. He says,

Whether sage or fool, whether good or bad, we simply have to give up the idea of estimating our own qualities or of depending upon self. . . . Our salvation is "natural, as it is," in the sense that it is not due to our own device or intention but provided for by the Buddha himself; everything has been arranged by the Buddha to receive us into his paradise. It is "natural" because his grace is intangible and invisible and yet works by "naturalness" (jinen hōni) to induce us to the highest attainment. The foundation of salvation has been laid down in Amida's vows. "Calling the Buddha's name" in pious devotion and absolute trust in him is the way thereto, but no idea whatever of invocation or supplication is to be cherished; it should be uttered as the expression of trust and gratitude toward his grace. Further, even this gratitude is a matter of reminding ourselves of the Buddha's primeval vows already completed, rather than of thanking him in anticipation of the bliss to be attained.[66]

QUESTION: What is the status of the individual in Mahāyāna Buddhism, and what is the status of the individual in nirvāṇa?

ANSWER: As Sir Charles Eliot has remarked, Japanese Buddhism, though imported from China, has a flavor of its own. Thus, any technical definition of Japanese Buddhism as a form of Mahāyāna is inadequate. Yet, having said this, says Eliot, it may be well to point out that the singularity of Japanese Buddhism is due partly to the fact that it is the only instance of Mahāyānism now flourishing as a vital religion among the people.[67]

In this context, in Japanese Mahāyāna Buddhism the individual is not annihilated nor does he disappear in his ultimate destiny or in nirvāṇa. Japanese Buddhism never uses the term "nirvāṇa" in its original negative meaning. The term "nehan" (Japanese pronunciation of nirvāṇa) has been used mainly to express the Buddha Śākyamuni's death. They usually use the terms "jōbutsu" and "satori" (enlightenment, becoming a buddha).

Only the Jōdo-Shin sect uses the term "nehan" as its final salvation. According to Jōdo-Shin theology, the schools of the "difficult way" and "salvation by one's own power" claim that jōbutsu, or satori, can be attained even in this world if one accumulates pure good and awakens absolute wisdom in oneself. But the Pure Land schools realize nirvāṇa through Amida's grace after birth in paradise. According to the explanations given by Fujiwara Ryōsetsu, the Jōdo sect usually states that nirvāṇa can be achieved after a long period of further practice in Amida's Pure Land. However, Shinran emphasized that birth in the Pure Land is "birthless birth," which means the end of saṁsāra, and that birth itself is indeed the realization of nirvāṇa. In this case, the term "nirvāṇa" has a positive meaning rather than its original negative meaning, because to attain nirvāṇa is to achieve complete buddhahood, which means the perfection of absolute wisdom and compassion, both for oneself and for all others. Fujiwara says that Shinran stressed the deep significance of two kinds of merit-transference, namely, "merit-transference of going forward" (ōsō ekō) and "merit-transference of coming backward" (gensō ekō). The former means that Amida transfers his own merit to enable us to attain buddhahood. The latter shows that it is also through his merit-transference that one who has attained *buddha*hood is given a special power to return to the defiled worlds and save all beings. According to the traditional Shin sect, theology, Fujiwara remarks, is the benefit to be given at the instance of attaining *buddha*hood. It is the crystalization of the Buddha's positive and compassionate mind to benefit all suffering beings.[68]

Notes

1. The concept of Japanese *kami* is very complicated, and so it should not be translated as "god" or "deity." Motoori Norinaga explained that "*kami*" was originated from "above," "upper," or "super" in its etymology (*Kojiki den,* chap. 1). "Hierophany" would be completely appropriate to express the concept of *kami.* Cf. D. C. Holtom, "The Meaning of Kami," *Monumenta Nipponica,* III (1940), No. 1, 1–27; No. 2, 32–53; and IV, (1941), No. 2, 25–68.
2. In the *Manyōshū* anthology, compiled about 770, we can find instances of the *ujigami* type of Shintō. See the *Manyōshū* (*One Thousand Poems Selected and Translated from the Japanese*) (Tokyo: The Nippon Gakujitsu Shinkōkai, Iwanami-shōten, 1940), pp. 151, 179.
3. In Japanese folk-belief, the spirit of the dead was conceived in terms of its loss of identity thirty-three years after death, when it joined with the community of ancestral spirits. The Buddhist memorial services to a personal spirit of the dead are stopped at the thirty-third anniversary service, called *tomuraiage* or *toikiri* (completion of the personal memorial service). After this, the spirit of the dead is believed to become an ancestral spirit, or *kami.* See Yanagita Kunio (compiler), *Sōsō shūzoku goi* (Folk Vocabulary Concerning Funeral and Memorial Rites and Ceremonies) (Tokyo: Iwanami-shōten, 1937), pp. 206–209.
4. The life of Pi-mi-ko, of the Yamatai kingdom, was clearly documented in the Chinese *Wei chih* compiled by Ch'en Shou (233–297), this book having been published by Professors Wada Kiyoshi and Ishihara Michiharu (Tokyo: Iwanami-shōten, 1951). Other examples in old Japanese historical legends should be seen in my *Nippon shūkyō no shakaiteki yakuwari* (Social Roles of Japanese Religion) (Tokyo: Miraisha, 1962), pp. 36–70; see also my *Wagakuni minkan shinkōshi no kenkyū* (Study of the History of Japanese Folk Religion) (Tokyo: Sōgensha, 1953) Vol. II.
5. Cf. my *Wagakuni minkan shinkōshi no kenkyū,* Vol. II, especially pp. 709–766: "The Concept of *Hitogami* in the Folk-belief and the Primitive Characters and Functions of Magico-religious Wanderers," written in Japanese.
6. Cf. Robert N. Bellah, *Tokugawa Religion, The Values of Pre-*

industrial Japan (Glencoe: Free Press, 1957), pp. 70–73.

7. Watsuji Tetsurō, *Fūdo* (Historico-climatic Characteristics of Culture) (Tokyo: Iwanami-shōten, 1935), pp. 236–257; cf. Hori Ichirō, *Minkan shinkō* (Japanese Folk-beliefs) (Tokyo: Iwanami-shōten, 1951), pp. 119–202.

8. For example, the Meiji Shrine was erected to enshrine the spirits of the deceased Emperor Meiji (d. 1912) and his Consort, Shōken; Nogi Jinja (Shrine) for the spirit of General Nogi Maresuke and his wife (d. 1912); and Tōgō Jinja (Shrine) for the spirit of Admiral Tōgō Heihachirō (d. 1938). Yasukuni Jinja (Shrine) was dedicated to the spirits of all of the unknown soldiers who had died in battle since the Meiji Restoration.

9. Sir Charles Eliot, *Japanese Buddhism* (2nd imp.; London: Routledge and Kegan Paul, 1959), p. 195.

10. The evidences of the influence of Confucianism upon the ruling class are seen in several legends in the *Nihongi*. See especially Vol. XI, in W. G. Aston, *Nihongi, Chronicles of Japan from the Earliest Times to* A.D. *697* (London: Kegan Paul, Trench, Trübner, 1896), Vol. I, pp. 273, 278–279.

11. *Nihongi*, Vol. XXII; Aston, *op. cit.*, Vol. II, pp. 129–130.

12. *Ibid.*, Vol. XXII; Aston, *op. cit.*, Vol. II, pp. 131.

13. *Jōgū Shōtoku-hōō teisetsu* (Collections of Biography and Legends of Prince Shōtoku, a Pious Lord of the Upper Palace), by Hanayama Shinshō and Iyenaga Saburō, with annotation (Tokyo: Iwanami-shōten, 1941), p. 82.

14. *Nihongi*, Vol. XXIII; Aston, *op. cit.*, Vol. II, p. 163.

15. *Ibid.*, Vol. XXIV; Aston, *op. cit.*, Vol. II, p. 183.

16. *Saddharma-puṇḍarīka-sūtra*, Nanjio Catalogue, No. 184 (Oxford: Clarendon Press, 1883) (*Hokkekyō* or *Myōhō rengekyō*, in Japanese).

17. Takurei Hirako interpreted the meaning of *Tenjukoku* as being the same as Amida's Pure Land, i.e., Muryōjukoku (Land of Everlasting Life), cited by Hanayama and Iyenaga, *op. cit.*, in their commentary of *Jōgū Shōtoku-hōō teisetsu*, p. 82.

18. See Hori Ichirō, *Nippon Bukkyō bunka shi* (Historical and Cultural Materials Concerning Japanese Buddhism up to the Nara Period) (Tokyo: Daitō-shuppansha, 1941), Vol. I, pp. 228-255.

19. For example, Katsuragidera was built as the tutelary temple for the Katsuragi Family; Kidera was for the Ki Family; Kofukuji for the Fujiwara Family; Hōryūji for the Jōgū-ō Family, whose ancestor was Prince Shōtoku; the Soga Family built their tutelary temple, named Hōkōji; the Sogakura Yamada Family built their tutelary temple, named Yamadadera; the Hata Family built their temple, Kōryūji.

20. *Gangōji engi* (Origin and History of Gangōji [Temple]) in *Dai*

Nippon Bukkyō zensho (A Complete Series of the Buddhist Documents in Japan), published under the editorship of Bunyū Nanijiō, Takakusu Junjirō, and others (Tokyo: Bussho-kankōkai, 1911–1922), Vol. 118 (1913).

21. *Nihongi,* Vol. XXII in Aston, *op. cit.,* Vol. II, p. 123.

22. In Japanese, *Ninno gokoku hannya haramittakyō* (or *haramitsukyō*); Nanjio Catalogue Nos. 17, 965.

23. In Japanese, *Konkōmyō saishōō kyō,* Nanjio Catalogue, No. 13.

24. *Nihongi,* Vol. XXIX: Aston, *op. cit.,* Vol. II, pp. 346 ff. See Hori Ichirō, "Nihonshoki to Bukkyō" (The *Nihongi* and Buddhism), in his *Nippon Bukkyōshi ron* (Essays on the History of Japanese Buddhism) (Tokyo: Meguro-shōten, 1940), pp. 6–76.

25. In Japanese, *Rengezō-sekai,* which was engraved on the calyx of the lotus leaves of the Mahāvairocana Buddha.

26. *Tōdaiji yōroku* (Historical and Legendary Documents Concerning the Tōdaiji [Temple]), supposedly completed about A.D. 1118. It was published by Tsutsui Eishun, with annotations (Osaka: Zenko-ku-shobō, 1944), pp. 11–12, 15. See also Tsuji Zennosuke, "Honji suijaku setsu no kigen ni tsuite" (On the Origins of the Manifestation of the Prime Noumenon), in his *Nippon Bukkyō shi no kenkyū* (Studies on the History of Japanese Buddhism) (11th imp.; Tokyo: Kinkōdō, 1931), Vol. I, pp. 49–194.

27. *Shoku-Nihongi* (Second Official Historical Document Continuing to the *Nihongi* from 698 to 794 compiled by the Imperial edict in 797), Vol. XV, Imperial edict in 734; also Vol. XVII, Imperial edict in 749.

28. *Ibid.,* Vol. XV, 734.

29. Another example is also seen in the *Nihongi,* Vol. XXV. Cf. Aston, *op. cit.,* Vol. II, pp. 233–234.

30. See *Shoku-Nihongi,* Vol. XXVII. Also Hori, *Wagakuni minkan shinkōshi no kenkyū,;* Vol. I (1955), pp. 256–293.

31. Ennin, *Nittō guhō junrei-kōki* (Ennin's Diary—The Record of a Pilgrimage to China in Search of the Buddha's Law); An English translation was published with annotations by Edwin O. Reischauer (New York: The Ronald Press, 1955); see also Reischauer, *Ennin's Travel in T'ang China* (New York: The Ronald Press, 1955).

32. See Hori Ichirō, *Wagakuni minkan shinkōshi no kenkyū,* Vol. II, Pt. II, chaps. 1–3, "Shoji jōgyōdō no konryū to fudan nembutsu no seikō" (The Buildings of the Jōgyōdō Seminaries at the Several Buddhist Temples and the Popularising of the Continuous Nembutsu Practices), pp. 255–256.

33. *The Great Sun Sūtra* was formerly called *Mahā-vairocanābhisambodhi* (*Ta p'i-lu-che-na cheng-fo shen-pien chia-chih ching* in Chinese, and *Dai birushana jōbutsu jim-pen-kajikō* in Japanese). This *Sūtra*

means "The Sūtra on Mahā-vairocana's Becoming Buddha and the Supernatural Formula called *Yugandhara* (literally, adding-holding)" according to the Nanjio Catalogue, No. 530, which was translated by Subhakarasimha in 724, and is usually called in Japanese *Dai-birushanakyō* or *Dainichikyō* (Oxford: Clarendon Press, 1883), p. 122.

34. "*Vajra-dhātu*" is translated as the "Realm of the Indestructibles" in Masaharu Anesaki (Anesaki Masaharu), *History of Japanese Religion* (Tokyo: Charles Tuttle, 1963), p. 127; or the "Diamond Element," in Eliot, *op. cit.*, p. 345; and *kongōkai* in Japanese. "*Garbha-dhātu*" is translated as the "womb-store" (Anesaki) and "womb-element" (Eliot), and is *taizōkai* in Japanese.

35. Cf. *Maitreya-vyākaraṇa* (*Mi-le hsia-sheng ching* in Chinese, and *Miroku geshōgyō* in Japanese) (*Sūtra* Spoken by the Buddha on Maitreya's Coming Down to be Born in This World), Nanjiō Catalogue, Nos. 205–208.

36. For example, *Sokushin jōbutsugi* (The Theory on Becoming a Buddha in One's Own Body), *Taishō daizōkyō*, Vol. 77, No. 2428; *Jūjū shinron* (The Ten Stages of Spiritual Development), *Taishō daizōkyō*, Vol. 77, No. 2425; and the later condensed work *Hizō hōyaku* (The Jewel Key to the Store of Mysteries), *Taishō daizōkyō*: Vol. 77, No. 2426, are Kūkai's major works. See *Kōbō Daishi zenshū*.

37. Cf. Anesaki, *History of Japanese Religion,* pp. 131–133.

38. By Annen (841–889 or 898) in his life work entitled *Sokushin jōbutsugi-shiki* (My Understanding of the Theory on the Sokushin jōbutsu), *Dai-Nippon Bukkyō zensho*, Vol. 24, "Tendai Section," No. 4; *Himitsu sokushin jōbutsu gi* (Secret Theory on the Sokushin jōbutsu), *Nippon Daizōkyō*, published under the editorship of Nakano Tatsue (Tokyo: Nippon Daizōkyō Hensankai, 1919–1921), Vol. 43, "Tendai Section," No. 3.

39. Nichiren's theory on becoming a *buddha* in one's own body is that there are three ways of achieving this state: the original nature of mankind is *buddha*hood as it is; the completion of self-enlightenment by holding the symbolic prayer of the Nichiren sect, i.e., *Namu myōhō rengekyō;* and, finally, the realization of perfect enlightenment after completing religious practices. The second was insisted on as the most efficacious means of actually becoming a *buddha* in one's own body. Cf. *Sōsho kōyō sakuryaku*, compiled by Nichidō (1724–1789), in Bukkyō taikei series (Tokyo: Bukkyō Taikei Kankō-kai, 1920).

40. *Shugen-dō* is a religious institution peculiar to Japan, which consists of a mixture of various religious elements, both indigenous and heterogeneous, including primitive beliefs and worship of mountains,

Shintō magic and ritual, Mantrayāna Buddhist theories and austerities in mountains both of Tendai and Shingon, Chinese astrology and divination (*inyōdō*, or Way of *Yin Yang*), Taoistic conceptions and practices of hermit or genie (*hsien-jen* or *hsien-tao* in Chinese; *sennin* or *sendō* in Japanese), and some elements of Confucian ethics as well as Chinese philosophy and metaphysics. See Wakamori Tarō, *Shugendō shi kenkyū* (A Historical Study on Shugendō), (Tokyo: Kawade-shobō) 1943; Murakami Toshio, *Shugendō no hattatsu* (The Development of Shugendō) (Tokyo: Unebi-shobō, 1943).

41. Ichirō Hori (Hori Ichirō), "Self-mummified Buddha in Japan," *History of Religions*, I, No. 2 (Winter, 1961), 222–242, especially 227.
42. See Hori, *Wagakuni minkan shinkōshi no kenkyū*, Vol. II, pp. 76–88.
43. Ichirō Hori (Hori Ichirō), "The Concept of *Hijiri* (Holy-man), *Numen*, V, fasc. 5 (1958), 214–215.
44. See Hori, *ibid.*, p. 205.
45. See Hori, *ibid.*, pp. 203–204. He wrote a book entitled *Nippon ojō gokuraku ki* (The Compiled Biographies about the Persons Who Went to Amida's Pure Land after Their Death) during 985 to 986.
46. Ryōnin (1072–1132) was the founder of the Yūzū Nembutsu school of the Tendai sect. Having integrated the Tendai and *Avataṁsaka* (*Kegon*, in Japanese) theories with the teachings of the Chinese Pure Land sects, Ryōnin systematized his own doctrine. This was that one person's merits, coming from faith and repetition of the Amida's name, circulated and were added to all other persons' merits, and all other persons' merits were transferable to one's own merits, so that all human beings could gain the benefit of rebirth into the Amida's paradise after death. This doctrine was based on the teachings of the Pure Land sects, the "One-and-All" idea of the *Avataṁsaka-sūtra*, and the "Salvation-for-All" idea of *The Lotus Sūtra*. See Hori, *Wagakuni minkan shinkōshi no kenkyū*, Vol. II, pp. 291–294; also Hori, "On the Concept of *Hijiri* (Holy-man)," p. 220.
47. See Hori, "On the Concept of *Hijiri* (Holy-man)," pp. 205–206.
48. He composed one poem in Chinese entitled *Kantei go* (Words About the Secluded Retreat), which really manifested his principle. See *Shosha-zankyūki*, Vol. II, in *Dai Nippon Bukkyō zensho*, Vol. 117, Temple-graphic Section, No. 1. See also Hori, *Wagakuni minkan shinkōshi no kenkyū*, Vol. II, pp. 19–20.

> Poor and also humble,
> Who is not ambitious after wealth and distinction;
> But love my own life.
> Though the four walls are crude,

The eight winds cannot trespass on them;
Though one gourd for wine is empty,
The *samādhi* is full to the brim spontaneously,
I do not know anyone,
[So that] there is neither slander nor praise;
No one knows me,
[So that] there is neither hatred nor affection.
When I lie down with my head resting on my arm,
[The] delight and happiness exist in it.
For what purpose should I wish again for
[The] unstable lap of luxury like a floating cloud!

See Hori, *Wagakuni minkan shinkōshi no kenkyū*, Vol. II, pp. 19–20.

49. For example, Jichin (1155–1225), *Gukanshō* (Outline of Japanese History), Vol. VII, in *Kokushi taikei*, Vol. 14, pp. 609–616; Kōen (1145–1150), *Fusō ryakki* (Collections of Japanese Historical Documents), Vol. XXIX, in *Kokushi taikei*, Vol. 6, p. 796; Fujiwara Sanesuke, *Shōuki* (Sanesuke's Diary), in 1023, 3 vols. *Shiryō taisei*, published under the editorship of Sasagawa Taneo (Tokyo: Chugai-shoseki, 1934–1935); Fujiwara Sukefusa, *Shunki* (Sukefusa's Dairy,) in 1052, in *Shiryō taisei*.

50. Hori Ichirō, *Kōya* (Tokyo: Yoshikawa-kobunkan, 1963), pp. 204 ff.

51. *Ojō yōshū* (A Selection of the Sacred Words Concerning Birth in Amida's Paradise). Edited by Hanayama Shinshō, with annotations (Tokyo: Iwanami-shōten, 1942); *Taishō daizōkyō*, Vol. 84, No. 2682. This work consists of ten chapters, the first two chapters being most famous because of the sharp contrast between the descriptions of hell and paradise which have sometimes been compared with Dante's *Divine Comedy* by contemporary Japanese Buddhist scholars.

52. The aim of the *Nijūgo zammai kesshū* was that the members of this fraternity could be reborn without fail to Amida's paradise after death as a result of the concentrated merit of *Nembutsu* by like-minded persons. *Nijūgo zammai kishō* written by Genshin in 986 and 988 A.D. See Hori, *Wagakuni minkan shinkōshi no kenkyū*, Vol. II, pp. 284–288.

53. *Ōjō yōshū, op. cit.*

54. Masaharu Anesaki, *History of Japanese Religion*, pp. 170–171.

55. *Senjaku hongan nembutsu shū* (A Selection of Passages Bearing on the Nembutsu of the Original Vow), *Taishō daizōkyo*, Vol. 83, No. 2608.

56. *Ichimai kishō mon* (One Sheet of Paper Expressing Genku's Final Enlightenment). *Jōdoshū zensho* (The Complete Works on the Jōdo sect), Vol. IX (Tokyo: Jōdoshū Shūten Kankōkai, 1911–1914). Translation in Eliot, *Japanese Buddhism*, p. 267.

57. The three states of mind are: (1) a most sincere heart, (2) a deep-believing heart, and (3) a longing heart which offers in the hope of attaining paradise any merits it may have acquired, the point being that *Ojō*, or birth in paradise, can be obtained merely by personal merit and without faith in Amida, but that any merit one may have obtained should not be devoted to any other object. The fourfold practice, as prescribed by Zendō (Shan-tao) is (1) to treat images and other sacred objects with profound reverence, (2) to practice the repetition of the *Nembutsu* only, (3) to practice it continually and, if any sin has been committed, at once to purify the heart by uttering it, and (4) to observe the above three rules continuously throughout one's life. Cf. Eliot, *op. cit.*, p. 267, note 2.

58. The two Holy Ones are Śākyamuni and Amida Buddha.

59. *Tannishō*, written by Yui-en, Shinran's disciple, Section 2, *Taishō daizōkyō*, Vol. 83, No. 2661.

60. *Tannishō;* see Anesaki, *History of Japanese Religion*, pp. 182–183.

61. The doctrine of "once calling" (*ichinen'gi*) and the doctrine of "many calling" (*tanengi*) were differentiated and disputed among Genkū's disciples. Kōsai was a representative of the "once calling" school, while Ryūkan was of the "many calling" school. The former doctrine was based on the metaphysical conception of the identity of our souls with the Buddha's, as taught in Tendai and Avataṁsaka philosophies. Being adapted to the inclination of easygoing believers, it found a number of advocates and grew in influence, joining hands with neglect of moral discipline. The other, on the other hand, imported scrupulous formalism into the religion of piety and insisted on the necessity of "many," i.e., constant, thoughts on the Buddha. This doctrine found some followers also and was identified with the prevalent method of mechanically repeating the Buddha's name, especially in company with many fellows (*ibid.*, pp. 179–180).

62. Cf. Eliot, *op. cit.*, p. 381.

63. Ofumi is also called *Gobunsho* (Honorable Writings) which was compiled by Ennyo, Rennyo's grandson, in five volumes. It included 80 letters that Rennyo gave his lay disciples and Shin-sect believers, using the spoken language and Sinico-Japanese writing for the purpose of easily understanding his doctrine. *Taishō daizōkyō*, Vol. 83, No. 2668, pp. 777 ff.

64. Max Weber, *Protestant Ethics and the Spirit of Capitalism*, English editions, by T. Parsons (3rd imp.; London: George Allen & Unwin Ltd.; New York: Charles Scribner's Sons, 1950). A remarkable paper on the ethics of the Shin sect and the spirit of Ōmi merchants was written by Naitō Kanji, who applied Weber's theory to this phenomenon in pre-industrial Japan: "Shūkyō to keizai rinri, Jōdo Shinshū to Ōmi shōnin" (Religion and Economic Ethics and the

Jōdo-Shin sect and the Merchants in the Ōmi (present Shiga Pre-fecture), in *Shakaigaku*, Vol. VIII (Tokyo: Iwanami-shōten, 1941). See Robert N. Bellah *op. cit.*, chap. V.

65. Cf. R. N. Bellah, *Tokugawa Religion* (Glencoe: Free Press, 1957), pp. 7–8.

66. Cf. Masaharu Anesaki, *History of Japanese Religion* (London: Kegan Paul, Trench, Trübner & Co., 1930), pp. 170–186.

67. Cf. Eliot, *Japanese Buddhism* (2nd imp.; London: Routledge & Kegan Paul, 1959), p. 179.

68. Cf. Fujiwara Ryōsetsu, *A Standard of Shinshū Faith.* Jōdo-Shin Sect Series, No. 22. (San Francisco: Buddhist Church of America, 1963), pp. 21–22.

FURUKAWA TESSHI   *The Individual*

in Japanese Ethics

I

THE EUROPEAN AND AMERICAN CONCEPTION of Japanese Bushidō
is derived chiefly from the memorable work on the subject by
Nitobe Inazō.[1] The truth is, however, that, as its subtitle, "The
Soul of Japan," shows, the book is not a treatise dedicated solely
to the treatment of Bushidō (way of the *samurai*) itself. It should
perhaps be regarded, rather, as an attempt, under the title of
Bushidō, at an introduction to Japanese morals in general. The
Bushidō to be taken up here is a little different from what Nitobe
meant to describe in his book. We shall deal with Bushidō in its
proper sense, or what may be called "orthodox" Bushidō, one of the
most typical expressions of which is to be found in a volume
entitled, *Hagakure*[2] (popularly known as *Nabeshima rongo* or
Analects of the Nabeshima Clan), written in the year 1716 or
thereabouts.

In this samurai bible we find a famous saying: *"Bushidō to wa
shinu koto to mitsuketari"* (Bushidō consists in dying—that is the
conclusion I have reached).[3] The correct interpretation of this
saying will enable us to grasp what the Bushidō of the *Hagakure*
means. The key words of the dictum *"shinu koto"* (dying) mean,
first, "becoming pure and simple" in the spiritual sense. "Becoming
pure and simple" in this sense means a mental attitude the *samurai*
takes when he acts spontaneously from pure first motives undefiled
by any secondary consideration of the possible consequences of his
act. From this standpoint, the *Hagakure* strongly supports the
speedy action taken in the incident of the Nagasaki Brawl in con-

trast to the deliberate vendetta of the noted forty-seven loyal *rōnin* of Akō and that of the Sōga brothers, which it views with grave distrust.

The forty-seven loyal *rōnin* avenged the wrongs to their lord, the feudal baron of Akō, an incident which was dramatized as the *Chūshingura* in Kabuki drama well known to and well loved by every Japanese. The Sōga brothers were the heroes of a celebrated vendetta in which they avenged their father, who had been murdered by one of his relatives seventeen years before. The *Hagakure* pronounces these two famous cases in history to be far from satisfactory from the viewpoint of Bushidō, because their avenging was carried out one to seventeen years after their lord or father had been wrongly killed, during the lapse of which time the objects of their avenging might have died a natural death. The *Hagakure* claims: "The right way of avenging is to strike at the enemy without delay or hesitation, even in the danger of being killed by him. In this case, it is no disgrace at all to be killed by the object of one's vengeance. It would be disgraceful, however, not to strike at once, thus losing forever the opportunity of vengeance in the vain hope of accomplishing one's purpose satisfactorily. While one is hesitating to fight against heavy odds, time is wasted, the opportunity passes away never to return, and the project of vengeance is given up for good. One has only to cast oneself at one's enemies, no matter how heavy the odds, with an unflinching determination to exterminate them all. That determined act alone will place the glory of success in one's hands." [4]

In sharp contrast with the deliberate tardiness of the foregoing two instances of *samurai* vendetta, the Nagasaki Brawl which took place in Nagasaki on December 20, 1700, ran its whole course with breathless speed. The origin was a very trifling matter. Two *samurai*, while walking down a street in Nagasaki, happened to pass a city official and his man-servant, who called them names for splashing the dirty half-thawed snow on the street and getting him soiled with it. Infuriated at the man's outrageous reviling, the two kicked him down into the snow and gave him a sound thrashing. Then, later that same night, the man-servant, together with some ten fellow-servants of his master, made a raid on the residence of the two *samurai* surrounding and mauling them mercilessly. They went to the length of robbing the *samurai* of their swords and marched off in triumph. The two, overwhelmed as they were by the superior number of their enemy, found themselves reinforced by fifteen friends and relatives who, at the alarm, hurried to their rescue, only to arrive at the scene too late. They at once rushed en masse to make a sudden descent upon the enemy's house, and, after slaughtering many people, including the city official and his man-servant, they put an end to their own lives by committing *harakiri*, as many brave *samurai* have done.

A remarkable feature that characterizes this Brawl is to be found, as the *Hagakure* points out, in the fact that the whole affair was conducted on the impulse of the occasion with no deliberation whatsoever. Not only the *samurai*, but their servants as well, rushed pell-mell into the valley of death in a reckless attack upon the enemy, paying no attention to the peril of their own lives or to the final outcome of the whole matter. The mental attitude shown here, to act without heeding the possible consequences, described above as "pure and simple," is the one that the *Hagakure* seeks as its ideal, and to become "pure and simple" in this sense is at least one of the basic meanings of the *Hagakure* multi-significant key word "dying."

II

"Bushidō consists in dying—that is what I have found out." If this "dying" in the *Hagakure* dictum really means "becoming pure and simple," as explained above, it is self-evident that "dying" in this sense is far removed from the so-called "dog's death." This conclusion naturally follows when we read the sentence that closes the whole passage from which the above quotation was taken: "When one eternally repeats his vow to die at any moment at the call of his duty every morning and every evening, one can act freely in Bushidō at a moment's notice, thus fulfilling his duties as a feudal vassal without a flaw, even to the very last moment of his life." [5] In the same volume, we also find such passages as these: "Bushidō is a single straight way to death, practicing over and over again every day and night how to die a *samurai's* death on every possible occasion and for every possible cause." [6] "Readiness to die at the call of one's duty should be kept ever fresh and alive by repeating the vow every day and every moment." [7] From such passages it is easy to conclude that the "death" in the *Hagakure* is not death in the ordinary sense, but is such that one can die every morning and every evening ever recurrently.

Then, what does it mean to say that one dies every morning

and every evening and keeps dying ever recurrently? It is clear, of course, that the "death" meant in this instance is not death in an ordinary or physiological sense. Nevertheless, it is equally indisputable that the word here means at least a kind of death which is the utmost limit of human existence. A human being essentially contains in his constitution such an utmost limit, which constantly presses upon him and makes him return to the daily possibilities of his real existence. And, in proportion to the intensity and sincerity with which a man tackles this utmost limit of his existence, its possibilities are just that much more enriched and diversified in content. It naturally follows that a man can enrich and enlarge the possibilities of his existence to their maximum by dying every morning and every evening and ever recurrently, that is to say, by keeping himself constantly face to face with the utmost limit of his existence in the world. This may be considered as a reasonable interpretation of the previously quoted sentence: "When one eternally repeats his vow to die at any moment at the call of his duty every morning and every evening, one can act freely in Bushidō at a moment's notice, thus fulfilling his duties as a feudal vassal without a flaw, even to the very last moment of his life." [8]

Instead of preaching abstract precepts, the *Hagakure* amplifies this truth with rich concreteness by relating numerous illustrative instances. Among others, here is one concerning a physician named Ikujima Sakuan. He was the attendant physician who administered medicine to his lord, Baron Nabeshima Mitsushige of the Soga Clan who had a severe attack of smallpox. Severe or slight, any illness of the liege lord was of serious concern to all his retainers. What a shock it was when they learned that their master's illness had taken a sudden turn for the worse. The attendant nurses, greatly disheartened at the critical condition of the invalid lord, sent in hot haste for Sakuan, who came without delay, and, after examination, declared, "Oh, thank Heaven! Our lord's illness is gone! His complete recovery is near. I, Sakuan, myself will answer for it. Let every one of you rejoice!" All the attendant people, hearing this, thought to themselves in dismay, "Sakuan must have gone mad. His pronouncement is utterly groundless." Sakuan, however, paying no heed to what they thought or said, surrounded himself with a screen and set about concocting his medicine. After a while he respectfully administered a dose of his concoction to his master, whose condition turned on a sudden for the better as soon as the medicine took effect. Later on, Sakuan is said to have given his own account of the matter thus: "Since I declared that I alone would answer for the recovery of our lord, I was prepared to immolate myself in order to attend on our lord beyond the grave by disemboweling myself on the spot, if my concoction should prove of no avail." [9]

The leading motif of this episode is evidently to be found in spotlighting the absolute potency that is given only to a man who is ready at any moment to relinquish his life—in emphasizing the all-powerful virtue of concentration that a man can bring to bear upon his task when he takes the whole responsibility upon his shoulders at the peril of his own life. And it is also evident that in this episode is narrated an instance of a man's life dedicated to "fulfilling his duties as a feudal vassal without a flaw even to the very last moment." Thus, we may perhaps be permitted to say that "dying," in the sense of *Hagakure*, means doing one's duty, ever ready to lay down one's life—concentrating upon one's task, taking all the responsibility upon oneself at the peril of one's life.

III

As seen above, the multi-significant word "dying" in the *Hagakure* means, first, "becoming pure and simple"; second, "doing one's duty, ever ready to lay down one's life—concentrating upon one's task, taking all the responsibility upon oneself at the peril of one's life"; and, third, it may be added that the word has another—perhaps central—meaning at bottom: "dedicating one's life unconditionally to one's master's service." That may be evidenced by a passage like this: "One can never be called a good vassal unless he dedicates himself to his lord, making it his sole object worth living and dying for, to consolidate the dominion of his lord by bravely dying to all other mundane desires and making himself a ghostly being who keeps worrying over his master's affairs around the clock and who stints no labor in putting them in order." [10] This clearly shows that the dictum "Bushidō consists in dying—that is, what I have found out"—can justly be paraphrased into the sentence: "Bushidō has its foundation in dedicating one's life unconditionally to one's master's service."

In the *Hagakure* this loyal devotion of a vassal to his liege lord is variously expressed in other passages: "I serve my master, not from a sense of duty, but out of a blind love of service; I hold my master dear simply because he is dear to my heart above everything else, not because he is kind to me or provides for my living." [11] "The *alpha* and *omega* of a *samurai's* life is service, service, service —nothing but service." [12] "A *samurai* has nothing else in his heart or mind but his master." [13] "To a *samurai* the pledge of loyalty is everything." [14] "A *samurai* gives himself up *in toto* at the free disposal of his master." [15]

The intensity and profundity of passion that strike us as we read these expressions in the original Japanese are past all translation and leave us in sheer wonder and admiration. What a single-hearted loyalty is expressed in the following: "Though Śākyamuni or Confucius himself were here in person to preach what we have never heard of before, we should not be a bit shaken in our conviction. Let them cast us into hell and eternal damnation: the one thing needful for us is loyalty to our liege lord." [16] What an earnest faith is confessed in these words: "I am only a vassal of my lord. Let him be kind to me or cruel to me as he will; let him not know me at all; it is all the same to me. For my part, not a moment passes without my heart being filled even to overflowing with the bliss of having him for my lord whom I hold dear with my eyes swimming in tears, being penetrated with an exulting sense of thankfulness." [17] Utterances like these have to our ears some unearthly sound from beyond our world. In the same book we find an anecdote about Suzuki Shōsan (1579–1655), a Buddhist priest of the Zen sect, noted in the early years of the Tokugawa Shōgunate (1615–1867) for his theory of the identity between spiritual and worldly laws. According to the anecdote, he is reported to have said, "What is there in the world purer than renouncing one's own life for the sake of one's lord?", when he heard the following narrative, which is originally to be found in a book entitled *Roankyō* (Crossing the Bridge on a Donkey): [18]

In the Province of Hizen there was once a warrior who was unfortunately suffering from smallpox when a war broke out and called him to arms. All his friends and relatives tried to dissuade him from leaving home for the front, saying, "Even if you were to go to the front, your illness would prevent you from being of any service." But he would not listen to their advice, saying in reply, "If I should die on my way to the front, I should be quite happy. When I think of my lord's kindness to me, I can never stay at home with an easy mind. How do you think I can ever be satisfied but by trying my very best to prove of what little service I can be to my dear lord?" It was mid-winter, and the cold was severe. But during the whole campaign he never had an overcoat on, never resorted to any means of cure or remedy; much less did he pay attention to any sort of sanitary measures. And yet, he got well all the sooner and distinguished himself on the field, as he had wished.

On this tale of loyalty, Suzuki Shōsan commented, it is said, "What is there in the world purer than renouncing one's own life for the sake of one's lord? At the sight of a man heedless of any danger to his life in the cause of loyalty, all the gods of heaven and of earth, to say nothing of the god of smallpox, would be moved to help him." [19]

That Bushidō has for its foundation the laying down of one's own life for the sake of one's lord is rightly pointed out by Josiah Royce in his *The Philosophy of Loyalty*. According to him, Japanese Bushidō regards loyalty as the centrally significant good, and its "loyalty discounts death, for it is from the start a readiness to die for the cause." [20] Then the central meaning of "dying" in the *Hagakure* dictum ("Bushidō consists in dying—that is what I have found out") is to be found in renouncing one's own life for the sake of one's lord, in dedicating oneself unconditionally to one's master. Becoming pure and simple; doing one's duty, ever prepared to die; devoting oneself to one's task, taking all the responsibility upon oneself at the peril of one's own life—all these, in the final analysis, come to this single principle.

IV

The Bushidō of the *Hagakure* found its centrally significant good in renouncing one's own life for the sake of one's lord, in dedicating oneself unconditionally to one's master. In short, it was a moral code of self-sacrifice and self-effacement in its extreme form. Then, what relations are there between such morals of Bushidō and the consciousness of the Japanese in general?

Professor Inatomi Eijirō [21] considers the Japanese to be devoid of "self-consciousness," and cites as evidence the lack of clear distinction between the parts of speech in Japanese as contrasted with the European languages. In English, German, and French, nouns, verbs, adjectives, and other kinds of words stand by themselves, clearly independent of one another; and, when they are written in sentences, each part of speech is written as a unit separate from the rest. Thus, all sentences are composed of individual words, each independent of one another. In Japanese, on the contrary, there are indeed some words (characters) that can be clearly distinguished as forming independent "parts of speech," but there are also not a few that cannot be strictly separated from other words. Consequently, there is great difficulty in writing Japanese sentences with all their elements strictly separate from one another. We experience this difficulty very keenly, especially when we try to write Japanese in roman letters, a proof that Japanese is not composed of individual words distinctly independent of one another. A Japanese sentence is a composite whole, and not an aggregate of individual words or phrases. This corresponds with the fact that in actual life a Japanese has no clear consciousness of his individual self, but recognizes his own existence only in the composite life of the world. So concludes Inatomi.

After examining the Japanese language from various angles, as described above, Inatomi concludes that it is a perfect symbol of the Japanese people in its peculiarity of lacking a definite sense of the individual self. To quote his own words, this "perfectly corresponds with the lack of the individual, the blank of the self, that is to be seen in the clothing, food, and shelter of the Japanese in their daily life." And as one of its greatest sources, Inatomi traces this lack of a clear sense of the individual self in Japanese character to the feudal system that governed our country for hundreds of years. Under the feudal system individual man could not have his own value. Instead, he could have his *raison d'être* only in the hierarchical system from feudal lord down to servants. In other words, man could have his own *raison d'être* only insofar as he had relationships of some kind with the feudal lord. His value as a human being increased as his position got closer to the lord and decreased as it got closer to the servants. Therefore, it was conceived that the highest virtue of the human being consists in serving the superior, the feudal lord, instead of regarding one's individual self as independent from others while living faithful to one's self. All the virtues consist in self-renunciation, self-annihilation, and unselfishness, and devotion and service to the lord. One should not take one's own happiness or unhappiness into consideration. In some cases it was regarded as the heroic deed to kill even one's own parents for the great cause.

After such arguments, Inatomi quotes the following passages from the *Hagakure* as the text most clearly expressing these basic virtues:

Whenever one is taken into service to the lord, he should serve the lord without any consideration of his own self. Even if one is dismissed or is ordered to commit *harakiri,* one should accept the action as one of the services to the lord, and should be sincerely concerned with the destiny of the lord's house wherever one may be. Such should be the fundamental spirit of the Nabeshima *samurai.* As far as I am concerned, I have never thought of attaining buddha*hood,* which would not fit me at all, but I am completely prepared to be born seven times as a Nabeshima *samurai* in order to work for the cause of the domain.[22]

If this theory of Inatomi is correct, it may be inferred that the self-sacrifice and self-effacement of Bushidō are closely connected with the lack of a clear sense of the individual self in the Japanese character.

V

In Royce's *The Philosophy of Loyalty* there is the following passage:

Now, Bushido did indeed involve many anti-individualistic features. But it never meant to those who believed in it any sort of mere slavishness. The loyal Japanese Samurai, as he is described to us by those who know, never lacked his own sort of self-assertion. He never accepted what he took to be tyranny. He had his chiefs; but as an individual, he was proud to serve them. He often used his own highly trained judgment regarding the applications of the complex code of honor under which he was reared. He was fond of what he took to be his rights as a man of honor. He made much, even childlike, display of dignity. His costume, his sword, his bearing, displayed this sense of his importance. Yet his ideal at least, and in large part his practice, as his admirers depict him, involved a great deal of elaborate cultivation of a genuine spiritual serenity. His whole early training involved a repression of private emotions, a control over his moods, a deliberate cheer and peace of mind, all of which he conceived to be a necessary part of his knightly equipment. Chinese sages, as well as Buddhistic traditions, influenced his views of the cultivation of this interior self-possession and serenity of soul. And yet he was also a man of the world, a warrior, an avenger of insults to his honor; and above all, he was loyal. His loyalty, in fact, consisted of all these personal and social virtues together.[23]

This description naturally leads us to conclude that in the life of a Japanese *samurai* the virtues of self-sacrifice and self-effacement were not necessarily incompatible with those of self-assertion and interior self-possession. This conclusion quite agrees with the fact that representative advocates of individualism in modern Japan—Fukuzawa Yukichi, Niijima Jōe, Uchimura Kanzō, Nitobe Inazō, and the like—came, without exception, of *samurai* stock and were ardent admirers of Bushidō. For instance, Uchimura Kanzo writes in the Epilogue to the German version of his work on Representative Japanese as follows:

> I am one of the least among the children of the *samurai* stock, and one of the least among the disciples of Jesus Christ our Lord. But one of the least as I am in both those capacities, the *samurai* that dwells in my present self will not suffer itself to be either overlooked or made little of. Just what benefits me as a *samurai's* son is self-respect and independence. It becomes me as a *samurai's* son to be a hater of all trickery, fraud, and dishonesty. The code of Bushidō is no less than the law of Christianity that tells us: "Love of money is the root of all evil." So what is becoming to me as a *samurai's* son is to confront, with my countenance steeled, that other law, "Money is power," which modern Christianity is so impudent as to declare in public. . . .[23a]

The self-respect and independence which are glorified by Uchimura in this passage are the very kernel and the supreme objective of modern individualism. And Uchimura calls them "just what befits me as a samurai's son." Then it is only natural that Bushidō should have served in Japan as a hotbed upon which our modern individualism has been reared. And it is also understandable why Royce says, "This Japanese loyalty of the *Samurai* was trained by the ancient customs of Bushido to such freedom and plasticity of conception and expression that, when the modern reform came, the feudal loyalties were readily transformed, almost at a stroke, into that active devotion of the individual to the whole nation and to its modern needs and demands—that devotion, I say, which made the rapid and wonderful transformation of Japan possible."[24] It seems, then that, we should perhaps re-examine the theory that ascribes a lack of a clear sense of the individual self in the Japanese character to "feudal loyalties."

However, we cannot ignore the fact that one of the most important factors which transformed the "feudal loyalties" into "active devotion of the individual to the whole nation and to its modern needs and demands" "almost at a stroke" was Christianity. How Christianity contributed toward modernizing Japan is evidenced by the fact that monogamy became an established moral principle only after Christianity was introduced into the country.

I should like to illustrate these statements with some factual examples:

In pre-Meiji (–1868) Japanese society, the guiding principle of moral life was Confucianism which developed in ancient Chinese society and was based primarily on the family system. The most important virtue in family-system-centered Confucianism is piety to one's parents and ancestors. To put this in more concrete terms, the highest virtue in Confucianism consists in preventing one's posterity from dying out—the effort not to break the family line. As a result, there became prevalent the idea that one might rightfully divorce a wife who did not give birth to a child within three years of married life. In line with this idea, it was regarded as only right that in case the wife would not agree to get divorced, her husband kept a mistress and let her bring forth his child. Polygamy was a commonplace matter in pre-Meiji Japan, in accordance with the moral control of Confucianism.[25]

At present, polygamy is not recognized morally. Such a drastic change in the morals of the Japanese might not have been brought about without the influence of Christianity. The following statement of Nishikawa Jōken [26] (1648–1724), who championed the idea of monogamy, which was extraordinary in the Tokugawa period, would fully support this view: "There are many people in China and Japan who keep mistresses besides their wives. However, I am told that in the West bigamy deserves criminal punishment. We should be ashamed of polygamy before the Western people." There will be no doubt that the idea of monogamy is ascribed to the influences of Western morality, the fundamentals of which are, as Arai Hakuseki, who appeared a little later than Jōken, also claimed, evidently based on Christianity.

As seen in the foregoing, we cannot locate the source of the idea of monogamy outside of Christianity. In this sense, we have to admit that the role Christianity played for the modernization of Japan was not insignificant. In relation to this, we are rather surprised to find that the exponents of individualism in modern Japan whom we mentioned above were ardent Christians, while they were still proud of being the sons of samurai. It is clear that in the minds of these exponents these two elements were harmoniously blended and produced "active devotion of the individual to the whole nation and to its modern needs and demands."

VI

But there is no denying the fact that the Japanese have certain habitual traits deeply rooted in their national character which may be called a "spirit of the governed" and "a spirit of the taught." By a "spirit of the governed" is meant that mental tendency of the Japanese which prevents them from exercising their sovereign rights and duties as autonomous people, a tendency which was fostered in their character during the long period of time when they were subjected to the iron rule of the sword. By a "spirit of the taught" is meant that moral habit of the Japanese which makes them content with the passive attitude, in which they do nothing but accept with a slavish docility that which is taught by the governing authorities. This is a habit which is devoid of positive initiative on the part of the masses to produce their own morals out of themselves and which is a result of the powerful leadership of the politically dominant, who have always been in the habit of setting themselves up as moral teachers of the populace.

The origin of these traits in the Japanese character must be traced to the deplorable fact that in Japanese society the individual has never been firmly established in his own proper rights. Prior to her defeat in August, 1945, Japan attached an almost almighty authority to the Imperial Edict on National Education (*Kyōiku Chokugo*) for the moral training of the people. It would not be too much to say that in prewar Japan that Edict was a virtual bible in national education. On every ceremonial occasion in every school throughout Japan, the Edict was read aloud in utmost solemnity by the principal or headmaster, with pictures of the emperor and the empress hung in the background before the boys and girls of the whole school assembled in a hall, with their heads bent low in an attitude of deepest respect and attention.

However, Inoue Kowashi (1844–1895), who drew up the original draft of the Edict, considered that, before everything else, this Edict "should not be treated as one of those ordinary edicts on political matters." Since freedom of conscience was granted to every citizen by the Imperial Constitution, the monarch was not in a position to interfere in the spiritual matters of the people. Accordingly, this Edict, intended to point out the righteous way of a citizen in nurturing the rising generation, should be regarded as "a written proclamation of the monarch on social affairs in distinction from his political ordinances." So, regarding the manner of its publication, too, Inoue thought "either of two ways should be adopted—first, that it should be given only to the Minister of Education, and not to the people at large; second, that, instead of being given to the Ministry of Education, it should be given in the form of an address to the Peers' School or to the Association of Educators at the royal visit paid by the monarch to those institutions." In short, the intention of the drafter of the Edict was far from positive for fear lest this imperial proclamation should be combined with a compulsive force to interfere with the freedom of a citizen's conscience. In the light of the actual developments of subsequent history, these fears on the part of the drafter were not in vain. The process of idolizing it and worshipping it as a document of absolute infallibility, which began shortly after its promulgation in 1890, took its ever-widening course with acceleration up to the catastrophe in 1945.

Who was responsible for such a state of affairs? Of course, those who were at the helm of the government were largely responsible for that state of things, it must be admitted; but no less responsible were the people in general, who could neither break themselves of their "spirit of the governed" nor free themselves of their "spirit of the taught," and remained abject followers of governmental guidance.

In the educational world of post-war Japan, which found itself freed from the overpowering authority of the Imperial Edict, there has again been raised a cry, though not so strong, to be sure, for something to replace the Edict in order to clarify the moral standards upon which the people may act. This cry, though not without plausible reasons in its favor, has its origin, after all, in the fact that in Japan the full establishment of the individual is yet to come.

It is of great interest that Takamura Kōtarō (1883–1956) and Saitō Mokichi (1882–1953)—two representative intellectuals modern Japan has produced—lived and died under the guidance of their life-long mottoes, "becoming pure and simple" and "doing one's utmost," both of which were mentioned at the beginning of this essay as constituting the essential meaning of the multisignificant phrase *"shinu koto"* (dying) in the *Hagakure*. Takamura, who was a poet as well as a sculptor, considered himself a sculptor pure and simple, declaring that he composed poems to make his sculpture pure and simple. In a note giving the reason why he "did not give up writing poems," he says that it was "because I composed poems for preserving my sculpture—making it pure and simple, untarnished by any extraneous influences, and, above all, making it independent of literature, whose influence . . . made sculpture sick."

Saitō, a poet in the traditional Japanese style, worshipped Kakinomoto-no-Hitomaro as the greatest of all Japanese poets, and wrote a work of five voluminous tomes on his life and achievement. His reasons for highly regarding the famous poet of ancient Japan were based upon the theory that Hitomaro was a poet who put into his poems all that was in him. In one of Mokichi's letters, written as a confession of his passionate love for a young woman when he was fifty-three years old, which were first published some time ago and which attracted universal attention, we can read passages such as the following: "There is nothing false or tricky mingled in the love of a true lover. It is because he puts in his love all that is in him."

In this way, Kōtarō maintained his principle of "becoming pure and simple", and Mokichi maintained his principle of doing one's utmost and putting all that is in oneself into life and artistic activities. Is it a mere coincidence that their principles were in complete agreement with the leading tenets inculcated in the textbook of Bushidō which had been written two centuries and a half before these modern intellectuals were born?

QUESTION: You emphasized Bushidō as of the essence of the Japanese ethical tradition, and, in that, you emphasized the ethics of duty and loyalty. Does this ethics of duty and loyalty violate the right of private or personal ethical convictions or conscience by requiring that the individual do whatever his duty—or the one in authority over him—requires, no matter what that is, and without any possibility of an ethical challenge if what is required seems to him to be unethical?

ANSWER: Even in Bushidō as a type of feudal morals in Japan, blind obedience was not required. A *samurai* could remonstrate with the lord about his misconduct, at the risk of his life. In reply to the question, I refer you to the quotation from Royce in my paper. As Royce observed: "The loyal Japanese *samurai* never lacked his own sort of self-assertion. He never accepted what he took to be tyranny."

QUESTION: In your exposition you emphasized Shintō and said little or nothing about the Buddhist aspect of Japanese ethics.

Buddhism has certainly contributed to Japanese ethics, has it not? What significant aspects of Japanese ethical thought and life may be ascribed to Buddhist influence?

ANSWER: Shintō was the essence of traditional Japanese ethics, although Buddhism has also played an important part in Japanese ethics, of course. For example, in Bushidō of the *Hagakure* there are four oaths:

1) We should not be inferior to others in Bushidō.
2) We should be loyal to our lord.
3) We should be obedient to our parents.
4) We should have mercy on others and do good to them.

The last oath had its origin in Tannen Oshō's (Priest Tannen) teachings. Tannen Oshō was the eleventh chief Zen priest of Nabeshima's family temple, the Kōdenji. According to him, a priest must be a man of charity, but without courage he cannot be a good priest. On the other hand, a warrior must be courageous, but, if he has no charity, he cannot fulfill his duty. Therefore, the priest and the warrior must help each other.

QUESTION: What is the status of the ethics of duty and loyalty in contemporary Japanese ethics: (a) up to 1945 and (b) since 1945?

ANSWER: One of the most familiar traits in postwar Japan is the tendency to revise tradition, to reconsider the foundations of old beliefs, and sometimes mercilessly to destroy what once seemed indispensable. This disposition is especially prominent in the realm of moral education. As stated in my paper, Japan attached an almost almighty authority to the Imperial Edict on National Education for the moral training of the people until her catastrophic defeat in August, 1945. The principal virtues in this Edict were loyalty to the Imperial Family and piety to parents and ancestors. These virtues were neglected almost entirely immediately after the war had finished. The Government felt that the moral hiatus must be filled. In June, 1963, the then Minister of Education, Araki Masuo, asked his advisory agency, the Central Council on Education, to formulate such an image. The Council then appointed a subcommittee to work on the project. Recently, the subcommittee submitted what it called an "interim draft" to the Council, which disclosed it to the public. In this draft we read, "We have carried the flag and sung the anthem and loved and revered the Emperor as symbols of Japan. This was not apart from our loving Japan and paying respect to her mission. The Emperor is a symbol of Japan and of the unity of the people. We must give our deep thought to the fact that our loving and revering our fatherland, Japan, is identical with loving and revering the Emperor."

Notes

1. Inazō Nitobe (Nitobe Inazō), *Bushidō: The Soul of Japan* (Philadelphia: The Leeds and Biddle Company, 1899; 10th ed.; New York: G. P. Putnam's Sons, 1905).
2. *Hagakure*, revised by Watsuji Tetsurō and Furukawa Tesshi. 3 vols. (Tokyo: Iwanami-shōten, 1940–1941).
3. *Ibid*, chap. I.
4. *Ibid.*
5. *Ibid.*
6. *Ibid.*
7. *Ibid.*, chap. XI.
8. *Ibid.*, chap. I.
9. *Ibid.*, chap. VIII.
10. *Ibid.*, chap. I.
11. *Ibid.*
12. *Ibid.*
13. *Ibid.*
14. *Ibid.*, chap. II.
15. *Ibid.*
16. *Ibid.*
17. *Ibid.*
18. *Roankyō*, revised by Suzuki Daisetz Teitarō (Tokyo: Iwanami-shōten, 1948), p. 254.
19. *Ibid.*, p. 173.
20. Josiah Royce, *The Philosophy of Loyalty* (New York: The Macmillan Company, 1930).
21. Inatomi Eijirō, *Nihonjin to Nihonbunka* (The Japanese and Japanese Culture) (Tokyo: Risōsha, 1963).
22. *Hagakure*, Introduction.
23. *The Philosophy of Loyalty*, pp. 72–73.
23a. Uchimura Kanzō, *Japanische Charakterkopfe* (Stuttgart: Gundert 1908).
24. *The Philosophy of Loyalty*, pp. 73–74.
25. This fact is clearly seen in the life of Sakuma Shōzan (1811–1864), a representative scholar of Western studies in the later Tokugawa period. *Sakuma Shōzan zenshū* (The Complete Works of Sakuma Shōzan), 4 vols. (Nagano: Shinano-Kyoikukai, 1943). As the case of Sakuma Shōzan shows, it was not an unnatural thing for the

Japanese people until the end of the Tokugawa period to have mistresses besides wives. It was against such a background that Ōhara Yūgaku, a thinker in the later Tokugawa period, gave the following precepts: "If a man cannot get a child, first he should treat his wife more kindly; next, he should inculcate the importance of the cause of his house, keeping her mind as calm as possible; then he should make her gradually worry about having no child; and, lastly, upon her complete understanding and agreement, he should try to seek after a mistress." *Ōhara Yūgaku zenshū* (The Complete Works of Ohara Yūgaku) (Chiba: Chiba-Kyoikukai, 1943), p. 21.

26. *Chōninbukuro* (Handbook for Merchants), revised by Iijima Tadao (Tokyo: Iwanami-shōten, 1942).

KŌSAKA MASAAKI *The Status and the Role of*

the Individual in Japanese Society

I. *Introduction*

BEFORE I BEGIN to treat the problem, I would like to clarify my procedure.

First, I am not going to consider the problem of the status of the individual in Japan from a sociological point of view, but from a historical point of view, or, to be more exact, from a topographical point of view.

Second, I would like to describe the frame of reference of my study of the status of the individual. Detailed examination is impossible here but can be included in the questions and answers at the end.

Third, I will treat the history of Japanese culture and society by dividing it into four periods. The characteristic which runs topographically through all the periods is aestheticism. This aestheticism should not be neglected when we consider the relations between individuals and the group, for here lie both the strong point and the weak point of the Japanese attitude.

II. *The Age of Aesthetic Culture (700–1200)*

The aestheticism which constitutes the core of the Japanese mind took definite form in the first period. Therefore, I would call it the age of aesthetic culture. But what was this age really like? I would like to characterize it, first, through the legendary stories of the Court, and, secondly, through the activities of the authoresses.

This first period, which covered nearly five hundred years,

began with the era of Empress Suiko, to which great splendor was added by her Prince Regent, Shōtoku Taishi (574–622). Many of the records which relate the achievements of Prince Shōtoku belong almost to legend. But these records, though legendary, or because they are legendary, show the kind of ruler the Japanese from olden times have regarded as ideal. Conversely, expectations on the part of the people prescribed the characteristics of the emperor.

One of the most famous stories was that he could listen to appeals from several persons at the same time. He was sagacious and fair, too. It may well be noted that the fundamental principle of his politics was the spirit of harmony. "Most prized is harmony" was the fundamental principle of the famous Seventeen-Article Constitution, which is ascribed to the prince. His ideal was not in power politics, but in moral politics (on this point he was influenced by Confucianism).

One of the articles of the Constitution states: "Highly respect the Three Treasures." The three treasures are the Buddha, the Law (*Dharma*), and the Assemblage (*Saṅgha*). The same spirit asserted itself in the words of Emperor Shōmu, who ordered the construction of Tōdaiji (Temple). He said, "We are the servants of the Three Treasures."

Even the most destructive historian, who doubts all the historical facts about Prince Shōtoku, accepts as his words the inscription which reads, "The world is fiction: only the Buddha is truth." It is considered to have been written by him in honor of his wife, Tachibana-no-Iratsume. This phrase expressed his outlook on life.

Prince Shōtoku said, "Highly respect the Three Treasures." And Emperor Shōmu declared, "We are the servants of the Three Treasures." They devoted themselvs to the supreme existence, to which they were only servants.

Reviewing Japanese history, we find many emperors noted as master calligraphers or masters of *tanka* (short poem) poetry. They were patrons of culture and at the same time were required to be well cultivated themselves. Even today, the New Year Poetry Party and the New Year Lectures are held. The former is the ceremony where *tanka* of emperor, empress, and princes and princesses are presented to the public, with those of the general public chosen from among the poems appropriate to the occasion. The New Year Lectures, which cover a wide range of subjects, from history, politics, and literature to natural science of the latest development, are given by prominent scholars and are attended by the royal families.

Historically, the actual power of politics was not in the hands of the emperor, but was for some time in the hands of the nobles and later for a longer period of time in the hands of the *samurai* class. When the emperor tried to regain political power, unfortunate incidents sometimes ensued. The role of the emperor was originally to venerate the gods. In other words, he was more symbolic than political. It is clear from this that the emperor was not an absolute monarch, who oppressed the people. The Japanese emperor was more humane. Note that the duties of emperors were basically ceremonial, while the nobles of the court and the Shōgunate served as actual rulers.

Parenthetically, there was no slave system in the full meaning of the word. The Japanese did not know how to conquer other races to make them slaves.

So far I have talked about the Imperial Household in the period which I call the age of aesthetic culture. Now, I will touch on the literary activities of women in this era.

There are two very old books which are popular among the Japanese even today. One is the *Manyōshū* (A Collection of Myriad Leaves), the other the *Genji monogatari* (*Tale of Genji*). The former is an anthology containing verses and *tanka* poems numbering more than forty-five hundred. This twenty-volume anthology is a collection of works of many years, perhaps over three hundred years, the main period being the seventh and eighth centuries. The latest one of the poems which was dated was composed in 759. It contained some very old poems whose dates cannot be precisely determined.

Now, from the sociological point of view, what are the characteristics of this anthology? The first feature is that the social background of the writers is highly heterogeneous. There are, of course, poems by emperors, empresses, and nobles of the Court. But there are also those of *sakimori,* those soldiers who were called up for defense of the Kyushu district, and those of their wives expressing their sorrow at parting from their husbands. There are poems of professional poets such as Kakinomoto-no-Hitomaro (7th century) and Yamabe-no-Akahito (8th century), who are respected as representative poets even today. There are also poems of nameless people. *Azumauta,* poems of people in the Kantō district, which had not been civilized in those days, and other folk songs are also included in the anthology. The variety of poets was the product of a highly democratic editing principle, and it also means that the society of Japan in those days was not stratified into strictly segregated classes.

The second feature is the status of women. Many poems by women are in this anthology. They must number one fourth or one fifth of the total. This is rare and has no parallel in the world. The form of marriage in those days was that wherein the intended husband visited the house of his intended wife to meet her. This type of marriage contributed to the production of love poems (*sōmon-no-uta*), and the status of women was not inferior to that of men in these poems.

Among these poets was a beautiful and talented woman, Nukada-no-Ōkimi, who was loved by two emperors successively. Some delicate, some passionate poems of such women rank highest in the anthology. Japanese culture in the Manyō era (8th and 9th centuries) was supported by women to a considerable extent. They were not slaves of the other sex.

But it was in the age of the *Genji monogatari* that the activities of women in the cultural field reached their apex. Women, rather than men, played a leading part. And it goes without saying that the woman who represented this tendency was Murasaki Shikibu (10th and 11th century), and that the masterpiece of the period was her *Genji monogatari*. Other women writers were Seishō Nagon (11th century), author of the *Pillow Books*, Akasome emon (11th century), Michitsuna-no-haha, mother of Michitsuna (10th century), and so on. Women writers appeared in great number and formed a new genre of literature, namely, diary literature. The literature of this age was made colorful and rich by their works. Many of them were women in the Court. We must remember, therefore, that there once existed in Japan a type of culture which may be called the woman-culture.

III.   *The Age of Religious Culture* (1200–1600)

As pointed out above, in the age of aesthetic culture, the emperor was never a tyrant with absolute power, but was at the center of cultural activities, and women were not slaves of men but were educated persons with brilliant personalities.

These facts are very much at variance with the patterns of

Japanese culture which Ruth Benedict described. Moreover, she said that Japanese culture was a shame-culture and not a guilt-culture, and that the Japanese had neither conscience nor guilt-consciousness. But is this true? I think not. Good evidence against her interpretation is given in the second period, the age of religious culture.

This second period began when Minamoto Yoritomo opened the *bakufu* (A.D. 1192), the federal government at Kamakura in the twelfth century, and continued until the seventeenth century, when the Tokugawa Government (1615–1867) was firmly established at Edo. The characteristics of this period can be best described by examining prominent priests and the *samurai* class, who were the *Kulturträger* of the age.

The sect of Buddhism which holds the greatest number of devotees in Japan is the Jōdo-Shin sect, which was founded by Shinran (1173–1262). It is safe to say that Shinran was the greatest of those who made Buddhism the religion of the common people in Japan. It was at the time of Prince Shōtoku that Buddhism was introduced into Japan. Five hundred years passed from the days of Prince Shōtoku to those of Shinran, and there were changes in the Japanese view of Buddhism and its functions after Shinran.

Buddhism of the first period was characterized by three features. First, it played the role of vehicle of continental culture. Perhaps it was more cultural than religious. It was not so different from the way the Japanese in the Meiji era (1868–1911) accepted Christianity. In the case of Prince Shōtoku, the Buddhist and Confucian elements were mixed together. As beautiful Buddhist images and Buddhist temples in Nara show, admiration for Buddhism was inseparable from the longing for beauty. It was, so to speak, an aesthetic religion. And the legends of Kōbō's spanning bridges, digging ponds, and curing diseases show that he was respected as an excellent engineer and doctor. In short, Buddhism was more cultural and aesthetic than simply religious.

Second, it was the religion of the aristocracy, the main believers being the courtiers and the nobles. Emperor Shōmu was said to have had temples and convents constructed all over the country, which should be considered as an enlightenment movement from the aristocracy. Priests played a very important part in it. And temples gradually became the privileged owners of vast lands and even had military power. Buddhism was not the religion of the people.

Third, it was a religion of mundane interests. Or, it would be better described as an incantatory religion. For individuals, the purpose was to cure disease and to avoid misfortune. For the nation, the purpose was to pacify and defend it. It was believed that floods, droughts, earthquakes, and epidemics could be avoided by the power of prayer.

However, this aesthetic, aristocratic, and incantatory religion was to be greatly changed by Shinran and others. Incantation gave place to genuine faith, and the purpose was no longer mundane interests but the relief of the souls of the individuals suffering from the consciousness of guilt. In this way, aristocratic religion became the religion of the common people. Its characteristics are as follows:

First, the types of priests were different. There were many excellent priests in the aesthetic and incantatory religion, and they sought relief in research on the philosophical principles in the scriptures, or by strict observance of moral commandments. But Shinran, who called himself "a silly man," realized that even the highest wisdom of man was haunted with errors and was nothing but an illusion, and that man was an incarnation of avarice and guilt or sin who would not keep any commandments perfectly. So, he concluded that there was no way of relief except through genuine faith. This was his view of Buddhist invocation.

Man could not be saved by knowledge or morality, but only by believing in the Buddha's love. Shinran called himself "a person who falls short of any austerities," and said, "Hell is the fixed dwelling." [5] Man is a lump of guilt. All men are essentially wicked. It is not the power of any man but the love of the Buddha, who pities such a wicked man, that can save him. His famous words— "Even a good person can attain *nirvāṇa*. Then, how much more so a wicked man" [6] originated from these ideas.

Second, this consciousness of guilt is deeply connected with the self-consciousness of the individual. Shinran said that it was not for his father and mother, and not for his country and society, that he prayed to Amida Buddha, but only for himself. So, he said, it was "solely for Shinran" that the Buddha pledged to save man. And he said, "Shinran will have no disciples." [7]

Third, accused of heresy, Shinran was driven from Kyoto and exiled to a rural district, where he married. This may remind us of Martin Luther. His new Buddhism (with the principle that man was not saved by the study of difficult traditional scriptures or by the observance of the minutely regulated commandments but only by praying to Amida Buddha) was spread among peasants and the common people.

My direct purpose here has been to show how mistaken Ruth Benedict is in saying that Japanese culture is a shame-culture and not a guilt-culture. The Japanese do have a consciousness of guilt. It is the nucleus of Shinran's religion, and Shinran's sect, the Jōdo-Shin sect, is the largest sect of all the Japanese sects of Buddhism.

I shall deal now with the *samurai* class to explain the kind of outlook they had on life and death. The *samurai* society was a defensive community, but it was based on two different principles. On the other hand, there existed a kind of affectionate relation like that between parents and children, as is shown by the phrase " *'Ie' no ko,*" (the children of the family), which was used to signify the rank and file of the *samurai* group. But, on the other hand, the relation was a contractual one like that of lord and vassal, employer and employee.

Accordingly, there appeared an interesting mixed relation in a *samurai* group, a mixture of a natural relation like that between parents and children and an obligatory relation like that between lord and vassal, employer and employee. The lord put his vassals under an obligation and had an obligation to compensate for it. There was a kind of implied contract composed of a presentation and a counterpresentation. This compound relation supported "an extended *'ie'*" (family or household) which formed the core of the *samurai* group. A lord does his vassals a favor, and they are loyal to him. The morality of devotion observable in this relation became Bushidō, or chivalry, in the course of time.

What was the status of the individual in *samurai* society? Was an individual like an atom buried in an extended or a small family? Not in the least. Even in the *samurai* group as an extended family, those who excelled in bravery were especially respected, for it was a fighting community, and there arose a rivalry for leadership. On the other hand, a *samurai* was required to be affectionate. Therefore, it can be said that a good *samurai* was one who was both brave and affectionate.

In the case of family succession, the eldest son was not always the heir. Sometimes the successor was he who was the ablest and most talented in the eyes of the parent. Similarly, in the field of the arts, the supreme secret of the family school was handed down, not only to the kindred of the family, but also to the eminent pupil.

However, it should be remembered that the status of women underwent a fundamental change as *samurai* families were gradually formed. The former type of marriage, in which the intended husband visited the house of his intended wife, was replaced by a new procedure in which the intended wife came to the house of her intended husband to live. With this change, men came to be more respected than women. Men are more important than women in an age of wars.

Also, the primogeniture system replaced the old parcenary system, in order to keep the fortune of a family intact. This change, together with the change of the status of women in the family, strengthened the power of the father. This new system continued through the Tokugawa period (1615–1867) up to the Meiji era (1868–1911). It is not true, however, that the rights of women were completely neglected. The Jōei Code (1232) (Collection of Maxims and Rules for Administrators) decreed that the rights of the wife be protected.

Also, it should not be forgotten that the people of those days attached great importance to the family and the family line. They were proud of their good lineage. However, there was a brief interlude in the growth of the authority of the family. At about the time of the civil war of Ōnin (1467–1477), there appeared the trend of the lower overpowering the upper. The former wrested the position of superiority from the latter. The *shugo daimyō* (protector feudal lords) were replaced by the *sengoku daimyō* (fighting feudal lords). For the *shugo daimyō* had been restricted to the "*Ie'-no-ko*" of the Genji family, but they had lost real power, so that they could not resist the onslaught of the *sengoku daimyō*, who gained power not by their status but by their ability. Some Japanese historians even assert that the social structure was completely changed during the time of the civil war ("Sengoku era," 1467–1560).

Toyotomi Hideyoshi, who conquered the whole country and unified it, was of peasant origin. Also, there was the example of Sakai City (later Osaka), the citizens of which gained power by wealth acquired in foreign trade. In those days the abilities of individuals were freely developed, as is evident in pictures and other works of fine art of the Azuchi-Momoyama era (1568–1615). But these free activities of individuals were to be restricted by the feudal system and by the national isolation policy of the Tokugawa Government.

IV. The Age of Politics (1600–1850)

The Japanese mind was thus formed in the first and second periods. As Watsuji Tetsurō rightly pointed out, Japanese culture has a multi-strata structure. The old element is not lost when a new one is introduced, but the new is added onto the old. When the third period began, at the beginning of the seventeenth century, the same pattern appeared, but with a slight difference. The Tokugawa era provided another stratum added to the Japanese culture already developed.

But it did more than that. It gave a framework to it, thereby giving it a certain character and modifying the preceding culture. Consequently, some contradiction appeared between the framework, namely, the feudal system, and the substance, namely, the emotional life, religion, and the arts. The contradiction, the symbol of which Ruth Benedict saw in her *The Chrysanthemum and the Sword*, was thus originated. Let us look at the several traits of this period.

First, this period was the age of politics, for political unity and control were effected for the first time in Japanese history. And the political mechanism rigidly regulated the arts, religion, morals, and thought.

Second, the *Kulturträger* of this period was the *samurai* and the *chōnin* (townspeople). The former had been the *Kulturträger* since the Kamakura era (1185–1335), but had undergone a very significant change. The *samurai* class in the Tokugawa era was not engaged in war, but was busy with administration. The *samurai* were bureaucrats of a kind. Two hundred and fifty years of the Tokugawa era consituted a period of undisturbed peace unparalleled in world history. It was natural that the *samurai* should become bureaucrats since they had to rule in peace.

While the center of this *samurai* bureaucracy was in Edo, the center of merchant activities was in Osaka. In the feudal system of Tokugawa, there was a rigid hierarchy of *shi-nō-kō-shō:* the *samurai* coming first, the peasant, the craftsmen, and the merchant, in order. The merchants were put at the bottom, since they were considered to produce nothing, but to gain huge benefits by simply trading the products of others. It was the same with the *samurai*, who also produced nothing. Then, wherein consisted the prestige of the *samurai?* *Samurai* were expected to act like gentlemen. That was the source of their prestige.

But, as the economy flourished in the peace of the Tokugawa era, the merchants gained real economic power. Even the *daimyō* refrained from offending the merchants of Osaka, for they were their debtors. As the culture of the Tokugawa era was that of merchants, Osaka became its center. Consequently, Osaka could compete with Edo, the latter being the center of politics and the former being the center of economics. In this sense, Japan was in a bipolar situation.

Third, "*ie*" stood above the individual as the ethical reality. The individual was the secondary existence within the structure of the "*ie*" to which he belonged. The wife and children were under the authoritarian rule of the father, who represented the ethical reality called "*ie.*" Everyone should serve the "*ie*" under the guidance of the father, and it was held a sacred duty of the family member to respect the name of "*ie.*"

This picture might give one a somber impression, but it does not follow from this structure of the "*ie*" that the individual was neglected. It is true that the *daimyō* succeeded as head of the house even if he was not competent. But the real power was not in his hands but in the hands of his retainers, whose duty it was to take good care of the *daimyō's* household. Naturally, real power passed into the hands of able retainers. The same thing happened in the households of big merchants, and the *bantō*, or head clerks, held real power. They served their master's house, of course. But, if it was necessary to keep the "*ie*" intact, they often remonstrated with the *daimyō*, their masters.

It can be said, therefore, that the power of the *daimyō* and the master was nominal rather than substantial. Knowledge and originality, ability and talent, were highly regarded among the merchants of Osaka. Successful merchants were entrepreneurs who gained through their originality and knowledge.

Fourth, the thought of Nakae Tōjyū, who was called the saint of Ōmi, had one aspect which has been unfortunately neglected, but throws clear light on the life and ethics of the Tokugawa era. He thought that *kō*, filial duty or piety toward parents, was the highest virtue of all. But he made a meaningful distinction between *daikō*, the great filial duty, and *shōkō*, the small filial duty. The latter was ordinary filial duty, that is to say, duty to serve the parents well.

But, according to him, the right filial duty was to admonish and make the parents amend their wrong attitude when the parents were in the wrong. This he called *daikō* (the great filial duty). Parents give birth to us, but there are more basic, greater fathers and mothers, who gave birth to the world. He called these greater parents *Tenkun* (the Lord of Heaven), and considered it our duty to serve him. Consequently, to remedy the error of our physical parents is to fulfill the duty of serving the greater parents through our conscience. Also, he deemed the human being a small cosmos, a microcosm, in contrast to the great cosmos, a macrocosm, which words remind us of Liebniz' monads, that the individual is the living mirror that reflects the great cosmos.

V. *The Age of Enlightenment* (CA. 1860)

The hundred years since the fall of the Tokugawa Government —to the present—is the *bunmei kaika* (the age of enlightenment). Tokyo, which name took the place of Edo, became the new capital, and the center of Westernization, modernization, industrialization, and urbanization. Tokyo became the symbol of the age. In this sense, this age might be called the age of Tokyo.

Several interpretations of the Meiji Ishin (Meiji Restoration) have been proposed, but it was a reform rather than a revolution. The reform began in the domain of politics and gradually expanded into social reform, economic reform, and, finally, spiritual reform. The general trend has been the industrialization and Westernization of the country. Seen from a different viewpoint, it has been the clash of what is Japanese and Oriental, on the one hand, and what is Western, on the other, the amalgam of the two being the result. Nevertheless, it has been predominately an age of modernization, (*bunmei kaika*). I will briefly treat of the characteristics of the age, especially the status and role of the individual, as follows:

First, the transition of the ideal person for the Japanese is very significant. In the first twenty years of the Meiji era, statesmen and soldiers were respected above all, the most prominent being Peter the Great, Napoleon, Bismarck, Washington, and Lincoln. But in the second twenties, the Japanese discovered the names of Shakespeare, Goethe, Heine, Byron, Hugo, Tolstoi, Descartes, Kant, Newton, and Darwin as ideal persons. The interests of the people were now expanded to include scholars, men of letters, and artists. It is interesting that Rousseau was known as the author of *The Social Contract* in the first twenty years of the Meiji era, but as the author of *Confessions* in the second twenties. Chief interest was now centered in man himself.

Second, individualism appeared in the twenties, which decade was called by Uchimura Kanzō the decade of spiritual revolution. Also, statism, nationalism, and socialism appeared. Socialism passed through three phases, that is, the phases of Christian socialism, French socialism, and Marxist socialism. It was also in the twenties that *heimin shugi* (presumably a translation of democracy), was introduced. After World War I, in the Taishō era (1912–1925), the translation was changed to *minshu shugi* and this became very popular. But this democratic movement was unfortunately overwhelmed by the tide of chauvinism. The problem that the Japanese have faced since the Meiji Restoration has been to find a suitable place for Japan and Japanese culture in the world, and a place for the individual in society.

Third, the emancipation of women was first advocated also in the twenties of the Meiji era, and in the thirties the Japanese "Blue Stockings" appeared. To them, the predominant problem was the relation between the family and the individual, on which the decisive change took place after the end of World War II. The reform by the Occupation Forces weakened the authority of the father and legally established the dignity of the individual. But it also effected the disintegration of the family ethic.

Fourth, Japan is now enjoying a considerably high social mobility. This is proved by the fact that the leaders since the Meiji Restoration came from the middle and lower classes. The Japanese are most enthusiastic about sending their children to the universities. For ability, instead of status, assures the child success in life.

Fifth, the problems to be solved are the relation between the individual and the state and that between the individual and the various social groups. As the Japanese has deemed strong self-assertion ugly, he seldom expresses his opinion in the presence of others. To eliminate what was bad is relatively easy, but to eliminate or alter what was good but is no longer deemed highly appropriate is very difficult. Here lies one of the fundamental problems for the Japanese. For the virtue of non-self-assertiveness that was once respected is now either inappropriate or insufficient for modern society.

Note

Shintō, the traditional Japanese religion, is a religion which detests impurity and tries to drive it out. It is more fundamental to the Japanese not to stain one's name than not to shame it. Strongly influenced by Shintō, the culture of ancient Japan was not a shame-culture but a culture of impunity. Nietzsche said, "*Jenseits von Gut und Böse.*" The Japanese in ancient times had no category of good and evil in the Christian sense of the words. It is, as mentioned above, under the influence of Confucianism and Buddhism, and especially since the middle age of Japan, that the Japanese have had the categories of good and evil. The most important categories for the Japanese were those of beauty and ugliness. The Japanese in ancient times esteemed health, life, and beauty more than anything else. In sharp contrast to this, it was disease, death, and ugliness that the Japanese disliked. Today we use such expressions as "Have a 'clean mind'!" or "Don't do a 'dirty' act!" It is clear from these expressions that the things explained under the categories of good and evil in later years fell under the categories of beauty and ugliness. Morality in ancient times was aesthetic, just as the culture of those times on the whole was aesthetic.

Supplementary Comments

The definition of the term "aestheticism": There are many kinds of values, for example, utility, pleasure, happiness, freedom, truth, and so on. If there is a culture or society wherein beauty stands at the top of the value system, such a culture is aesthetic. This is what I mean by the term "aestheticism." But what I mean by beauty is not limited to physical beauty, i.e., beautiful flowers, beautiful women, but involves spiritual beauty, also. Therefore, Japanese ethics demands purity of mind, refinement of tastes, harmony of individuals, mutual love.

Morality based upon sympathy and love: It has been said that there are two basic orientations in the Western tradition. One involves the pursuit of ends or goals. It is primarily value-oriented. The other involves the recognition of laws, of duties and obligations. This may be called duty-oriented.

But there is still another, a third orientation. This involves love, mercy, kindness, and so on. This morality may be called love-oriented, and its basic principle is sympathy. We can very easily find such morality in Christian, Buddhist, Hindu, Chinese, and Japanese ethics. But there are slight differences among them; however, sympathy is basic to them all.

Now, when we sympathize with each other, so far we become one. But this does not mean that we lose our individualities. We are not melted into simple oneness. I am I, you are you. In this sense, individuals do exist in the East. "One in manyness, many in oneness" is the fundamental principle of Japanese ethics and metaphysics.

Concerning the alleged emphasis upon rights in the West and duties in the East: Before the introduction of European political thought into Japan, the Japanese did not use such terms as "rights" and "duties." Instead of such terms, we used the term "righteousness." Righteousness, or justice, is required from those at the top and those below at the same time. They are equal from the point of view of justice and righteousness. From the Western standpoint, this equality is limited to morality but not extended to law. This is true, indeed, but I wonder whether it is very desirable to make such a strict distinction between morality and law.

QUESTION: You have emphasized the aesthetic point of view as specifically characteristic of the Japanese mind. What significance does this have for the status of the individual?

ANSWER: The aesthetic point of view, which I emphasize as specifically characteristic of the Japanese mind, causes people to recognize the value of personality. The value of the individual is not dissolved into that of the group, as one can see in the literature of ancient Japan.

QUESTION: How do you make your interpretation accord with the almost universal—of Japanese and outsiders—interpretation to the effect that in Japanese social thought and practice or culture the individual does not have significant status, but only group status, chiefly family, even labor or employee group, and ordinary political unity?

ANSWER: The aim of my paper is to refute the interpretation which you consider almost universal and to provide a different point of view.

QUESTION: The point has been made that guilt is individual, whereas shame is social. Have you a comment on this?

ANSWER: It has been the basic principle in Japan, as well as in China, that one should feel shame in one's conscience. Therefore the dictum "Control yourself" has been emphasized. The same philosophy is found in the expression, "Even if others do not know, Heaven knows, Earth knows, and I myself know."

QUESTION: Aren't you, near the end of your paper, confirming Ruth Benedict's point of view?

ANSWER: Ruth Benedict's error lies in her generalizing those points which are true about the Tokugawa period or part of it. She has taken these points as characteristic of the whole history and the entire society of Japan. If Ruth Benedict had limited her assertion to the Tokugawa period or to a part of Japan during the World War II, I would not deny that there is some truth in what she has said.

Chronology

I. THE AGE OF AESTHETIC CULTURE (*ca.* 700–*ca.* 1200)

552	Introduction of Buddhism to Japan
592–628	Reign of Suiko Tennō; Shōtoku Taishi, regent
604	*Seventeen-Article Constitution*
645	Taika Reform
710	Establishment of the first permanent capital, Nara
712	*Records of Ancient Matters* (*Kojiki*)
720	*Chronicles of Japan* (*Nihongi*)
752	Dedication of the Great Buddha at the Tōdaiji in Nara
ca. 770	*Manyōshū* (A Collection of Myriad Leaves: An Anthology)
794	Heian-kyō (Kyoto) becomes the capital
ca. 990–1020	*Tale of Genji* (*Genji monogatari*) and *Pillow Book* (*Makura sōshi*)

II. THE AGE OF RELIGIOUS CULTURE (*ca.* 1200–*ca.* 1600)

1192	Founding of Kamakura Shōgunate
1232	The Jōei Code (Collection of Maxims and Rules for Administrators)
1262	Shinran (1173–1262), founder of the True Pure Land sect (Jōdo-Shinshu)
1274	First Mongol invasion
1281	Second Mongol invasion
1338	Ashikaga Takauji becomes *Shōgun*

1467 Ōnin War. Commencement of endemic civil wars throughout Japan

1568 Oda Nobunaga controls the capital

1571 Nobunaga destroys the Enryakuji on Mt. Hiei

III. THE AGE OF POLITICS (*ca.* 1600–1860)

1582 Toyotomi Hideyoshi succeeds to power

1598 Death of Hideyoshi

1603 Establishment of Tokugawa Shōgunate

1637–1638 Shimabara Revolt

1640 Europeans excluded

1648 Nakae Tōjyū (1608–1648)

1685 Yamaga Sōkō (1622–1685)

1688–1704 Genroku Period (Saikaku, Chikamatsu, Bashō, and Ukiyoe prints)

1705 Itō Jinsai (1627–1705)

1801 Motoori Norinaga (1730–1801)

1858 United States–Japanese commercial treaty.

IV. THE AGE OF ENLIGHTENMENT (*ca.* 1860)

1868 Meiji Restoration

1912 Death of Emperor Meiji

1920 Prewar liberalism (Taishō Democracy)

1925 Universal male suffrage

1931 Manchurian "Incident"

1941–1945 Pacific War

1952 End of military occupation by Allied forces.

Notes

1. *Nihonshoki* (Chronicles of Japan), section on Emperor Suiko, April, 12th year.
2. *Zoku Nihonki* (Records of Japan, continued) section on Emperor Shōmu, April, 1st year.
3. *Tenju koku shikuchō* (Works on the Felicitous Land).
4. Ruth Benedict, *The Chrysanthemum and the Sword* (Boston: Houghton Mifflin Co., 1946).
5. *Tannishō*, sec. 3.
6. *Ibid.*, sec. 2.
7. *Ibid.*, secs. 5, 6.
8. *Watsuji Tetsurō zenshū* (Collected Works of Watsuji Tetsurō), Vol. IV.i. *Zoku Nihon seishinshi kenkyū* (Supplement to Studies on the

Spiritual [Intellectual] History of Japan), chapter entitled "Nihon bunka no jūsōsei" (Multiple Characterization of Japanese Culture) (Tokyo: Iwanami-shōten, 1962).

9. *Nakae Tojyu sensei zenshū* (Collected Works of Professor Nakae) (Shiga: Toju-shoin, 1928) Vol. 1, p. 192. Also Vol. III, pp. 84–85.

KAWASHIMA TAKEYOSHI   *The Status of the*

Individual in the Notion of Law, Right,

and Social Order in Japan

I. Introduction

PROFESSOR F. S. C. NORTHROP once pointed to a very important correlation between non-normative assumptions or epistemology, and legal and ethical theory, and in connection with this he emphasized the contrast between the epistemology of naïve realism and that of logical realism. The former accepts images of man and society, with their immense variety of attributes, as they are perceived by the senses naïvely and with radical empirical immediacy. The latter construes the images of men and society through abstractions with concepts by postulation. Each of these assumptions finds its respective counterparts in legal and ethical philosophy.[1]

When we look at the traditional notions of the Japanese people about Nature as well as society, what impresses us most in contrast with the prevailing view of contemporary Western society is the fact that, in the traditional culture of the Japanese, Nature and society are accepted as they appear to the senses in their empirical immediacy. The indeterminateness of Nature and society with immense variety and subtle nuances is therefore their everlasting attribute, and, hence, it is to be valued because it is in its very nature unlimited and contains infinite possibilities for development and expansion.[2]

The basic assumption of empirical immediacy and the evaluation based on it permeate traditional Japanese culture. Probably this is evidenced by the peculiar nature of the Japanese language habit, since language is a vehicle for conveying ideas. The language habit of the Japanese people is not suitable for detailed and determinate expression or communication, for, as the novelist Tanizaki Junichirō pointed out, the *Tale of Genji* (*Genji monogatari*) had to be translated into English with longer sentences containing numerous detailed expressions so as to make it understandable to Western readers. He says:

In the English manner of writing, the meaning becomes clear, but at the same time it becomes limited and shallow. . . . We do not make such useless effort, but use those words which allow sufficient leeway to suggest various things, and supplement the rest [that which is not expressed with words] with sensible elements such as tones, appearance of letters, rhythms, etc., . . . of the sentence . . . [whereas] the sentence of the Westerners tries to restrict its meaning as narrowly and detailedly as possible and does not allow the smallest shadow, so that there is no room at all for the imagination of the reader.[3]

Viewed from this cognitive and evaluative perspective of naïve realism, men and society appear with immense variety in their subtle nuances and do not fit the abstractions with concepts by postulation. Each individual appears as a discrete entity with its own status and value. There is in this viewpoint no room for the existence of the image of an individual who is "equal" to every other on the ground that he is "independent" of every other. In a society with such assumptions, law and ethics aim at maintaining the social order consisting in the statuses of men with immense variety as they actually exist and not at imposing a social order which is postulated by intellect or ideal. The basic philosophy of law commonly held by the Japanese is in this respect in striking contrast with that of Western society at large.[4]

II. On the Level of Social Life

The Japanese traditionally expect that, in principle, social obligations will be fulfilled by a voluntary act on the part of the person under obligation, usually with particular friendliness or benevolence. They consider it improper for the other party [5] (beneficiary) of an obligation to demand or claim that the obligated person fulfill his obligation. An obligation is considered valueless, if, although it is fulfilled by the obligated person, he does not fulfill it in addition with a special friendliness or favor toward the other party. In other words, the actual value of social obligations depends upon the good will and favor of the obligated person, and there is no place for the existence of the notion of "right"; [6] in the

Japanese vocabulary there was no equivalent word for "right" or "*Recht,*" "*droit,*" and so on, of Western languages,[7] until the Dutch word "*Regt*" was translated into Japanese as "*kenri.*" Social obligations in the traditional culture are, in their very nature, indeterminate. "When a Japanese makes a promise with another, not the promise as such, but the kindness and friendship with which the promise is made is crucial for him, and, as long as he holds such *magokoro* (an ambiguous term meaning something like true-heartedness), it is all right even if he does not fulfill the promise exactly as the verbal expressions of the promise require." [8]

The indeterminateness of social obligations is idealized in the concept of "*wa*" (harmony, concord). The classical statement of this notion is the well-known, frequently quoted, phrase of Article I of the "Seventeen-Article Constitution" of Prince Shōtoku: "*Wa* is to be esteemed." [9] But with particular reference to law and the status of individuals, as well as in contrast with law and social order in Western society, the following statements are to be noted.

In individualism there can exist co-operation, compromise, self-sacrifice, and so on, in order to adjust and reduce contradictions and oppositions, but in the final analysis there exists no real harmony (*wa*). . . . The *wa* of our country is not mechanical co-operation, starting from reason, of equal individuals independent of each other, but the grand harmony (*taiwa*) which maintains its integrity by proper statuses of individuals within the collectivity and by acts in accordance with these statuses. . . . After all, oppositions of opinions, as well as differences of interests deriving from [various] standpoints, are integrated into a unity of grand harmony proper to Japan and originating from a common source. Not conflicts, but harmony is final.[10]

"Harmony consists in not making distinctions; if a distinction between good and bad can be made, then there *wa* (harmony) does not exist." [11]

In a concept of social obligation which does not have the counterbalancing notion of "right," the interest of the individual is not made distinct and fixed. Here, an individual is not considered to be an independent entity. Rather, his interest is absorbed in the interest of the collectivity to which he belongs, and the interest of the collectivity is recognized as having primary importance, while the interest of the individual has merely a secondary importance.

Under this notion of the individual, there has been no place for the concept of "human rights." This does not mean, however, that a sense of respect for the honor, life, and feelings of other persons did not exist in traditional Japan. Buddhism taught the virtue of "*jihi*" (mercy) [12] and Confucianism taught the virtue of *jin* (Chinese *jen*; human-heartedness).[13] The doctrine of "the spirit of *wa*" which has been taught as the traditional spirit of Japan, also contains some notion of human love. But what makes these notions differ from the idea of "human rights" in Western society is that the essential element of the concept of "human right" is the emphasis on the notion of "right" in the sense that every individual is endowed as a human being *per se* with human "rights" by which he can *demand* that other people, particularly his own government, respect, or refrain from infringement upon, the interests which are vital for his existence as a human being. This very nature of a human right never occurred in the traditional culture of the Japanese until the early years of the Meiji period (1868–1912). (See below.)

Nevertheless, the above should not be construed as contending that there has never been a notion of "right" in Japan. With respect to some kinds of interests (e.g., land, forests, personal effects, etc.), the Japanese have for centuries had a notion of "entitledness." [14] What is to be emphasized, however, is that there has been no clear and definite notion of "right" to the effect that the person who has the right is entitled to demand other persons to act in conformity with his interest invested in "right." Expressions such as "a right which is not a right," [15] which looks like a verbal absurdity, actually convey the idea of what the traditional Japanese has conceived to be his entitled interest.

The fact that the traditional notion of social obligation has not had, in principle, the notion of "right" as its counterpart means that in the traditional culture of Japan a law, in the sense of the *Recht* or *droit*, etc., of the continental European countries, was not differentiated from morality,[16] whereas the differentiation of law from morality has been characteristic of the culture of Western society since ancient Roman law. Related to this may also be the fact that the history of Japan lacks an equivalent for the notion of the "law of Nature" or "philosophical law," which has been recognized as an independent system of its own, which provided determinate positive standards for criticizing a positive legal law, and in which the belief that people had the right to criticize the positive law was incorporated.[17]

Moreover, illustrative of these beliefs and this value of social obligations and rights are the following facts:

In the world of business, people in Japan traditionally avoid defining the contractual obligations and rights in the process of negotiations prior to the conclusion of a contract. Even to think of a possible dispute in the future between contractual parties, not to mention actual negotiations on the terms for eventual resolution of disputes, would indicate a mistrust of the other party to the contract and would damage the relationship of *wa*, the most valid reason, in the minds of the contractual parties, for compliance with the obligations assumed under the contract. Therefore, contracts were rarely documentated.[18] Whenever a dispute arises out of a contract, both parties expect to reach an *ad hoc* agreement through negotiations to settle the dispute, because the parties combined in the contract are not merely "persons who pass one another by on the street," [19] but are instances of the proverb: "When people touch each other at the sleeves, it is by the *en* (tie) in their past lives." [20] Contractual parties are supposed to participate in the relationship of *wa* as expounded by Prince Shōtoku in his "Seventeen-Article Constitution" about 1,360 years ago,[21] so that the only, if any, contract clause foreseeing the possibility of future disputes may reasonably be that which provides that they have to negotiate in case of a dispute.[22] Western people would surely feel insecure with such a contract clause, but the Japanese feel insecure with any contractual clause which provides for contractual obligations in specific and determinate terms, because under such a clause there is no place at all for them to make adjustments for the specific contingencies which may arise in the case.[23]

The concept of social obligations in traditional Japanese culture, as described above, has been closely related with patterns of the social life out of which social obligations arose. In the past, social obligations arose in most cases out of close, face-to-face social relationships of a high degree of particularism and more or less long duration,[24] such as the family, kinship groups, landlord and tenant relationships, employer and employee relationships (particularly domestic servants, master-apprentice, etc.).[25] Even employee-employer relationships in modern business firms or factories [26] and merchant-customer relationships were in principle of the same nature in the past.[27] The social tie in these relationships was considered, so to speak, to be predestined by the *en* in the past lives of the individuals concerned. The term *"giri"* indicates obligations arising out of these relationships.[28]

In social obligations of this sort there has been no place for a settlement based upon a judgment determined by fixed, objective standards, namely, the administration of justice.[29] In other words, social obligations of this sort do not fit the lawsuit, which will inevitably bring about a breach of the close personal relationships based on the spirit of *wa*. "With the Code of Civil Procedure," once argued a member of the House of Representatives in the Diet, "the bureaucrats of the Meiji government destroyed the peaceful society of Japan." [30]

III. On the Level of Law

In Western society, it is taken for granted that in principle there exist tensions between legal rules and the social world, and that the latter is evaluated and controlled by the former.[31] The most striking, or exaggerated, expression of this idea is *"Fiat iustitia pereat mundus."* Japan, however, does not have the idea of this determinate dualism. What has existed in Japan is not a tension between these two antitheses, but a continuum from one to the other, or, rather, a compromise between these two antitheses. As Northrop points out, what the people of the West approve as "sticking up for one's rights" would be regarded in Japan as "trouble making," and lawsuits which the people of the West would approve as "law enforcement" would be viewed by the Japanese as unjustified resort to political power, which would not help to settle disputes.[32]

In Western society, particularly in America, it is expected that statutes, once promulgated, will function like a machine. A typical example of this idea was the Volstead Act (the Prohibition Amendment) of 1919 in the United States, which, from the Japanese point of view, seemed to be an extremely unrealistic legislative attempt in view of the strong and widespread alcoholic habits of the nation, but the United States Government persistently made an effort to enforce the law in spite of the hopelessness of the actual effectiveness of the law.[33]

In Japan, however, a statute is considered, according to the prevailing view, to be nothing but a *denka no hoto* (a sword handed down from ancestors as a family treasure), which means that it is not for actual use, but for symbolic manifestation of the prestige of the family. In fact, the government has usually been reserved in enforcing statutes. (The first case of prosecution in compliance with the Prostitution Surveillance Law [Law no. 118

of 1956] was in 1958.[34]) Even during the *"Totalkrieg"* of World War II the enforcement of the Food Control Law (Law no. 40 of 1942), which prohibited the sale of staple food outside of the legally sanctioned channels, was fairly liberal. The enforcement of the Road Traffic Law (Law no. 105 of 1960; prior to this Law, Road Traffic Surveillance Law no. 130 of 1933), which has no actual effect unless it is enforced like a machine, has been almost as liberal as the enforcement of the Food Control Law; from time to time a "Traffic Safety Week" was declared by the police, during which violations of traffic regulations were watched strictly, but the rest of the time violations were only occasionally noticed and prosecuted. Apparently the police have hesitated to enforce the Traffic Regulation Law in a machine-like manner.

The lack of the concept of "right" was particularly evident on the level of court practices with respect to infringement by the government upon the interests of private persons or their associations. When the translation of the French civil code, in which the expression *"droit civil"* was translated into Japanese for the first time as *"minken"* (right of a subject or citizen), was under debate in a conference of the Ministry of Justice in 1870, some of the members of the conference were not familiar with the concept that citizens have any rights whatsoever, and raised the question: "What on earth does it mean to say that a citizen has a right?" [35] This point is expressed in exaggerated form in *Kokutai no hongi* (Grand Principles of National Polity) as an authoritative statement by the government:

To conceive of relationships of dominance and obedience or rights and duties is a rationalistic view which based on an individualistic viewpoint considers everything to be relationships between equal persons. Our relationship between the emperor and his subjects is not a shallow flat one at all in which the emperor and his subjects confront each other, but a relationship of identification through self-denial which, starting from this very base (*konpon*), never loses this base (*konpon*). It can never be apprehended by the individualistic way of thinking.[36]

Until the new constitution became effective in 1947, it had been taken for granted that the government by its very nature transcended the law insofar as the exercise of administrative powers was concerned, and that neither the government nor its functionary was responsible for any act of the functionary performed in the capacity of an administrator, regardless of whether the functionary did it intentionally or by negligence.[37]

This basic attitude to law is illustrated by various actual practices of the administration of justice.

First, the Penal Code allows the court wide discretionary powers in meting out punishment in specific cases. The most striking example is Article 199, which provides for capital punishment, life imprisonment, or imprisonment for over three years for all kinds of murder without making a distinction between first-degree murder and any other kind of murder or assault (i.e., indeterminateness with respect to both the definition of crime and the nature of its punishment). The court can reduce the period of imprisonment or the amount of fine up to half of the legal minimum, in case it recognizes the existence of mitigating circumstances, without making a distinction in the nature of the crimes. Furthermore, the court is allowed such a wide discretion in suspending executions of the punishment that ultimately the effect is to cancel the sentence itself (Article 25, Penal Code). Therefore, in case the court recognizes the existence of mitigating circumstances, it is legally possible for the court to render a sentence with suspended execution even for cases of first-degree murder.

The important point, however, is not that there are such provisions, but that the enactment of these provisions was possible from the first with no opposition worth mentioning. On the contrary, the legislation of a law which introduced the institution of suspended execution as early as 1905 and the amendment of the Penal Code for liberalizing the punishment of murder in 1947 were both welcomed by legal specialists.[38]

Second, court practices in criminal cases are apparently illustrative of the Japanese high regard for the indeterminate, as is also found in the expressions of the provisions of the Penal Code. The wide discretionary power which is allowed the court is actually exercised to a high degree, and the actual sentenced punishments are frequently very light. Particularly, sentences with suspended execution are quite frequent. (See Table 1, p. 270.)

Those who cause the death of, or bodily injury to, other persons in automobile accidents, e.g., are rarely prosecuted for murder or manslaughter but almost always for negligent bodily injury or negligent homicide, and prosecutions on the ground of *dolus eventualis* are extremely rare, though it is admitted in principle. Most of the cases of bodily injury caused by intoxicated drivers are prosecuted as crimes of negligence, and the punishment provided in the Penal Code for negligent bodily injury is a fine under 1,000

TABLE 1

Crime	1951 A	1951 B	1951 per cent	1952 A	1952 B	1952 per cent	1953 A	1953 B	1953 per cent	1954 A	1954 B	1954 per cent	1955 A	1955 B	1955 per cent
a	917	617	67.3	773	452	58.5	729	432	59.3	643	405	63.0	648	405	62.5
b	1,327	903	68.0	1,197	507	42.4	1,155	389	33.7	1,277	462	36.2	842	350	41.6
c	1,157	427	36.9	958	351	36.6	1,011	385	38.0	1,160	390	33.6	1,403	459	32.7
d	27,774	2,211	8.0	32,775	2,071	6.3	38,419	2,103	5.5	44,092	2,432	5.5	55,227	2,791	5.0
e	6,651	234	3.5	9,588	266	2.8	15,795	308	1.9	22,373	366	1.6	30,077	507	1.7
f	61,859	24,754	40.0	56,726	22,263	39.2	47,415	17,860	36.7	46,173	18,576	40.2	52,692	21,301	40.4
g	3,525	698	19.8	2,615	438	16.7	2,144	345	16.1	2,032	353	17.4	2,546	383	15.0
h	11,595	5,318	45.9	11,530	4,670	40.5	11,272	4,566	40.5	11,249	4,750	42.2	11,764	5,017	42.6
i	2,724	1,362	50.0	2,699	1,129	41.8	2,428	994	40.9	2,846	1,249	43.9	3,505	1,573	44.9
j	7,150	4,328	59.3	6,743	4,005	59.4	6,633	3,492	52.6	5,829	3,291	56.5	5,355	3,130	58.5
k	6,001	4,177	69.6	5,770	3,647	63.2	4,631	3,030	65.4	3,383	2,212	65.4	3,632	2,443	64.5

Crime	1956 A	1956 B	1956 per cent	1957 A	1957 B	1957 per cent	1958 A	1958 B	1958 per cent	1959 A	1959 B	1959 per cent	1960 A	1960 B	1960 per cent
a	808	485	60.0	801	504	62.9	717	461	64.3	702	465	66.2	762	516	67.7
b	921	441	47.9	835	354	42.4	659	307	46.6	740	366	49.5	802	353	44.0
c	1,295	449	34.7	1,261	410	32.5	1,474	462	31.3	1,581	447	28.3	1,404	426	30.3
d	62,885	2,972	4.7	68,025	3,031	4.5	71,825	3,298	4.6	71,441	3,355	4.7	69,628	3,613	5.2
e	41,527	630	1.5	51,468	761	1.5	59,031	866	1.5	73,343	1,027	1.4	84,771	1,482	1.7
f	55,126	24,080	43.7	51,474	22,872	44.4	45,896	19,422	42.3	43,987	18,902	43.0	40,350	17,949	44.5
g	2,473	378	15.3	2,208	347	15.7	2,486	380	15.3	2,330	305	13.1	1,901	327	17.2
h	10,532	4,726	44.9	9,753	4,339	44.5	8,867	4,357	44.2	9,227	3,957	42.9	8,467	3,806	45.0
i	4,096	1,925	47.0	4,097	2,060	50.3	4,966	2,520	50.7	5,420	2,759	50.9	5,407	2,777	51.4
j	4,908	2,954	60.2	4,424	2,739	61.9	3,864	2,287	59.2	3,694	2,100	56.8	3,590	2,098	58.4
k	4,078	2,797	68.6	3,643	2,534	70.0	2,987	1,848	61.9	2,962	1,899	64.1	3,203	2,135	66.7

A = Number of persons found guilty
B = Number of persons found guilty and sentenced without suspended execution
Per cent = 100 B/A
Source: Saikō Saibansho Jimusōkyoku (General Secretariat of the Supreme Court), Shihō Tōkei Nenpō (Annual Report of Judicial Statistics), 1951–1960.

a = documentary forgery
b = official corruption
c = homicide
d = bodily injury
e = bodily injury through negligence
f = larceny
g = robbery
h = fraud
i = extortion
j = embezzlement
k = crime regarding stolen property

yen (approximately three dollars), and for negligent homicide imprisonment from two up to fifteen years (Articles 210 and 205, Penal Code), and consequently the sentences of the courts result in relatively light sentences.[39,40]

Third, in civil affairs, the parties in dispute are reluctant to sue in the court, and not simply because lawsuits are expensive and time consuming.[41] They expect, and are ready, to settle disputes by compromise (either judicial or extra-judicial),[42] and the courts also usually try to effectuate a compromise.[43] In Western society, people also seem to be inclined to avoid lawsuits if possible and tend to prefer compromise ("A lean compromise is better than a flat lawsuit"). But, when we look at the percentage of compromises in civil cases in Japan, we have to take into consideration the fact that people usually try to reach a compromise by any means, and that they sue in court only in case they feel a solution by compromise is hopeless and only if they do not care if their opponents become bitter enemies.

It is probable that every society generally endeavors to make the meaning of its statutes clear and determinate in order that the latitude of the court to interpret the meaning of the statutes is limited. In Japan, however, the indeterminateness of the meaning of the statutes is taken for granted, and so scope for widening or narrowing the meaning of the statutes has been almost limitless. In Japan, it has been extremely rare for a court to explain the reason for a decision on grounds which cannot be derived by interpretation of the statutes. In connection with this, it is to be noted that the movement for "free interpretation of statutes" (*Freirechts-bewegung*) in Germany after World War I was readily accepted by Japanese jurists.

IV. *Historical Change*

The above description of the characteristics of the Japanese notion of social obligation and right should not be taken as meaning that these characteristics are, so to speak, inborn or racially pre-destined in the Japanese.[44] By the late nineteenth century there had emerged some changes in attitudes in the direction of some patterns of Western thought. The French ideology of "human rights" based on the Law of Nature was introduced by philosophers and political scientists and readily accepted by political leaders of the strong nation-wide political movement for democracy (Jiyū

Minken Undō, Movement for Freedom and People's Rights).[45]

Though the government almost succeeded in oppressing this movement by about 1890, a new wave for democracy and human rights emerged toward the end of World War I, when the traditional social system became disorganized to some extent as a result of the industrialization brought about by the war. Labor unions, farm-tenants' associations, house-tenants' associations, land-lessees' associations, etc., were organized against the oppression by the government and claimed the recognition and confirmation of their "rights" on the level of actual interpersonal relationships, as well as on the level of law, particularly statutes.[46] Facing this situation, the government tried to suppress this historical change by reorganizing and intensifying the education of the ideology of familial "piety" in primary and secondary schools, as well as by introducing the procedure of chōtei (mediation) by legislation for disputes of farm tenancy, house tenancy, land tenancy, and labor, by which the claim on "rights" was expected to be absorbed into the "harmonious" relationship reorganized through the compromise reached by mediation on the principle of indeterminate social obligations.[47] In the period of more extensive disorganization of the traditional social system as a result of the industrialization after the Manchurian Incident, the government moved further in intensifying the inculcation of the ideology of familial "piety," and denounced self-assertion and individualism by issuing official textbooks on authorized totalitarian ideology, such as Kokutai no hongi (Grand Principles of National Polity), Shinmin no michi (The Way of Subjects), and Senji katei kyoiku shidō yōryō (Basic Principles of Wartime Home Education).[48] The spirit of wa was proclaimed as a supreme value,[49] and the argument (kotoage) for private interest was condemned as a vice.[50]

Nevertheless, these attempts did not succeed in suppressing the growth of the notion of "right." This is evidenced by the fact that the notion of "human rights" was accepted universally when the political power which had suppressed its growth collapsed with the defeat in 1945.[51]

The notion of "right" developed also with respect to relationships between private persons. A very interesting study on this point was made by Professor Sasaki Yoshio,[52] who made a survey of the attitudes of rural and urban areas toward lawsuit and mediation. Its result shows that, of the total samples, 25 per cent (urban) were reluctant to resort to court on the grounds that "to make a distinction between black and white with respect to a dispute is not proper" or "both parties of a dispute have their reasons," and that a large portion of the samples were ready to resort to court only if a lawsuit would have been less expensive and time-consuming than they are now.[53]

The change in this respect is illustrated more evidently in the official statistics of the Supreme Court: filings of mediation cases have decreased, whereas those of lawsuits have increased in recent years. (See Table 2, below.)

TABLE 2

	Lawsuits and Other Court Cases	Mediation Cases
1948	54.2	45.8
1949	61.5	38.5
1950	70.5	29.5
1951	71.6	28.4
1952	73.4	26.6
1953	74.9	25.1
1954	78.5	21.5
1955	79.2	20.8
1956	79.6	20.4
1957	80.7	19.3
1958	81.8	18.1
1959	82.9	17.1
1960	83.1	16.9
1961	83.9	16.1
1962	84.4	15.6

SOURCE: *Hōsō jihō* (Lawyers' Association Journal), XV, No. 12, (1963), 60

Another indication of this change will be found in the revision, 1962, of Standard Stipulated Terms for Contracts for Work in Construction Projects, which was effectuated by the proposal of the representatives of the construction industry, whereas in former years amendments in the same direction had been rejected by the representatives of the construction industry itself. The Central Construction Industry Council of the Ministry of Construction passed a resolution to change the clause which had provided that the amount of the damage or change of the remuneration be contingent upon conferral between the parties into a more determinate clause according to which the right for change of the remuneration and the right for damages be recognized *ipso iure* (without conferral be-

tween the parties) under specific circumstances provided in the
clause and the amount of damages be also fixed by specific standards provided in the clause.[54]

Furthermore, indicative of this change is the frequency of
reports of judicial cases in an ordinary newspaper and the degree
of interest the editor feels in reporting judicial cases (as the index
of which I use the size of headlines), which, I presume, will indicate the extent to which society at large is interested in judicial
decisions. In the period 1962–1963, the frequency of news reports
on judicial cases was 59 and 61, respectively, whereas the frequency
in 1930 was 29, and in 1935 was 43. The average size of headlines
and standard deviation of news reports on judicial cases was
3.34 ± 4.11 in 1962, and 3.44 ± 5.66 in 1963, whereas it was
2.37 ± 1.56 in 1930, and 1.98 ± 2.41 in 1935.[55]

In view of these changes, it is clear that the Japanese attitude
toward law, right, and social order will continue to undergo changes
in the direction of the patterns of Western society and probably
other nations of Asia also will not be able to avoid changes in more
or less the same direction, though probably to a different degree
from Western societies, when the traditional social structure becomes disorganized as the process of industrialization proceeds.

V. Conclusion

In traditional Japanese culture, the individual is conceived as
an existence which appears to the senses in its empirical immediacy
—hence with an immense variety of attributes and subtle nuances.
Consequently, there is no place for the concept of the individual as
an independent entity equal to other individuals. In such a culture,
the social order consists of social obligations, which are defined, not
in specific, determinate terms, but in diffuse, indeterminate terms,
and the indeterminateness of social obligations of this nature contains the possibility of flexible adjustment to contingent circumstances. The indeterminateness of social obligations—hence the lack
of concepts of equality and independence of individuals—does not
allow the existence of the concept of "right" as the counterpart of
social obligations.

In view of such an image of the individual, there is lacking the
antithesis between the actual social world and legal rules which is
characteristic of Western society. Given such an image, law is not
expected to function with the precision of a machine. A lawsuit,

which in its nature makes distinctions between right and wrong, is in contradiction to the social order, based on diffusely defined indeterminate social obligations; hence, it is undesirable; and mediation is the means which fits the indeterminate social order.

Japanese society, however, continues to move in the direction of Western society with respect to these notions, presumably as a result of industrialization and disintegration of traditional social structure. This would lead to the assumption that other nations of Asia also will not be able to avoid the same or similar changes of thought, once they expose themselves to the influence of industrialization.

Furthermore, the case of Japan suggests that the image of the individual which a society holds is the key concept with which it is possible to understand the basic characteristics of legal thought and the structure of the law of the society.

QUESTION: You have associated the emergence of the individual in Japan with the loss of community, citing industrialization as the cause. I feel a kind of anguish about this, because I would judge that you have had community in a more significant sense than we in the West in recent years, but you are losing it, as we have lost it. If one can achieve the individual only by losing the community, that is a very high price to pay. Furthermore, there is a kind of dialectic in this, for, having lost significant community, you will lose the individual, too; there will be a loss of depth in the kind of individual then possible.

You cited some new types of community relationship appearing in Japan. I recognize all of these types, because we have them in America. The meeting of the housewives: this is the morning coffee hour, the *Kaffeeklatsch*. They meet in one or another of their almost identical houses to discuss one or another of their almost identical problems. And the business men have weekly meetings of the Lions, the Elks, etc. But the point is that these are forms of nominal community, casual, uninspired, and almost rootless. What we need, of course, is significant individuality and profound community. But we do not have it, and you do not have it. This is a deep problem for every nation. I do not know the answer; but, if you have insight on this problem, I would like to have that insight.

ANSWER: Those "communities" or *Gemeinschaften*, which were disorganized as a result of the development of free, independent individuals, have maintained their existence by exercising various kinds of group pressures which were in contradiction to the independence and freedom of individuals who were members of the groups.

QUESTION: It seems to me that even in "communities," or *Gemeinschaften,* in which the principle of *wa* prevails it is possible to make a distinction between right and wrong. Why do people in these social groups not want to maintain their social order by way of deciding right or wrong?

ANSWER: Of course, in many cases it is possible to make a judgment of right or wrong on behavior within the group. But, at the same time, such a decision is more or less difficult in such a group, because the standard according to which a decision of right or wrong is to be made depends in its nature on the contingent circumstances of the case, particularly the subtle nuances of the temperament, mood, feeling, etc., of the parties involved.

QUESTION: The politics of Japan was taken up in your paper. I have been wondering if the democracy in Japan is merely a veneer without sufficient background. The prevailing view in the West rather tends to consider that Japan is lacking sufficient foundation or background for genuine and lasting democracy.

ANSWER: I am afraid that my paper might have given the impression that I support the view which you mention. But I cannot agree with that view. Japan is now in the process of transition from pre-modern to modern society, and there co-exist in social and political life in Japan pre-democratic elements along with democratic elements. The existence of pre-democratic elements which are the remnants from the feudal period does not mean that democracy in Japan has a merely superficial or temporary existence. We should not overlook the fact that Japan experienced, in the past, three major democratic movements. The first was the Jiyū Minken Undō (Movement for Freedom and People's Rights) in the 1870s and 1880s, a large-scale movement which arose and spread all over Japan, and its outcome, and, in a sense, a peace treaty of the government with it, was the Constitution of 1889. The second was the Democratic Movement (Minpon Shugi, and, later on, the Socialist Movement) since around 1914, the main outcome of which were the Jury Law (*Baishin hō*) of 1923 and the Universal Suffrage Law (*Futsū senkyo hō*) of 1925. The third was the democratic movement after World War II, which was released by the

Occupation Forces from suppression by the government after General Tōjō Hideki's regime, in which a large variety of people were involved, i.e., not only intellectuals and workers, but also women and rural people. In other words, the desire for democracy and civil rights has existed ever since the Meiji Reform on a national scale, though we might get an opposite impression when we look at the official ideology disseminated and imposed upon the nation, which was nothing but a means of the government to overcome the democratic ideas persisting within the nation, which constituted the evidence of the existence of democratic ideas. Democracy in Japan is now firmly grounded in the minds of the people, and any political attempt to infringe upon democracy and civil rights will encounter the strong opposition and the resistance of the people in the future.

Notes

1. See F. S. C. Northrop, "Comparative Philosophy and Science in the Light of Comparative Law," in Charles A. Moore, ed., *Philosophy and Culture—East and West* (Honolulu: University of Hawaii Press, 1962), pp. 251 ff.
2. Northrop points out in his pioneering work that this is characteristic of Oriental culture in general. See F. S. C. Northrop, *The Meeting of East and West* (New York: The Macmillan Co., 1953), pp. 381 ff., particulary p. 386: "The good which is identified with the indeterminate, all-embracing factor is the only good which is absolute in the sense that it holds for all people under all circumstances. It has this absolute character because in fact it is not transitory or different in one person or thing from what it is in another. The good which is identified with the determinate, limited, differentiated factor is relative, not varying merely from person to person or from thing to thing but also, for a given person, from circumstance to circumstance and from time to time."
3. Tanizaki Junichirō, *Bunshō tokuhon* (Reader of Composition), in *Tanizaki Junichirō zenshū* (Collected Works of Tanizaki Junichirō), Vol. 21 (Tokyo: Chuokōronsha, 1958), pp. 34 ff., particularly p. 44.
4. In this paper I use the term "West" or "Western" as meaning the modern West-European and American society in its ideal type in the sense of Max Weber.
5. This became most evident when Mediation Laws were under debate in the Diet in the period immediately after World War I. A member of the House of Representatives urged: "By endeavoring to be sympathetic and by expressing harmony, we amicably reap rights which are not actually rights in themselves." (*Dai 45 kai teikokugikai*

shugiin iinkai sokkiroku, Stenographic Record of House of Representatives' Committee in the 45th Session of the Imperial Diet, Category 5, no. 5, 2nd session, at p. 4, 1922.) Another member urged: "Handling this matter as merely a determination of the problem of the rights of a lessee of land or a tenant of a house so that the owner may assert his own rights even to the point of rapacity, in a period such as that of today when a shift in society in the harmony of supply and demand brings only shortages, with anyone being able to assert his own rights exclusively, makes it quite difficult, in the final analysis, to obtain true stability of rights. Therefore, the establishment of the Mediation Law is not so that someone by sticking to the law can determine the relationship of rights among the parties. That is, the relationship between a tenant and a houseowner, a land lessee and a landowner differs from that between people passing by on the street [complete strangers]. Therein is the personal expression of sympathy; therein is morality. And in the sense that it attempts to base settlement on these things exists the *raison d'être* of mediation." (*Ibid.,* 3rd session, at p. 1, 1922.) Another member argued: "Shōtoku Taishi, who drafted the 'Seventeen-Article Constitution' wrote [in Article 1] that harmony is to be honored. Japan, unlike other countries where rights and duties prevail, must strive to solve interpersonal cases by harmony and compromise. Since Japan does not settle everything by law as in the West but rather must determine matters, for the most part, in accordance with morality and human sentiment (*ninjō*), the doctrine of mediation is indigenous to Japan. . . . The great three-hundred-year peace of the Tokugawa era (1615–1867) was preserved because disputes between citizens were resolved harmoniously through their own autonomous administration, avoiding, so far as possible, resort to court procedure. . . . However, later the judicial bureaucrats, assuming upon the appearance of the Code of Civil Procedure that the bureaucracy should attempt to settle all problems in dispute, extremely perverted the thought of the People." (*Dai 51 teikokugikai shugiin inkai sokkiroku,* Stenographic Record of House of Representatives' Committees in the 51st Session of the Imperial Diet, Category 5, no. 18, 3rd session, at p. 2. 1926.)

6. "In recent publications, original as well as translated works, we encounter words such as *"kenri"* (right, power, and interest), *"kengen"* (competence, or authorized rights), *"kenryoku"* (power), *"kenri"* (right, power, and reason), *"kokken"* (state power), *"minken"* (civil right), etc., which are intelligible to those who understand foreign languages or to scholars who have studied and translated books extensively, but which are not easy for laymen to understand because in China as well as in Japan these Chinese characters were very rarely used in the meanings they have

now." Fukuzawa Yukichi, *Tsuzoku minkenron* (Treatise on Civil Rights), originally published in 1878, in *Fukuzawa Yukichi zenshū* (Selected Works of Fukuzawa Yukichi) (Tokyo: Iwanami-shōten, 1952,) Vol. IV, p. 30. "But perhaps the most interesting feature of the new Japanese code [Civil Code] is not the similarity of some of its provisions to those of one foreign code or another, but, rather, its adoption of one characteristic principle of modern European law which introduces an entirely new concept into Japanese legislation. This is the concept of rights as contrasted to obligations. Here we have a distinct and undoubted case of the exertion of direct Western influence upon Japanese culture, for the notion of rights is foreign to the jurisprudence that Japan borrowed from China in the seventh century and on which all her subsequent legislation was based. Instead, not only in its laws but in its customs the social system of Japan was penetrated by the idea of duties to the exclusion of the ideas of rights. So unfamiliar was the concept of the rights of the individual subject that in purely Japanese legal writings there is no term that closely corresponds to the word "rights" as expressing something that is due a person and that he can claim; nor indeed did familiar speech include such a word in its vocabulary." Sir George Sansom, *The Western World and Japan* (New York: Alfred A. Knopf, 1950), p. 446.

7. When the Dutch word *"Regt"* (right) was introduced into Japan in the late nineteenth century, there was no equivalent for this word in the vocabulary of the Japanese language, and a scholar had to create a new word, *"kenri,"* by a combination of two Chinese characters, *"ken"* (power) and *"ri"* (reason, logic). Later on, the latter character, *"ri,"* was changed to another *"ri,"* which means interest, thereby maintaining the pronunciation (*kenri*) of the word as it had been originally.

8. Hattori Shirō (Professor of Linguistics at the University of Tokyo), "Hōritsu to yakusoku ni tsuite" (On Law and Promise), in *Asahi Shinbun* (Newspaper Asahi), December 20, 1952, 12th ed., p. 6.

9. On the authoritative statement by Buddhist Prince Shōtoku Taishi, see Nakamura Hajime, "Basic Features of the Legal, Political, and Economic Thought of Japan" (cited hereafter as "Basic Features"), in Charles A. Moore, ed., *Philosophy and Culture—East and West*, p. 633.

10. Monbushō (Ministry of Education), *Kokutai no hongi* (Grand Principles of National Polity) (Tokyo: Naikaku-insatsukyoku [The Cabinet's Printing Office], 1937), pp. 50, 51, 57.

11. Ono Seiichirō, *Nihon hōri no jikaku teki tenkai* (Self-conscious Development of Japanese Philosophy of Law) (Tokyo: Yuhikaku, 1942), p. 300.

12. On the virtue of *jihi* (mercy), see Nakamura Hajime, "Basic Features," p. 632; Nakamura Hajime, *Jihi* (Mercy) (Tokyo: Heirakuji-shōten, 1955), pp. 124 ff.

13. On teachings on *"jin"* (*"jen"* in Chinese) by Japanese Confucian scholars, see Robert N. Bellah, *Tokugawa Religion: The Values of Pre-industrial Japan* (Tokyo: The Free Press, 1957), pp. 94, 141, 156. See also Clarence Burton Day, *The Philosophers of China* (New York: Philosophical Library, 1962), pp. 304–305.

14. The lack of a word which is the equivalent of "right," however, does not necessarily mean that words which signify "right" to any limited extent did not exist at all. In any society there exists some kind of property, and the notion of right existed in that sense and to that extent. In Japan, also, prior to the introduction of Western legal systems, there were in usage words such as *"nauke," "mochiji," "mochigiri,"* etc. *"Nauke"* means registration in the *Kenchichō* (tax register, equivalent of *Domesday Book* in medieval England) of the name of a farmer who was obliged to pay rent or tribute to the *daimyō* (provincial feudal lord) which at the same time functioned as recognition of the property of the farmer whose name was registered. *"Mochiji"* meant the actually owned land. *"Mochigiri"* meant common land in use by the village community as a collectivity. The fact that, besides these words which signify each specific kind of property, there did not emerge a general term which corresponds to the word "right" draws our attention. Probably this was because in each of these interests there were contained at the same time restrictions or obligations which were so inherently combined with these interests that the concept of right could not emerge as such. See also F. S. C. Northrop "Linguistic Symbols and Legal Norms," in L. Bryson, L. Finkelstein, H. Hoagland, and R. M. MacIver, eds., *Symbols and Society, Fourteenth Symposium of the Conference on Science, Philosophy and Religion* (New York: The Conference on Science, Philosophy and Religion in their Relation to the Democratic Way of Life, Inc., 1955), pp. 55 ff.

15. See note 5. The expression "a right which is not a right" sounds very strange, of course, not only to Westerners, but also to present-day Japanese. This expression was probably intended to point to an interest which is defined by indeterminate social obligations, and so it can hardly be called a right in the proper sense, but still contains some elements of a right, or resembles a right.

16. See, for example, Ono Seiichirō, *Nihon hōri no jikaku teki tenkai*, p. 64. On the undifferentiated state of law and morality in contemporary China, see Jean Escarra, *Le droit chinois* (Paris: Sirey, 1936), Part I, chap. 4; John C. H. Wu, "Chinese Legal and Political

Philosophy," in Charles A. Moore, ed., *Philosophy and Culture—East and West*, pp. 616 ff.

17. See Reinhardt Bendix, *Max Weber, An Intellectual Portrait* (New York: Doubleday & Co., 1962), pp. 398–399. For a comparison with Japanese tradition, the following statement by Paul Vinogradoff about the emergence of the Law of Nature in ancient Greece is particularly interesting: "It is at a later stage—with the advent of Stoicism, especially in its Roman form—that the law of nature began to be considered as a source of law in the practical sense of the term. The explanation of this fact may be found, I think, in the powerful development of equity in the jurisdiction of the democratic courts of the classical period, which left to the popular juries great latitude in the interpretation and application of positive law." Sir Paul Vinogradoff, *Outlines of Historical Jurisprudence* (Oxford: Oxford University Press, 1922), Vol. II, p. 42.

18. Kawashima, "Hōken teki keiyaku to sono kaitai" (Feudal Contracts and Their Disorganization) (cited hereafter as "Hōken teki keiyaku"), in Kawashima, *Hōshakaigaku ni okeru hō no sonzai kōzō* (The Structure of Law in Sociology of Law) (Tokyo: Nihonhyōron-shinsha, 1950), pp. 201–202.

19. See note 5.

20. Undoubtedly, this remark originates from the Buddhist belief.

21. See notes 5 and 8.

22. Examples of a contract clause of this kind are as follows: "In the case of the prior paragraph, if B has sustained damage, A shall compensate him for this damage, the amount of compensation to be determined by *conferral* between A and B." *Kensetsu kōji hyōjun ukeoi keiyaku yakkan* (Standard Stipulated Terms for Contracts for Work in Construction Projects), Feb. 21, 1950, Ruling of the Third Meeting of the Central Construction Industry Council, as amended through the Oct. 3, 1956, Ruling of the Twenty-first Meeting, Second Session of the Central Construction Industry Council, Article 16. (Italics mine.) The same expression is also found in Article 22 of the same Standard Stipulated Terms. On details, see Kawashima Takeyoshi and Watanabe Yōzō, *Dōken ukeoi keiyakuron* (Treatise on Construction Contracts) (Tokyo: Nihonhyōron-shinsha, 1950), note 13, pp. 57–70, 140–143; Kawashima, "Dispute Resolution in Contemporary Japan" (cited hereafter as "Dispute Resolution"), in Arthur von Mehren, ed., *Law in Japan* (Cambridge: Harvard University Press, 1963), pp. 46–47.

23. See Kawashima, "Dispute Resolution," p. 47.

24. Most of these relationships or groups can be characterized (a) as "familistic" or "patriarchal" in the sense that the superior (landlord,

employer, etc.) has a power of indeterminate scope and intensity contingent on *ad hoc* circumstances, and (b) as "feudal" in the sense that the power of the superior over the inferior is founded on and legitimized by "*on*" (special favor or benevolence which corresponds to "*beneficium*" in the feudal society given by a lord to a vassal, to which the vassal in turn is indebted by a limitless obligation to reciprocate). See Kawashima, "Hōken teki keiyaku," pp. 190 ff., 208 ff.

25. See Kawashima, "Hōken teki keiyaku," pp. 185 ff. on the patriarchal or familistic nature of farm tenancy; Ishino Iwao and John W. Bennett, *The Japanese Labor Boss System: A Description and a Preliminary Sociological Analysis* (mimeographed, Columbus: Department of Sociology, Ohio State University, 1952); and John W. Bennett, *Social Aspects of Japanese Forestry Economy: Two Case Studies* (mimeographed, Department of Sociology, Ohio State University, 1953), pp. 26 ff. on the same nature of forestry labor.

26. James C. Abegglen, *The Japanese Factory* (Glencoe, Illinois: The Free Press, 1958), pp. 17, 66, 94; Kawashima, "Hōken teki keiyaku," pp. 205–206.

27. Kawashima, "Hōken teki keiyaku," p. 206.

28. See Ruth Benedict, *The Chrysanthemum and the Sword* (New York: Houghton Mifflin Co., 1946), chaps. 7, 9; Kawashima, "Giri," *Shisō* (Thought), No. 327 (September, 1951), 21 ff.

29. See Kawashima, "Dispute Resolution," pp. 44 ff.

30. See note 5.

31. Reinhard Bendix, *Max Weber, An Intellectual Portrait*, pp. 115 ff.

32. F. S. C. Northrop, *The Taming of the Nations* (New York: The Macmillan Co., 1954), chaps. 2, 3, 7, 10; Gray L. Dorsey, "Influence of Philosophy on Law and Politics," in Charles A. Moore, ed., *Philosophy and Culture—East and West*, pp. 538 ff.

33. Comparing the situation with that in America, Professor Hattori Shirō writes: "The Americans observe law, regulation and promise, whereas the Japanese do not have a clear notion of these things; instead, they value and rely on *jōjō* (situational circumstances), *giri, ninjō* (friendship) *magokoro.* . . . It seems to us very strange that Americans are sensitive to law and make thorough precautions to prevent crimes committed by out-maneuvering the law. . . . The American society is mechanical, not only materially but also socially; for those Japanese who are not used to this the interpersonal relationships [in America] might seem too mechanical and *mizukusai* (officious, austere). . . . The Americans make a promise for promise's sake; hence the promise has to be fulfilled faithfully." Shirō Hattori, "Hōritsu to yakusoku ni tsuite" (On Law and Promise), in *Asahi Shinbun* (Newspaper Asahi), Dec. 20, 1952, 12th ed., p. 6.

("*Magokoro*" is hard to translate. "True sincerity" or "true-heartedness" is close to the implied meaning.)

34. According to unpublished statistics of the Tokyo District Prosecutor's Office.

35. Hozumi Nobushige, *Hōsō yawa* (Night Stories from a Study of a Law Professor) (Tokyo: Yuhikaku, 1916), pp. 212–213.

36. Monbushō (Ministry of Education), *Kokutai no hongi* (Grand Principles of National Polity), pp. 35–36.

37. Murakami Setsuko vs. State (Osaka City), Grand Court of Judicature, IV Civil Department, August 31, 1953, *Hōritsu Shinbun*, no. 3886, p. 7; Takeuchi Yoshi vs. Takahashi Katsuchika (judge), Great Court of Judicature, Civil Department, May 14, 1906, 12 *Daishinin minji hanketsuroku* (Collection of Civil Great Court of Judicature Cases), 817: Naitō Tsunejirō vs. Itō Junzō (president of Kyoto Medical College Hospital), Osaka Court of Appeals, I Civil Department, December 19, 1905, *Hōritsu Shinbun*, no. 338 p. 7; Awaya Kumatsuchi vs. Tsurumi Moriyoshi, *et al.* Tokyo District Court, III Civil Department, January 10, 1916, *Hōritsu Shinbun*, no. 1064, p. 27. For details see Kawashima, *Nihon no shakai to seikatsu ishiki* (Japanese Society and Mentality) (Tokyo: Gakuseisha, 1955), pp. 30 ff.

38. Professor Miyauchi Hiroshi points out that the enactment of Law Regarding Suspended Execution, 1905, was not an outcome of the growth of democracy or individualism, as was the case in Europe and America, but, rather, an attempt by political leaders to liberalize or enlarge the discretionary power of the court and to correct the provisions of the so-called Old Penal Code of 1882 based on individualism and democracy, drafted under the strong influence of the French philosophy of a Law of Nature. See Miyauchi Hiroshi, *Shikkō yūyo no jittai* (Actualities of Suspended Execution) (Tokyo: Nihonhyōron-shinsha, 1957), p. 90; Takikawa Haruo, Nakatake Yasuo, Hiraba Yasuji, and Miyauchi Hiroshi, "Nihon keihō no ōiyumi" (Historical Changes in Japanese Criminal Law) in *Hōritsu jihō* (Law Journal), XXIV, no. 11 (1952), 35–36. The law of 1905 was kept valid even after the New Penal Code of 1907 was promulgated. Miyauchi raises the question that the institution of suspended execution and its liberalization in later years are to be studied from the viewpoint of the liberalization of the discretionary power of the court—in other words, as an illustration of the ideology of law which is specifically Japanese. (*Ibid.*, p. 90.)

39. Some examples: the Yokohama District Court sentenced to imprisonment for terms of two years and one and a half years, respectively, two criminal defendants who had left their intoxicated friend on the track of an electric railway to be run over and killed by a train. The prosecution had demanded a two-year sentence. *Asahi Shinbun,*

Nov. 28, 1961, 12th ed., p. 15, emphasized the fact that these defendants were sentenced to imprisonment without suspended execution by a three-column headline, "Sentence without suspended execution to two criminal defendants of a joint crime." At the end of this report, the paper referred to another decision by the Nagoya District Court which sentenced to one-year imprisonment (presumably without suspended execution) a *sewayaki* (a foreman who controlled his workers' room and board) who had left an intoxicated worker under his care outside of the barracks during the winter and the worker thereupon froze to death; the Tokyo District Court sentenced to two-year imprisonment a criminal defendant who had run over a young man and dragged him some distance with his truck while driving at 50 kilometers an hour, though the young man repeatedly cried, "Stop the car." *Asahi Shinbun* commented in its report on this decision that this was the first decision ever rendered by the Tokyo District Court which recognized the intention of bodily injury resulting in death—*n.b.*, not the intention of homicide—in an automobile accident and which sentenced the defendant to imprisonment (Dec. 11, 1962, 3rd ed., p. 7); a bus driver, pulling up to a bus-stop, hit a 72-year-old man, thereby seriously injuring his head and other parts of his body while he was crossing the road and signaling the driver by raising his left hand. The driver, sentenced to a fine of 5,000 *yen* by summary procedure, appealed for regular trial and was acquitted on the ground that the victim was also at fault. (This reminds us of the adage, *"kenka ryōseibai"*—Both parties of a dispute are to be punished.) The Court of Appeals sentenced him to a fine of 3,000 *yen*. *Mainichi Shinbun* (Newspaper Mainichi) commented in its report on this decision: "In traffic-regulation cases drivers tend to attribute the responsibility of the accident to the fault of the victim. In view of this fact, this decision draws our attention as it imposes 'strict' liability on the drivers from the standpoint of the victim (Dec. 6, 1961, 13th ed., p. 13). In this connection, an epoch-making decision was rendered by the Niigata District Court, which was upheld by Tokyo Court of Appeals on June 28, 1963. A criminal, driving a truck without a license, struck and killed a young woman carrying her baby on her back at an intersection in the city of Nagaoka and drove on about 300 meters, dragging her husband, who had jumped on the truck and asked the driver to stop. The Niigata District Court sentenced him to five years imprisonment for homicide with *dolus eventualis* (eventual intent), and the Appellate Court upheld this decision. This was the first case in which a hit-and-run driver was prosecuted for intentional homicide "after careful deliberation" in the prosecutor's office (see *Mainichi Shinbun*, December 6, 1961, 13th ed., p. 13). *Asahi Shinbun*, June 28, 1963, 12th ed., p. 15, commented on this case in its report on the decision of the Appellate Court that this was the fourth decision ever rendered by the court which, in a hit-and-run automobile accident case, imposed punishment for homicide, and noted that this "severe attitude of the court was noteworthy."

40. "It is (*jihi*) (the mercy) of the East to embrace criminals of every kind of crime and not to cast them away. . . . It is the philosophy of law of the East, and Japan as well, to abstain from inflicting punishment." Ono Seiichirō, *Nihon hōri no jikaku teki tenkai* (Self-conscious Development of Japanese Philosophy of Law), pp. 108, 110. "When [Vice President] Nixon apologized, 'It was the fault of U.S., by mistake,' we are moved all at once and think 'we have to save his face.' Even a raped girl or her parents, if the criminal visits them early in the morning and apologizes with tears, are easily moved and inclined to forgive him." (Anonymous comment in *Asahi Shinbun*, November 23, 1953, 12th ed., p. 3).

41. Sasaki Yoshio, "Minji chōtei ni okeru 'Goi' no kentō" (Analysis of "Agreement" in Civil Mediation), in *Kanagawa Hōgaku* (Kanagawa University Study of Law), IX, No. 1–2 (1963), 6 ff.

42. See Kawashima, "Dispute Resolution," pp. 50 ff.

43. See *ibid.*, p. 55. For statistics, see Kawashima, "Dispute Resolutions," table 12, II at p. 69.

44. Sometimes the racial or inborn nature of these characteristics has been emphasized by nationalist writers. See particularly Monbushō (Ministry of Education), *Kokutai no hongi* (Grand Principles of National Polity), p. 97; Toda Teizo, *Ie no michi* (The Way of the House) (Tokyo: Shakai-kyōiku-kyōkai [Social Education Association], 1942), p. 43.

45. See Sir George Sansom, *The Western World and Japan*, pp. 343 ff.

46. See Kawashima, "Kenri no taikei" (Systems of Rights), in Kawashima, *Kindai shakai to hō* (Modern Society and Law) (Tokyo: Iwanami-shōten, 1959), p. 1963, n. 17.

47. Leased Land and Leased House Mediation Law, Law No. 41 of 1922; Tenant Farming Law, Law No. 18 of 1924; subsequently Monetary Obligation Temporary Mediation Law, Law No. 26 of 1932; Personal Affairs Mediation Law, Law No. 11 of 1939.

48. Monbushō, *Kokutai no hongi* (Grand Principles of National Polity); Monbushō *Shinmin no michi* (The Way of the Emperor's Subjects) (Tokyo: Shakai-Kyōiku Kyōkai); Monbushō, *Senji katei kyōiku shidō yōryo* (Basic Principles of Wartime Home Education) (Tokyo: Monbushō, 1942).

49. "Tracing the development of our country since its foundation, we always find the spirit of *"wa"* (Monbushō, *Kokutai no hongi*, p. 50).

50. "Even a cup of rice or a kimono is not my own property; even during play or sleep there is no self apart from the country; everything exists in its bond with our country." (Monbushō, *Shinmin no michi*, p. 63).

51. See Kawashima, "Dispute Resolution," pp. 58 ff., on some of the findings in the survey of the social attitude by the Ministry of Labor. *Hōkensei ni tsuite no chōsa* (A Survey Regarding Feudal Characteristics), No. 7 of *Fujin kankei shiryō* (Materials relating to Women Series, 1951) and the survey by Kokuritsu Yoron Chōsajo (National Public Opinion Research Institute). *Shakai kyōiku ni tsuite no yoron chōsa* (A Public Opinion Survey Regarding Social Education), 1953.

52. Sasaki Yoshio, "Minji chotei ni okeru 'Goi' no kento" (Analysis of "Agreement" in Civil Mediation) in *Kanazawa Hōgaku* (Study of Law at Kanazawa University), IX, Nos. 1–2, (1963), 1 ff.

53. In a sampling of an urban area (Osaka City), 31.6 per cent gave as the reason for avoiding lawsuit that it is time-consuming and 44.9 per cent that it is too expensive; and in a sampling of a rural area (13 districts of Shimane Prefecture) 28 per cent alleged that lawsuit is time-consuming and 40.5 per cent that it is too expensive. See Sasaki Yoshio, *op. cit.*, p. 14.

54. Article 19 (B) and Article 23 of the Standard Stipulated Terms for Contracts for Work in Construction Projects as amended by the Central Construction Industry Council on September 15, 1962.

55. The frequency shows the number of news reports of *Asahi Shinbun* on judicial cases for civil, labor, and administrative cases (excluding criminal cases, which were often reported in the newspaper with particular interest in the scandalous nature of the case). The size of headlines shows the length of headlines in terms of the number of columns covered by the headlines. In counting the frequency, news reports on the same case in the same issue of the newspaper are counted as 1, and, in counting the size of headlines, the length of headlines regarding the same case in the same issue of the newspaper is regarded as a headline of a single report as stated above and totaled. The distribution of the size of headlines is shown in the chart on p. 287.

Size of headlines	1930	1935	1962	1963
1	3	13	11	16
2	18	20	8	12
3	5	8	22	17
4	2	2	7	6
5	0	0	5	1
6	0	0	0	4
7	1	0	3	0
8	0	0	1	0
9	0	0	1	1
10	0	0	0	1
11	0	0	0	1
13	0	0	1	0
15	0	0	0	1
21	0	0	0	1
total	29	43	59	61
mean	2.37	1.98	3.34	3.44
standard deviation	1.56	2.41	4.11	5.66

CHARLES A. MOORE   *Editor's Suppliment:**

The Enigmatic[1] Japanese Mind

THE TWO MOST fundamental characteristics of the Japanese thought-tradition and of Japanese culture, even today, may be summed up in the expressions "direct (or immediate) experience," the general experiential point of view, and "indirect thinking," "indirectness," or "indeterminateness in thought," called variously "irrationalism," anti-intellectualism, "non-rationalistic tendencies," etc. (The universal and equally significant presence of *both* of these is what makes Japan enigmatic.) The two go together, of course, as two aspects of a single basic perspective. Both of these attitudes take many forms. Illustrations are readily available representing practically every aspect of Japanese life and thought, now and traditionally. (Many such illustrations will be found herein.)

EXPERIENTIAL

On the positive side—and this is their way of seeing the situation—the Japanese have primary interest in experiencing, in living, in doing, and in enjoying life. As explained in Dr. Kishimoto's chapter herein, a Shintō worshipper is interested exclusively in his

* This Supplement constitutes an attempt to state and describe widely-accepted general characteristics of Japanese thought and culture. Frequent references are deliberately made to Japanese and non-Japanese authorities in the field (those in this volume and others) so as to support what might seem to be controversial interpretations. Strictly personal interpretations and observations, some of which will bring out more realistic aspects of the situation than are usually noted, are for the most part relegated to the notes (reference to these notes is requested) or to parenthetical statements in the text—except for the "Conclusion."

spiritual experience before the shrine; he is not interested in intellectual explanations or arguments about matters of religion. Kishimoto also explains how the Japanese, by one word, can—by pregnant suggestiveness—describe a significant experience or feeling without any elaboration or explanation such as might be required by the more intellectual or critical-minded observer, and by the more intellectual and analytical and literal languages such as those of the West (and India).[2] Zen Buddhism is so prominent in Japan, not primarily because of its apparent anti-intellectualism, as so many think, but because of its positive attitude toward living naturally rather than intellectualizing life, since such intellectualizing falsifies and distorts life.

Nakamura Hajime has elsewhere [3] explained this point of view by saying that the Japanese simply accept life as it is, with all its confusions, incompatibilities, contradictions. They always emphasize the intuitive and emotional tendencies.[3a] (In technical Buddhism, too, there is the attempt—or even the goal—to realize reality as it is or things as they are in themselves—"thusness," "suchness." There is no explanatory Absolute beyond, and there is no intellectual formulation within, life and reality *themselves*.) This is expressed technically by Nakamura, somewhat herein but more elaborately in his *Ways of Thinking*, by calling attention to the fact that for the Japanese the only Absolute they know is found within the phenomenal world.[4] The idea that *nirvāṇa* and *saṁsāra* are identical is present in much of the history of Buddhist thought, but at no time and in no tradition has it achieved the almost exclusive significance it has in Japan, because the Japanese made it conform with traditional and indigenous Japanese attitudes.

Immediate experience—"radical empiricism"—as of primary importance seems to be the key to the situation. And for the Japanese this is the most positive and realistic point of view one can adopt; any other attitude, such as, for example, the intellectual (the conceptual, the analytic, even the explanatory), is unnatural, impractical, and a distortion, a getting away from—a deliberate refusal to face—things as they actually are. It seems almost as if Japan differs from the rest of the major traditions of the world, all of which would accept the Socratic dictum that "the unexamined life is unfit to live." Japan might even counter by saying that it is the examined life that is unfit to live, because it is not *life*. This may be an extreme illustration, but it seems pertinent and sound.

ANTI-INTELLECTUAL

The "negative" aspect of this over-all attitude is the rejection of—or lack of concern with—the intellectual or intellectualistic, the rationalistic, the determinate, approach. It is surprising how many Japanese interpreters of their own tradition emphasize this point. There are striking illustrations and explanations of this point of view in some of the chapters in this volume and in a special short passage quoted herein from a paper Dr. Suzuki presented at the Third East-West Philosophers' Conference in which he contends that the East (the Far East and especially Japan) differs almost completely from the logical West.[5] The East tries to grasp reality "in its suchness or isness, or in its totality," seeing things as they are in themselves, as contrasted with logicians and scientists and Westerners generally. This is the non-logical and anti-intellectual attitude of the Far East. He says, "The Western mind abhors paradoxes, contradictions, absurdities, obscurantism, emptiness, in short, anything that is not clear, well defined, and capable of determination."[6] To the Far East, these are not to be abhorred; in fact, they represent reality as it is—and truth. Its emphasis is always on the concrete—and directness of living.

Several authorities have cited the characteristic of simplicity as basic to Japanese thought and life. They cite the three ideals of simplicity, purity, and sincerity. (See Furukawa and Kishimoto herein.) Simplicity is basic as contrasted with or even opposed to conceptual and intellectual complexity, of course. It is further illustrated in what Nakamura and Suzuki call the Japanese tendency toward *natural* living.[7]

The positive emphasis upon experience naturally minimizes the significance of intellectual examination and analysis of life and experience. Dr. Yukawa Hideki (a Nobel Prize winner in physics!) goes so far as to say, here, that "the Japanese mentality is unfit for abstract thinking." Precision, determinateness, direct logical analysis and/or exposition, and direct confrontation of any sort are simply out of order. Indirectness, suggestiveness, evasion or evasiveness, the smile rather than a logical argument,[8] sentiment rather than logic and objectivity,[9] a polite affirmative answer rather than frankness or challenging opposition, symbolism in many aspects of life and art and literature—these are all telling examples of the point. It has been said of recent political Japan—and, if sound, this is indicative of the fact that traditional Japanese ways are still the ways of Japan—"Japan has too often deluded the U.S. by hiding its true beliefs behind a mask of courtesy . . . respect transcends frankness in the scale of customary values." [10] This is nothing new to Japan. In history there has traditionally been the facade of the power of the Emperor, who had the traditional right to absolute power by virtue of divine origin and mandate, *along with* the "indirect" or "hidden" real power of others ruling him—right up to 1945.[11]

Here—in all this, and more—we find a substantial and comprehensive challenge to the entire attitude of intellectualism—and even rationalism—so dominant in and so demanded by the West, so prominent but sometimes transcended in India, and dominant but with significant limitations in China, but rejected almost completely in Japan. (One is impelled to add: except, perhaps, in the more mechanical sides of life, where the Japanese seem to show no lack of intellectual capacity, ingenuity, and precision.) Perhaps—despite Yukawa and others—it is not that they are incapable of, but that they are not interested in, the abstract and intellectual approach—in concepts, universals, abstract principles, absolutes. Perhaps they are simply interested in other things: living, doing, experiencing, enjoying [12]—and inner tranquillity or serenity, the "spiritual" side.

The two major aspects of this basic attitude, namely, the emphasis upon actual experience, actual living, and second, the rejection of the intellectualistic examination of life and experience, are closest to our problem in attempting to describe and understand as best we can the philosophical and psychological essence of the Japanese mind. And they make such understanding most difficult. (Or, do they really? The West has had comparable attitudes and points of view, of course, and still has. The Japanese views are different, yes, but not unintelligible.)

One of the most significant features of this anti-intellectualism—as possibly both cause and effect—is either the incapacity to think in terms of absolute or universal abstract principles or at least the ignoring of such universals or absolutes in thinking, even in thinking about life—and, as a matter of fact, in living. At one place, not here, Nakamura refers to Japanese Buddhism's rejection of even the basic principles of Buddhist discipline, because principles are meaningless and objectionable to the Japanese.[13]

This "inability" to think in terms of absolutes and universals and concepts is sometimes explained in part (by Japanese) as either caused by or reflected in the Japanese language—discussed herein in three distinct papers (those by Dr. Nakamura, Dr. Furukawa, and Dr. Kōsaka)—because the very language they use to express their ideas does not lend itself to absolutes or universals or abstract principles.[14] In a sense, then, the attitude is practically inescapable.

In studying the Indian mind, the Chinese mind, and the Japanese mind—in the three volumes in this series—the purpose of such study and the values to be derived therefrom are two: to learn about and to learn from. First, such a study is indispensable (and highly fruitful) as a basis of fundamental understanding of the people concerned, and, second, the more strictly philosophical purpose and value is that of enlarging the sum total of philosophical knowledge and wisdom and of broadening the horizon of philosophers of all traditions and cultures by the discovery of new experiences, new insights, new interpretations, perhaps even new meanings for philosophy itself, in the thought-tradition being examined. (Surely no two cultures and/or traditions are identical. Nor are the experiences of their thinkers, nor the thought-processes, the insights, the "intuitions," the perspectives, the attitudes, and even the methods of perception and thinking, including the form and degree of perceptiveness.)

Both India and China unquestionably have much to contribute to the total perspective of philosophy, because in each there is a substantial and well-defined philosophical tradition. On the contrary, it has been contended widely—it is the consensus— that little is to be gained in this direction by a study of Japanese thought, because of its essential lack of a genuinely (and indigenous) philosophical tradition.

Actually, this derogatory interpretation of Japanese philosophy might well be rather tragically incorrect, in both fact and interpretation, almost a typical false cliché about Asia. This is especially true if we are willing to face realistically and openmindedly the realization that the very concept of philosophy itself might well need broadening and greater comprehensiveness instead of being limited to any single interpretation required by one's own particular traditional point of view, be it Western, Indian, Chinese, or whatever. Furthermore, Japanese thought, both as a whole and in its specific basic characteristics, has much to contribute to the total perspective that is—or is required of—philosophy. In many of the essential points of view, attitudes, and methods of thinking that are characteristic of the Japanese way, in the principles which have provided the basis for the adaptation rather than the mere adoption of alien points of view, and in what unquestionably must be called their over-all *Weltanschauung*, the Japanese offer valuable unique ideas and ideals. Let it be philosophy or not, strictly—or Westernly—speaking, this is a thought-tradition and a cultural tradition which may well be the most suggestive and the most provocative of the major traditions of Asia—simply, and paradoxically, because it does not conform either in general or in detail to what might be called the orthodox or usual philosophical attitude which permeates—and, in fact, dominates—the philosophical scene in the West, nearly so in India, and, yes, also in China, though to a somewhat lesser degree. (Even Japanese Zen is very different from Chinese Zen—a long and complicated subject.)

The *sheer novelty* of the total point of view and of many of the particular attitudes and methods of thought and attitudes toward life can be both exciting and substantially valuable to the open-minded philosopher of both East and West. The very facts that constituted the enigma and paradox that are Japan are the same facts that may well be of greatest significance to those whose thought-traditions and cultures differ so markedly from the Japanese. There are extreme exaggerations of Chinese points of view but one must never underestimate the inestimable influence of China upon Japan.

And now for some specific at least alleged characteristics.

EXOTIC

The consensus is that there is a dearth of substantial, original, and creative philosophy in the history of Japanese culture and the Japanese thought-tradition.[15] Japan's thought-tradition is usually labeled "exotic" because practically all of its basic philosophical points of view—and this includes almost the entire fabric of cultural life—are taken from outside sources, chiefly, of course, China, Korea, and India (and recently the West, especially German idealism and American pragmatism). According to this interpretation, Japanese "philosophy" has been essentially a matter of study and interpretation of alien points of view and their adaptation so as to make them useful and fitting for the Japanese.

This deprecatory judgment about Japanese philosophy finds some substantiation in a study of the course of development of Japanese thought, a development which reveals little substantial philosophy that is indigenous and original or creative. It is also evidenced in certain basic characteristics of Japanese mentality which seem to militate against the development of philosophical thought in its critical, thoroughgoing, fundamental, intellectual, and logical aspects.

It is these indigenous characteristics of the Japanese mind and culture which serve as the basis of the process of adapting the several outside philosophical points of view to the Japanese situation. In taking from the outside world, Japan has very thoroughly adapted "borrowed" alien philosophies to its own needs and its own mentality, sometimes so much so that the Japanese versions are hardly close enough to the original to be recognizable—as best illustrated perhaps in the case of Japanese Buddhism.[16] (One might mention here also the many significant modifications and excessive —or exaggerated—interpretations of basic Chinese, Confucian, points of view, but this is a long story.) The Japanese are the most openminded people in the world in welcoming ideas and ideals from alien sources, and are seemingly less dogmatically proud of their *thought*-tradition.[17] But it is this tradition itself that provides the restrictive and interpretive principles of adaptation when alien ideas are brought in—and they are of special importance for us.

It seems appropriate and advisable to provide here a preliminary exposition and explanation of these basic principles of the Japanese mind—its thought and its psychological tendencies.[18] The principles presented here will be primarily a set of guidelines for the over-all perspective and comprehension of the tradition which is described in detail in the essays in this volume. These essays are studies of particular aspects of the over-all picture of Japanese thought and culture and do not attempt to provide the type of comprehensive or outlined picture which the reader might find useful. It is the purpose of this Introduction to provide such an over-all picture, whether the details are discussed in this volume or not—and many of them are not.

Emphasis herein will be placed upon explaining and understanding the Japanese tradition rather than concentrating upon or giving exclusive attention to contemporary . conditions as such. This is not due to mere antiquarian interest in history. It is based upon the general conviction that the present cannot be understood except in relation to the past, the tradition, upon which the present is based. And this is strongly so in the case of Japan, which has such a strong cultural tradition. As her most respected philosopher,

Nishida Kitarō has said, "In order to explain what Japanese culture is like, we must look back on its history, studying its institutions and civilization." [19]

Practical-mindedness and worldliness.[19a] Japan has been worldly and realistic from the very beginning. (See Dr. Sakamaki's paper herein.) This probably the most significant clue to the wide range of attitudes that constitute the Japanese perspective. It seems to be the most enlightening general attitude and the most pervasive, and the significant, thread that tends to hold together a wide variety of attitudes and practices. (This point will be much in evidence in the chapters here, where it will be revealed in its many ramifications. It therefore needs not further elaboration here.)

ECLECTIC

Japanese thought is significantly and widely described as "eclectic." And here we find further evidence of practical-mindedness—as we have already found it, in fact, in the adaptation rather than the adoption of alien points of view.[19b] The basis of such adaptation has not been intellectual. It has been strictly in terms of practical suitability for Japanese life. The Japanese tend to combine points of view which are incompatible in strictly intellectual and logical precision—for example, Confucianism, Taoism, Buddhism, and Shintō. Each of these seems to provide a basis for the practical adjustment to some one aspect of life, and all, together, provide a comprehensive philosophy of life, logically compatible or not—and they are not compatible unless and until they are interpreted so as to *make* them so, if that is at all possible.[20]

HARMONY

Most Japanese would use the word "harmony" instead of the somewhat derogatory term "eclecticism." Like the Indians and the Chinese, the Japanese stress harmony and tolerance—and try more than others to minimize both practical and intellectual cleavages and confrontation. In Japan, this tendency is dominant. In most of the adjustments to life, whether they are in philosophy, religion, or practical affairs, there are clear intellectual incompatibilities, but to the Japanese mind they are not so—or it does not matter if they are—in the name of intellectual and practical harmony (and tolerance). (Whether tolerance-harmony is cause or result of the eclectic tendency is a question). Sometimes there seems to have been little serious realization of the problem, little attempt to overcome the incompatabilities, and even less genuine success when the effort has been made.

In this matter of eclecticism (or uncritically accepted harmony), and in the emphasis upon practical-mindedness as opposed to the more intellectual approach to life and the world, we immediately sense the unavoidable and inevitable difficulty that any outsider encounters in his attempt to understand the Japanese people and their mentality. Although there is no such thing as the inscrutable East or the inscrutable Oriental, the Japanese are perhaps the most difficult of all Asians to understand in any substantial and comprehensive manner or degree [21]—as will be more and more evident as we proceed.

AESTHETIC

A famous illustration of the non-intellectualistic approach to life and reality, another evidence of the positive emphasis upon direct experience, is the Japanese emphasis upon the aesthetic point of view and attitude in practically all aspects of life and culture. Tagore has called aesthetics Japan's unique *Dharma*.[22] Kishimoto, here, speaks of the aesthetic as being so significant as to be identical with the religious in Japan, in what is surely a unique emphasis upon the aesthetic. Kōsaka, here, points to the *essential* aesthetic emphasis in Japanese culture practically throughout its history—such that Japanese culture *is* an aesthetic culture. And Nakamura, here and elsewhere, stresses what he calls the primacy of the aesthetic, the intuitive, the emotional,[23] and the simple symbolic tendencies of the Japanese.[24]

So important is the aesthetic in Japanese culture that it has been accepted by many students of Japan as the outstanding positive characteristic of Japanese culture as a whole [25]—as of the very essence of Japanese life. In comparison with other cultures, the aesthetic has been considered to be the essentially unique expression of spirituality in Japan, as is ethics in China, religion in India, and, possibly, reason in the West.[26] Their love of beauty; their extreme and seemingly universal love of Nature; their attempt to express beauty in all aspects of life (the tea ceremony, flower arrangement, gardens, etc.); the spirit and fact (or, at least, ideal) of harmony in philosophy, in religion, and in the social and political order; their obvious emphasis upon feeling and emotion; their almost all-pervading romanticism; and, possibly, the "feminine" characterization that is so often cited [27]—these are all well known and accepted as characteristic. (It is interesting, and perhaps typical, that even the liquor menu on a Japanese airline takes the form of a beautiful fold-up Japanese fan!) And, perhaps of special significance, the ugly and the evil seem to be identical (see Kōsaka's paper herein).[28]

RELIGION

These same characteristics are evidenced in Japanese religions, where eclecticism, flexibility, lack of intellectual concern, lack of universality, and the down-to-earth realism and practicality of the Japanese are predominant. Ultimate concerns seem to be of little importance to the Japanese. There is no transcendentalism or universalism in Japanese religion. The major problems are the achievement of inner tranquillity and the serene facing of the problems of life. (And as will be seen later, aesthetic experience and religious experience are apparently equally effective here.) Transcendentalism of any sort is unwelcome. Shintōism, Confucianism, and Buddhism go hand in hand—for practical purposes, or is it tolerance and harmony, or is it intellectual indifference? Japan is often called the land of Buddhism, but the Buddhism of Japan seems a far cry from original Buddhism or even from present-day Buddhism in South and Southeast Asia—and even from that developed in humanistic China. In one chapter in this book—Kishimoto's —Buddhism is described as a joyful religion, because the Japanese are a life-enjoying people.[29] The rejection or major modification of so many basic principles of Buddhist philosophy, religion, and ethics could happen only in Japan.

ETHICS

Japanese ethics is also characteristically unique. There is no attempt to find a philosophical or metaphysical or religious basis for ethics. Ethics in Japan is merely a pattern of social living— more so than in humanistic China. It is realistic, almost opportunistic, apparently without absolutes or universals, except for the one basic ethical principle of duty-loyalty to the group and to the superior-dominated and exclusively Japanese social nexus—and whatever actions are required thereby. Spontaneity—not intelligently planned action (see Furukawa's paper)—and inwardness, inner purity, serenity, and emphasis upon motive, rather than following basic thought-out principles seem to be of the essence.

To an outsider, the ethical complex of Japan is quite confusing: for example, the status of freedom of individual conscience as compared with the demands of absolute loyalty and duty, although here again the Japanese do not find confusion or conflict (see Furukawa's chapter)—external performance is based upon inner positive willingness and desire to do one's duty.

It is to be noted that this traditional ethics is far from dead in Japan. There is confusion now, as one writer in this volume (Furukawa) says, as to just what are the values worth seeking in life—the old or the new? (At another place in this volume it is noted that defeat in the war and occupation by the victorious army "legitimized" the dignity of the individual but at the same time destroyed traditional Japanese ethics—in what would seem to be a significant remark.) Just as the Japanese remade Buddhism to fit the Japanese scene, so Dr. Kenneth Saunders could say, "Confucius would have been surprised" if he had known how the Japanese adapted his virtue of loyalty to the "glorification of warriors and feudal chieftains, over scholars and philosophers." [30] To some, Japan's ethics is little beyond the ethics of pure utility and expediency and the acceptance of sociological principles and mores in which the basic Western virtues lose status. In name of duty, loyalty, etc., truth and conscience would seem to lose status.

SOCIAL NEXUS

Still another aspect of the practical and the antiuniversal perspective in what Naskamura calls (see page 143 ff. herein) the Japanese emphasis upon the social nexus (or human relationships) and, beyond that, "complete devotion to the exclusive social nexus of Japan." This attitude works against giving attention to universals that transcend either the social nexus itself—in which attitude Japan has much in common with humanistic China, where it has been said, "People come first"—and specifically the Japanese social nexus. This is the reason given for the non-acceptability of any universal religion except after adapting it to the Japanese social nexus. As noted earlier, it is also found in the rejection of the *principles* of Buddhist discipline. This attitude has ramifications in almost all aspects of life and also, it would seem, in reference to international relationships, political and diplomatic relationships, and to ethical principles, as well as to religion. In traditional Japan, the Emperor (or the state), the personal (or "official") embodiment of the exclusive Japanese social nexus, was completely dominant in life and thought up to 1945.[31]

ANTI-INDIVIDUAL

Very closely related to this matter of social nexus—and also the exclusive social nexus of Japan—is the problem of the status of the individual as related to the various group-patterns to which he belongs, from the family up to the state. As said in the Preface of this volume, the problem of the status of the individual is so fundamental that the entire Fourth East-West Philosophers' Conference was devoted to it (as are six chapters herein). This was done partly because there is so much uncertainty concerning the status of the individual—and of democracy—in the several Asian traditions (perhaps especially in Japan) in the past and even at the present time. All of these traditions seem to belittle the individual in terms of group relationships, perhaps especially Japan.[32]

The status of the individual in Japan is a problem that leaves one bewildered because of the widely varying interpretations available. The emphasis has always seemed to be on the group rather than on the individual, on duties rather than rights, on loyalty to group or hierarchical superior, and this emphasis has seemed to be stronger in Japan than in any other major tradition. There it leads up to the dominance of the state to such an extent that one paper in this volume (Nakamura's 1959 paper [32a]) makes the point that the state traditionally determined all thought in Japan, a concept which falls in line with the idea of absolute devotion to the unique social nexus of Japan.

There are many additional aspects or indications of this feature of Japanese culture: the hierarchical structure of society generally; the universal sense of social rank—as evidenced even in language usage; the many-sided fact of and demand for discipline (inner and outer); the sense for control (inner and outer); and the over-all spirit and fact of authoritarianism (allegedly adopted from Confucianism but, if so, reaching an extreme degree that Confucianism would certainly have rejected) in all walks of life and in thought.

This notion of the dominance of the group over the individual seems to be the consensus.[32b,33] But in this volume (see Nakamura, Kōsaka, Kawashima) we find abundant evidence strongly to the contrary. And so, the problem persists—and so does the confusion. (There is also the interesting fact of group inferiority—the class known as "outcasts" and the Okinawans. These conditions are now illegal, but, like caste prejudice in India, persists strongly.)

There is *a substantial* paradox here—especially in terms of the previously noted emphasis on experience *and* the anti-intellectual-istic rejection of concepts, universals, etc. Both of these aspects of the Japanese mind—see Kōsaka's and Nakamura's chapters herein for numerous illustrations—would, one would think, provide a basis for individualism, and so would the language and the "logic" of the Japanese, which reject universals and concepts. And yet, the groupism which unquestionably prevails from family to state and the monism which so many interpreters find in Japanese culture would seem to conflict seriously with individualism—in another serious and difficult-to-escape paradox. Part of the solution comes, perhaps, from the fact that, to the Japanese, the family is not a conceptual group or universal and that the state is not an institution or a universal comprehending all individuals as members, but an all-inclusive family in which the emperor is not a sovereign as such but a person, the head of the family of all the people—and so superior, as one Japanese has said that the very problem of the relative status of the individual could not even arise.[33a] But the conflict between what seem to be the individualistic implications of these basic traits, on the one hand, and the tendencies or facts that are so anti-individualistic, on the other, remains and is seriously puzzling: just where does the individual stand?

DEMOCRACY

One of the major concerns in this connection has to do with the foundation upon which democracy in contemporary Japan has been built, the question being whether such democracy is com-patible with Japanese tradition relative to the status of the individ-ual, whether it is established on a solid or, at least, an adequately solid foundation in that tradition, or whether it is merely the result of external pressure, military dictation, and/or the psychology of the times—and thus possibly uncertain in terms of permanence.[34] Hasegawa is frank enough to say, "Now, when Japan is beginning on a new footing as a free and democratic state (as a result of the directions and guidance imposed upon us by America), it may be wondered whether instead of making intellectual judgments based on a strictly objective cognition of the realities facing Japan, there is not a tendency to indulge in a subjective, cerebral development of the abstract ideas of 'freedom' and 'democracy'! We may also wonder what the practical results will be." [35] It has been said, "Democracy exists here [in Japan] but its roots are scarcely deep." On the other hand, it may well be that Japan's traditional practice of "borrowing" from other cultures and traditions, plus its equally traditional practice of adapting alien ideas to its purposes, may enable Japan, without much of a traditional basis otherwise, to adopt and adapt in this case also. The result will (or would) be, not American democracy—that seems practically impossible for Japan—but Japanese democracy, with all the qualifications that expression implies. These are questions which must be faced but which do not seem to be subject to clear-cut answers—as seems to be the case with so many problems in the context of Japanese tradition.

LAW

In the legal "system" of Japan we find another paradox—and more confusion—with respect to this same problem. On the political side, we seem to find domination by the group all the way up to the state, which traditionally dominated completely and essentially made the individual insignificant because of the demand for absolute loyalty and duty. On the other hand, surprisingly perhaps, we find in the legal area—see Dr. Kawashima's paper—a much greater emphasis upon and concern for the individual personality than in the mechanical or universalistic and strictly conceptualistic laws of the West.[36] (And the idea of harmony versus conflict applies here, too.) The point is that nothing is mechanical or absolute—or conceptual—in Japan, not even the law (except, traditionally, the rather ultimate dominance of the state and the demand for absolute loyalty on the part of the individual). But all this is in a state of great flux and transition today—with more confusion and uncertainty. But, if Japan continues to go toward the West in its legal system, will not Japanese law also become mechanical and forgetful of the real person versus its entire tradition, or which it is proud?

In this seeming conflict between the individual and the group, from family to state, the outsider finds strongly undemocratic and anti-individualistic tendencies, as he finds also in the strong emphasis upon duties rather than rights. But, as in all cases, the attempt must be made to understand this situation as far as possible as the Japanese themselves understand it. As mentioned before, seeming conflicts in the Japanese complex are generally overcome or dissolved by the attitude of harmony, which apparently pervades the whole of Japanese thought and culture. At least two points here explain this the positive essence of this spirit and fact of harmony, and Nakamura indicates the same thing even when he speaks of "ultra-nationalistic tendencies to absolute *devotion* [not submission]to a specific [superior] individual." [37] But there is another fact of significance, too. This is that the Japanese have apparently always found in their social and political system from family to state—as perhaps also in their eclectic philosophical and religious perspectives—a degree of peace of mind and security and harmonious living that the rest of the world does not achieve and frequently even condemns. From the family to the state, the individual "belongs." He finds protection, warmth, security, dependability, and, what seems to be most important to the Japanese, peace of mind, inner tranquillity, and personal serenity.[38] These are the values which underlie and explain the *willing* acceptance of social, political, religious, and ethical customs and practices which are most difficult for the outsider to understand and appreciate.

Before the statement of what might constitute a justifiable conclusion of this Introduction, one or two factual qualifications should be noted.

For one thing, the emphasis upon harmony in Japanese thought and culture—and in practically all accounts—must not blind us to certain elements of disharmony that prevail in Japanese thought and culture, past and present. It has already been mentioned [39] that the characterization of Japanese culture as aesthetic is faulty because it ignores the realistic fact that there is also crudeness, rudeness, loudness, roughness and sheer sensuality. Reference has also been made, elsewhere, to "the influence of the harsh feudal laws . . . on the thinking of the Japanese people." One could also note the factual domination of the lower classes, the marked subordination or women (despite disclaimers), the "cheapness" of life—recall "recently" the capture of Singapore— and historically infanticide as examples.[39a] All is not sweetness and light, or agreement and harmony, or respect for the dignity of man as an individual, in Japanese thought and/or culture. The tendency to overlook the realistic, the inharmonious, the unaesthetic, the ethically unscrupulous, even the unspiritual, is met with protest, but the protest is not sound.

Secondly, it might be well to note also that, even in the realm of thought, historically speaking, as well as in the area of religions, there has not been nearly so much harmony and lack of intellectual antagonism and opposition, or lack of the intellectual investigation and acumen, as ordinarily maintained. But this lack of harmony is of value—to human knowledge. Many speak about the dearth of philosophy and intellectual ability and activity and about the sheer eclecticism of Japanese thought and culture. One Japanese scholar's interpretation is that this eclecticism is sheer eclecticism, essentially an unexamined chaotic jumble of conflicting attitudes ("leaving borrowed cultures in irrelevant juxtaposition"). Also, there seems to be little doubt that there has been less polemical thinking and writing in Japan than in most any other major tradition. However—a strong "however"—there have also been almost throughout Japanese history, certainly not later than the coming of Confucianism and Taoism from China and then Buddhism from India (via China and Korea), constant intellectual conflicts and numerous intellectual efforts at synthesis which were not merely eclectic but actually much more argumentative and mutually critical and apparently much more intellectual in their methods than many seem to realize. In fact, the very process of adapting alien views, theories, and practices to Japan's needs, including theoretical modifications of Buddhist doctrines and the achievement of "synthesis" between Buddhism and Shintō has, itself, required genuine intellectual activity and ability.[40] This whole point deserves much further consideration, but not here.[41]

Conclusion

Because of its eclectic tendencies and because of its non- or anti-intellectualistic attitude, Japanese thought and culture—the Japanese people and Japan, that is, and the Japanese mind—have been variously described by authorities as "enigmatic," "paradoxical," "ambiguous," "flexible," etc. These are terms which, if correct, emphasize the difficulty of achieving genuine understanding of the Japanese. And, to make matters worse, all of these terms, and similar ones, seems justified in the light of the historical and even the contemporary situation. Present-day Japan is obviously a culture in great transition, and one which almost of necessity feels the significant co-presence of conflicting and even contradictory or at least significantly differing tendencies. Also, practically throughout Japan's history (after an early era of simplicity, perhaps), there have always been conflicting major tendencies which made and make clarity of understanding and clear interpretation next to impossible. This is not unique to Japan, of course; no advanced culture is simple enough to justify clear-cut descriptions or characterizations. But the Japanese situation seems to be truly unique because of its excesses in this direction. There seems to be not one single basic quality or characteristic or attitude which clearly expresses or embodies the character of the people and which does not co-exist with its very opposite—except, probably, the *felt* "Spirit of Japan," the "Japanese Spirit," or what Dr. Takakusu Junjirō has called the "Culture of the Blood" [42]—this, and perhaps the deeply engrained and very-difficult-to-eradicate tradition, or assumption, or even the now officially denied myth, of racial and national superiority.

We thus find Japanese thought and culture presenting an assemblage of ideas, ideals, attitudes, practices, and methods of thinking—astoundingly different, in their totality or unity, from every other major Asian tradition and from the West. There are here more challenges to "orthodox" points of view of both East and West than are presented by any other major tradition. This is the key to the profound difficulties to be encountered in seeking understanding. But it is also the essence of the contributions which Japanese thought and culture can make to human knowledge and to a much-needed wider philosophical perspective.

Since contemporary students of the Asian cultures are—and almost must be—vitally interested in the significance of whatever knowledge and understanding we can achieve on the practical level of world affairs and intellectual affairs, it might be appropriate to offer an interpretive observation or two here. If looked at realistically—and we must do this—this confusing and sometimes mystifying composite of characteristic attitudes and tendencies and values does not augur well for dependability, stability, and assured co-operation on the world scene; instead, it would seem to indicate unpredictability, without even basic points of view—or even standards, goals, and values—that can be counted on to prevail and/or persist. And the seriousness of the problem might well be increased by the fact that the prominent presence of such Western tendencies as economic progress, liberalism, and political democracy becloud the judgment of the West to the great degree to which traditional values still guide the lives and thought of the people of Japan.

Present-day Japan—as well as traditional Japan in its way—is, or presents, a most complicated state of affairs. The contrast of Tokyo and Kyoto has been cited as symbolic of the conflict in contemporary Japan—Tokyo, of course, representing the modern, much-Westernized, city, whereas Kyoto represents traditional Japan (and perhaps some 80 per cent of the people of the country), largely unaffected by Westernization and modernization. But there is much more to the contemporary situation than this. And it is noteworthy that, in all this, despite contentions to the contrary by Japanese and non-Japanese outside observers alike, traditional Japan—certainly right up to 1945, and not likely to die or be abandoned "over it"—is still very much alive and the conflict between tradition and modernization is very real. What, then, is "the Japanese way"? (See footnote no. 5—the last sentence.)

There is in present-day Japan, a co-presence of—and perhaps conflict between—the traditional *and* the modern; progressiveness and traditionalism or conservatism; the Eastern *and* the Western; what might be termed "outlawed" "ultra-nationalism" [43] (again, certainly up to 1945) *and* an unquestioned revival of political nationalism and even of nationalistic religion in the strong revival of Shintō (and the development of militant Buddhist movements); the aesthetic *and* the mechanical; the strongly feminine *and* the equally strongly masculine; the inner attitude *and* the outer expression; the alleged attitude of naturalism or naturalistic activity and the expected complete control of emotions, at least as far as external expression is concerned; basic internal conflicts of values; "delicate" *and* militant; a non-militant constitution and, some say, a traditional extra-legal tendency to revive a military force; the idea of peacefulness in Buddhism *and* the ever-present and persisting spirit of the *samurai* (and recall in this connection the paradoxical —to outsiders—study of Zen by the warrior); also "the readiness to defend the social nexus by means of force," [44] and, to bring this up to date, we may recall the typical Japanese theory and practice of fighting to the death and no surrender, and also the spirit of the *kamikaze* pilot; non-intellectualism *and* the scientific and technological progress that is so characteristic of contemporary Japan (in war and in industry); democracy *and* groupism, and hierarchy of various degrees and on all levels; and, to be more specific, emphasis upon the significance of the individual, his freedom and dignity, on the one hand, *and*, on the other, the ineradicable emphasis upon strong group tendencies despite some contemporary breakdown or lessening of the significance of such relationships.

This situation presents serious confusion and almost unintelligibility to an outsider looking at Japan through the eyes of intellectualism and the either/or type of thinking which demands clarity and determinateness and the rejection, as Dr. Suzuki says, of paradoxes, contradiction, and the like.

But the situation does not seem to be confusing to the Japanese themselves. To them, with their eclectic perspective, with their non-intellectualistic tendencies, and with their strong sense of uncritical harmony, this seeming confusion is not serious confusion—though one wonders. (This was probably much truer of classical and relatively simple Japan, of course, than it could possibly be of contemporary Japan.) And it is the intellectual and human obligation of "outsiders" to understand—or feel—with the Japanese, to try to see them as they see themselves. Then "understanding" may be achieved—possibly.

The significant questions here, of course, are: (1) whether—and/or just how far—traditional ideas and ideals and methods are and will continue to be effective for the Japanese (at home and in international relations)—despite internal and external pressure to create a "new Japan"—and (2) whether Japan can and will escape from or rise above, or overcome, the paradoxes that make understanding so difficult to outsiders and seem to prevent a clear-cut and unanimous attitude even by the Japanese themselves?

But, even if full understanding and clarity of description are next to impossible, there is the very significant philosophical point that some of these "peculiar" attitudes and perspectives and methods may be the very essence of Japan's significant contribution to man's knowledge about man, society, and life itself—and to philosophy and to our understanding of the human situation *in its totality*.

The *big* question is can and will the Japanese *in Tokyo* retain their new interest in the new Japan—or will they really want to? Opinion differs considerably on this basic question but the chances are that the basic Japanese "tendency of thinking persists to this day." [44a]

A nmemonic clue—a rather remarkably fitting one—is offered to help pinpoint certain apparent tendencies, in spite of complexity and confusion. It reminds one of the key descriptions cited here which start with the letter "E"—exotic, eclectic, enigmatic, evasive, extra-legalistic, earthly (or worldly), "Emperor Institution," experiental, enjoyment (hedonistic), empirical, esthetic, economically (or materially) oriented [45]—and energetic. And, possibly most important of all, the genuine and basic *esprit* of Japanese tradition and culture—the "Culture of the Blood," the exclusive social nexus, or ethnocentrism, call it what one will.

Notes

1. A number of terms were considered as the key characterization to be used here: ambiguous, enigmatic, paradoxical, etc. "Enigmatic" seems to be the most appropriate.
2. A similar suggestiveness, rather than literalness, is embodied in much of Japanese literature, especially poetry, and specifically in *haiku* (the 17-syllable poem).
3. Hajime Nakamura (Nakamura Hajime), *Ways of Thinking of Eastern Peoples: India, China, Tibet, Japan*, Philip P. Wiener, ed. (rev. ed., Honolulu: East-West Center Press, 1964), pp. 531–576.
3a. *Ibid.*, p. 551.
4. *Ibid.*, pp. 350–576.
5. See Suzuki, "Basic Thoughts Underlying Eastern Ethical and Social Practice," in Charles A. Moore, ed., *Philosophy and Culture— East and West* (Honolulu: University of Hawaii Press, 1962), pp. 428–447.
6. *Ibid.*, p. 429.
7. See Nakamura, *Ways of Thinking*, pp. 372–380; also Suzuki, *op. cit.*
8. An interesting presentation of this point is by Nakane Chie, in her "Logic and the Smile—When the Japanese Meet Indians," *Japan Quarterly*, XI, No. 4 (October–December, 1964).
9. Ambassador Edwin O. Reischauer was quoted as saying this (with specific reference to the Japanese attitude toward Communist China) in an interview at the time his resignation was announced.
10. C. L. Sulzberger, "Look Mama San, No Hands," *The New York Times* (May 20, 1966).
11. Minoru Shinoda (Shinoda Minoru) has called this the "extra-legalistic" handling of political matters. (See also reference to this point in its contemporary setting and significance in the "Conclusion" of this Supplement.) See also G. B. Sansom, *Japan: A Short Cultural History of Japan* (rev. ed., New York: D. Appleton-Century Company, 1943), p. 207.
12. Hasegawa Nyozekan has contended that, among other changes which must be made by the new Japan, "the hedonism generally characteristic of Japanese culture must be changed." In this *Ushinawareta Nihon*, quoted in Wm. Theodore de Bary, ed.,

Sources of the Japanese Tradition (New York: Columbia University Press, 1958), p. 897.

13. For an enlightening discussion of emphasis upon things and events rather than principles, see Nakamura, *Ways of Thinking*, especially chap. 34. A noted agricultural economist has made this point repeatedly in referring to the Japanese tendency to accumulate facts and data without any interest in a competence for determining logical implications.

14. One reviewer of Nakamura's *Ways of Thinking* has pointed out that, true, the original or native Japanese language was unsuited for absolute, universals, and abstract principles, but that for hundreds of years the Japanese language has incorporated Chinese terms and in this sense has not thereafter been incapable of expressing such principles. See review of Nakamura, *Ways of Thinking* by Philip Yampolsky, *Philosophy East and West*, XIV, No. 2 (April 9, 1965), 181.

15. This widely held view will be examined, though not adequately, later in this Supplement, but it is noted here and now that the interpretation is open to challenge.

16. Nakamura says, "It was within the framework of their own peculiar nationalistic standpoint and orientation that the Japanese accepted Buddhism. . . . They were not converted to Buddhism. They converted Buddhism to their own tribalism." *Ways of Thinking*, p. 528. See also pp. 434–449.

Nakamura, pp. 345–587, presents an excellent survey of the fundamentals of the Japanese way of thinking. (Frequent references will be made to this volume for the convenience of those interested in looking further into some of the points made here.) According to Nakamura, the three essential comprehensive characteristics are: "the acceptance of phenomenalism" (including "this-worldliness"), "the tendency to emphasize a limited social nexus," and "non-rationalistic tendencies," all of which are explained fundamentally and extensively.

These, to be sure, are characteristic of *traditional* Japan, but we must keep in mind Nakamura's "warning": "The Japanese way of thinking is undergoing a change, *but their thinking is an inheritance, a tradition.*" The past is far from dead in Japan—such a strong tradition cannot be destroyed by military defeat or by edict from on high [although this "procedure" is almost typical of Japan!], be it alien or native—and, yet, Japan is, nevertheless—again, paradoxically—unquestionably the most progressive and modern nation in Asia.

17. See Yoshikawa Kōjirō, "The Introduction of Chinese Culture," *Japan Quarterly*, VIII, No. 2 (April–June, 1961). "Thought" is

italicized here, because this lack of pride does not apply to the political tradition.

18. One feels guilty here of indulging in the possibly questionable procedure of attempting to "define" or characterize an entire tradition and culture. It is doubtful, of course, that any culture can or should be subjected to the oversimplification that is almost required in any such attempt. But this is especially true of Japan because its two *basic* characteristics are completely opposite. To the completely contrary, see Pearl S. Buck, *The People of Japan* (New York: Simon and Schuster, 1966). (One investigator recently wrote: ". . . the Japanese 'worship' the Emperor in their hearts if not on paper.") One should be ever conscious of what has been called "the inherent limitations of the national-character approach." However, it is within reason—and experience—to contend that every people does have a character—a national character—by which it can be identified and distinguished. Any people or culture must have a basic set of norms or values and principles that identify it as a people; self-identity is impossible otherwise, and no people would admit lack of distinctive identity. It is on this basis that the attempt is here undertaken to suggest certain "characteristics" of the Japanese mind. Generally speaking, they are continuing major emphases, regardless of historical modifications and admitted complexity and ambiguity.

19. From his *Nihon bunka no mondai,* quoted in Wm. Theodore de Bary, ed., *Sources of Japanese Tradition,* p. 859.

19a. Could her trading with Communist China and her developing warm relationships with Russia be examples?

19b. Maruyama Masao calls special attention to the Japanese "special way" of thinking and of reacting to new ideas. Speaking of their "lack of reflection" and "tolerance," and of the primacy of practical application, he says, ". . . a Japanese may embrace and adopt a limitless variety of ideas and academic propositions, even when some of them are contradictory. "Japanese Thought," *Iwanami kōza: gendai shisō,* XI (1957), 3–46, especially pp. 41–43.

20. While Chinese thought and culture are also given to eclecticism, the Chinese were more intellectually conscious of the need for synthesis, and the achievement in Chinese philosophy was substantial synthesis rather than mere eclecticism. For example, see Wing-tsit Chan (Chan Wing-tsit), "Syntheses in Chinese Metaphysics," in Charles A. Moore, ed., *Essays in East-West Philosophy* (Honolulu: University of Hawaii Press, 1951), chap. VIII.

21. There is an opposite possible interpretation, however. This is that the Japanese are not at all difficult to understand if one will only realize that they are dominated by matter-of-fact practical-minded-

ness, or even worldliness, that they are not especially concerned with the intellectual aspects of their culture, and thus that there is no "mystery" or "enigma" about their mentality or culture.

22. *The Religion of Man* (New York: The Macmillan Company, 1931), pp. 150–152.

23. *Ways of Thinking*, pp. 551–557; 564–573.

24. Hasegawa Nyozekan says, "The fact that national movements do not assume an intellectual direction is a reflection of the intuitive culture. Japanese religions and academic culture have similarly tended to be governed by primitive mysticism and illogicality." He goes on to say even that "the war was started as the result of a mistaken intuitive 'calculation' . . . the characteristic reliance on intuition by Japanese blocked the objective cognition of the objective world." *Op. cit.*, pp. 895–896.

25. "Aesthetic" was strongly suggested as the key terms of the title of this Introduction, but was rejected on the basis of its inadequacy or possible incorrectness, in the light of the total situation. (See note 28, below.)

26. See Charles A. Moore, "The Spiritual Approach to East-West Understanding," in Swami Sivananda, ed., *The World Philosophers Congress* (Dt. Tehri-Garhwal, India: The Yoga-Vedanta Forest Academy, 1961), pp. 46–71.

27. This is only half accurate, however; one must not ignore that very strong "masculine" characterization, too—"a man's world."

28. This characteristic—the aesthetic attitude—is perhaps the best known of all Japanese emphases, but even it is not an adequate or accurate basic characterization, though it may well be a tendency and emphasis. It is often exaggerated (and idealized) out of the true perspective by ignoring the realistic and unaesthetic—and even the unharmonious—aspects—"secular and profane," "rowdy," "crude," "loud," "boisterous," "vulgar"—that are also there in some abundance. (It would not have been necessary to point to this darker side were it not for the fact that it is almost always ignored—quite unrealistically.) The aesthetics of the elite is not the aesthetics of Japan—the elite do not constitute Japan, by far. There is no doubt about the aesthetic spirit in Japan but it is not the essence of the culture as so many believe.

29. Recall also the quotation of the hedonistic tendencies of Japan from Hasegawa—note 19 above. See also Nakamura, *Ways of Thinking*, pp. 372–380.

30. *The Ideals of East and West* (Cambridge, England: University Press, 1934), p. 88. He could also have mentioned extreme authoritarianism, statism, anti-intellectualism, etc.

31. For the significance of the Emperor Institution, see Nakamura, *Ways of Thinking*, pp. 467–481.

32. See Nakamura, "Basic Features of the Legal, Political, and Economic Thought of Japan," herein, pp. 143–163.

32a. *Ibid.*

32b. For example, see Matsumoto Yoshiharu's monograph, "Contemporary Japan: the Individual and the Group," Transaction of the American *Philosophical Society,* new series, Vol. I, Part 1 (January, 1960).

33. The traditional use of the family name first, the personal name or names thereafter, is an interesting possible indication or illustration of this non-individual and non-personal emphasis. Only in the Far East is this custom followed.

33a. Nakamura, *Ways of Thinking,* section on "Emperor Worship" (pp. 467–490), especially pp. 477, 489.

34. See several significant statements made by Japanese authorities (in several fields)—as quoted in de Bary, *op. cit.,* as cited in the index of that volume.

35. Hasegawa, "Now, when Japan is beginning on a new footing as a free and democratic state (as a result of the directions and guidance imposed upon by America), it may be wondered whether instead of making intellectual judgments based on a strictly objective cognition of the realities facing Japan, there is not a tendency to indulge in a subjective, cerebral development of the abstract ideas of 'freedom' and 'democracy.' We may also wonder what the practical results will be." In de Bary, *op cit.,* pp. 897–898.

Ohe Seizo holds that what is happening in Japan at the present time is, at most, "a socio-political experiment," and says, ". . . this ideal of the pre-war Japanese state itself must be the central problem of any socio-political reform-experiment in Japan. . . ." "The Socio-Political Experiment in Postwar Japan," *Ethics,* LXVI, No. 4 (July, 1966), 255. This is a frank and interesting study.

36. For example, see F. S. C. Northrop, "Comparative Philosophy and Science in the Light of Comparative Law," in C. A. Moore, ed., *Philosophy and Culture—East and West,* pp. 251 ff. His *The Meeting of East and West* (New York: The Macmillan Co., 1946) and his *The Taming of the Nations* (New York: The Macmillan Co., 1952) provide a technical philosophical background for this point of view.)

37. Italics mine.

38. See Matsumoto, *op. cit.,* especially pp. 60–63.

39. See note 28, above.

39a. See G. B. Sansom, *Japan: A Short Cultural History of Japan,* p. 516.

40. Even a cursory "glance" at the numerous major thinkers referred to in the papers in this volume—and in Nakamura's *Ways of Thinking* and de Bary's *Sources of Japanese Tradition*—must convince one that much *thinking* has gone on in the Japanese tradition,

despite numerous interpretations that tend to belittle such activity. This is true even though it must be admitted, however, that, relatively speaking, there has been less polemical and original philosophical thinking and writing in Japan than in other major traditions.

Nishida Kitarō has another suggestion—although he, too, admits that Japanese tradition has been excessively intuitive as contrasted with the intellectual attitude and method. He suggests that "'not to be argumentative' should be understood as not to be self assertive, but to bend one's head low before the true facts"—and that not being argumentative "means only that argument is not indulged in for argument's sake and concepts are not bandied about for their own sake." *Op. cit.*, p. 859.

41. The writer understands that Nakamura has been "commissioned" to write a comprehensive history of Japanese philosophy, and it is almost assured in advance that the point made here, and earlier in this Introduction, will be abundantly vindicated by that survey. It is also understood that Professor Frederick P. Harris is contemplating the preparation of a source book in Japanese philosophy, and the results of this work will probably be strongly in the same direction.

42. Takakusu (writing during the tense times around 1938, and therefore calling special attention to basic traditional beliefs) says, ". . . the soil of the Japanese spirit . . . is no other than the sacred message of the Imperial Ancestress." (See Sakamaki's chapter herein.) He explains this "spirit" as exhibiting itself in "four forms of expression . . . *ara-mitama* (strong spirit) is an expression of bravery. *Nigi-mitama* (quiet spirit) is an expression of benevolence, *saki-mitama* (active spirit) is an expression of intelligence which is the origin of ecconomical activities, and . . . *kushi-mitama* (mysterious spirit) is an expression of wisdom." He also finds crucial the Three Treasures of Shintō tradition, the Mirror, the Jewels, and the Sword. These constitute "the age-old inheritance of ours." There is in the spirit of Japan, he says, a consciousness of the "Culture of the Blood." "The Imperial Japan has its own land, state structure and people who are conscious of the Culture of the Blood." For Takakusu, the Culture of the Blood—which he compares with the similar attitude of Germany—takes priority over the culture of the intellect, but, in some distinction from other interpreters quoted here and writing here, he says that the Japanese spirit calls for both in mutual and effective harmony. (And he never speaks of any incapacity of the Japanese for intellectual achievements.) He brings together the nationalism of traditional Shintō and the "totalistic" view of Kegon Buddhist philosophy is another achievement of harmony—with interesting overtones and implications. *The New Japanism and the Buddhist View on Nationality*, Maekawa Kiyoshi

and Kiyooka Eiichi, trans. (Tokyo: Hokuseido Press, 1938), pp. 9, 10, 14–16, and p. 41, where Takakusu says, "The Culture of the Blood is crystalized in the Japanese Spirit."

43. Those who wish to look somewhat further into this point of view are referred to several passages in de Bary, *op. cit.*, as cited by index references on "nationalism," and "ultra-nationalism"; see also Nakamura, *Ways of Thinking*, pp. 434–449.

44. Nakamura says, "When the existence of the system of human relationships to which one belongs is endangered, one is apt to defend it even by recourse to force. . . . High esteem for arms has a very important place among the thought-tendencies in Japan, at least in the past." *Ways of Thinking*, p. 490.

45. This point has been emphasized by Takakusu, as just mentioned, as herein by Nakamura, pages 143–163, and is as old as Shintō itself—see Sakamaki herein, pages 24–32. Could the contemporary and ever-increasing tendency of Japan to trade with communist China be an illustration of this tendency?

＊　＊　＊　＊　＊　＊　＊　＊

Editor's Note: Some lately discovered interesting ideas found in recently published books and journals.

(1) One writer speaks of "how deeply the cult [of Shintō] pervades the life of the Japanese." Ono Sokyo, *Shinto: The Kami Way* (Tokyo: Bridgeway Press, 1962).

(2) Fundamental was the influence of Fukuzawa Yukichi in setting the Japanese toward the West and against the Chinese. See, e.g., Carmen Blacker, *The Japanese Enlightenment: A Study of the Writings of Fukuzawa Yukichi* (Cambridge: Cambridge University Press, 1964).

(3) "The problem, it seems, is . . . one of the—albeit unconscious—confidence of a people in its own traditional culture, its pride, and its sense or spiritual security, which make themselves apparent in its everyday behavior. Before the tide of Westernization, self-confidence, pride, and assurance all went by the board." Ishida Eiichirō, "Japan Rediscovered," *Japan Quarterly*, XI (1964), No. 3, 276–282.

(4) If the folk legends of a country are indicative of its character, the double-mindedness of Japan is clear: Richard M. Dorsm, *Folk Legends of Japan* (Tokyo: Charles E. Tuttle Co., 1962).

(5) Not all Japanese admire Western humanism, which some consider a complete differentation between Japan and the West: Aida Yūji, "The Limitations of Western European Humanism," *Journal of Social and Political Ideas of Japan*, II, No. 2 (August, 1964), 31.

Romanization and Corresponding Japanese Characters

Akitsu Mikami 現御神
Akō 赤穂
Amaterasu Ōmikami 天照大御神
Amida Butsu 阿弥陀仏
Amidakyō 阿弥陀経
Anesaki Masaharu 姉崎正治
Annen 安然
Arai Hakuseki 新井白石
Ashikaga Takauji 足利尊氏
Azuchi-Momoyama jidai 安土桃山時代

bakufu 幕府
Bashō 芭蕉
Baso 馬祖
bettōsō 別当僧
bombu 凡夫
bosatsudō 菩薩道
Bukkōji 仏光寺
Bukkyō taikei 仏教大系
bunmei kaika 文明開化
bushi 武士
bushidō 武士道
Busshinshū 仏心宗
Butsudō 仏道
Buzan 豊山

Chikamatsu 近松
chōnin 町人
Chūshingura 忠臣蔵

Dai Nippon Bukkyō zensho 大日本仏教全書
Daigu 大愚
Daimuryōjukyō 大無量寿経
daimyō 大名
Dainichi Nyorai 大日如来
Dainichikyō 大日経
Daiye 大慧
Dazai Shundai 太宰春台
Dengyō Daishi 伝教大師
dō 道
Dōgen 道元
Donran 曇鸞
dōri 道理

Edo 江戸
Eisai 栄西
Eka 慧可
ekō 廻向
en 縁
engi 縁起
Engo 円悟
Ennin (Jikaku Daishi) 円仁

Ennyū 円融
Enō 慧能
Enryakuji 延暦寺
Eshin Sōzu 恵心僧都

Fu Daishi 傅大士
Fūdo 風土
Fukuzawa Yukichi 福沢諭吉
Fusō ryakki 扶桑略記

Gangōjiengi 元興寺縁起
Gankai 顔回
Genji monogatari 源氏物語
Genjō kōan 現成公案
Genju Daishi 賢首大師
Genkō shakusho 元享釈書
Genkū 源空
Genroku jidai 元禄時代
Genshin (Eshin Sōzu) 源信
gensō ekō 還相廻向
giri 義理
Gobunshō 御文章
Godaisan 五台山
gongen 権現
Gukanshō 愚管抄
Gyōgi 行基

Hagakure 葉隠
haibutsu kishaku 廃仏毀釈
Hakuin 白隠
harakiri 腹切り
Heian jidai 平安時代
Heian-kyō 平安京
Hekiganshū 碧巌集
Hidenin 悲田院
Hieizan 比叡山
hijiri 聖
Himitsu sokushin jōbutsu gi 秘密即身
　成仏義
Hirako Takurei 平子鐸嶺
Hirata Atsutane 平田篤胤
hitogami 人神
Hizō hōyaku 秘蔵宝鑰

hōjin 報身
hōkkai engi 法界縁起
Hokke gengi 法華玄義
Hokkekyō 法華経
Hokke mongu 法華文句
Hōnen 法然
Hongwanji 本願寺
hōni dōri 法爾道理
honji suijaku 本地垂迹
hōon 報恩
Hōryūji 法隆寺
Hossō Shū 法相宗
Hōtan 鳳潭
Hyakujō 百丈

Ichijitsu Shintō 一実神道
Ichimai kishō mon 一枚起請文
Ichinen tanen shōmon 一念多念証文
ichinen gi 一念義
ie 家
igyō 易行
inmyō 因明
Inmyō nisshōriron myōtōshō 因明入正
　理論明燈抄
innen 因縁
Inoue Kowashi 井上毅
Inoue Tetsujirō 井上哲次郎
Ippen Shonin 一遍上人
Isan 潙山
Ise 伊勢
Ishida Baigan 石田梅巌
Itō Jinsai 伊藤仁斎
Izanagi 伊奘諾
Izanami 伊奘冉

ji 自
ji 事
Jichin 慈鎮
jihi 慈悲
jiji muge 事事無礙
jiji muge hokkai 事事無礙法界
Jikaku Daishi (Ennin) 慈覚大師
jin 仁

Jinen 自然
Jinen hōni 自然法爾
jinen hōnishō 自然法爾章
Jingikan 神祇官
jinja 神社
Jinmu Tennō 神武天皇
Jinnō shōtōki 神皇正統記
jiriki 自力
Jōdo monrui jushō 浄土文類聚鈔
Jōdo Shin Shū 浄土真宗
Jōdo Shū 浄土宗
Jōdoron 浄土論
Jōdoshū zensho 浄土宗全書
Jōei shikimoku 貞永式目
Jōgū Shōtoku hōō teisetsu 上宮聖徳法皇帝説
jōgyō zammaidō 常行三昧堂
jūgen engi 十玄縁起
Jūjū shinron 十住心論
Jūshichijō kempō 十七条憲法

Kaijō 戒定
Kakinomoto-no-Hitomaro 柿本人麻呂
Kakunyo 覚如
Kamakura jidai 鎌倉時代
kami 神
Kamo-no-Mabuchi 賀茂真淵
Kanō Motonobu 狩野元信
Kegon gokyōshō 華厳五教章
Kegon Shū 華厳宗
Kegonkyō tangenki 華厳経探玄記
Keitoku dentō roku 景徳伝燈録
Kenchi 顕智
kengyō 顕教
Kennyo 顕如
kenri 権利
Kimmei Tennō 欽明天皇
Kishimoto Hideo 岸本英夫
Kitabatake Chikafusa 北畠親房
kō 孝
kōan 公案
Kōbō Daishi 弘法大師

Kōbō Daishi zenshū 弘法大師全集
Kōchū Nippon Bungaku Taikei 校註日本文学大系
Kōfukuji 興福寺
Kojiki 古事記
Kojiki den 古事記伝
Kokan Shiren 虎関師錬
Kokka Shintō 国家神道
Kokugakuha 国学派
kokutai 国体
Kōmō tōki 講孟箚記
Kōmyō Kōgō 光明皇后
Kongōchōkyō 金剛頂経
kongōkai 金剛界
Konkōmyō saishōō kyō 金光明最勝王経
Kōryūji 広隆寺
kotoage 言あげ
Kōyasan 高野山
Kudara 百済
Kūkai 空海
Kumazawa Banzan 熊沢蕃山
Kwanmuryōjukyō 観無量寿経
Kwannon 観音
Kyōgyōshinshō 教行信証
Kyōiku chokugo 教育勅語
Kyōzan 仰山

Makashikan 摩訶止観
Makura no sōshi 枕草紙
Manyōshū 万葉集
mappō 末法
Mattōshō 末燈鈔
Meiji ishin 明治維新
Meiji jidai 明治時代
Meji Jingū 明治神宮
Meiji Tennō 明治天皇
mikkyō 密教
Minamoto-no-Yoritomo 源頼朝
Minpon Shugi 民本主義
minshu shugi 民主主義
Miroku 弥勒
Miroku geshōgyō 弥勒下生経

mitama 御霊
Miura Baien 三浦梅園
Miura Chikkei 三浦竹渓
mondō 問答
mono 物
Motoori Norinaga 本居宣長
muge 無礙
Murakami Senshō 村上専精
Murasaki Shikibu 紫式部
Muromachi jidai 室町時代
Musō (Sōseki) 夢窓
Myōhō rengekyō (*Hokkekyo*)
　妙法蓮華経

Nabeshima rongo 鍋島論語
Nakae Tōjyu 中江藤樹
Namu Amida Butsu 南無阿弥陀仏
Namu myōhō rengekyō 南無妙
　法蓮華経
nangyō 難行
Nanjō Bunyū 南条文雄
Nansō 南宋
Naobi no mitama 直毘霊
Nara jidai 奈良時代
nehan 涅槃
Nembutsu 念仏
Nichiren 日蓮
Nihongi 日本紀
Nihonshoki 日本書記
Niijima Jō 新島襄
Ninigi-no-Mikoto 瓊々杵尊
Ninnō gokoku hannya haramittakyō
　仁王護国般若波羅密多経
Ninomiya Sontoku 二宮尊徳
Nintoku Tennō 仁徳天皇
Nippon daizōkyō 日本大蔵経
Nishida Kitarō 西田幾多郎
Nitobe Inazō 新渡戸稲造
Nittō guhō junrai gyōki 入唐求法
　巡礼行記
Nogi Maresuke 乃木希典
Noguchi Hideyo 野口英世
Nyorai Zen 如来禅

Ōbaku 黄檗
Oda Nobunaga 織田信長
Ofumi 御文
Ogyū Sorai 荻生徂徠
ōjō 往生
Ōjō yōshū 往生要集
on 恩
Ōnin no ran 応仁の乱
Onmyōdō 陰陽道

rei 礼
Rennyo 蓮如
ri 理
riji muge 理事無礙
Rinzai 臨済
Rinzai roku 臨済録
Ryōbu Shintō 両部神道

Saichō 最澄
Saigusa Hiroto 三枝博音
Saikaku 西鶴
saisei icchi 祭政一致
Saitō Mokichi 斎藤茂吉
Sakuma Shōzan 佐久間象山
samurai 侍
Sanron Shū 三論宗
Sasaki Gesshō zenshū 佐々木月樵
　全集
satori 悟
Sei shonagon 清少納言
Sengoku jidai 戦国時代
Senjaku hongwan nenbutsushū 選択
　本願念仏集
seppuku 切腹
Seyakuin 施薬院
Shaka 釈迦
Shakamuni 釈迦牟尼
shi hokkai 四法界
shijūshichi gishi 四十七義士
Shimabara no ran 島原の乱
Shimaji Daitō 島地大等
Shingon Shū 真言宗
shinōkōshō 士農工商

Shinran 親鸞
Shin Shū 真宗
Shinshū taikei 真宗大系
Shinshū zensho 真宗全書
Shintō 神道
Shippei 竹箆
Shitennōji 四天王寺
Shōbōgenzō 正法眼蔵
shōdōmon 聖道門
shōgun 将軍
shōki 性起
Shoku Nihongi 続日本紀
Shōmangyō gisho 勝鬘経義疏
Shōmangyō 勝鬘経
Shōmu Tennō 聖武天皇
Shōtoku Taishi 聖徳太子
shōzō matsu no sanji 正像末の三時
shugendō 修験道
shugenja 修験者
shugyō 修行
Shūha 宗派
Shūha Shintō 宗派神道
Shūkō 周公
shumisen 須弥山
Shutsujō shōgo 出定笑語
Sōdai 宋代
Soga uji 蘇我氏
Sokushin jōbutsu gi 即身成仏義
Sōseki 疎石
Soshi Zen 祖師禅
sōsoku 相即
Sōtō Shū 曹洞宗
Sugawara-no-Michizane 菅原道真
Suiko Tennō 推古天皇
Susanoo-no-mikoto 素盞鳴(命)
Suzuki Daisetz Teitarō 鈴木大拙
　(貞太郎)
Suzuki Shōsan 鈴木正三

Tachibana-no-Ōiratsume
　橘大郎女
Taihō ritsuryō 大宝律令
Taika no kaishin 大化改新

Taishikō 太子講
Taisho jidai 大正時代
taizō kai 胎蔵界
Takada Senjuji 高田専修寺
Takakusu Junjirō 高楠順次郎
Takamagahara 高天原
Takamura Kōtarō 高村光太郎
Tanizaki Junichirō 谷崎潤一郎
Tanka 丹霞
Tannishō 歎異鈔
tariki 他力
Temmu Tennō 天武天皇
ten 天
Tendai Daishi 天台大師
Tendai Shū 天台宗
tenjukoku (maṇḍala) 矢寿国
　(曼荼羅)
Tenrikyō 天理教
Tōdai 唐代
Tōdaiji 東大寺
Tōgō Heihachirō 東郷平八郎
Tōjō Hideki 東条英機
Tōju sensei zenshū 藤樹先生全集
Tokugawa Ieyasu 徳川家康
Tokugawa jidai 徳川時代
Tokugawa Shōgun 徳川将軍
Tosotsuten 兜率天
Tōyōjin no shii hōhō 東洋人の思惟
　方法
Toyotomi Hideyoshi 豊臣秀吉
Tsuji Zennosuke 辻善之助
Tsukiyomi 月読

Uchimura Kanzō 内村鑑三
Ui Hakuju 宇井伯寿
Uiyamabumi うひ山蹈
ujidera 氏寺
ujigami 氏神
ukiyoe 浮世絵
Umehara Shinryū 梅原真隆
Ummon roku 雲門録
Urabe Kanetomo 卜部兼倶

wa 和
wasan 和讃
Watsuji Tetsurō 和辻哲郎

Yamabe-no-Akahito 山部赤人
yamabushi 山伏
Yamaga Sokō 山鹿素行
Yamashiro-no-Ōye 山背大兄 (王)
Yamatai 耶馬台
Yamazaki Ansai 山崎闇斎
Yanagida Kunio 柳田国男
Yasukuni Jinja 靖国神社
Yoshida Shōin 吉田蔭松
Yūgaku Ōhara 大原幽学

Yui-en 唯円
Yuiitsu Shintō 唯一神道
Yuimagyō 維摩経
Yūzū Nembutsu 融通念神

zazen 座禅
Zen 禅
Zendō 善導
Zenmui 善無畏
Zenne Daishi 善慧大師
Zen no kenkyu 善の研究
Zonkaku 存覚
Zonnyo 存如
Zuidai 随代

Who's Who

FURUKAWA TESSHI

Professor of Ethics, Tokyo University.

Graduated from the Imperial University of Tokyo, 1935. D. Litt., Tōhoku University, 1962.

University of Tokyo; 1949– Has also lectured at Tōhoku University, Okayama University, and Kumamoto University.

Director, Japanese Society for Ethics; Director, Japanese Society for Moral Education.

Member, Fourth East-West Philosophers' Conference, 1964.

Publications (in Japanese): *A Study of Modern Japanese Thought; A Study of French Ethical Thought; History of Japanese Ethics; Idea of Yearning for the Heian Period and Its Tradition; Idea of Bushidō and Its Background; Ethics for Young Peoples; Heroes and Saints.*

Editor: *Ethics; History of Japanese Thought; History of Moral Education in Japan;* and *History of Ethics.*

Also author of many articles in professional journals, such as, *East Asian Studies in Japan, Recent Trends of East Asian Studies in Japan,* and *Philosophical Studies of Japan* (UNESCO publication, Tokyo).

HANAYAMA SHINSHŌ

B.A. Tokyo Imperial University, 1921; D. Litt. Tokyo Imperial University, 1942.

Professor of Japanese Buddhism (Indian Philosophy), Tokyo Imperial University (University of Tokyo), 1934–1959. Professor Emeritus, University of Tokyo, 1959. Professor of Japanese Buddhism, Tokyo University, 1923–1959. Lecturer, Buddhism, Nippon University, 1923–1959. Lecturer and Professor of Japanese Buddhism and Religion; Kokugakuin University, 1926–1959. Lecturer, Japanese Buddhism, Kyushu Imperial University, 1931, 1933, 1934, 1936, 1941, 1950; Tōhoku Imperial University, 1937, 1939; Hokkaido University, 1953.

Imperial Award, Japan Academy, 1935.

Member, East-West Philosophers' Conferences, 1949, 1964.

Publications (in Japanese): *Prince Shotoku and Japanese Buddhism; A History of Japanese Buddhism; Concerning the Distinctive Character of Japanese Buddhism; Japanese Development of Ekayan Thought; Japanese Buddhism; Orientation in the Study of Japanese Buddhism; Bibliography on Buddhism;* (in English) *Buddhism in Japan; The Way of Deliverance.*

HORI ICHIRŌ

Professor and Chairman, Department of the History of Religion, Tōhoku University; Professor of the History of Religion, Kokugakuin University; Lecturer of the History of Religion, University of Tokyo.

Educated at the Imperial University of Tokyo. D.Litt., University of Tokyo, 1954.

Member, National Institute for the Studies of Japanese Culture, 1939–1947; Professor of the History of Religion, Kokugakuin University and Lecturer of the History of Japanese Religion, University of Tokyo, 1948–1952; Associate Professor of the History of Religion, Tōhoku National University.

Research Fellow of the Rockefeller Foundation, Harvard University, 1956–1957; Visiting Professor of the History of Religion, University of Chicago, 1957–1958; Research Fellow of the Rockefeller Foundation, Europe, 1958.

Awarded Honored Prize of the Mainichi Press for his book, *Japanese Folk-Beliefs*, 1952, and of the Japan Academy for his book, *A Study of the History of Japanese Folk Religions*, 1956.

Managing Director: Japanese Association of Religious Studies, Japanese Society of Ethnology, Japanese Folklore Society. Member

of the Board of Trustees, Japanese Association of Indian and
Buddhist Studies.

Member, Fourth East-West Philosophers' Conference, 1964.

Among publications (in Japanese): *Essays on the History of
Japanese Buddhism; Japanese Culture and Buddhism; Historical and
Cultural Materials concerning Japanese Buddhism; Biography and
Evaluation of Dengyo Daishi; Japanese Folk-Beliefs; A Study of the
History of Japanese Folk Religions; Social Roles of Japanese Reli-
gion; Control of the Life and Attitude of Japanese People by the
Religions and Folk-ways.*

KAWASHIMA TAKEYOSHI

Professor of Law, University of Tokyo.

Graduated from Imperial University of Tokyo, Faculty of Law,
1932; LL.D., University of Tokyo, 1959.

Visiting Professor, Stanford University, 1958–1959.

Director, Japanese Association of Private Law and Japanese
Association of Sociology of Law; Councillor, Japanese Association
of Ethnology and Agrarian History Society; Member, Research
Committee of Sociology of Law (Subcommittee of the International
Association of Sociology).

Member: Legislative Council of the Ministry of Justice and
of the Central Council of Construction Industry of the Ministry of
Construction.

Member, Fourth East-West Philosophers' Conference, 1964.

Publications (in Japanese): *Treatise on the Civil Code of the
Republic of China; Familistic Structure of Japanese Society;
Theory of the Law of Property; Structure of Law in the Theory of
Sociology of Law; On the Contracts of Construction; The Study of
Law as an Empirical Science; Dissolution of the Rights on Com-
mon Land; Sociology of Law; Modern Society and the Law;
Treatise on Civil Code of Japan.* Also articles in English and
Japanese.

KISHIMOTO HIDEO

Professor of Religion, Tokyo University.

B.A., Tokyo Imperial University, 1926; M.A., Harvard University, 1934; Ph.D., Tokyo University, 1945.

Lecturer at Tokyo University, 1934–1945; Associate Professor,

Tokyo University, 1945–1947; Professor, Tokyo University, 1947 to present.

Member, Third East-West Philosophers' Conference, 1959.

President, Japanese Association for Religious Studies, 1950–1954; Visiting Professor at Stanford University, 1953–1954; Haskell Lecturer, University of Chicago, 1954; participated in UNESCO Conference, San Francisco, 1957; Executive Secretary, The International Congress for the History of Religions, 1958; UNESCO Lecturer for North Europe and U.S. for East-West program, 1958–1959. Frequently represented his country at international conferences.

(Died 1966.)

KŌSAKA MASAAKI

President, Tokyo Gakugei University.

Graduated from Kyoto University, 1923; Ph.D. Kyoto University, 1940.

Taught at Kyoto Furitsu (Prefecture) College of Medicine, Tokyo Bunrika (Arts and Sciences) University, Kyoto University, and Kansei Gakuin University. Director, Center for Humanistic Studies, Kyoto University, 1941–1946. Dean, Faculty of Education, Kyoto University, 1955–1960.

Member: Central Advisory Council of Education; Board of Directors, Institute for Democratic Education; Board of Directors, Philosophy of Education Association. President, Teacher's Training College Association.

Member, Fourth East-West Philosophers' Conference, 1964.

Publications (in Japanese): *Historical World; Kant; A Study of Mythology; Nishida Kitarō, His Life and Thought; From Kierkegaard to Sartre; Existential Philosophy; Modern Philosophy; Pragmatism; Philosophy of Nishida and Philosophy of Tanabe; History of Japanese Thought in the Meiji Era; Nishida Kitarō and Watsuji Tetsurō.*

MIYAMOTO SHŌSON

Professor Emeritus of Buddhist Philosophy, Tokyo University.

M.A., Otani University, 1918; Ph.D., Oxford University, 1929; D. Litt., Imperial University of Tokyo, 1942.

Imperial University of Tokyo 1928–1954; Professor Emeritus, 1954–. Professor, Waseda University, 1955–1964; Komazawa University, 1955–. Visiting Professor, University of Chicago, 1958–1959.

Member, East-West Philosophers' Conferences, 1959, 1964; Science Council of Japan, 1954–1959; Chairman of the Directors, Japanese Association of Indian and Buddhist Studies, 1951–1965; Executive Board, International Association for the History of Religions, 1955–1965; Executive Director, The Center of Religions, 1965–.

Publications (in Japanese): *Ultimate Middle and Voidness; Mahāyāna and Hīnayāna; Middle Way Thought and Its Development.*

Editor, *A Study of the Formative History of Mahāyāna Buddhism; The Fundamental Truth of Buddhism.*

Also many articles in English.

NAKAMURA HAJIME

Professor of Indian and Buddhist Philosophy and Dean of the Faculty of Letters, University of Tokyo.

Graduated from the Imperial University of Tokyo, 1936; D.Litt., University of Tokyo, 1943.

President, Japan-India Society; Director, Japanese Association for Indian and Buddhist Studies; Director, Japanese Association for Religious Studies; Life Member, Bhandarkar Oriental Research Institute, Poona; Honorary Fellow, Government Sanskrit College, Calcutta.

Visiting Professor of Philosophy, Stanford University, 1951–1952; Visiting Professor of Religion, University of Florida, 1961; Senior Scholar, East-West Center, University of Hawaii, 1962; Visiting Professor of World Religions, Harvard University, 1963–1964; Summer Session Lecturer, University of Hawaii, 1959 and 1964. Lectured at the University of Michigan, Yale University, University of Chicago, Delhi University, Banaras Hindu University, Columbia University.

Delegate to Congress on Cultural Freedom in Asia, Rangoon, 1955; Delegate to the Buddhist Symposium sponsored by the Government of India, New Delhi, 1956; Delegate to the UNESCO-PAX ROMANA Conference, Manila, 1960; Tour of India at invitation of the Government of India, 1960.

Panel Member, East-West Philosophers' Conferences, 1959, 1964.

Awarded the Imperial Prize by the Japan Academy, 1957, for *A History of Early Vedānta Philosophy* (4 vols.).

Publications include: *Ways of Thinking of Eastern Peoples, Selected* [Japanese] *Works of Hajime Nakamura* (10 vols.), *Comparative Thought.*

Formerly editor of *The Bulletin of the Okurayama Oriental Research Institute* and of *Science of Thought;* Associate Editor, *Monumenta Nipponica;* Contributing Editor, *Journal of the History of Ideas* and *United Asia;* Member, Board of Editors, *Philosophy East and West.*

SAKAMAKI SHUNZŌ

Professor of History and Dean of Summer Session, University of Hawaii.

B.A., M.A., University of Hawaii, Ph.D., Columbia University.

Taught at: Doshisha University; Columbia University (summer session); University of Hawaii since 1936; Dean of Summer Session, 1955–.

Friend Peace Scholar, 1923–1927, 1928–1931.

Member, Phi Beta Kappa, Phi Kappa Phi, Omicron Delta Kappa, Sigma Delta Rho.

Member, Board of Directors, Association for Asian Studies, 1964–1967. General Chairman, International Conference on General Semantics, 1960.

Member, Fourth East-West Philosophers' Conference, 1964.

Publications: *Japan and the United States, 1790–1853; A Study of Japanese Contacts with and Conceptions of the United States and Its People Prior to the American Expedition of 1853–1854; Asia* (with John A. White); *Ryukyu: A Bibliographical Guide to Okinawan Studies, Surveying Important Primary Sources and Writings in Ryukyuan, Japanese, Chinese, and Korean; Ryukyuan Names: Monographs on and Lists of Personal and Place Names in the Ryukyus* (Editor and co-author); *Ryukyuan Research Resources at the University of Hawaii;* and articles in several scholarly journals.

Conference papers presented at International Conference on General Semantics, Mexico City, 1958. Association for Asian Studies, 15th Annual Meeting, Philadelphia, 1963. American Historical Association, Pacific Coast Branch, Annual Meeting, San Francisco, 1963. 20th International Congress of Orientalists, New

Delhi, 1964. International Conference of Asian Historians, Hong Kong, 1964. 11th Pacific Science Congress, Tokyo, 1966.

SUZUKI DAISETZ TEITARŌ

Professor Emeritus, Otani University; Director, Matsugaoka Bunko.

Educated at Tokyo Imperial University, 1891–1894. D.Litt., Otani University, 1933; LL.D., University of Hawaii, 1959 (honorary).

Taught at Gakushu-in, Tokyo Imperial University, and Otani University.

Lectured at various British universities under the auspices of the Japanese Foreign Ministry, 1936; University of Hawaii, 1949; Claremont College, 1950, 1951; as Rockefeller Foundation Lecturer at Yale, Harvard, Cornell, Princeton and other universities, 1950; Columbia University, 1951, 1952–1954, 1955–1957; University of Munich, 1953; Mexico City College, 1956; University of Mexico, 1957; and in many cities of Europe and the United States.

Elected member of the Japan Academy and awarded the Cultural Medal by the Emperor of Japan, 1949; received the Asahi Cultural Award, 1955; invited as State Guest of India, 1960; received the Rabindranath Tagore Birth-Centenary Medal, Asiatic Society, Calcutta, 1964.

Member, East-West Philosophers' Conferences, 1939, 1949, 1959, 1964; 13th Symposium of the Conference on Science, Philosophy and Religion, Columbia University, 1952; Eranos Conference, Ascona, Switzerland, 1953 and 1954; Conference on Zen and Psychoanalysis, Cuernavaca, Mexico, 1957; Massachusetts Institute of Technology Conference, "New Knowledge in Human Values," 1957.

His publications number over 125, among which are (in Japanese): On "No-Mind"; Studies in the Pure Land Thought; Studies in the History of Zen Thought, 2 vols.; The Awakening of Japanese Spirituality; Bankei on the Unborn; The East and the West; (in English): Essays in Zen Buddhism, 3 vols.; Studies in the Laṅkāvatāra Sūtra; Manual of Zen Buddhism; An Introduction to Zen Buddhism; Living by Zen; Outlines of Mahāyāna Buddhism; Zen and Japanese Culture. Editor, The Eastern Buddhist, 1921–1939; and many essays in learned journals.

(Died in 1966.)

TAKAKUSU JUNJIRŌ

Professor Emeritus, Tokyo Imperial University.

Graduate, Kyoto Imperial University; Oxford, 1890–1894. Honorary D. Litt. Heidelberg, D. Litt., Oxford.

Member, Imperial Academy of Japan; First East-West Philosophers' Conference, 1939.

Author, translator, and editor of many works on Buddhism and Indian philosophy.

Editor, *Dictionary and Buddhism.*

UEDA YOSHIFUMI

Professor of Buddhist Philosophy and Chairman, Department of Indic and Buddhist Studies, Nagoya University.

Graduated from Imperial University of Tokyo, 1933; D.Litt., University of Kyushu, 1948.

Professor, Ryukoku University, 1945–1949; Lecturer, Hiroshima University, 1952–1956; Hokkaido University, 1954; Kyoto University, 1957; Tōhoku University, 1961.

Director, Japanese Association of Indian and Buddhist Studies.

Member, Fourth East-West Philosophers' Conference, 1964.

Publications (in Japanese): *A Study of the History of Buddhist Thought; On the Concept of "Karma" in Buddhism; On the Fundamental Structure of Mahāyāna Buddhist Thought; An Introduction to Yogācāra Philosophy;* and articles in learned journals.

YUKAWA HIDEKI

Professor of Physics, Columbia University, 1951–.

Educated at Kyoto University, Sc.D.

Professor of Physics, Kyoto University; awarded Imperial Prize of Japan, 1940; Oppenheimer Professor at Princeton University, 1948; Professor of Physics at Columbia University and awarded the Nobel Prize for his researches in meson, 1949. Director, Research Institute for Fundamental Physics, Kyoto University, 1953–. Professor Emeritus, Osaka University.

Member, Third Philosophers' Conference, 1959.

His works include "Research in Neutrons," "Introduction to Quantam Theory," and "Infinitesimal World."

Index

PREPARED BY E. MURIEL MOYLE